International Humanitarian Law

Protecting the Rights of Women in Armed Conflicts in Africa

Vol. 1

NIGERIA, DR CONGO AND SIERRA-LEONE

EMMANUEL CHINWEIKE IBEZIM, Ph.D

First Edition

Published by The Lighthouse books, Agape Inc.

For information regarding permission, write to:
The Lighthouse Books,
13721 E. Rice Pl,
Aurora,
CO 80015.

ISBN: 978-1-950320-24-0

Visit us at: www.thelighthousebooks.com
Printed in the USA

Dedication

This book is dedicated to all the women who have suffered so disproportionately in all the armed conflicts the world has witnessed in recent times, especially in Africa. It is also dedicated to my beloved parents of blessed memory, Sir & Lady Hezekiah and Priscilla Ibezim, and to my loving wife, Pastor Chioma Millicent Ibezim (Ph.D), who stood by me all through the period of writing this book.

Table of Contents

Table of Cases

Frolova v USSR 761 F.2d 370 at 373 (7th Cir. 1985	214
Greifelt and others, (the Rusha Case), Nuremberg, 10th March 1984, TWC, vol.5, 88-173	136
Hamdan v Rumsfeld, Secretary of defense et.al., 548. U.S. 557 (2006), NO.5. 184, 29 June, 2006	120, 411
Hoess (1948) 7 LRTWC II (Supreme National Court of Poland) Greifelt and Others [The Rusha Case], Nuremberg, 10 March 1948, TWC, Vol. 5, 88 – 173	136
Hoess (1948) 7LRTWC II (supreme National of Poland	136
Hostage Trail. LRTWC. Vol. viii. 1949	165
Hostage Trial. LRTWC. Vol. viii 1949	165
Ibidapo v Lufthansa Airlines, (1997) 4NWLRC	210
ICJ, Application for the Genocide Convention (Bosina-Herzegovina v Yugoslavia), Judgment, ICJ Reports 2007	118
ICJ, Military and Paramilitary Activities in and Against Nicaragua (Nicaragua v United state of America), Judgment, ICJ Reports 198	109, 112, 118, 221, 218
ICTY, prosecutor v Gotovina ana Markac, case No.IT 06-90-A, judgment (Appeal Chamber) 16th November 2012	322
ICTY, prosecutor v Kunarac, Kovac and Vukovic, Paras (IT-96-23), AC, 12 June 2002	21, 60, 108
ICTY, prosecutor v Perisic, Case No.IT-04-18-A, Judgment (Appeal Chamber), 28th February, 2013. 246	109, 322
ICTY, the Prosecutor v Delatic et.al., Paras 475ff	60
Idowu v State (2008) vol.1 WHRC 467	341

Trans World Airlines Inc. v Franklin Mint Corporation. 466 US 234 at 32 (1984)	168, 214
U.S v Lebb. Nuremberg Trials, Vol. II, 1950	60, 161, 164, 386
Ubani v Director of State Security Services (1999) 11NWLR (Pt. 625), 129	211
Ukeje v Ukeje (2014) 11NWLR (Pt. 1418), S.C. 384	338–339
Umar v Federal Republic of Nigeria & Ors. (2014), LPELR – 24051 (CA), Court of Appeal Abuja Division	276
United State Diplomatic and Consular Staff in Tehrar (United States of America v Iran), Judgment, ICJ Reports, (1980), p.42, para. 91	94
University of California v Bakke (438 U.S. 268 ct. 2733 57L2d 750) (1978)	366
US v Alfried Krupp von Bohlen UndHalbach, Jan. 21, 1984	163, 164, 165
USA v Wilhelm List, Volume XI, Trials of war Criminals, 757	164
Walikale Case, ASF 2009 Study (n.61), Annex, ICTJ	289
Washington v Washington State commercial passenger Fishing Vessel Association 443 US 56 58 at (1979)	214
Weinberger v Rossi 456 US 25 at 32 (1983)	214

Table of Statutes

Draft Equality Law, 2013	190, 224, 227, 267, 332
Law on the Prohibition of Sexual Repression Law No. 06/019, 2006	227
Portant Code Judiciaire Militiere, Act No. 023-2002, 2002 (Congolese Military Penal Code)	291, 296
Sexual Violence Law, Law No. 06/018	229

SIERRA LEONEAN STATUTES

Anti Human Trafficking Act, 2005	234
Anti-Human Trafficking Act, 2005	234
Child's Right Act (2007) of Sierra Leone	235
Christian Marriage Act, Cap. 95 of the Revised Law of Sierra Leone, 1960	234
Constitution of Sierra Leone (1991) Laws of Sierra Leone	233, 262, 333, 334, 363
Section19(1)	233
Convention on the Elimination of All Forms of Discrimination Against Women Act, 2007	234
Correction Act of Sierra Leone, 2014	234, 260
Domestic Violence Act, 2007 of Sierra Leone	234, 334
Legal Aid Act of Sierra Leone, 2012	26
Lome Peace Accord, 1999 (Peace Agreement between the Government of Sierra Leone and the Revolutionary United Front of Sierra Leone (1999)	103, 115, 199, 200, 221
Malicious Damages Act, 1861	190, 234, 265
Offences Against the Persons Act, 1861	234
Article 3	263
Article 4	263
Article 4(a) – (c)	264
Article 5	263, 264
Article 7	263
Article 8	263

Prevention of Cruelty to Children Act (1926)	189, 264
Right to Access Information Act, 2013	234
Right to Access Information Act, 2013	234, 334
Sexual Offences Act, 2012	234, 334
Sierra Leone's Penal Code	24, 69, 321
Sierra Leonean Criminal Procedure Act, 1965	276
Statute of the Special Court of Sierra Leone	182, 189, 311, 315, 316, 319
Article 1(2)	261
Article 2	189, 263
Article2(a)–(i)	189

FOREIGN STATUTES

1958 French Constitution	215
Article 55	215
1992 Constitution of Ghana	215
Constitution of Cape Verde, 1992	215, 242
Constitution of the United States of America	213, 214
Article VI, Clause 2	214
International Crimes (Tribunal) (2013 Amendment) Act of Bangladesh	294
International Military Tribunal Charter of the Nuremberg Tribunal	136, 176
Article 6	136
Article VII	171
Nuremberg Laws for the Racial Purification of the Greater Reich	158
Official United State Code, "Congressional and Administrative News", Oct. 19, 1984, Vol.2, para 3077	124
Representation of the Peoples Act, 1867 (U.S.A.)	103
Re-Statement of the Foreign Relations Law of U.S.A.	80

Sierra Leonean Statutes

Congolese Statutes

Foreign Statutes

Treaties and International Instruments

Convention on the Elimination of All Forms of Discrimination Against Women (CEDAW), 1979	191, 192, 193, 194, 198, 206, 217, 218, 223, 226, 230, 231, 232, 234, 328, 351, 352, 354, 368
Article 1	192
Article 2(a)	192
Article 2(f)	192
Convention on the Nationality of Married Women	331
Convention on the Non-applicability of Statutory Limitation to War Crimes Against Humanity, 1968	369
Convention on the Political Rights of Women, 1952	331
Convention on the Prevention and Punishment of the Crime of Genocide 1948	82, 96, 137, 167, 168, 218
Article 2	139
Article 111	167
Convention on the Prohibition of the Development, Production, Stockpiling and Use of Chemical Weapons and on their Destruction	206
Convention on the Rights of Persons with Disability (CRPD)	231
Convention on the Rights of the Child, 1989	139, 206, 208, 209, 218, 223, 230, 232, 328, 352
Convention on the Sale of Children, Child Prostitution and Child Pornography	231
Convention Relative to the Status of Refugees, 1951	206

Declarations

Beijing Declaration and Platform for Action (1995)	197, 198, 328, 331, 337, 352, 368, 370
Brussels Declaration on the Laws and Customs of War 1874	131
Declaration on the Elimination of Violence against Women (DEVAW)	194, 195, 328
Article 1, 4	177, 212, 365
Declaration on the Protection of Women and Children in Emergency and Armed Conflicts, 1974	190, 191, 328, 331
International Declaration Concerning the Laws and Customs of War (As Amended in 1880)	130, 131
Article 9	125, 131, 137, 232
Oxford Manual on the Laws of War, 1880	131
Universal Declaration of Human Rights	87, 88, 90, 93, 94, 178, 190, 242, 328
Vienna Declaration and Programme of Action (1993) UN Doc A/COF.157/24 (13th October, 1993)	195

Reports

Gender Equity Reports, Vol.23, No. 2, July 1995	101
Human Rights Watch (HRW) 2010, World Report (n.40)	285
McDougall, Final Report of the Special Rappateur for the Commission on Human Rights Contemporary forms of Slavery: UN Doc E/CN.4/Sub.2/1998/13 (22 June, 1998) Appendix para. 31	196
McDougall, Final Report on Thematic Issues Related to Sexual Violence during Armed Conflict	195
Report of Fourth World Conference on Women, Action for Equality, Development and Peace Beijing Declaration and Platform for Action, UN Doc A/COF.177/20 (1997)	196, 328, 331, 337
Report of the International Federation of Human Rights on the DR Congo (DRC) titled Breaking the Circle of Impunity	252
Report of the National Human Rights Commission of Nigeria on State of Compliance with International Minimum Standards of Human Rights by Nigeria under the Universal Periodic Review Mechanism, 2013	231, 242
Report of the office of the Prosecutor International Criminal Court (ICC) on 'Situation in Nigeria' dated 5 August, 2013	15, 239, 280
Report of the Secretary General on the Principles of Individual Criminal Responsibility, Para. 54	169
Report on Violence against Women in North and South Kivu in the DR Congo. Alternative Report for the Committee on the Elimination of All	9, 227

Principles/Policies

Resolutions

Acknowledgements

May I from the outset acknowledge my erudite and tireless Supervisors, Professor Sam Erugo and Dr. I. Okoronye, who effectively guided and supervised my research and read through the entire manuscript of this book and advised me on necessary corrections. My special gratitude yet again, goes to Professor S. Erugo, as the Dean of the Faculty of Law, and Dr. Haglar Okorie, the Coordinator of Post Graduate Studies in the Faculty, who respectively facilitated the successful completion of this work. Special debt of gratitude is also owed to the following Heads of Department and senior members of the Faculty, who individually and collectively contributed immensely to the writing of this book, through their constructive criticisms and suggestions namely, Professor E.C.Ngwakwe, Dr. M.O. Unegbu (Reader),Dr. I. Okoronye (Reader), Mr. P.C Ugochukwu, Dr. C.E Odoemenam and Dr. Collins O.Chijioke, Dr. (Mrs.) Chizoba Okpara and Dr. Steve A. Amaramiro. Besides their role in the research and writing of this book, Professor U.U. Chuckwumaeze and Dr. M.O. Unegbu (Reader) taught me Comparative International Criminal Law (at the Doctorate degree level) and International Humanitarian Law (at the Masters Degree level), respectively. Thus, I owe them much gratitude for my knowledge of the law in these areas. I also owe my other colleagues in the faculty appreciation for encouraging me in their different ways. In the same vein, I must also acknowledge my colleagues in the Society for International Humanitarian Law Teachers, for their inspiring and scholarly presentations during our annual workshops at Abuja, which are organized by the Abuja Delegation of the

International Committee of the Red Cross. The International Committee of the Red Cross is hereby also acknowledged.

These acknowledgements would not be complete without me thanking my darling wife, Pastor Mrs. Chioma Emma Ibezim (Ph.D), who prayerfully and sacrificially supported me throughout the period of this work. So also would I acknowledge our lovely children, Samuel and Emmanuella Ibezim for understanding that 'daddy' must not be disturbed, whenever he was engaged in the research and the writing of this book.

Finally, I wish to acknowledge my responsibility for any error or omission that might be found in this work, while giving all the glory to Almighty Jehovah for successfully producing this book.

Foreword

It is in sincere appreciation of Dr. Emmanuel Chinweike Ibezim that I write this foreword. I feel honoured, and congratulate him for publication of *International Humanitarian Law Protecting The Rights of Women in Armed Conflicts: Nigeria, DR Congo and Sierra Leone Volume 1.*

My relationship with Dr. Ibezim dates back to the late 1970s in the University of Jos, Jos, Plateau State, Nigeria where he obtained his Bachelor of Arts degree in English. When later he completed his Bachelor of Laws degree at the University of Nigeria Nsukka, Enugu campus and was called to the Nigerian Bar in 1993, our relationship as professional colleagues became galvanized and same flourished as co-members of Society of International Humanitarian Law Teachers.

The author is an Associate Professor of Law in Abia State University, Uturu and currently in the Faculty of Law of the University in Umuahia campus, Nigeria. A seasoned university administrator who successfully veered into the legal profession and scholarship, the author has distinguished himself as an academic to be reckoned with in the true sense of the use of the word. His educational background in English Language always ignites seamless communicative effectiveness in his writings. He has written, published and presented numerous specialized works in Gender and International Human Rights Law. This book is an addition to the *corpus juris* of the laws on the subject matter of his research area.

The theme and focus of the book are answers to questions raised by the insensitivity of the language of the law especially in the material content of the Geneva Conventions and their Additional Protocols which seem to operate to limit substantive coverage of the law to men alone. It is commendable that the book delves into "a gender-sensitive interpretation and implementation of International Humanitarian Law as a vital mechanism for responding adequately to the needs of both men and women, and more especially women who are disproportionately affected in the event of armed conflicts". In order to achieve the aim of the author, the book is structured in seven chapters. The introductory chapter deals with, *inter alia*, challenges for International Humanitarian Law while chapter two espouses theories, thoughts and concepts in the legal protection of women. Historical evolution of the impact of war on women in ancient, medieval and modern era is the focus of chapter three. In striking a chord on the main subject of research in the book, the author examines the protective laws and institutions for women victims of armed conflicts in Africa. Nigeria, DR Congo and Sierra Leone are vividly used as case studies in assessing the standard of protection afforded by the relevant laws and institutions. The assessment is expanded in chapter five where judicial enforcement of the rights of women in armed conflicts in the selected countries is undertaken. Chapter six is a verdict on the effectiveness of implementation measures on legal protection of women in the armed conflicts in the three countries for comparative studies. The final chapter draws salient conclusions from the premise of the research, and offered recommendations.

I congratulate the author for venturing into the chosen area of research and achieving the aim of the research. The book is an immense contribution to knowledge and an academic resource material to students, jurists, legal practitioners and members of the public at both national and international levels. It is highly recommended.

Prof. A. D. Badaiki, SAN
B. A. (Hons); LL.B (Hons.) (BENSU); LL.M (Lagos); LL.M (EDSU); PhD; B.L;
PGDM; AMNIM, MNIMN; FCIArb; FCITN; FIMC; CMC
Professor of Law, President Society of International Humanitarian
Law Teachers of Nigeria, Legal Practitioner, Arbitrator, Tax
Consultant and Notary Public,
former Dean, Faculty of Law,
and School of Postgraduate Studies,
Ambrose Alli University,
Ekpoma, Edo State,
Nigeria.

This book titled *International Humanitarian Law: Protecting the Rights of Women in Armed Conflicts* is quite timely. Armed conflicts have devastating consequences on the entire population but its impact is mostly felt by women who have become targets for both state and non-state actors. The incidences of abductions, rapes and other acts of sexual violence against women in times of armed conflict are unprecedented. Rapes and other forms of sexual violence are used as a method of warfare by armed groups. These women who are victims of these crimes often do not seek justice due to the attendant consequences of rejection, shame. Coupled with this is the fact that these women are traumatized and are victims of sexually transmitted diseases and infections and lack knowledge on what steps to take in addressing the issue.

This book is very apt as noted earlier as it has articulated the legal and institutional frameworks available for redress in situations of violations of the rights of women in times of armed conflict. The book is presented in well-articulated and easy to read prose, an evidence of the fact that the author is a master of his game. Dr Emmanuel Ibezim is an expert in Gender and Law studies especially International Humanitarian Law (IHL) having taught IHL for 25 years. He has also attended national and international conferences on IHL and served as Ad hoc judge in the annual International Humanitarian law national moot court competitions organized by the Abuja Regional Delegation of International Committee of the Red Cross (ICRC). He has also groomed and led students to national and international competitions and moot court trials on IHL.

The author writes from a standpoint of knowledge and expertise. This book is an invaluable material for both IHL teachers and students and I want to encourage all to get copies for themselves and the Law Librarians of law faculties should purchase copies for the law libraries. Relatively few textbooks on gender and IHL exist. Certainly this book will contribute in filling the existing gap.

Prof. Theresa Akpoghome
Dean, Faculty of Law,
Benson Idahosa University,
Benin City, Nigeria.
Member, Society of International Humanitarian Law Teachers
of Nigeria.

Preface

As the branch of public international law that protects victims of armed conflicts, International Humanitarian Law (IHL) has become of great importance to war-torn Africa. This is reflected in the increasing number of Law faculties in Africa that offer the course, especially through the promotional activities of the International Committee of the Red Cross (ICRC). The ICRC has continued to champion the publication of books and periodicals on IHL and facilitated interactions within academic circles.

Granted that ICRC has published considerable reading materials on the impact of armed conflicts on women, this book reaches farther by viewing their experiences from the prism of gender, and challenges the present limited state of the law, which is based on formal equality of the sexes. This is the more so, because women suffer more as their rights are violated disproportionately in relation to men's, during armed conflicts. This is why this book has integrated a gender perspective, which also reflects feminist impulses. This has offered the expanded advantage of treating women in armed conflicts as women qua women, on the one hand and, women in the face of their respective social and cultural situations or roles, on the other hand.

A number of formidable limitations were faced in the writing of this book. Firstly, the dangers and violence of war prohibits direct or personal study tours of war zones, thereby limiting one's research studies to *ex post facto* descriptions of the impact of war on women. Definitely, such *ex post facto* narratives of the war may have lost vital and critical facts, or such facts may have been underplayed or exaggerated. Secondly, the history of women as subjects of law is rather very short. That of research or even concern for the legal protection of women, especially during armed conflicts is even much shorter. Consequently, relatively few researches had been conducted on the legal protection of women during armed conflicts, thereby resulting in a relative paucity of researched materials and information. The problem is exacerbated by the fact that the legal systems collapse completely in times of armed conflicts making it difficult, if not impossible for the courts to operate.

This book focuses on the legal protection of women in armed conflicts in Africa and has in this 'volume one' captured Nigeria, DR Congo and Sierra-Leone. Other countries in Africa that have experienced armed conflicts should be expected in subsequent volumes.

However, it remains to state that this book is an adaptation of the author's Ph.D thesis, and thus has necessarily retained some of its relevant features.

Emmanuel C. Ibezim
2021

List of Abbreviations

AC - Appeal Cases.

AD - Anno Domini (Since Christ was born; after the birth of Christ)

ADFL - Alliance of Democratic Forces for the Liberation of Congo

AFRC - Armed Forces Revolutionary Council

AG - Attorney General

AIDS - Acquired Immune Deficiency Syndrome

AP - Additional Protocol

ASF - Avocats Sans Frontiers

AYIHL - African Year Book of International Humanitarian Law

BC - Before Christ

CA - Circa (around/about)

CAE - Special African Chamber

CC - Criminal Code

CCSSP - Common Wealth Community Safety and Security Project.

ICT - International Crimes Tribunal

CDF - Civil Defense Forces

CEDAW Convention on the Elimination of All Forms of Discrimination against Women

CF - Compare (Latin, confer)

CFS - Congo Free State

CO. - Company

DDR - Disarmament, Demobilization and Reintegration.

DFID - Department for International Development

DRC - DR Congo

ECOMOG - Economic Community of West African States Monitoring Group.

Ed. - Editor or Edition

Edn. - Edition

Eds. - Editors

Eg - For example, for instance (Latin, Exempli Gratia)

Et.al. - And others (Latin, Et Alii)

Etc - And so Forth (Latin, Et cetera)

FAWE - Forum of African Women Educationalist

FDD - Forces for the Defense of Democracy

Feb. - February

Fn - Foot note

FSUS - Family Support Units.

Gov. - Government

HCJ - High Court of Justice

HIV - Human Immuno…. Virus

HRW - Human Rights Watch http ----Hyper Text Transfer Protocol

http - Hyper Text Transfer Protocol

https - Hyper Text Transfer Protocol Secure

IACHR - Inter-America Commission on Human Rights

Ibid - *Ibid*em (In the same Already Specified Place, Book or Material)

ICC - International Criminal Court

ICJ - International Court of Justice

ICRC - International Committee of the Red Cross

ICTR - International Criminal Tribunal for Rwanda

ICTJ - International Center for Transitional Justice.

ICTY - International Criminal Tribunal for Yugoslavia

IDP - Internally Displaced Persons

IEDs - Improvised Explosive Devices

IHL - International Humanitarian Law

Inc. - Incorporated

Internet - International Network of Computers

IOM - International Organization of Migration

IRRC - International Review of the Red Cross

LL.M - Master of Laws Degree

LTD - Limited

LTTE - Liberation Tyers of Tamil Ealam

MLC - Movement for the Liberation of Congo

MONUC - United Nations Organisation Mission in the DR Congo

NLPF - Liberian National Liberation Patriotic Front

No. - Number

OMCT - World Organization against Torture

OSISA - Open Society Initiative for Southern Africa.

OSJI - Open Society Justice Initiative

Op.cit - Opera Citatus (In the Work Cited Before)

P. - Page

Para - Paragraph

P. C - Penal Code

Ph.D - Doctor of Philosophy

PHR - Physicians for Human Rights

Pp. - Pages

RCD - Congolese Rally for Democracy

REJUSCO - European Union Programme for the Restoration of Justice in Eastern Congo.

RLA - Rwandan Liberation Army

RPA - Rwandan Patriotic Army

RUF - Revolutionary United Front

RULAC - Rule of Law in Armed Conflicts Project.

S - Section

SCS - Special Court of Senegal

SCSL - Special Court for Sierra Leone

Supra - Above

UDHR- Universal Declaration of Human Rights

UN - United Nations

UNESCO - United Nation Educational, Scientific and Cultural Organization.

UNDP - United Nations Development Programme

UNFPA- United Nations Fund for Population Activities

UNHCR- United Nation High Commission for Refugees

UNICEF - United Nations International Children Education Fund

UNIFEM - United Nations Development Fund for Women

UNITA- National Union for the Total Independence of Angola

US - United States of America

USAID - United States Agency for International Development

USD - United States Dollar

v - Against (Versus)

Vol. - Volume

WHO - World Health Organization.

www - World Wide Website.

Abstract

Existing laws on armed conflicts, otherwise embodied as International Humanitarian Law, are mostly gender insensitive to women. This insensitivity is reflected in the language of the law. The linguistic disposition of the law, which goes to the root of legal draftsmanship, seems to operate to limit its substantive coverage, that is, its material content (especially those of the Geneva Conventions and their Additional Protocols), to men alone. This problem raises number of questions. Thus the aims and objectives of this research are to answer these questions and seek to foster a gender-sensitive interpretation and implementation of International Humanitarian Law as a vital mechanism for responding adequately to the needs of both men and women, and more especially women who are disproportionately affected in the event of armed conflicts. To achieve these, information and data have been processed with a keen sensitivity to the plight of women in the armed conflicts in selected African countries namely: Nigeria, DR Congo and Sierra Leone. Research findings reveal that the Geneva Conventions and their Additional Protocols are not gender-sensitive enough to protect women in armed conflicts. While subsequent legal instruments like the Rome Statute of International Criminal Court (1998), the Convention on the Elimination of All Forms of Discrimination Against Women (1979), the Protocol to the African Charter on the Rights of Women (2003), etcetera, are couched in gender-specific language in favour of women they are defeated in their effects by conflicting national laws that are discriminatory of women, and governments lack of political will to domesticate them. Moreover, patriarchal customs and traditions that discriminate against women still pervade in Africa and militate against the implementation and enforcement of International humanitarian law rules that are protective of women. The courts should therefore declare such customs and traditions as contrary to natural justice, equity and good conscience, and therefore null and void, while governments should repeal legislations that discriminate against women and enact legislations that are gender-sensitive to them. Such legislative actions should also target the cultural component of the law by providing for sustained enlightenment campaigns, etcetera aimed at mainstreaming gender in the implementation and enforcement of the law.

CHAPTER ONE

Introduction

❦

1. 1 General Background.

Women form part of the most vulnerable groups in the event of armed conflicts.[1] It is therefore apparent that they, do not only need protection, but also deserve to be specially protected as an imperative state or international policy. The basic instrument of protection has been law, especially the Law of Armed Conflicts or International Humanitarian Law (IHL), which is complemented by International Criminal Law, and International Human Rights Law. However, until recently the ability of States and international agencies or authorities, especially the United Nations to implement these laws, and bring criminals to justice, by enforcing them, has been quite questionable. This is more so, in relation to women whose access to justice has been further curtailed or hampered by elements of gender discrimination inherent in the relevant laws. Such discrimination can be found both in the language and the material content of the laws. Of course, the present state of the law is consistent with gender discrimination against women as a norm.

In the event of an armed conflict, this norm is exacerbated by the culture of impunity that characterizes armed conflicts and conduces to the targeting of girls and women, as objects of sexual abuse and

---

[1] Other vulnerable groups are decidedly children, the aged, the wounded and the sick.

rape. The historical fact that women have been regarded as booties of war and non-legal persons against whom sexual violence could be perpetrated encourages impunity against them. The equally historical fact that perpetrators of atrocities against women were hardly prosecuted emboldens them to systematically commit even greater atrocities against women.

The recent developments in International Criminal Law, which have seen increasing prosecution of war criminals and for the first time the prosecution of sexual crimes against women during the armed conflict in the Former Yugoslavia and the armed conflict and genocide in Rwanda, are thus a welcome relief.

In the face of the long lull between the Nuremberg, and the Tokyo trials of 1945 – 1948, the establishment of the International Criminal Tribunals for former Yugoslavia and Rwanda (1993 and 1994), respectively, and the ultimate establishment of the International Criminal Court (ICC) under the 1998 Rome Statute,[2] the world witnessed horrendous violations of International Humanitarian Law. War crimes, crimes against humanity, and genocide were committed with impunity, in the many armed conflicts that the world has witnessed, since the end of the Second World War. In all these violations, women were disproportionately affected, and in fact deliberately targeted as a strategy of war.

The negatives and legal analysis in this book are against the backdrop of the those armed conflicts, most of which have been prosecuted with utmost brutality, and which have targeted women as a deliberate strategy of war, and in furtherance of the genocidal

---

[2] *Rome statute of the International Criminal Court* (1998), entered into force on 1 July, 2002.

phenomenon of ethnic cleansing. Africa has been the setting for most of such wars, where mass rapes and the targeting of civilians have been reported. The genocide and the armed conflict in Rwanda saw rape of women as a weapon of war, and ethnic cleansing. In Darfur, the Sudanese-sponsored *Janjaweed* militias routinely brought out and gang-raped women of three African tribes, then cut-off their ears or mutilate them to mark them forever as rape victims.[3] During the armed conflict in Sierra Leone, half of the women in that country were reported to have 'endured sexual violence or the threat of it, while 90 percent of girls and women over the age of three were reported to have been sexually abused in parts of Liberia during the Civil War there'.[4] On the other hand, eastern Congo has been declared the world capital of rape. There, militias consider it risky to engage in fire fights with other gunmen, so instead they assault civilians.[5] Particularly, they rape women with stunning brutality in their bid to terrorize civilian populations.[6]

In the face of use of widespread rape in these armed conflicts in Africa and those in the former Yugoslavia and Bosnia, in 2008, the United Nations formally declared rape as a 'weapon of war'. Speaking of spread of rape as a war tactic, Major General Patrick Cammaert, a former United Nations Force Commander made the following haunting statement: 'it has probably become more

---

[3] Kristof, N. D. and WuDunn, S., *Half of the sky: Turning Oppression into Opportunity for Women Worldwide*, New
York, Vintage Books, 2010, 83.

[4] *Ibid.*

[5] *Ibid.*, 84.

[6] *Ibid.*

dangerous to be a woman than a soldier in an armed conflict'.[7] This ominous statement seems to have been underlined in Nigeria as the *Boko Haram* Islamic sect[8] target women for abduction and rape, in their bid to terrorize civilian populations. The terrorist attacks which started in 2009 as religious riots and insurrections have long assumed the status of an armed conflict between the Federal Republic of Nigeria and the *Boko Haram* Islamic sect.[9] It was the abduction by *Boko Haram* of about two hundred girls, from the Government Secondary School in Chibok, Borno State, on April 14, 2014, which drew an overwhelming global attention to the armed conflict in Nigeria. The sect refused to release the girls who were abducted, in a dusk raid upon their school, in spite of national and international public outcry.

The *Chibok* girls' experience soon became a pattern, and a strategy of war as the sect continued to abduct girls and women, with their children, ostensibly as sex objects, forced labourers, and human shields. For instance, the insurgents abducted seventy women in June, 2014, from Kummabza village in Damboa Local Government Area of Borno State. Fortunately, sixty-three out of the seventy women escaped from captivity and returned to their homes,

---

[7] *Ibid.*

[8] The *Boko Haram* (Books are evil) sect, otherwise known as Jama'atul Ahlus Sunnah Lidda Awatiwal Jihad was founded in 2002 by one Mohammed Yusuf, who had since been killed, in controversial circumstances.

[9] The International Criminal Court (ICC), Prosecutor had in 2013 declared that Nigeria was in a state of armed conflict with *Boko Haram*. The International Committee of the Red Cross had also in the same year, independently declared that Nigeria was in a state of armed conflict with *Boko Haram*, and went further to characterize it as an armed conflict of non-international character, while in 2014, the Nigeria, National Human Rights Commission confirmed the assertions.

when the insurgents left them in the camp to embark on an operation against military formations.[10] Another notorious case of *Boko Haram* abduction was that of *Dapchi* school girls.[11] The school girls, numbering one hundred and ten (110) and aged between 11 – 19 years old were abducted by the *Boko Haram* terrorists on February 19, 2018, at about 5:30p.m. Fortunately, the girls were released on 21st March, 2018, in controversial circumstances, while five (5) of them were presumed dead.[12]

More recently, in December, 2020, *Boko Haram* struck again, this time allegedly abducting more than three hundred school boys from an all-boys Government Secondary School in Katsina State, North-West of Nigeria. Again, they were released in controversial circumstances.[13]

The number of girls and women that have been abducted and raped or killed by the insurgents, may never be known, but there are reports that more than six hundred and seventy-seven women and girls were freed, when soldiers destroyed more than a dozen insurgents' camps in the Sambisa forest.[14] Tragically, out of two hundred and thirty-four women and children that were rescued by the Nigerian Army, from one of the camps in the forest alone, two

---

[10] See the Punch Newspaper of Monday, July 7, 2014, 9 & 19.

[11] See 'Dapchi School girls kidnapping', available at https://en.m.wikipedia.org (Accessed on 21-08-2018)

[12] UN report, 'Huge ransom paid for release of Dapchi girls' available at https://punchng.com (Accessed on 21-08-2018)

[13] See 'Nigeria official: 'More than 300 abducted school boys freed', (17-12-2020)available at apnews.com (Accessed 30-12-2020)

[14] Yusuf, U., 'Boko Haram stones captives to death', [Monday, May 4, 2015], *Vanguard Newspaper*, (Vol. 25, No. 62397), 5.

hundred and fourteen were visibly pregnant.[15] In this connection, the then Executive Director, United Nations Fund for Population Activities (UNFPA), Professor Babatunde Osotimehin disclosed that in the last one year, the organization had taken deliveries of over sixteen thousand pregnancies in the troubled North East of the country.[16]

Some of the women who survived the ordeal narrate how the terrorists stoned many women and children to death as the military approached to rescue them.[17] Clearly, for *Boko Haram* insurgents, targeting of women and children is a deliberate strategy of war, aimed at demoralizing the government, and terrorizing the entire Nigerian population. So also is their use of mostly women as suicide bombers, a phenomenon that has been described as the "weaponization" of women. This form of mortal objectification of women seems to serve a number of tactical purposes, namely: 1. The women serve as effective smugglers (in the present case bombs) and arouse less suspicion while moving in civilian areas; 2. Their attacks have high propaganda value and are more likely to be sensationalized by the media than attacks by men. In other words as a human bomb mission, 'it attracts higher shock value and more media coverage if it involves a female martyr.'[18]

---

[15] *Ibid.*, 58.

[16] *Ibid.*

[17] *Ibid.*

[18] Blogger, Q., and Campbell, J. 'Women and the Boko Haram Insurgency', available at
http:blogs.cfc.org/cambell/2015/08/11/women-and-the-boko-haram-insurgency (accessed on 10th April, 2016). See

This same effect of demoralizing government and terrorizing a whole population may have been achieved by the Nigerian government against Igbo's during the Nigeria Civil War (1967 – 1970), as civilians, especially Biafran women and children were targeted.

Besides being deliberately targeted by air raids on markets, schools, churches, *etcetera,* the Nigerian government's policy of starvation, as a legitimate strategy of war, operated to affect women and their children, disproportionately, leaving in its wake, grotesque pictures of hunger, sufferings and death. This was an experience that evoked widespread sentiments and vocal allegations of genocide against Nigeria.

1.2 Background to the Armed Conflicts.

It may be necessary at this point to briefly state the background to the Nigeria-Biafra Civil War. Nigeria gained independence from the United Kingdom in 1960. Just like most enclaves in colonial Africa, its boundaries were arbitrarily demarcated to serve the competing claims of the imperial powers. At inception, it thus could hardly be described as a nation. For instance, in 1948, Sir Abubakar Tafawa Balewa, a prominent Northern Nigerian, who later became the Prime Minister of Nigeria remarked:

Since 1914, the British Government has been trying to make Nigeria into one country, but the Nigerian people themselves are historically different in their backgrounds, in their

___

also 'Boko Haram Turn Nigerian Girls to Female Suicide Bombers, available at https:/www.naij.com/275853-boko-
haram-nigerian-girls-suicide-bombers.html (accessed on 2oth May, 2016).

religious beliefs and customs and do not show themselves any signs of willingness to unite…. Nigerian unity is only a British invention.[19]

A year earlier, Obafemi Awolowo, the Yoruba leader, who dominated Western Nigerian politics for more than thirty years, wrote:

Nigeria is not a nation. It is a mere geographical expression. There is no "Nigerian" in the sense as there are "English", "Welsh, or "French". The word "Nigerian" is merely a distinctive appellation to distinguish those who live within the boundaries of Nigeria and those who do not.[20]

However, Nigeria was composed of semi-autonomous Muslim feudal states in the desert north, and once-powerful Christian and animist kingdoms in the south and east.

Nigeria's independence constitution comprised of three regions made up of the principal ethnic groups in the country – the Hausa and the Fulani in the north, Yoruba in the south-west, and Ibo in the south-east. However, the emergent political class mismanaged the polity, while nepotism and corruption became the order of the day. This led to military coups in 1966.

On the 15th of January 1966, some young military officers led by Major Chukwuma Nzeogwu carried out a bloody coup de'tat which resulted in the death of some senior military and civilian leaders.[21]

---

[19] Martin, M., *The State of Africa: A History of the Continent since Independence*, New Delhi/Sydney, Simon & Schuster, 2011, 8.

[20] *Ibid*.

[21] Madiebo, A. A, *The Nigerian Revolution and the Biafran War*, Enugu, Fourth Dimension Publishing Co. Ltd., 1980, 17-19.

The dead included the Prime Minister, Sir Abubakar Tafawa Belewa, the Premier of Northern Region, the Sarduana of Sokoto, Sir Ahmadu Bello, the Minister of Finance, Chief Festus Okotie-Eboh, the Premier Western Region, Chief S. O. Akintola, Brigadier Ademulegun, Colonel Ralph Shodeinde, the commandant. The three most senior Northern officers, Brigadier Maimalari, Lt. Col. Pam (Adjutant-General) and Lt. Col. Largema (Commander, Fourth Battalion), were also killed. Lt. Col. Unegbe, an Ibo who was in charge of the ammunition store at Ikeja barracks was killed for refusing to hand over the keys to the store.[22]

Major General Aguiyi Ironsi who seemed to have been on the list of those to be eliminated foiled the coup in Lagos and according to Walter Schwarz in his book, Nigeria:

> The failure of the coup in Lagos had scotched the one in Enugu. Whether the presence of Archbishop Makarios had saved Okpara's life, or whether Ibo soldiers had, after all, found it impossible to kill one of their own tribesmen, is not yet clear.[23]

The North was the only region where the coup succeeded as planned. This, and the fact that those killed were mostly westerners and northerners may have been responsible for the sentiment that the coup was an Igbo coup carried out by mainly Igbo officers, so as to hijack power for the Igbo race.[24] This claim has been thoroughly

---

[22] Uwechue, R., *Reflections on the Nigerian Civil War: Facing the Future*, Paris, Jeune Afrique, 1971, 24.

[23] *Ibid.*, 26.

[24] See, Ezeani, E., *In Biafra Africa Died: The Diplomatic Plot* (2nd ed.), London, Veritas Lumen Publishers, 2013, 22-   23 for arguments on the theory of the 'Igbo Coup'.

debunked by many objective observers that include non-Igbos, and particularly some principal actors in the 15th January coup.[25]

However, it was against the background of this theory of an 'Igbo coup' that northern elements staged the counter coup of 29th July 1966. That counter coup proved to be very bloody with the mass killing of officers and men of the Nigerian army who were Igbos. The killings took place in the 2nd Brigade in the south, precisely in Abeokuta, Ibadan and Ikeja barracks. Generally, operations in the North did not start until about twenty-four hours after they had begun in the south. Officers and men of Eastern Nigerian origin were also targeted and killed. Meanwhile, the Supreme Commander, Major General Aguiyi Ironsi, and Lt. Col. Adekunle Fajuyi had been tortured and killed in Ibadan. The planners of the coup installed Lt. Col. Yakubu Gowon as the Head of state and commander-in-chief of the Armed Forces of Nigeria.

Subsequently, in waves of violence, the northern troops in collaboration with northern civilians and civilian authorities massacred easterners and mainly Igbos in virtually all parts of the North.[26] This resulted into the first armed conflict in Nigeria, namely the Nigerian civil war. Boko Harram insurgency constitutes the second.

---

[25] *Ibid.*, 22 – 37.

[26] The massacre was so extensive that some commentator described it as a pogrom. The statistics of the dead was estimated at between 30,000 – 50,000 persons (men, women and children). In fact, according to Chinua Achebe, Colin Legum of the observer (UK) was the first to describe the massacre as a pogrom. See Achebe, C., *There was a country: A personal History of Biafra*, London/New York, Allen Lane/Penguin Books, 2012, 82.

The Nigerian Civil War otherwise described as the Nigeria-Biafra War was therefore a fall-out of the successive military coups of January 15, 1966, and July 29, 1966. Following the counter-coup of July which witnessed the cold-blooded murder of one hundred and eighty-five Igbo military officers and the massacre of thirty thousand Igbos and Easterners in pogroms that started in May 1966 and lasted over a period of four months without the emergent military regime led by Gowon, a Northerner doing anything to stop the massacre, the Igbos and Easterners generally lost faith in the Federal Government.[27] The Igbos and Easterners 'fled "home" to Eastern Nigeria to escape all manner of atrocities that were inflicted upon us and our families in different parts of Nigeria, we saw ourselves as victims.'[28]

The fact that the Federal Government did not respond to calls to end the pogrom, nor did it care much about the internally displaced persons of Igbo origin spurred the Igbos and Easterners on to consider secession. Ultimately, the government of Eastern Nigeria became resolute and declared the birth of the sovereign state of Republic of Biafra,[29] while, the Federal Military Government purported to have restructured the polity by creating twelve states out of the existing four regions, thereby balkanizing Eastern Nigeria

---

[27] Achebe, C., *Ibid*.

[28] *Ibid*.

[29] The historic declaration of the Republic of Biafra as an independent state was made on 30th May, 1967. For more information on events in Biafra, see, Ojukwu, C. O., *Biafra: Selected Speeches with Journals of Events*, New York, Harper & Row Publishers, 1969.

and the other regions into disparate states.[30] Consequently, the Nigeria Civil War broke out in July 1967, when military units from Nigeria that attempted to advance into secessionist Biafran territory, in what the then Federal Military Government of Nigeria had termed 'Police measure or action', were repelled by Biafran troops. This recourse to the use of armed forces amounted to an armed conflict in the eyes of the law, and an armed conflict of international character, if the recourse to armed forces was indeed between two states.[31] That is however doubtful in this case as the fledgling nascent Republic of Biafra was not recognized as an independent state by Nigeria, and the international community was also yet to recognize it as such.

However, one arm of the *Tadic* definition of armed conflict recognizes 'protracted armed violence between governmental authorities and organized armed groups or between such groups within a state', as also an armed conflict, but that of a non-international character.[32] Thus, as at July 1967, the Nigeria-Biafra conflict could be described as an armed conflict of non international character as the Nigerian forces could at least be described as 'governmental authorities', while the Biafran forces could at worst be described as 'organized armed groups'. The issue of protractedness, though factual, is more or less subjective. However, that the conflict lasted for about three years leaves no one in any doubt that it was protracted and thus qualified as an armed conflict.

---

[30] Eastern Region was divided into three states, namely, East Central State, Rivers State and South East State.

[31] See again *Prosecutor v Tadic*, Decision on the Defence Motion for Interlocutory Appeal on Jurisdiction, Tadic (IT-94-1), October 1995, s.70.

[32] *Supra*

The name 'Biafra' is said to have been taken from the name of an ancient kingdom in Africa which encompassed the then Eastern Region and part of the Western Region of what later became Nigeria.[33] The Federal Military Government of Nigeria responded by declaring war against the nascent republic ostensibly in a bid to force Biafra back into the Nigerian union.[34] The *Biafran* government fought to defend the territorial integrity of the nascent nation and cried out that the Nigerian aggression was a war of genocide. The war which ended in January, 1970 with the formal surrender of secessionist Biafra took a great toll on the *Biafran* civilian population, especially children, women and the elderly. The situation was exacerbated by the adoption of a policy of starvation as a weapon of war by the Nigerian government.

Boko Haram terrorist insurgency in the North East of Nigeria constitutes the highest internal security challenge that Nigeria has faced since the end of the Civil War in 1970. By the end of 2012, *Boko Haram* was said to have killed three thousand people.[35] The number

---

[33] Ezeani, E., *Op.cit*, 39. However, the name 'Biafra' had survived in the name of a body of water called 'Bight of Biafra', which had since after the war been renamed *Gulf of Guinea by the Nigerian government.*

[34] Nigeria declared war against *Biafra* on 6th July, 1967, and boasted of crushing Biafra in 48 hours. She imposed sea and air blockade against *Biafra*, making it difficult for food, weapon and other essential materials to come into Biafra.

[35] See Muhammad Bello, and others, 'Boko Haram has killed 3,000 people says Army chief', Nigerian Thisday Newspaper, November 6, 2012. Available at http://www.thisdaylive.com/ articles/bokoharam-has killed-3-000-people-says-army-chief/129809/ (Accessed January 11, 2013) and cited in Udounwa, S. E. 'Boko Haram: Developing New Strategies to combat Terrorism in Nigeria', A Research Project submitted in partial fulfillment of the requirement of the Master of Strategic Studies Degree at the United States Army War College, 2013, endnote 3.

may have doubled by now.[36] They bombed Churches, Mosques, Police Stations, Government properties, Markets and Crowded places.[37] Consequently, the Federal Government declared a State of Emergency in the three worst-hit states of the North East that is Borno, Yobe and Adamawa.

In spite of the State of Emergency, the group grew from strength to strength, as it fought 'with renewed energy and ruthlessness'[38] and carried out deadly attacks in the states, as well as in some other Northern states in the country including the Nation's capital, Abuja. They even occupied a number of towns in the states, until a reinvigorated Nigerian Armed Forces routed the group and largely degraded their military capability. However, the remnants of the Boko Haram fighters retreated deep into the Sambisa forest from which they carry out sporadic attacks, and have resorted to laying land mines on stretches of farm land in their desperate bid to unleash terror on the people.[39]

Meanwhile, the Nigerian Police reports to have fully taken over four liberated towns and cities in Borno State from *Boko Haram*; and also announced that it has concluded plans to take over other nineteen liberated towns in the state before the end of April 2016.[40] Clearly, the war is not yet over, as *Boko Haram* has continued to

---

[36] Unfortunately, no reliable statistics may be available.

[37] Peterside, Z. B., 'The Military and Internal Security in Nigeria: Challenges and Prospects', [2014], *Mediterranean*

Journal of Social Sciences, (Vol. 5, No 27), 1304.

[38] *Ibid.*

[39] Kilete, M., 'Boko Haram: Police take over 4 liberated towns in Borno ...', [Wednesday, April 27, 2016], *DailySun*, (Vol. 10 No. 3393), 2.

[40] '... Insurgents Launch new uniform, ID: Soldier Kill Kingpin, 6 others', *Ibid.*

launch surprise attacks through bands of terrorists, or through suicide bombers, whilst insidiously recruiting new combatants or insurgents. They even have recently launched new uniforms.[41]

Clearly Boko Haram insurgency and Nigerian war against terrorism started as an internal disturbance, which is normally classified in International Humanitarian Law under 'Other Situations of Violence'. However, its violent attacks against Christians, government personnel and even fellow Muslims perceived as uncooperative with them, and their confrontations with the Nigerian army, in their bid to impose an exclusive Islamic system of government continued until they reached an unprecedented scale and intensity which has been considered to reach the threshold of an armed conflict.

The Office of the Prosecutor ('OTP'), International Criminal Court ('ICC') which is responsible for determining whether a situation meets the legal criteria established by the *Rome Statute* to warrant investigation by the court has examined the situation in Nigeria and published its Article 5 Report on the situation in Nigeria, including the situation relative to Boko Haram.[42] The report states as

---

[41] *Ibid.*

[42] See Article 5 Report on 'Situation in Nigeria' dated 5 August, 2013, published by the Office of the Prosecutor, International Criminal Court. According to the report, in order to distinguish the situations that warrant investigation from those that do not, the office has a filtering process comprising four consecutive phases:

In phase 1, the Office conducts an initial assessment of all information on alleged crimes received under article 15 of the Rome Statute ('article 15 communications') to filter out information on crimes that are outside the jurisdiction of the court.

In phase 2, the Office analyses all information on alleged crimes received or collected to determine whether the preconditions to the exercise of jurisdiction under article 12 of the Rome Statute are satisfied and whether there is a reasonable

follows with regard to the conflict and clashes between the Boko Haram insurgents and the Nigeria security operatives:

> At the time of writing, analysis suggests that the security operation against Boko Haram may still fall under the category of 'internal disturbances' as opposed to a non-international armed conflict. However, the issue remains subject to on-going analysis. The Office will seek additional information on the types and the geographical spread of security operations and the structure and organization of the JTF and other relevant security forces in order to fine-tune its assessment.[43]

Apparently, since that investigation and report, the prosecutor must have accessed additional information on the situation as it later on declared in late 2013, that Nigeria was in a state of non-international armed conflict with *Boko Haram*. On its own part, and independently too, the International Committee of the Red Cross (ICRC), also declared the situation in Nigeria, as an armed conflict

---

basis to believe that the alleged crimes fall under the subject-matter jurisdiction of the court as per article 5 of the Rome Statute.

In phase 3, the Office analyses admissibility in terms of complementarity and gravity as per article 17 of the Rome Statute.

In phase 4, having concluded from its preliminary examination that the case is admissive *prima facie*, the Office, taking into account the gravity of the crimes and the interest of victims, examines under article 53(1)(c) whether there are nonetheless substantial reasons to believe that an investigation would not serve the interests of justice.

[43] See ICC Article 5 Report on 'Situation in Nigeria', para 113. According to Para 83, 'available information appears sufficient to establish that Boko Haram could be considered as an "organization" capable of defining and implementing a policy of committing crimes against humanity. The group appears to be under a responsible command, namely the leadership exerted by Abubakar Shekau'.

of non-international character in 2013, while in 2014, the National
Human Rights Commission in Nigeria confirmed that the country
was engaged in an armed conflict of non-international character, as
had been established by the prosecutor, International Criminal
Court and the International Committee of the Red Cross.[44] Besides,
extant precedent on levying of war in Nigeria supports the view that
Abubakar Shekau-led *Boko Haram* insurgency against the
government and peoples of Nigeria amounts to levying of war
against Nigeria.[45] In *Adaka Boro and Others v The Republic*,[46] Isaac
Adaka Boro (the 1st defendant/appellant) proclaimed an
independent Niger Delta Peoples Republic with a flag of its own and
an emergency constitution. He formed a band of fighters (which
included the other appellants) and trained them in the use of arms
and explosives. They attacked a police station, blew up the armory,
and took rifles and ammunitions; blew up two oil pipelines; and had
a gun battle with the police. They were prosecuted for treason
contrary to *section* 37(1), of the *Criminal Code of Nigeria* which reads:
'Any person who levies war against the State, in order to intimidate
or overawe the President or the Governor of a Region, is guilty of
treason, and is liable to the punishment of death'.[47]

---

[44] The foregoing classification of the conflict situation in Nigeria was reported by
Professor Anselem Odinkalu, Chairman of the National Human Rights
Commission in an interview broadcast nation-wide on Channels Television, on
24th February, 2015.

[45] See *Boro and Others v The Republic*, (SC.377/66), All NLR, 263-273.

[46] *Supra.*

[47] 'Following the events of mid-January 1966, the former civilian government of
Nigeria handed over power to the military authorities, and the government of
Nigeria became the Federal Military Government. From the 17th January, 1966, by
virtue of Section 12 of Decree, No. 1 of 1966 and paragraph 2 of the Second

The court held that 'the defendants (appellants) levied war against the State and did so in order to frighten the Government of Nigeria into acquiescence in their carving out of an area of Nigeria as an independent republic, and that was an offence against s.37 (1); and that it did not matter that Government had a superior force or that its Head was too far to be frightened'.[48] They were therefore convicted of treason and sentenced to death.

On appeal, counsel to the appellants agreed that they had levied war against the State, but submitted that the object of *section 37* (I) of the *Criminal Code* was to protect the personal safety of the Head of State and that to sustain the charge, it must be proved (but was not) that he was intimidated or overawed by fear of injury to his person.[49] In dismissing the appeal, the Supreme Court held as follows:

1. The Head of State is the embodiment of the State, and to intimidate [or overawe] him is the same as intimidating [or overawing] the State.

2. In section 37(1) of the Criminal Code, to overawe the Head of State connotes the creation of a situation in which Government feels compelled to choose between yielding to force and exposing its members or the public to very serious danger; it is not necessary that the danger should be the danger of personal injury to the Head of State.

Schedule thereof, the reference to the President in Section 37(1) of the Criminal Code is to be construed as a reference to the Head of the Federal Military Government – hence the reference in the information.' (*Boro and others v The Republic, Supra, at 266*).

[48] *Supra, 263.*

[49] *Supra, 263-264.*

3. The evidence established an intent to overawe the Head
    of the Federal Military Government when interpreted as
    the embodiment of the state.[50]

The court also observes that appellants' counsel cited *sections* 121
and 124 of the *Indian Penal Code* in aid of his argument, and notes
that *section* 121A of the Indian Penal Code, which he did not refer to
is more relevant. It therefore, notes the case, *Mir Hasan Khan v The
State*,[51] which deals with the section, and quotes Shearer J, as follows:

> The word 'overawe' clearly imports more than the creation
> of apprehension or alarm or even perhaps fear. It appears to
> me to connote the creation of a situation in which the
> members of the Central or the Provincial Government feel
> themselves compelled to choose between yielding to force or
> exposing themselves or members of the public to a very
> serious danger. It is not necessary that the danger should be
> the danger of assassination or of bodily injury to themselves.
> The danger might as well be a danger to public property or
> to the safety of members of the general public.

Judged against the background of the foregoing case, it is
abundantly clear that Abubakar Shekau and his cohorts have levied
war against Nigeria. It is equally clear that the Boko Haram/
Nigerian war against terrorism is an armed conflict of non-
international character. Applicable laws may include *Article* 3
common to the *Geneva Conventions*; the *Geneva Conventions Act of
Nigeria* (1961); Customary International Humanitarian Law;
Nigerian national laws, especially, the *Criminal and Penal Codes*[52];

---

[50] *Supra*, 264.

[51] (1951) A. J. R. (Patna) 60, at 65.

[52] The list covers ratifications as at 30th may, 2013.

Refugee Laws, and Guidelines for the treatment of internally displaced persons.[53]

The following historical facts may be given as a background to the armed conflict in DR Congo. The country was first known as the Congo Free State (CFS), in 1885.[54] In November, 1908, the Congo Free State was colonized by Belgium, which changed her name to Belgian Congo. However, the colony gained independence on June 30, 1960, as the Republic of Congo. Following the adoption in 1964 of a constitution, the nation's name was changed to DR Congo (Democratic Republic of Congo), but in 1971 President Mobutu renamed the country as Zaire. When Laurent Kabila became president in 1997, after the seven-month civil war that toppled Mobutu, he restored the name, DR Congo.

In August, war broke out again in DR Congo with Rwanda and Uganda this time fighting against Kabila in support of a local insurrection. Angola, Namibia and Zimbabwe intervened on the side of Kabila. Thus, DR Congo became the battle ground for what many commentators have called 'Africa's First World War.'[55] The

---

[53] Ratified 20-6-1961.

[54] Kisangani, E.F., 'DR Congo', [2009], *Encyclopedia of Human Rights,* (Vol.2), 12.

[55] *Ibid.* see also Prunier, G., *African's World War: Congo, Rwandan Genocide, and the Making of a Continental*

Catastrophe, Oxford, Oxford University Press, 2010, See also US Government Accounting Office, 'U.N. Peace Keeping executive branch Consultations with Congress did not fully meet expectations in 1999-2000'(2000) <http://Fas:org/irp/gac/do/917.pdf> Accessed on 25 August 2010, p:52("[on"] 2000 January 24 [the] U.N. Security Council met to consider the conflict in DR Congo. At the meeting the US secretary of state asserted the Congo conflict could be called "Africa's first world war", because of DR Congo's location and size and the number of states involved.

conflict is so called, because it involved four countries, and a number of rebel groups. At the least, six separate wars were simultaneously fought on the Congolese territory: Rwanda against the Rwandan Liberation Army (RLA); Uganda against its own rebel groups; Angola against the National Union for the total Independence of Angola (UNITA); Burundi against the forces for the Defense of Democracy (FDD); the Mai Mai against the Congolese Rally for Democracy (RCD) and Rwandan troops operating in DR Congo in support of the government against its own rebel groups, including the Congolese Rally for Democracy, the Congolese Rally for Democracy-Liberation movement (RCD-ML), and the Movement for the Liberation of Congo (MLC).[56]

In July 1999, a cease fire was agreed upon, paving way to a United Nations peace keeping mission in DR Congo, the United Nations Organization Mission in DR Congo (MONUC). In January 2001, Laurent Kabila was assassinated and his son Joseph became President. Rwandan and Ugandan forces withdrew in late 2002, leaving their proxies in the form of rebel groups.[57]

The conflict in DR Congo was clearly an armed conflict under international humanitarian law, as there was recourse to armed forces by the parties to the conflict.[58] 'Forces led by Laurent Desire

---

[56] *Ibid*.,, See also 'The war within the war: Sexual Violence Against Women and Girls in Eastern Congo', [2002], *Human Rights Watch*, 1

[57] *Ibid*.

58 See Commentary on Common Article 2 to the Geneva Conventions; *Prosecutor* v *Tadic*, Decision on Defence Motion for Interlocutory Appeal on Jurisdiction, *Tadic* (IT-94-1), October 1995, 70). See also Judgment, *Furuundizija* (IT-95-17/1-T), TC, 10 December 1998, 59; Judgment, *Kunarac* and others (IT-96-23), AC, 12 June 2002, $ 56.

Kabila fought the Mobutu government since 1993'.[59] The tensions were further fueled in 1994, by the massive inflow of refugees fleeing the conflicts in Rwanda and Burundi.[60] The Kabila forces, which were backed by neighbouring Rwanda and Uganda brutally, dismantled the refugee camps in the North and South Kivu provinces, where Rwandan Hutus settled in the aftermath of the 1994 Rwandan genocide.[61] Still fighting alongside Rwanda and Uganda, Kabila's forces ousted the Mobutu regime and installed Kabila as president of DR Congo.[62] However, Kabila subsequently fell out of favour with Rwanda and Uganda, for asking their militaries to leave DR Congo.

War broke out again in DR Congo, with Rwanda and Uganda who had refused to leave the country, this time around fighting against Kabila in support of a local insurrection.[63] On the other hand, Angola, Namibia and Zimbabwe intervened on the side of Kabila.[64]

Considering the foregoing factual situation, the armed conflict started in 1993 as a non-international armed conflict between dissident armed forces led by Laurent Desire Kabila against the government forces under Mobutu, and remained so until November 1996, when Rwandan and Burundi forces entered the fray on the side of Kabila's forces, thereby internationalizing the armed conflict, which ended in May 1997 in victory for Kabila and his forces. The

---

59 Horovitz, S., 'DR CONGO: Interaction between International and National Judicial Responses to the Mass Atrocities', [2012], DOMAC (Vol. 14), 16.
60 *Ibid.*
61 *Ibid.*
62 *Ibid.*
63 *Ibid.*
64 *Ibid.*

same situation of internationalized armed conflict was repeated when war broke out again in DR Congo in August, 1998 between government forces led by Kabila, and dissidents that were supported by Rwanda and Uganda. The fact that Angola, Namibia and Zimbabwe intervened on the side of Kabila reinforced the internationalized character of the conflict. Thus, the four *Geneva Conventions* of 1949 (with the exception of Common *Article 3*) and the *Additional Protocol 1* of 1977 would apply to govern the international armed conflict, while Common *Article 3* of the *Geneva Conventions* and the *Additional Protocol* II would apply to govern the non international armed conflicts, *Geneva Conventions* and the 1977 *Additional Protocol* II would apply to govern the non international armed conflict.[65].

In the case of Sierra Leone, the War began on 23rd March 1991, when a small rebel group, the Revolutionary United Front (RUF) led by Foday Sankoh attacked and entered diamond rich South Eastern Sierra Leone from Liberia.[66] The war which has been described as one of the most brutal in the late twentieth century raged on in varying degrees of intensity throughout the 1990s, until peace was officially declared on 18th January, 2002.[67]

---

[65]See 'Qualification of armed conflict', by RULAC available at http://www.geneva-academy -ch.RULAC/qualification-of-armed-conflict.php (Accessed on 12-06-2016). On the qualification of armed conflicts under international humanitarian law, see Vite, S., 'Typology of Armed Conflicts in international humanitarian law: legal concepts and actual situations', [March 2009], International Review of the Red Cross, (Vol.91, No.673)

[66] Coulter, C., *Bush Wives and Girl Soldiers: Women's Lives Through War and Peace in Sierra Leone*, New York, Cornell University Press, 2009, 5. See also, Ruteere, M., 'Sierra Leone', [2009], *Encyclopedia of Human Rights (Vol. 4)*, 446.

[67] Ruteere, *Ibid*.

Sankoh started the war with the support of 'Special Forces' from Charles Taylor led Liberian National Liberation Patriotic Front (NLPF), and mercenaries from neighboring Burkina Faso. Sankoh, Taylor and Burkina Faso's president, Blaise Compaore were products of Qaddafi's guerilla training school.[68] Ruteere observes that the Sierra Leonean civil war can only be properly understood when viewed within the geopolitics of the West African region.[69] He recounts:

> In neighbouring Liberia, Taylor's NLPF rebels had been fighting for control of the government since 1989. The Economic Community of West African States (ECOWAS) had deployed its Cease-Fire Monitoring Group (ECOMOG) to Liberia in August 1990, to forestall the capture of the capital, Monrovia, by Taylor's NLPF rebels. Angry that the intervention of ECOWAS had denied him military victory, Taylor threatened Sierra Leone that it would soon get a "taste of war". Moreover, for Taylor, Sierra Leone was a potential source of diamonds that he could exploit to support his war in Liberia. Indeed, Sierra Leone's diamonds became the main source of war revenue for the RUF rebels and Taylor's regional war machine.[70]

Thus, it is clear that the Sierra Leonean war was instigated and encouraged by Charles Taylor.

That war witnessed serious violations of international humanitarian law. Granted that such violations were committed by

---

[68] *Ibid.*

[69] *Ibid.*

[70] *Ibid*, 446 – 447.

all the warring parties,[71] the Revolutionary United Front (RUF) rebels are said to have 'plumbed new depths of brutality with their gruesome and often gratuitous attacks on civilians', and civilian objects.[72] Again Ruteere observes:

> As the war progressed, however, the RUF took to the indiscriminate execution of men, women and children and the razing of whole villages. They also destroyed infrastructure in areas under their control without regard for its military value. Water towers were pulverized with rocket launchers, and hospitals, schools and administration buildings were destroyed.[73]

However, the war seems to have disproportionately impacted upon women and the girl-children. It would of course be erroneous to view women in the war as victims all the time as may have been the case in the past, as there is increasingly ample evidence of the participation of women in armed conflict, including direct combat. In spite of this, 'the perception of rebels and soldiers as males remains, signifying the endurance of gendered ideas of war and peace'.[74] This, notwithstanding, it is clear that women remain more vulnerable to sexual violence of all sorts, and forced labour, just for being women.[75]

---

[71] Ruteere acknowledges that like the rebels, the government forces summarily executed captured combatants, in violation of international humanitarian law. He also acknowledges that there were reported cases of government forces executing civilians, including women and children, suspected of collaborating with the rebels.

[72] *Ibid.*, 447.

[73] *Ibid.*, 448.

[74] Coulter, *Op.cit.*, 10.

[75] *Ibid.*

The armed conflict in Sierra Leone was clearly an armed conflict of non-international character, despite the involvement of foreign elements. It was an armed conflict between a rebel group, the Revolutionary United Front (RUF) led by Sankoh and government forces. The intervention of the Charles Taylor led Liberian National Liberation Patriotic Front (NLPF) and mercenaries from neighbouring Burkina-Faso,[76] on the side of Sankoh and his rebel group did not internationalize the armed conflict. This is precisely because they were not state actors. Thus, the armed conflict has generally been characterized as a civil war, that is, a non-international armed conflict.[77]

1.3 Challenges for International Humanitarian Law:

Existing laws on armed conflict, otherwise embodied as International Humanitarian Law, seem plagued by formidable problems, which militate against the legal protection of women in armed conflicts. Consequently, the question as to whether women's rights are adequately secured by existing legal provisions on armed conflict arises. Equally pertinent is the question of patriarchy which ensures that women are discriminated against on account of their gender, both in law, and in practice, and disproportionately targeted

---

[76] Ruteere, M., 'Sierra Leone', [2009], Forsythe, D.P., *Encyclopedia of Human Rights* (Vol. 4), New York, Oxford University Press, 446.

[77] Human, Rights Watch, 'Sierra Leone: "We'll Kill You If You Cry" – Sexual Violence in the Sierra Leone Conflict', [2003], *Human Rights Watch Report*, (Vol. 15, No. 1(A)), 55. Even though the armed conflict in Sierra Leone has generally been characterized as internal or non-international armed conflict, the fighting in 1997-98 between West African ECOWAS forces and the RUF/AFRC government may have met the criteria for an international armed conflict.

as objects of abuse within the culture of impunity that characterizes armed conflicts, for the same reason – their gender.

Regrettably, it has been observed that, in addressing humanitarian needs in armed conflicts, International Humanitarian Law assumes a population in which there is no systematic gender inequality, and fails to recognize the unequal situations of men and women in society, generally.[78] This seems to have been reflected and consolidated in the language of the law. For instance, most of the law is couched in gender neutral terms, by employing such phrases as "a person", "a "prisoner" and so on, but regrettably ending up using the masculine gender of pronouns, such as "he", "his", 'him' and 'himself' in specifying those who are covered or protected by the law. This linguistic disposition of the law, which goes to the roots of legal draftsmanship, seems to operate to limit the law's coverage that is its material content (especially those of the *Geneva Conventions* and the *Additional Protocols*) to men alone, subject to limited special provisions seeking to protect women's "honour", and granting special protection to expectant and nursing mothers.

Being treaty-based, International Humanitarian Law requires re-enactment, into the domestic law of most state-parties, to become enforceable within such states. Thus, in the event of a state neglecting to, or reneging on incorporating the treaty by re-

---

[78] Gardam, J. and Jarvis, M., *Women, Armed Conflict and International Law*, The Hague, Kluwer Law Int'l, 2001, 97. See also Durham, H., 'Women, Armed Conflict and International Law', [September 2002], *International Review of Red Cross IRRC*, (Vol. 84, No. 847), 657.

enactment or by any other means, it denies its citizens, the benefit of the law.[79]

For clarity the problems in the law could be stated as follows:

1. Women's rights are not adequately secured by existing legal provisions on armed conflicts, despite some specific or special provisions for the protection of women, as the laws are essentially male-oriented and sexist and exclude women substantially.

2. The law does not adequately protect women in Africa, as shown in the poor implementation of relevant international law provisions in the domestic legislations of the following countries: Nigeria, DR Congo, and Sierra Leone.

Thus, this book seeks to critically examine and analyze International Humanitarian Law and other relevant laws vis-à-vis the protection they offer women, who form part of the most vulnerable persons in times of armed conflicts. This is so as, generally, women suffer disproportionately, in comparison to men, in the event of armed conflicts. Regrettably, injuries against them are largely unrecognized by most existing legal instruments, and thus remain unpunished, a fact that may have warranted feminist criticisms of International Humanitarian Law.[80] Therefore the

---

[79] Fortunately, most International Humanitarian law rules have acquired the status of *opinio juris*, and thus evolved

into customary international law, which binds every state and everyone.

[80] Askin, K. D., 'The International Criminal Tribunal for Rwanda and its treatment of Crimes against Women',

Carey, J., *et.al.* (ed.), *International Humanitarian Law: Challenges*, New York, Transnational Publishers, Inc.,

2004, 33-34.

challenge remains to integrate a gender perspective in the law of armed conflict in such a way as to accommodate the rights of women, as much as those of men and foster a gender - sensitive interpretation and implementation of International Humanitarian Law as a vital mechanism for responding adequately to the protection needs of both men and women, and more especially women, in the event of armed conflicts[81].

This book focuses on the armed conflicts in Nigeria, DR Congo, and Sierra Leone - armed conflicts that have taken place between the late twentieth century and the present twenty-first century. However, repeated references are made to the armed conflict in the former Yugoslavia, and the genocide and armed conflict in Rwanda, because they are contemporaneous to the foregoing armed conflicts in focus, and especially because of the contributions of the *Ad hoc* International Criminal Tribunals for the former Yugoslavia and that of Rwanda to the jurisprudence of International Humanitarian Law. References are also made to lessons from the International Military Tribunals at Nuremberg and Tokyo, respectively. Such references are more or less, comparative and deductive.

It remains to justify the focus on the armed conflicts in Nigeria, DR Congo, and Sierra Leone. The armed conflicts in Nigeria (the Nigerian Civil War, and the Nigerian War against *Boko Haram* Insurgency) present interesting opportunities for assessing the legal protection of women in the armed conflicts in Africa for two major reasons. Firstly, echoes of the Nigerian Civil War have continued to

---

[81] Pfanner, T., 'Editorial, (Women; Humanitarian Debate; Law; Policy; Action)', *International Review of the Red Cross (IRRC)* volume 92, number 877, March 2010, 7.

resonate based on the charge of genocide by the defunct Biafran government against the then Nigerian government. The charge is mostly anchored on the Nigerian government's resort to starvation as a policy of war against the predominantly Igbo population of Biafra – a policy which had a disproportionate effect on Igbo women and children, who were also targeted by air raids. Secondly, *Boko Haram* targeting of women and girls for abduction, forced marriages, sexual violence and rape raises serious issues on the legal protection of women in armed conflicts, especially in the face of what may be termed 'faith cleansing'[82], as the women are forced to convert to *Boko Haram's* variant of Islam, and bear rape children who may be socialized into their mode of Islam. The foregoing reasons are accentuated by the strategic importance of Nigeria to Africa. The armed conflict in DR Congo witnessed a resort to sexual violence and rape, especially of women in an unprecedented scale. This sensitized the United Nations Organization, which for the first time declared that rape has been used as a weapon of war. Besides, the armed conflict in DR Congo consists of six separate wars that were simultaneously fought by forces from at least five African countries, and other armed groups, a situation that has made some commentators to qualify the armed conflict as Africa's First World War. Finally, the armed conflict in Sierra Leone provided an opportunity for experimentation with a hybrid court – the Special Court for Sierra Leone -, and thus deserves special attention.

This study is significant for a number of reasons, which includes that it will enhance and enrich the literature on the legal protection of women in armed conflict, as relatively few studies have been

---

[82] The term "faith cleansing" is based upon its parallelism with the idea of "ethnic cleansing".

undertaken on the legal protection of women in armed conflicts,[83] in spite of the fact that women are disproportionately abused during armed conflicts and even deliberately targeted as a strategy of war, even when they hardly take direct part in hostilities. Secondly, the study is ground breaking and thus significant for seeking to develop and promote an understanding of a gender perspective of the law in order to further strengthen and enhance the legal protection of women, under relevant laws. Thus, it considers the sensitivity or otherwise of the law to such "gendered" themes or issues as the use of sexual violence and rape against women during times of armed conflict, and the response of the law to such impunity.

Finally, this study is significant for being useful for Lawyers and Judges respectively, as tools for legal advocacy and judicial enforcement of International Humanitarian Law and other relevant laws. Beyond targeting law officers, law students, and the legal system, this work promises to be useful to everyone who seeks to study the impact of armed conflicts on women, students and advocates of peace and conflict resolution and even relevant non-governmental organizations.

---

[83] Some of the studies were carried out by the International Committee of the Red Cross (ICRC), or facilitated by the organization, and include: Lindsey-Curtet, C. et.al., *Addressing the Needs of Women Affected by Armed Conflict: An ICRC Guidance Document*, Geneva, ICRC, 2004; Lindsey, C., *Women Facing War*, Geneva, ICRC, 2001.

CHAPTER TWO

Theories, Thoughts and Concepts in The Legal Protection of Women

2.1 Introduction:

This chapter, establishes the theoretical and the conceptual framework for the legal protection of women, especially in the event of armed conflicts. It discusses a number of feminist and gender-based legal theories, on the one hand and certain relevant concepts on the other, while making the case for the special protection of the law for women victims of armed conflicts.

2.2 Theoretical Framework

Theories must be evaluated by their success in practice. This is so, as social facts, and in this case, those about women, exist only within a certain theoretical context.[1] Jaggar and Struhl observe that the theoretical presuppositions of our ordinary ways of thinking and talking are not always conscious and contend that a large part of the feminist critique of contemporary society has consisted in uncovering the presuppositions of those who deny the need for

---

[1] Jaggar, A., and Struhl, P.R., *Feminist Frameworks: Alternative Theoretical Accounts of the Relations between Women and Men*, New York, McGraw-Hill Book Company, 1978, x.

change.[2] They raise the question of precisely what changes should be made, and note that it is in order to answer the question that feminists have felt the need to construct a new theoretical framework in which to locate the critique of the contemporary position of women and the recommendations for how that position should be altered.[3] However, it is clear that the feminist legal theory is an offshoot of the Natural Law theory, which emphasizes morality and natural justice based on reason. It is necessary to commence with a review of the Natural Law theory, before discussing relevant feminist and gender-based legal theories.

Natural Law Theory: The Natural Law theory is said to have been developed by the Stoics, a school of philosophers led by Zeno.[4] The Stoics believe 'that man as part of nature is governed by reason.'[5] For them, man should not rely on his own reason alone but also on divine reason, which ultimately disposes him to morality and natural justice.[6] Thus, inspirationally, the natural law theory draws from nature and reason, while historically, as Friedman notes, it is 'a tale of the search of mankind for absolute justice and truth.[7] However, the theory is premised on the assumption that there is a

---

[2] *Ibid*.

[3] *Ibid*.

[4] Nnabue, U.S.F., *Understanding Jurisprudence and Legal Theory*, Owerri, Bon Publications, 2016, 67.

[5] *Ibid*,

[6] *Ibid*.

[7] Russel, B., *A History of Western Philosophy*, New York, Simon & Schuster, 1945, quoted in Martn D., and Hashi,

F., 'Law as an Institutional Barrier to the Economic Empowerment of Women', Working Paper No. 2, New York,

World Bank, 1989, 14.

law of nature according to which tenets and principles, all things including man himself ought to behave. In this case, the ought proposition is obligatory and not idealistic. For instance, natural law theories hold that there are fundamental, universal, compelling forces which guide human behaviour independently of enacted law, and that these forces grow out of and conform to nature, and form the basis for rules of conduct which have been established by the divine author of human nature.[8] In other words, for the Stoics, the course of the universe is '... ordained by a lawgiver ... and rigidly by the laws of nature.'[9] This is to say that laws and legal principles are deducible from nature through reason.

The natural law theory has over the years developed into 'a wide range of theories or theoretical insights from Greek thinkers, through to the Romans and up to the present day.'[10] For instance, the Roman orator, Cicero (106BC – 43BC) has been acclaimed to have offered the best known ancient formulation of the natural law concept.[11] He states *inter alia*:

> True law is right reason in agreement with nature; it is of universal application, unchanging and everlasting; it summons to duty by its commands, and averts from wrongdoing by its prohibitions. And it does not lay its commands or prohibitions upon good men in vain, though neither have any effect on the wicked. It is a sin to try to alter

---

[8] Garner, B.A., *Blacks Law Dictionary*, (5th edn.), St. Paul, West Publishing Company, 1979.

[9] Russel, B., *Op.cit.*

[10] Nnabue, U.S.F., *Op.cit.*, 59.

[11] Bix, B., Jurisprudence: Theory and Context (4th edn.), London, Sweet and Maxwell, 2006, 66.

this law, nor is it allowable to attempt to repeal any part of it, and it is impossible to abolish it entirely….[12]

It is at this point necessary to review the implications of natural law theories for the rights and status of women. Basically, the Stoics believe that according to the law of nature, all human beings are equal. Paradoxically though, they discriminated between men and women on the ground of what they saw as men's apparent superiority of strength and stamina,[13] as demonstrated in warfare. They reasoned that women were generally smaller and weaker than men and thus precluded by nature rather than nurture or convention from featuring in wars.[14] While acknowledging the importance of war to the survival of any society, they concluded that those who were physically best suited for fighting were superior also in other respects.

However, anthropologists disagree with the foregoing assertion. They see male physical superiority and the prevailing pattern of division of labour consequent upon it as nothing but environmentally and culturally determined. To buttress this, Kathleen Gough's work on primates indicates that males are larger and stronger than females and clearly dominate in societies where defence is not important.[15] She, however, concluded that attributes

---

[12] *Ibid.*

[13] Craik, E.M., "Marriage in Ancient Greece", Craik, E.M. (ed.), *Marriage and Property*, St. Andrews, Aberdeen University Press, 1984, 22. See also Ibezim, E.C., *The Beijing Conference and the Human Rights Protection of Women: A Critical Review*, 2000 (An Unpublished LL.M Dissertation), 24.

[14] *Ibid.*

[15] Gough, K., "The Origin of the Family", Freeman, J. (ed.), *Women: A Feminist Perspective*, Palo Alto, Mayfield Publishing Company, 1979, 49.

and phenomena used to indicate male superiority are not exclusively male traits; and that the environment is important in determining which sex acquires male superiority traits and to what extent.[16]

Early Roman and Christian interpretations of the principles of natural law followed the Stoic's discriminatory attitude against women.[17] But later day interpretations of the natural law theories which considered the principle of equality as an important element in the Stoic's concept of natural law inspired a change in Roman legal attitude. The roman lawyers became convinced that men were essentially equal and that any discriminations between them based on sex, class, race or nationality were unjust and contrary to the law of nature. These humanitarian ideas affected the legal status of the Roman wife positively, and gradually led to her emancipation from her husband's autocratic power of life and death over her.[18]

Emperor Constantine's decision in the third century BC to adopt Christianity as the state religion was another milestone in gender politics. The foundations of the Christian legal philosophy were laid several centuries before the beginning of the Middle Ages. It is commonly believed that St. Paul's '…Law written in (men's) hearts'[19] is a reference to "natural law". According to Russel, 'within the confines of its own morality and value, Christianity emphasized that part of Stoicism which addressed equality and governmental respect

---

[16] *Ibid.*

[17] This attitude of the Roman Law was reflected in the Twelve Tables which was the earliest code of Roman law written around 45 and 450 BC and which contained the most important rules which served as the basis for later legislations.

[18] Ibezim, E. C. *Op.cit.*, 26.

[19] See Romans 2:14 – 15 (New King James Version of the Holy Bible (2nd edn.))

for the rights of those governed.[20] When preaching to the Romans, St. Paul spoke of equality between husband and wife. He enjoins: 'the husband should give to the wife her conjugal rights, and likewise the wife to her husband. For the wife does not rule over her own body, but the husband does; likewise the husband does not rule over his own body, but his wife does.[21] However, this advocacy for equality suffers a set-back when the same St. Paul urges: 'wives be subject to your husband, as to the Lord. For the husband is the head of the wife as Christ is head of the Church, his body, and is himself its saviour. As the church is subject to Christ, so let wives also be subject in everything to their husbands'.[22] This rather ambivalent attitude of St. Paul's seems to derive from his belief in women's physical inferiority to men and the need to protect them.[23]

The spread of Christianity was enhanced by the political ascendancy of the Roman Empire (*Civitas Romana*). Dias summarizes the achievement of the Roman Lawyers thus: 'The enduring monument of the Roman Lawyers was their wonderful synthesis of practical rules and principles for the solution of everyday problems.[24] "Everyday problems" must have included the legal status of women and their attendant disability within the roman family, and the society at large.

---

[20] Russel, B., *Op.cit.*, 270.

[21] See 1 Corinthians 7:3 – 4 (The Revised Standard Version of the Holy Bible).

[22] See Ephesians 5:22 – 23 (The Revised Standard Version of the Holy Bible).

[23] Ibezim, E. C., *Op.cit.*, 27.

[24] Dias,R.W.M., *Jurisprudence* (4th edn.), London, Butters-worth, 1976, 85.

By the end of the reign of Emperor Justinian (527 – 65AD), the Roman Lawyers had made some improvements in the law with respect to the status of women. Such improvements include:

(i)   a married woman could reclaim her dowry on a showing of squandering by her husband;

(ii) the ban on marriage for women which came into force around 50 AD, because women were deemed married forever, was lifted during this period.[25]

Christianity is not the only religion that was influenced by Natural Law theories vis-à-vis the rights and status of women in society. Most other religions also reflect Natural Law principles. For instance, Islamic legal philosophy follows the Natural law theory and promulgates rules based on divine guidance.[26] Those rules which constitute the Islamic legal system known as Sharia (path ordained by God) regulate family relations, inheritance, divorce, dress codes, diet, hygiene, relationship between the sexes[27] and even warfare.

During the 9th century,[28] the Qur'an improved the lot of women in Southern Arabia, and provided for women's right to their bride price, and inheritance (even though daughters could only inherit half as much as sons). It also provided for protection of the woman

---

[25] Robinson, O.F., "The Historical Background", McLean, S. and Burrows, N. (ed.), *Relevance of Gender: Some Aspects of Sex-Based Discrimination*, London, MacMillan Press, 1988, 49.

[26] Martin, D. and Hashi, F., *Op.cit.*, 14.

[27] For a discussion of Islamic Law, see generally Hammerton, A.R., *"An Introduction to Islamic Law"*, *Modern Legal Systems Encyclopedia*, Vol. 6A, 1989.

[28] Islamic Religion was founded about the late 6th Century AD.

in cases of divorce by their husbands. However, the Qur'an reinforced the tenets of natural female domesticity and incapacity by emphasizing the need for men to serve as guardians over women.[29] This Qur'anic imposition of men over women accounts for the denigrated position of women in most, if not all Islamic communities of the world and encouraged the seclusion and veiling of women as a common Islamic practice.

Like Christianity and Islam, Hinduism which is the dominant religion in India believed in the Natural law principle of equality. However, like both religions, it regressed from a much more egalitarian status of women to the height of subjugation around 700 AD when 'Suttee' (the practice of burning widows on their husband's pyre) was considered a religious duty.[30] Therefore, there may be some credence in the claim that the subjugation of women did not begin until the advent of religions, and that it only became more intense as the centuries went by.[31] This and other apparent contradictions, which made the Natural Law theory imprecise and not all together just signaled its decline,[32] and the preference for the Positivist (Imperative) Law Theory. But the positivist law theory proved to be the worse instrument of oppression, hence the resurgence of natural law principles, as a means to check the excesses of positivist laws.[33]

---

[29] See The Qur'an 4:35.

[30] Tomansevski, E., *Women and Human Rights*, London, Zeb Books Ltd., 1993, 95. See also Eze, O.C., *Human Rights in Africa: Some Selected Problems*, Lagos, Nigerian Institute of International Affairs (NIIA), McMillian Publishers, 1984, 141.

[31] *Ibid*.

[32] Nnabue, U.S.F., *Op.cit.*, 102.

[33] *Ibid*.

This development saw the emergence of a crop of new writers who have been described as Neo-Naturalists. They include: Stammler, Del Vecchio, Finnis and Lon Fuller. These writers re-echo the tenets of Natural Law principles, thereby spinning theories that have been described as modern natural law theories. However, John Finnis's re-statement of natural law has been acclaimed as the most authoritative in modern times.[34] Essentially, natural law doctrines or theories of the era focused attention on the individual and seek to uphold the dignity of the individual against dictatorship. This led to the concept of democracy, and consequently the recognition of human rights and their 'expressions in constitutions and charters of the United Nations, which built on the idea of universality.'[35]

Nnabue observes that the quest for justice led to the re-discovery that there is a moral order to which all laws must conform.[36] This natural law idea has found expression in modern theories of justice which sees feminism as justice.[37] Thus feminism and the feminist legal theories are off-shoots of modern natural law theories. This is clear from the dicta of Roscoe Pound and Morris Cohen as captured in Black's Law Dictionary:[38]

---

[34] Freeman, M.D.A., *Lloyd's Introduction to Jurisprudence* (7th edn.), London, Sweet and Maxwell Ltd., 2001, 132.

[35] Nnabue, U.S.F., *Op.cit.*, 103. According to Nnabue, this gave birth to the *Universal Declaration of Human Rights*, the *Declaration of Delhi on the Rule of* Law (1959), and the *African Charter on Human and Peoples Rights*.

[36] Nnabue, *Ibid.*

[37] Freeman, M.D.A., *Op.cit.*, 548 – 556.

[38] Garner, B.A., *Black's Law Dictionary*, (8th edn.), St. Pauls, West (a Thomson Business), 2004, 1055.

Natural Law, as it is revived today, seeks to organize the ideal element in law, to furnish a critique of old received ideals and give a basis for formulating new ones, and to yield a reasoned canon of values and a technique of applying it...[Roscoe Pound, The Formative Era of American Law 29 (1938)] [39]

[N]atural law is often an idealization of the opposite to that which prevails. Where in-equality or privilege exists, natural law demands its abolition. [Morris R. Cohen, Reasons and Law 96 (1961)[40]

Feminist Legal Theory: The emergent feminist framework has been described as having a dual aspect. It simultaneously 'offers a description of women's oppression and a prescription for eliminating it. It is empirical insofar as it examines women's experience in the world; but it is normative insofar as it characterizes certain features of that experience as oppressive and offers a new vision of justice and freedom for women'.[41] It is therefore possible to understand the feminist legal theory as a reaction to the jurisprudence of modern legal scholars, who are mainly male scholars, and who tend to see law as a process for interpreting and perpetuating a universal, gender-neutral public morality.[42]

It has also been acknowledged that the 'feminist legal theory is diverse and anything but monolithic',[43] but that in spite of such diversity, the feminist scholars appear united in their claim that

---

[39] *Ibid*

[40] *Ibid*

[41] *Ibid*, xi.

[42] *Ibid*.

[43] *Ibid*.

'masculine jurisprudence of all stripes' fails to acknowledge, let alone respond to, the interests, values, fears, and harms experienced by women.[44] Thus, feminist theories focus attention on the subordinate status of women in many societies. Consequently, feminist sociologists and feminist lawyers have developed theories on gender inequality. However, the focus has in recent times changed from emphasis on inequality to that on difference[45], but the inequality approach still holds much appeal for feminist lawyers in search of feminist jurisprudence.[46]

The following are some of the feminist approaches: Conservative feminism; Liberal feminism; Radical feminism; Socialist feminism; Post Modern Feminism; Essentialism Feminist Theory; Anti-Essentialism Feminist Theory; Dominance Feminist Theory and African Feminism Theory.

The first theory, Conservatism, attempts to defend women's position in contemporary society by arguing that it is in accord with some kind of biological imperative.[47] Thus, for conservative feminists, freedom for women comes through the knowledge and acceptance of biological necessity.

On the contrary, liberal feminists argue that liberation for women requires that women have opportunities for education and

---

[44] *Ibid.*

[45] Haralambos, M. and Holborn, M., Sociology: Themes and Perspectives, (7th edn.), London, Harper Collins Publishers Ltd., 2008, 100.

[46] Scales, A.C, "The Emergence of Feminist Jurisprudence: An Essay", Bridgeman, J and Millns, S, Feminist

Perspectives on Law: Law's Engagement with the Female Body, London, Sweet & Mawell, 1998, 80-82

[47] Jaggar, A. M. and Struhl, P. R, *op. cit.*.xii.

professional advancement, which are equal with those of men.[48] For Marxist (traditional) feminists, the liberal analysis is too superficial. They see women's oppression as a mere symptom of the pervasive oppression that is endemic in a class society. They therefore argue that liberation can be achieved for women, only within a classless society.[49] However, radical feminists reject this argument. They assert that the oppression of women may exist within any type of economic system; blame it, on the social institution of gender, calling for its abolition, and indeed the elimination of the biological fact of sex itself.[50] The socialist feminist takes it a little further by re-establishing the classical Marxist connection between class society and sexism, but denies the contention that sexism is the less fundamental.[51] For them, 'women will not be able freely to determine the conditions of (their) own lives without the elimination both of class society and of the institution of gender'.[52]

Postmodern Feminism is an approach to feminist theory that incorporates postmodern and poststructuralist theory, and sees itself as moving beyond the modernist polarities of liberal feminism and radical feminism. Moreover, it has been regarded as having an affinity to postmodern philosophy through shared interest in 'speech acts, and on the enacted, performative aspects of languages'.[53] Perhaps, postmodern feminism's major departure from

---

[48] *Ibid.*

[49] *Ibid.*

[50] *Ibid.*

[51] *Ibid*, xiii.

[52] *Ibid.*

[53] See Appignanesi, R. and Garratt .C., *Postmodernism for Beginners* 1995, 100 – 101, available at en.m.wikipedia. org, accessed on 5-4-2016. See also Frug, M. P.,

other branches of feminism is the argument that sex, or at least gender is itself constructed through language, a view notably propounded in Judith Butler's book, titled *Gender Trouble*.[54] She draws on and critiques the work of Simon de Beauvoir, Michael Foucault, and Jacque Lacan, as well as on Luce Irigaray's argument that what we conventionally regard as 'feminine' is only a reflection of what is constructed as masculine.[55] She went on to criticize the distinction drawn by previous feminisms between sex (biology) and gender (socially constructed gender), and wondered why the assumption that material things, such as the body, are not subject to processes of social construction themselves. She therefore asserts that this does not allow for a sufficient criticism of essentialism. Finally, while agreeing with the fact that gender is a social construct, she criticizes the fact that feminists assume that it is always constructed in the same way.

Butler's argument implies that women's subordination has no single cause or single solution. Hence, postmodern feminism is criticized for offering no clear path to action. Butler herself rejects 'postmodernism' for being too vague to be meaningful.[56]

'Postmodern feminist Legal Manifesto (An unfinished Draft)', Bridgeman, J. O. and Millns, S., *Feminist Perspectives on Law: Law's Engagement with the female body*, London Sweet & Maxwell, 1998, 103.

[54] Butler, J., *Gender Trouble*, (1990), available at en.m.wikipedia.org. (accessed on 5-4-2016).

[55] *Ibid.*

[56] Butler, J., 'Contingent Foundation', Behabid, S. *et.al.*, *Feminist Contentions: A Philosophical Exchange*, New
York, Routledge 1995, 35 – 36.

However, Frug argues that although postmodernism resists characterization, it is possible to identify certain themes or orientations that postmodern feminists share: she suggests that one 'principle' of postmodernism is that human experience is located 'inescapably within language'. She therefore theorizes that power is exercised not only through direct coercion, but also through the way in which language shapes and restricts our reality. In her opinion, because language is always open to re-interpretation, it can also be used to resist this shaping and restrictions, and so is a potentially fruitful site of political struggle.[57]

Her second postmodern principle is that sex is not something natural, nor is it something completely determinate and definable. She argues that it is rather part of a system of meaning produced by language, and that 'cultural mechanisms encode the female body with meanings', and that these cultural mechanisms then go on to explain these meanings 'by an appeal to the "natural" differences between the sexes, differences that the rules themselves help to produce'.[58] This idea is also somewhat reflected in Essentialism Feminist theory, which focuses on women from a general perspective.

According to Olomojobi, Essentialism Feminist model or approach emphasizes that the essential feature that distinguishes men from women is based on biological and physiological differences.[59] She observes that essentialists argue that this biological

---

[57] Frug, M. J. *op. cit.*

[58] *Ibid.*

[59] Olomojobi, Y., *Human Rights (on Gender, Sex and the Law)*, Nigeria, Lagos, Princeton Publishing Company, 2015, 13.

difference puts women under a common umbrella of sexuality, which is assumed to be a significant determinant of desire, sex and control of women. Thus, issues such as gender discrimination are regarded as peculiar to all women. However, a classical illustration of essentialism is the universal social norm that women give birth and care for their children.[60]

Perhaps, more importantly, essentialism interrogates women from the perspective of westernized concepts. This approach has been criticized for being collective and presumptuous in nature. But Mackinnon defends the theory by explaining that 'the male power is elastic; its defenders love the accusation that feminism is "essentialist", even though they don't really know what it means'.[61] However, she is noted for being rather too essentialist, based on her illustration of women's experiences. This, it has been observed may pose problems in analyzing excluded groups, such as women of African origin.[62] It has also further been argued that essentialism 'indoctrinates one to see the world through the eyes of the fortunate, Caucasian woman and to accept their interests, way of life and viewpoints on the same footing as that of the African women'.[63]

On the whole, what Mackinnon has attempted to do, is 'universalized women's oppression without considering race, cultural and social analysis'[64] or identities. In view of this, Olomojobi, contends that one may be correct to say that the

---

[60] *Ibid*.

[61] *Ibid*., 14.

[62] *Ibid*.

[63] *Ibid*.

[64] *Ibid*.

essentialist is indeed unrealistic as: 'it cannot plausibly be maintained that women's experiences have any common character, or that women share any common location in social and cultural relations, or sense of psychic identity ....'[65] However, Mackinnon is credited with having exposed the law as constructed from a male point of view despite the claim that the law is gender-neutral and objective[66].

Anti-Essentialism Feminist Theory challenges the essentialism feminist theory by adopting a view point of diversity in explaining gender disparities in different societies. Thus, for this theory, women should not be generally categorized, in other words one woman's identity or challenges should not be used as a criterion to categorize all women. To this end, Smart's assessment of the "Category of Women" is illuminating.

Smart's assessment involves revealing first how law is "gendered" and second how law operates as a "gendering strategy". In the first place, Smart reveals three phases in identifying law as a gendered phenomenon: the first is that "law is sexist", the second is that "law is gendered"[67]. For her, the "law is sexist" approach deals with the liberal feminist's agenda of addressing the disadvantages women suffer in law through their differentiation. She observes that this insight, while important, misrepresents the problem. According to her:

[65] Stone, A.,' Essentialism and Anti-Essentialism in feminist Philosophy', [2004], *Journal of Moral Philosophy*, (Vol. 1, No. 2), 135 cited in Olomojobi, *Ibid*.

[66] Scales, A. C., *Op.cit.*, 84

[67] Smart, C., 'The Woman of Legend Discourse', [1992], Journal of Social and Legal Studies, (Vol. 1), 29.

The concept of sexism implies that we can override sexual difference as if it were epiphenomenal rather than embedded in how we comprehend and negotiate the social order.... If eradicating discrimination is dependent on differentiation, we have to be able to think of a culture without gender. Thus what seems like a relatively easy solution such as the incorporation of gender-neutral terminology into the law, masks a much deeper problem. Moreover, as many feminists have argued, it is not at all certain that the desired outcome of feminism is some form of androgyny.

Secondly, she captures the "law is male" approach as follows:

The idea that "law is male" arises from the empirical observation that most law-makers and lawyers are indeed male. It transcends this starting point however because of the realization that maleness or masculinity, once embedded in values and practices, need not be exhaustively anchored to the male biological referent, i.e. men.... Thus, in comparison to the 'law is sexist' approach, this analysis suggests that when a man and woman stand before the law, it is not that law fails to apply objective criteria when faced with the feminine subject, but precisely that it does apply objective criteria and these objective criteria are masculine.[68]

Like the first approach, Smart observes that this approach is not also unproblematic. According to her, in the first place, it 'perpetuate the idea of law as a unity rather than problematizing law and dealing with its internal contradictions'.[69] Secondly, she criticizes the approach for presuming that 'any system founded on supposedly universal values and impartial decision making (but which is now

---

[68] *Ibid*, 32.

[69] *Ibid*.

revealed to be particular and partial) serves in a systematic way the interests of men as a unitary category'.[70] Furthermore, she observes that any argument that commences with 'ceding priority to the binary division of male/female or masculine/feminine walks into the trap of demoting other forms of differentiation, particularly differences within these binary opposites.'[71] This naturally leads to what she considers the third problem in the approach, which is 'that divisions such as class, age, race, religion tend to become mere additives or after thoughts'.[72]

Having identified these problems, Smart proceeds to the third stage in her analysis which is to take 'law as gendered'. She opines:

> The shift between taking "law as male" and taking "law as gendered" is fairly subtle, and the transition does not entail a total rejection of all the insights of the former. But while the assertion that 'law is male' effects a closure in how we think about law, the idea of it as gendered allows us to think of it in terms of processes which will work in a variety of ways and in which there is no relentless assumption that whatever it does exploits women and serves men.... But further, the idea of 'law as gendered' does not require us to have a fixed category or empirical referent of Man and Woman. We can now allow for the position which is not fixed by either biological psychological or social determinants to sex. Within this analysis we can turn our focus to those strategies which attempt to do the 'fixing' of gender to rigid systems of meaning rather than falling into this practice ourselves.[73]

---

[70] *Ibid.*

[71] *Ibid.*, 32 – 33.

[72] *Ibid.*

[73] *Ibid.*

From this analysis of "law as gendered" flows Smart's key argument that law operates as a "gendering strategy". He explains what this concept entails thus:

> ...Yet first we must concede a distinction between Woman and women. This is familiar to feminists who have for some centuries argued that the idea of Woman (sometimes the ideal of Woman) is far removed from real women. Moreover, feminism has typically claimed an access to real women denied those who perceive the world through patriarchal visions. So the distinction between Woman and Women, is not new but it has become complex. ... Feminism does not represent women.... So if we accept that woman/women are not reducible to biological categories or at the very least- that biological signs are not essences which give rise to a homogenous category of women we can begin to acknowledge that there are strategies by which Woman/women are brought into being...[74]

There is of course, a distinction to be made between 'the discursive production of a type of Woman and the discursive construction of woman. The (legal) discursive construction of a type of Woman might refer to the female criminal, the prostitute, the unmarried mother, the infanticides mother and so on. The discursive construction of Woman, on the other hand, invokes the idea of Woman in contradistinction to Man'.[75] The former construction captures the Anti-essentialism approach and focuses on the premise that women are constructed by their distinctive realities of

---

[74] *Ibid.*

[75] *Ibid,* 33-34

experience. That premise is in consonance with African Feminism as a theory.

African Feminist theory which rests on the notion that women in Africa are socially constructed by different cultural components evolved in Africa in the 1990s.[76] It is in stark contrast with western feminist theories, 'as it searches deep into the social, economic and political forces that oppress women'.[77] According to Berger and Luckman the construction of reality in western societies is different to that in non-western societies.[78] As a result, the theory 'attempts to shift away from misleading notions of equating western value with non-western societies'.[79] For instance, it has been noted that African women have different identities and primordial attachment to religion and cultural determinants than women from western societies.[80]

Amadiume has been acknowledged as the pioneer of African feminism. She explores pre-colonial and post-colonial patriarchal institutions through an anthropological approach, and illustrates how these institutions have redefined roles for women in the Igbo ethnic group.[81]

According to Badeji', African feminism is based on 'the principles of traditional African values that view gender roles as

---

[76] *Ibid.*, 16.

[77] *Ibid.*

[78] Berger, L. P. and Luckman, T., *The Social Construction of Reality: Everything that passes for knowledge in society*, Allen Lane, the Penguin Press, 1966, as cited in Olomojobi, *Ibid.*

[79] *Ibid.*

[80] *Ibid.*

[81] *Ibid.*

complementary, parallel, asymmetrical, and autonomously linked in the continuity of human life.[82] It has been observed that this approach maybe suitable for explaining the situation of women of African heritage who are in diasporas, and particularly, women on the African continent. This approach emphasizes the effect of western influence on social systems, in most parts of Africa, and its consequences on the life of African women; consequences, which include, the feminization of poverty, and a re-adjustment of her role, as an equal companion with men.

Based on this notion, Mekgwe defines African feminism as:

a discourse that takes care to delineate those concerns peculiar to the African situation. It also questions features of traditional African values without denigrating them, understanding that these might be viewed differently to the different classes of women.[83]

This definition contemplates the complexities of the social realities of women in African societies. Such complexities have been observed in the dichotomous classification, in Africa, of the elite and the educated woman. Whereas, the educated woman understands the essence of her legal rights, the rural woman is confined to patriarchal institutions, with all their complex realities.[84]

Badeji has attempted to delineate the characteristics of African feminism as follows:

---

[82] *Ibid.*, 17, Badeji, D. L., 'African Feminism: Mythical and Social Power of Women of African Descent', [1998], *Research in African Literatures*, (Vol. 29, No. 2), 94.

[83] *Ibid.*, Mekgwe, P., 'Theorizing African Feminism(s): The Colonial Question', [2008], *Journal for African Culture and Society*, (Vol. 3), 167.

[84] Olomojobi, *Ibid.*

African feminism embraces feminity, beauty, power, serenity, inner harmony, and a complex matrix of power. It is always poised and centered in womaness. It demonstrates that power and feminity are intertwined rather than antithetical. African feminity complements African masculinity, and defends both with the ferocity of the lioness while simultaneously seeking male defense of both as critical, demonstrable, and mutually obligatory.[85]

However, apart from analyzing patriarchy as an institution in Africa, African feminism tends to 'critique the lesions of colonialism; the intrusion of imperialism and protracted nationalistic struggle for independence'.[86] This has made the exploitation of the African man and woman 'a crucial variable in explaining African feminism';[87] meaning 'that unlike western feminists who view women's oppression as the cause-effect of man's patriarchal institutions',[88] this approach interrogates independent determinants, such as racial struggles, classism, and western forms of patriarchy. This may have motivated Arndt to observe thus:

Generally speaking, African feminism gets to the bottom of African gender relations and the problems of African women illuminating their causes and consequences and criticizes them. In so doing, African feminism aims at upsetting the existing matrix of domination and overcoming it, thus transforming gender relationships and conceptions in

---

[85] *Ibid.*, Badeji, *Op.cit.*, 94.

[86] *Op.cit.*, 19.

[87] *Ibid.*

[88] *Ibid.*

African societies and improving the situation of African women.[89]

Ogundipe – Leslie, offers a clearer perspective of African feminism when she observes that men and women can have economic and social progression if they have the ability to have equal and valuable relationships.[90] Olomojobi believes that this explains why we had several anti-colonialist movements by women in Nigeria as is exemplified by the 1929 Aba women riots, which sought to protest against the levies and taxes that were imposed on market women by the colonial government.[91]

No doubts this theory has been received as a useful guide in explaining how colonial and post-colonial institutions engendered gender discrimination, but it has also been criticized as being ethnocentric, as it is based on just the experiences of women from particular ethnic backgrounds. This is so as Amadiume 'contextualizes African feminism in terms of the Igbo ethnic group, whilst Badeji... situates the theory within the paradigm of the Yoruba and Akan cultural norms'.[92] Olomojobi, on his part summarizes it when he asserts:

---

[89] *Ibid*. See also Arndt, S., 'Perspectives on African Feminism: Defining and classifying African Feminist Literatures, [2002], *Agenda: Empowering Women for Gender Equity*, (Vol. 17, No. 54), 32.

[90] *Ibid*. See also Ogundipe – Leslie, M., *Re-Creating Ourselves: African Women & Critical Transformations*, Trenton NJ, Africa World Press, 1994.

[91] Olomojobi, *Ibid*. See generally, Dike, P.C., *The Women's Revolt of 1929: Proceedings of a National Symposium to mark the 60th Anniversary of the Women's Uprising in South- Eastern Nigeria*, Lagos, Nelag and Co.Ltd,1995.

[92] *Ibid*.

However, African feminism theorizes the 'what?', the 'why?', and the 'how?' enquiries about gender discrimination and the complex interconnected relationship between women and men in the African context. Most important, it reveals that African women are the chaperones of the burden of the African people.[93]

There have been opponents of feminism, both as a theory and a concept. Both males and females have been found in the ranks of these opponents. Notable among them, is Chinweizu. Chinweizu acidly attacks feminists' notions of gender oppressive discrimination against women and attempts to debunk the feminist notion of patriarchy, in his treaties titled *Anatomy of Female Power*.[94]

He contends that what exists in reality is matriarchy and cites certain pronouncements in his epigraphs and prologue in support:

The object of women's existence is not to war with man, or allow man to war with her, but simply to conquer him and hold him in subservience without so much as a threat or a blow. Clever women always do this; clever women have always done it.

Marie Corelli, British novelist.

What woman hasn't been able to wrap a man around her fingers, if she puts her mind to it?

Regina Joseph, Nigerian Columnist.[95]

He goes on to state in his prologue that as a rule, the few women who have bothered to acknowledge female power over men have not been taken seriously. He cites women like Denyse Plummer, the

---

[93] *Ibid.*

[94] Chinweizu, *Anatomy of Female Power*, Lagos, Pero Press, 1990.

[95] *Ibid.*, vi.

Trinidadian calypso singer, who proclaims that 'woman is boss', the expatriate Nigerian actress Patti Boulaye, who says 'most men are controlled by women' and the Argentine, Esther Villar, who said, 'women let men work for them, think for them and take on their responsibilities – in fact, they exploit them'.[96]

He further contends that in the face of this 'great division of opinion among women'[97] one should be prompted to ask: 'which kind of claim is true, which picture is the illusion, and which reality?'[98] According to him, this is so especially, as conventional modern opinion, as well as the social science consensus, would appear to support the feminist picture, which assumes that female power, if it exists would be wielded by women, through some public system authority.[99] He also observes that conventional expert opinion, as portrayed by the Concise Oxford Dictionary (6th Edition, 1976) and the Encyclopedia Britannica, (15th Edition, 1986) hold that matriarchs (who would be the natural wielders of female power) are illusory; and that matriarchy (a system of females wielding authority) does not exist.

However, he rejects the foregoing expert opinion on matriarchs and matriarchy for 'flying in the face of the examples cited above.'[100] He argues that, though some feminists find it in their interest to have the world believe that women are less powerful than men, by pointing to the public structures of political, economic and cultural

---

[96] *Ibid*.

[97] *Ibid*., 9.

[98] *Ibid*. 10

[99] *Ibid*.

[100] *Ibid*. That is, his examples of those women who claim that women rule over and control men.

power, and showing that they are almost exclusively occupied by men, those public structures do not exhaust the modes and centre's of power in society. There are other modes and centre's of power, he contends, which are monopolized by women through sex and their sexual organs and roles.[101] He views the female sexual organs and their role in procreation and nurturing of the young as giving her the power over the man, to 'control scarce resources, commodities and opportunities; and ... distribute them.'[102] He asserts that they exercise this power through education (educating the girl-child to control the male folks with her power of sex and the male child to submit to that power), propaganda, directives, suggestions, rewards and punishments (with offer or denial of sex).

The whole essence of Chinweizu's logic is the objectification or the "commoditization" of the female sex and its inherent power to captivate, a logic that could be considered as being grounded on a flawed premise, that of the woman having "evolved" purely as an object of sex and nothing more.[103] Thus, for him, the male is preoccupied with all that he could ever do to gain access to the sexual favours of the female sex object (a legal non-person, a sex machine and a child "factory" and a "commodity") and is ready to give her anything in return, including laying all his achievements, acquisitions and earthly possessions at her feet, just to gain access to

---

[101] He enumerates five conditions which enable women to get what they want from men, which he describes as five pillars of female power as; women's control of the womb; women's control of the kitchen; women's control of the cradle; the psychological immaturity of men relative to women; and man's tendency to be deranged by his own excited penis.

[102] *Op.cit.,* 11.

[103] From his language, Chinweizu seems to believe in the theory of evolution of the human species.

her vagina and her womb or purchase her sexual favours. This for him constitutes real female power of control and domination over the male folk and male power. This indeed, is a brilliant, but absurd and convoluted logic which smacks of extreme male chauvinism.

Gender-based Legal Theory: Generally, gender theorists distinguish between sex as physiological, and gender as a cultural or social construct. Thus, for these theorists, 'sex refers to biological maleness and femaleness, or the physiological, functional, anatomical differences that distinguish men and women, whereas gender refers to the traits assigned to a sex-what maleness and femaleness stand for – within different societies and cultures.'[104] In other words, unlike the feminist theory, which is exclusively concerned with the rights of women, and measures to empower women, Gender-based legal theory is concerned with fostering equitable balance in gender relations.

That women are more vulnerable than men in times of armed conflict is a notorious fact, which derives from their peacetime conditions of life which are anchored on gender. Therefore, both in peace time and in times of armed conflict women deserve special protection of the law, because they are more vulnerable and are disproportionately affected by the effects of armed conflicts.

Unfortunately, the law in its present state is viewed by gender legal scholars as patriarchal, and hardly conceived to protect women, notwithstanding token special provisions ostensibly aimed at protecting them. Not even its policies of non-discrimination and equality before the law redeems this view, as they have been held to

---

[104] Litosseliti, L, *Gender and Language: Theory and Practice,* Hodder Arnold Education, London, 2006, 10-11.

perpetuate injustices against women by requiring that historically unequal genders, male and female, be treated equally, and without any discrimination as to sex. For instance, the Geneva Convention require that women benefit from the same protection that the law offers to men and without any discrimination as to sex.[105] Sassoli et.al acknowledge that and further observe that International Humanitarian Law first protects women as wounded, sick or shipwrecked, civilians, members of the civilian population or as combatants, and according to their gender status.[106] By their gender status, they imply special protection against attack on their sexual integrity, and in particular rape, enforced, prostitution or any form of indecent assault.[107] Purportedly, they are equally protected

---

[105] *Geneva Convention I-IV, Common Article 3; Geneva Conventions I-II, Art.12; Geneva Convention III, Art.16; Geneva Convention IV, Arts.13 and 27(3).*

[106] Sassoli, M., *et.al.*, How Does Law Protect in War?: Cases, Documents and Teaching Materials on Contemporary Practice in International Humanitarian Law, Geneva, International Committee of the Red Cross, 2011, 213. For specific provisions for the special protection of women, see *Geneva Conventions I-II, Art.12; Geneva Convention III, Arts.14, 25, 88, 97 and 108; Geneva Convention IV, Arts.14, 16, 21-27, 38, 50, 76.*

[107] *Geneva Conventions IV, Art. 27.* The International Criminal Tribunal for Rwanda (ICTR) and the International Criminal Court (ICC) has included rape and other forms of sexual violence in their list of war crimes. *See ICTR Statute, Art. 4(e) and International Criminal Court Statute, Art.8(2)(b)(xxii).* Although the *statute of the International Criminal Tribunal for the former Yugoslavia* (ICTY) does not explicitly mention rape as a war crime, the Trial Chamber in the *Celebici case* nevertheless recognized it as a grave breach of the *Geneva Conventions,* and declared that it could constitute torture. See also *ICTY, the Prosecutor v. Delalic et.al., paras 475 ff.,* where rape was also condemned by the ICTY as a crime against humanity. See also case No. 217, *ICTY, The Prosecutor v. Kunarac, Kovac and Vukovic,* paras 127-186, 1919 at 1923 – 1926 of Sassoli *et.al.*

against the effects of war in cases of pregnancy and maternity,[108] even during times of occupation, and such preferential treatment is not to be hindered by the occupying power.[109] These provisions of the *Geneva Conventions* have recently been recognized as having attained the status of customary international law.[110]

However, the gender-sensitivity demonstrated by the fore-going provisions of the *Geneva Conventions* is rather simplistic. It has failed to take account of the complexity and dynamism of gender, and gender relations. Gender Legal Scholars are increasingly becoming aware of this.

While analyzing the principles of non-discrimination and special protection, Lindsey Curtet sums-up the protection that IHL affords women as follows:

> Ever since its inception, International Humanitarian Law has accorded women general protection equal to that of men. [...] women who have taken an active part in hostilities as combatants are entitled to the same protection as men when they have fallen into enemy hands. [...] Besides this general protection, women are also afforded special protection based on the principle outlined in Article 14, paragraph 2 [of Geneva Convention III], that 'women shall be treated with all the regard due to their sex'. This principle is followed through in a number of provisions which expressly refer to the conditions of detention for women in POW camps [...]. Women (and men) who, as members of the civilian

---

[108] *Geneva Conventions IV, Arts 14, 16, 21, and 22.*

[109] *Geneva Conventions IV, Art. 50.*

[110] Sassoli, *et.al., Op.cit.,* 214. See, Henckaerts, J. & Doswald-Beck L. (ed.), *Customary International Humanitarian Law,* Vol. II, (Part C; Rules 124 and 93), Geneva, ICRC, (2005), 642.

population, are taking no active part in hostilities are afforded protection under the fourth Geneva Convention […] and under Additional Protocol 1. […] In addition to this general protection, women are afforded special protection under the said Convention and Protocol 1, which stipulate that 'women shall be especially protected against any attack on their honour in particular against rape, enforced prostitution or any form of indecent assault'. International Humanitarian Law also lays down special provisions for pregnant women and mothers of small children […].[111]

However, Lindsey-Curtet has since discovered that in spite of the fore-going provisions, women are on the contrary targeted and suffer violations of International Humanitarian Law precisely because they are women.[112] She acknowledges that, this is now the trend in recent and present armed conflicts, which have seen the erosion and ultimate destruction of the once perceived sense of security that a woman, particularly a mother had that she would be spared the excesses of warfare.[113] Besides, she observes that civilian men are also targeted, even when they have not taken up arms in resistance,[114] while women take up arms as members of the armed forces in many armed conflicts, and thus are not always civilians. In spite of this, the tendency has been to classify women and children within the same category of vulnerable persons, as a result of their

---

[111] Lindsey-Curtet C., 'Women and War', *International Review of the Red Cross (IRRC)* [2000], (N0. 839), 580. Sassoli, *et.al; Ibid*, 216.

[112] Lindsey-Curtet C., "The Impact of Armed Conflict on Women", Durham, H., & Gurd, T. (ed.), *Listening to the silences: Women and War*, Leiden, Martinus Nijhoff Publishers, 2005, 21.

[113] *Ibid*.

[114] *Ibid*., 21 – 22.

gender. Of course women are not necessarily vulnerable in situation of armed conflict. Admittedly, they have peculiar needs but their experiences and roles during armed conflicts differ from those of children.[115] This made Lindsey-Curtet to remark that women display remarkable strength, as evidenced by their role as combatants or agents for peace, or by the roles they assume in wartime to protect and support their families'.[116] Reviewing the contribution of gender legal scholars promise to enrich the theoretical frame-work for protecting women in the event of armed conflicts. In this regard it is noteworthy that the ICRC sponsored a study on the impact of armed conflict on women – a study that was 'undertaken as part of the ICRC's endeavour to draw attention to the plight of women in wartime'.[117] The study is rather near comprehensive in its coverage of needs of women affected by armed conflict, and proceeds by adopting a methodology that considers the various needs under the following headings: (a) Overview of Problem; (b) Review of (relevant) International Law; (c) the ICRC's operational response and (d) key points.

At the end of that study, Lindsey – Curtet led the International Committee of the Red Cross (ICRC) Women and War team, which comprises herself, Florence Tercier Holst – Roness; and Letitia Anderson to produce an International Committee of the Red Cross (ICRC) Guidance Document titled *Addressing the Needs of Women*

---

[115] *Ibid.*, 22.

[116] *Ibid.*

[117] *Ibid.* (See Dr. Kellenberger's comment in the foreword to the book).

Affected by Armed Conflicts.[118] The term urges that the text be seen as a complement to the ICRC Women Facing War study, which should be referred to for a more in-depth enquiry into specific problems confronting women and the law affording them protection, especially as its structure is coherent with the study.[119]

Judith Gardam and Michelle Jarvis' *Women, Armed Conflict and International Law*[120] is another very important source book on women and the laws that protect them during armed conflicts. The book is divided into seven chapters: 'Women, Armed Conflicts and International Law', 'The Impact of Armed Conflict on Women', 'International Humanitarian Law, Women and Armed Conflict, 'A Gendered view of the shaping of IHL' 'UN Developments concerning Women and Armed Conflict', International Redress', and 'The way forward'. Essentially, the book 'provides a comprehensive description of the impact on women of modern armed conflict and compares that experience with the current legal framework for protection'.[121] It judges the framework as inadequate for being based on a notion of formal equality, which pays little attention to the differential impact of armed conflict on women and men. However, the authors acknowledge and welcome the more recent developments in the law that has seen increased prosecution

---

[118] Lindsey – Curtet, C. *et.al.*, *Addressing the Needs of Women Affected by Armed Conflict: An ICRC Guidance Document,* Geneva, International Committee of the Red Cross, 2004.

[119] *Ibid.*, 6.

[120] Gardam, J. G. and Jarvis, M. J., *Women, Armed Conflict and International Law, The Hague, Kluwer Law* International, 2001.

[121] *Ibid.*, xiv (Foreword to the book, by Angela E. V. King, United Nations Assistant Secretary-General, Special Adviser on Gender Issues and Advancement of Women.

of sexual violence, especially against women, on the basis of their gender.

Nevertheless, they challenge the current IHL rule that require that its general rules be applied without discrimination, and that provides limited special provisions that deal with the peculiar needs of women. They go on to argue that the requirement of non-discrimination in the application of the provisions relating to all civilians and combatants disguises the reality of a regime that reflects a male perspective of armed conflict,[122] and end up concluding that IHL is not of general application, as 'its design reflects a certain male experience',[123] and thus 'a thoroughly gendered system'.[124] For them, even the special provisions in relation to women take the male perception of not only what it is to be a woman, but also what it is about women that warrants protection.[125] In conclusion, they assert that what has been overlooked, so far, in analyses of IHL is the impact of gender, which has accepted the social construction of the masculine and feminine as a given variable upon which to construct the regime. Unfortunately, they go no further. They should have advocated a total deconstruction of the law, in a way as to also make it cater for the female or feminine norm rather than just the male or masculine norm. They also stop short of advancing or recommending credible strategies for changing the law, either through formulation of new legislations or consequential amendments which might target the language of the law, and interpretations thereof, by the courts. This is important as language

---

[122] *Ibid.*, 9.

[123] *Ibid.*, 10.

[124] *Ibid.*, 11

[125] *Op.cit.*

is acknowledged as being constitutive of reality.[126] Therefore the importance of re-engineering the language of the law, with its socio-linguistic and psycho-linguistic implications cannot be over-emphasized.

Whereas, most of the literatures already reviewed provide descriptions of the impact on women of modern armed conflict, generally in relation to the current legal framework for protection, Coulter presents an ethnographic or 'anthrop graphic' account of women's lives during and immediately after the armed conflict in Sierra Leone.[127] Particularly, she examines the wartime and postwar experiences of young women in northern Sierra Leone who were abducted by the rebels, and notes that even though the young women had strategies and options, 'their choices were circumscribed in ways different than for men'.[128] In the course of analyzing gender and war, she deals with such phenomena as abduction, rape and female fighters as well as postwar issues like demobilization, impoverishment, stigma, and healing, within the larger processes of humanitarianism and the local social context.

Even though she focuses exclusively on women, 'the women's experiences were articulated in relation to their social environment, with an emphasis on gender, age, kinship, and socioeconomic position, and on the social aspects of being a woman'.[129] However,

---

[126] Shepherd. L. J., 'Women, armed conflict and language – Gender, violence and discourse', [2010],, *International Review of Red Cross (IRRC)*, (Vol. 92, No. 877), 144 – 147.

[127] Coulter, C., *Bush Wives and Girl Soldiers: Women's Lives through War and Peace in Sierra Leone*, Ithaca and London, Cornell, University Press, 2009.

[128] *Ibid.*, 4.

[129] *Ibid.*, 230

she pays little attention to the legal protection of these women,[130] but this is understandable as the work is more or less an ethnographic study. Thus, her mention of the fact that some Sierra Leonean national legislations criminalize rape of under-aged girls, and, the fact that Sierra Leone is a signatory to, and have ratified many international legal instruments enriches the study and makes it somewhat relevant to the legal protection of women. Regrettably though, she does not mention the legislations and the legal instruments in question.

However, Turshen's 'Women's War Stories'[131] is not as limiting in its coverage as the foregoing study on Sierra Leone. On the contrary, it attempts to capture most of the armed conflicts that Africa has witnessed. For instance, it catalogues:

> Wars of liberation were fought by Algeria, Angola, Eritrea, Guinea Bissau, Kenya, Mozambique, Namibia, South Africa, Western Sahara and Zimbabwe. Civil wars have broken out in Algeria, Angola, Burundi, Chad, Congo (Kinshasa), Djibouti, Ethiopia, Gambia, Liberia, Mali, Mozambique, Niger, Nigeria, Rwanda, Senegal, Sierra Leone, Somalia, South Africa, Sudan, Tanzania and Uganda.[132]

But the wars are not systematically discussed. The author's narrative is rather panoramic and kaleidoscopic, and anchored on salient themes like gender, gendered violence, feminism, especially

---

[130] *Ibid.*, 228 – 230.

[131] Turshen, M., 'Women's War Stories', Turshen, M. & Twagiramariya, C., (eds.). *What Women Do in Wartime: Gender and Conflict in Africa,* London & New York, Zed Books Ltd., 1998.

[132] *Ibid.*, 6.

rape, displacement and dislocation, widowhood and isolation, health and political violence.

In the final analysis, though Turshen's work acknowledges that the legal implications of abuses of women by non-State actors are different from those of State violators, as the former cannot formally subscribe to existing conventions, it fell short of critiquing the extant laws. However, she notes that while the *Geneva Conventions* and the *Additional Protocols* have no effective enforcement mechanisms, just a few African states have signed *Protocol* II, because they are unwilling to be bound by restrictions over the conduct of domestic affairs.[133]

Nevertheless, Turshen's narrative is not focused on war situations in particular countries because it is limited to an introductive chapter. The rest of the chapters contributed by different authors, focus on situations in particular countries, with respect to gender and armed conflicts. In chapter two, we have Goldblatt, and Meinties', 'South African Women Demand the Truth', which graphically describes how militarized constructions of masculinity and feminity became more pronounced in South Africa's apartheid era, and the gendered violence that characterized the ensuing conflict. Along with other chapters on South Africa, the chapter presents the case for a gendered approach to women's testimony before the Truth and Reconciliation Commission. The chapter on Sudan evokes 'the suffering of Southern women, as warriors, kidnap victims, sexual slaves and refugees, while a Rwandan woman describes the complex sexual pressures on women in a civil war that has been obscured by simplistic tribal

---

[133] *Ibid.*, 3.

explanations'.[134] There are also contributions on the Chadian civil war that started in 1965 and the 'brutality against women in the civil war in Liberia'.[135] The contribution by a Namibian woman recalls her eight years as guerilla fighter for SWAPO, 'while the final chapter analyzes the militarization of Africa and places the conflicts in the framework of international relation'.[136] On the whole, the book has been acknowledged as the first to examine rape and other forms of gendered political violence in African Civil Wars,[137] but it scarcely addresses legal protection against gendered violence.

Kristof and WuDunn's *Half the Sky: Turning oppression into opportunity for Women Worldwide* also draws attention to the brutality of gendered violence in some recent armed conflicts in Africa. In the chapter on 'Rule by Rape' they reveal that one study suggests that women perpetrators were involved, along with men, in one quarter of the gang rapes in Sierra Leone civil war.[138] Typically, in Sierra Leone, women fighters would lure a victim to the rape site, and then restrain or hold her down as she was raped by male fighters.[139] However, 'the author of the study cites evidence from Haiti, Iraq, and Rwanda to suggest that female participation in Sierra Leone's sexual violence was not an anomaly'.[140] She went on to argue that ubiquitous gang rape in civil wars is not about sexual gratification,

---

[134] See the Review on the back page cover of the book.

[135] *Ibid.*

[136] *Ibid.*

[137] *Ibid.*

[138] Kristof, N. D and WuDunn, S, *Half the Sky: Turning Oppression into Opportunity for Women Worldwide*, New York, Vintage Books, 2010, 67 – 68.

[139] *Ibid.*

[140] *Ibid.*

but rather a way for military units, including their female members, to bond, by engaging in sometimes 'brutally misogynistic violence'.[141] They also draw attention to gang-rapes in Darfur, and mass rapes and other sexual violence that affected about half of the women in Sierra Leone, including the aggravated use of sexual violence against women in the armed conflict in DR Congo, which saw eastern Congo declared as the world capital of rape.[142]

Chukwumaeze joins the ranks of gender legal scholars who agree that women are the most vulnerable to human rights abuses and humanitarian law violations, and cites the examples of the rape of about two million women by the Russian forces during the Second World War, the atrocious gang rape of women during the war in Sierra Leone, and the rape of Biafran women, and the disproportionate effect of economic sanctions or blockage on women in Biafra. Besides, he lauds the adoption of the *Rome Statute*, and the establishment of the International Criminal Court pursuant to that statute. He also acknowledges that significant advances have been made in International Humanitarian Law, particularly in the protection of women during times of armed conflict, but observes that significant gaps remain[143]. He cites the negligible role of women in decision making during times of conflict and their minimal involvement in peace deals and rebuilding process as a key

---

[141] *Ibid.*

[142] *Ibid.*, 84.

[143] Chukwumaeze, U. U., "Protecting the Rights of Women in Armed Conflict: A Legal Perspective", Njoku, S. A. (ed.) Essays on Contemporary Issues of Law, Owerri, Peacewise Systems, 2010, 305-306. Also see generally, Okorie, H., 'The Protection of Women in Armed Conflict: An Examination, available at https://www.nchii nim.nihi gov 2014 (accessed on 10-11-2018)

lacunae.[144] It is however, submitted that beyond the negligible role of women in decision making during conflicts and in peace deals, there is an over-ridding need for an integration of a gender perspective in the law. Particularly, this calls for the mainstreaming of gender in international humanitarian law.

Most of the contributions on the subject of 'women' published in *International Review of the Red Cross*[145] encourage a gender perspective in relation to women in armed conflicts, but fail to recommend strategies for integrating a gender perspective and mainstreaming gender in the relevant laws. For instance, Herrmann and Palmieri recount the long history and the multiple facets of women's involvement in war from two angles, namely women at war (participating in war) and women in war (affected by war), and examines the merit of a gender-based division of roles in war with reference to the traditional practice of armed violence.[146] They however conclude 'that war and the violence associated with it are not a matter of gender, but first and foremost of individuals, and that we must therefore regard aggression as a human rather than a male activity'.[147] This conclusion has implications for the discriminatory perception of aggression and violence by women, a perception that views aggressive or violent women as monsters.

---

[144] *Ibid.*, 318.

[145] Pfanner, T. (ed.), 'Women' [March 2010], *International Review of Red Cross*, (Vol. 92, No. 877).

[146] Herrmann and Palmieri, 'Between Amazons and Sabine's: a historical approach to women and war', [2010] *International Review of the Red Cross*, (Vol. 92, No. 877), 19.

[147] *Ibid.*, 30.

Durham and O'Byrne examines the meaning and potential usefulness of a 'gender perspective' on international humanitarian law, and suggest 'that further development and understanding of a gender perspective will contribute to the resilience and effectiveness of international humanitarian law and will strengthen the protection of those who are victimized and disempowered during times of war'.[148] However, the learned authors fail to recommend measures or strategies for developing a gender perspective. Sjoberg also fell into the same trap by advocating gender mainstreaming in the military without suggesting ways of achieving it.[149]

In analyzing women's participation in the Rwandan genocide, Hogg situates her discourse in the context of gender relations in pre-genocide Rwandan society. She observes that 'many "ordinary" women were involved in the genocide but, overall, committed significantly fewer acts of overt violence than men', while 'women in leadership position played a particularly important role in the genocide, and gendered imagery, including of the "evil woman" or "monster", is often at play in their encounters with the law'.[150] She finds that despite the existence of patriarchy in Rwandan culture, gender relations at the time of the genocide were more complex than is often depicted. She warns that seeking to excuse the conduct of women who participated in the genocide or condemning it for breaching gender norms draws us into stereotyping women and undermines the complex realities of women's experience of mass

---

[148] Durham, H., and O'Byrne, K., 'The dialogue of difference: gender perspective on international humanitarian law', *Ibid*, 31.

[149] Sjoberg, L., 'Women' fighters the 'beautiful soul' narrative, *Ibid.*, 53 – 68.

[150] Hogg, N., 'women's participation in the Rwandan genocide: mothers or monsters?'. *Ibid.*, 69.

violence.[151] However, Hogg leaves many questions unanswered. Haeri and Puechguirbal also dwell on the need to move away from stereotypical depictions of women in war towards a better understanding of the plurality of roles, responsibilities and challenges that shape the way women experience armed conflict.[152] Clearly, contemporary experiences of women in armed conflicts expose the limitations inherent in international humanitarian law.

Barrow acknowledges that while the *Geneva Conventions* contain gender-specific provisions, the reality of women's and men's experiences of armed conflict has highlighted gender limitations and conceptual constraints within international humanitarian law.[153] Particularly, she acknowledges that judgments at the International Criminal Tribunal for the former Yugoslavia (ICTY) and International Criminal Tribunal for Rwanda (ICTR) have gone some way towards expanding the scope of the definitions of sexual violence and rape in armed conflict. However, she notes that more recent developments in public international law, which includes the adoption of Security Council Resolutions 1325 and 1820 which focus on women, peace and security, have sought to increase the visibility of gender in situations of armed conflict.[154] But she understands that although the Resolutions are significant, 'they may not be radical enough to expand constructions of gender within international

---

[151] *Ibid.*, 101.

[152] Haeri, M., and Puechguirbal, N., 'From helplessness to agency: examining the plurality of women's experiences in armed conflict, *Ibid.*, 103.

[153] Barrow, A., 'UN Security Resolutions 1325 and 1820: constructing gender in armed conflict and international humanitarian law', *Ibid.*, 221.

[154] *Ibid.*

humanitarian law'.[155] Tachou – Sipowo agrees with her.[156] After having analyzed the foundations on which the Security Council has been able to assume responsibility for protecting women in situations of armed conflict, and having considered the actual protection it provides, he concludes that the council has had varying success, pointing out that the thematic and declaratory resolutions on which it is largely based are not binding.[157] According to the learned author, they are relatively effective only with regard to their provisions that commit the United Nations bodies. She recommends that the council's role could be better accomplished through situational resolutions than through resolutions declaratory of international law.[158]

However, the following are perceived gaps in existing literature on the subject of legal protection of women in armed conflicts generally, and in Africa in particular: 1.None of the reviewed literature advocates or recommends a total reform of existing laws on armed conflicts, which in its present state are basically male-oriented and gender blind to women, having been based on historically unequal gender power relations; 2.None recommends strategies for achieving equitable gender mainstreaming in the law generally, and in the law of armed conflict, in particular. Thus, the law as presently constituted seems unable to protect women and their physical integrity during armed conflicts. Of course, the problem is foundational and thus fundamental, as law evolved as a

---

[155] *Ibid.*

[156] Tachou – Sipowo, A., 'The Security Council on women in war: between peace building and humanitarian protection', *Ibid.*, 197.

[157] *Ibid.*

[158] *Ibid.*

male concept, which views women (the female gender) as non-legal persons, who were outside the protection of the law. This mood of the law which has been reflected in gender-neutral or gender-specific terms in favor of the male gender has persisted. Consequently, whenever women's rights are not provided for in gender-specific language and guaranteed by law, they tend to be unrecognized and unprotected. Even when guaranteed by law, gender discrimination attends the implementation and enforcement of the law which has continued to reflect a male perspective or idea of what it is about women, which deserves or warrants protection. This is the case, despite the special provisions of the law which seeks to protect women's "honor", pregnancy and unborn children (foetus), which of course are essentially the male owner's interests. The problem demands a total reform of the legal system, a reform which should target its components, namely: the substantive; the cultural; and the structural components.

The substantive component consists of the content of the law, while the cultural and the structural components, respectively consist of shared ideas, attitudes and behaviours about the law, on the one hand, and the courts, administrative and law enforcement agencies, on the other hand.[159] The three components are integrally linked to one another, so that activities aimed at changing the *status-quo* within the different components interact with and affect all the components and produce a change in the whole legal system. To bring about the desired change, such activities must target the three components simultaneously. The desired change in this case, is the

---

[159] Ibezim, E. C., 'Strategies for the Achievement of Gender Equality Under the Law',[2007/2008], Millennium Journal of Intetrnational Studies (Vol. 1, No. 1), 265

integration and mainstreaming of gender in the relevant laws that protect women in situations of armed conflict.

Uncoordinated activities or activities that target one or two of the components alone will not bring about the desired change, neither will such change take immediate effect, especially in the cultural component of the law, which involves attitudinal and behaviourial changes. However, one thing is certain. Once the aforementioned strategies are engaged, they will inevitably trigger a psycho-social change in attitudes and behaviours towards women and girls in society, and in armed conflicts in particular. Such a change will in turn trigger a change in law and practice in relation to women's rights.

2.3 Conceptual Framework:

The basic concepts that constitute the framework for this research are "Law", (especially Laws relating to armed conflicts), "Gender", "Women", "Feminism", and "Armed Conflicts". Thus, our review on concepts will focus on them, and certain derivative concepts, such as "International Law", "International Humanitarian Law", "International Human Rights Law", "International Criminal Law", "Terrorism", "Insurgency", "Belligerency", "Combatant", Genocide" and the doctrine of "Non-Discrimination".

Law:

Enquiries into the meaning and nature of law have generated enormous literature in the field of Jurisprudence.[160] However, for the present purpose, it is proposed to steer away from any jurisprudential enquiry into the meaning of law as that would be rather distractive, in the circumstances. Appraising or reviewing the lexical meaning of "Law" promise to be a more rewarding exercise, for the purposes of this book.

Law has been defined as:

The regime that orders human activities and relations through systematic application of the force of politically organized society, or through social pressure, backed by force, in such a society; the legal system... the aggregate of legislation, judicial precedents, and accepted legal principles; the body of authoritative grounds of judicial and administrative action;... the set of rules or principles dealing with a specific area of a legal system... the judicial and administrative process; legal action and proceedings...[161.]

This definition is near comprehensive. It speaks of law as that body of rules and regulations that orders human activities and relations through systematic application of force or social pressure. It also portrays it as denotative of a legal system; while among other things embodying legislations or statutes, judicial precedents or case

---

[160] Freeman, M.D.A, *Lloyd's Introduction to Jurisprudence* (7th ed.). London, Sweet & Maxwell Ltd; 2001; Bix, B., *Jurisprudence: Theory and Context*, London, Sweet & Maxwell, 2006; Ogwurike, C., *Concept of Law in English Speaking Africa*; Eso, K., *Further Thoughts on Law and Jurisprudence*, Ibadan, Spectrum Law publishing, 2003, etc.

[161] Garner, B.A, *Op.cit.*, 900.

law and principles of law. Law may also be described as authoritative bases of judicial and administrative action or process, as well as the set of rules or principles that deal with a specific area of a legal system.[162] Thus, we have International Humanitarian Law, Human Rights law, Constitutional Law etcetera. Interestingly, law has also been defined from the point of view of its efficacy or potency as: 'The enforceable body of rules that govern any society [or] one of the rules making up the body of law, such as an Act of Parliament'[163].

Though simple, this later definition emphasizes the fact that for rules to amount to law, they must be enforceable. In other words, unenforceable rules that are meant to govern a society may not be said to be laws. However, there is doubt that this meaning is intended, as enforceability or unenforceability touches on the quality of the Law, rather than on its status.

International Law: International Law has been defined as:

The legal system governing the relationships between nations; more modernly, the Law of international relations, embracing not only nations but also such participants as international organizations and individuals (such as those who invoke their human rights or commit war crimes).[164]

In a bid to further buttress the meaning of international law, Garner cites Jessup's definition of International Law as follows:

[I]International Law or the Law of nations must be defined as Law applicable to states in their relations with states.

---

[162] *Ibid*.

[163] Martin, E.A (ed), *A Dictionary of Law* (5th ed.), Oxford, Oxford University Press, 2003, 280.

[164] Garner, *Op.cit*, 835.

International Law may also, under the hypothesis, be applicable to certain interrelationships of individuals themselves, where such interrelationships involve matters of international concern.'[165]

Another learned lexicographer defines it as:

The system of Law regulating the interrelationship of sovereign states and their rights and duties with regard to one another. In addition, certain international organizations (such as the United Nations), companies, and sometimes individuals (e.g. in the sphere of 'human rights') may have rights or duties under international law. International Law deals with such matters as the formation and recognition of states, acquisition of territory, war, the Law of the sea and of space, treaties, treatment of aliens, human rights, international Crimes and international judicial settlement of disputes.[166]

He acknowledges that International Law is also known as Public International Law, so as to distinguish it from Private International Law, which does not deal with relationships between States.[167]

Some other learned authors have also attempted to define international Law. For instance, Shaw views Public International Law as covering relations between states in all their myriad forms, from war to satellites, and regulates the operations of the many international institutions.[168] He went on to observe that it may be

---

[165] *Ibid.*

[166] Martin, *Op.cit.*, 260.

[167] *Ibid.*

[168] Shaw, M.N., *International Law* (5th ed.), Cambridge, Cambridge University Press, 2003, 2.

universal or general, meaning that a group of States linked geographically or ideologically may recognize special rules applying only to them.[169] He cites the example of practice of diplomatic asylum that has developed to its greatest extent in Latin America.[170] Emphasizing an alternative view, Brierly opines:

> The best view is that international Law is in fact just a system of customary law, upon which has been erected, almost entirely within the last two generations, a superstructure of 'conventional' or treaty-made law, and some of its chief defects are precisely those that the history of law teaches us to expect in a customary system.[171]

Thus, for Brierly, international law is just a system of customary law. This justifies the term 'Customary International Law'. Customary International Law has been defined as international law that derives from the practice of states and is accepted by them as legally binding. This is one of the principal sources or building blocks of the international legal system.[172]

However, in order to be considered customary international law, a provision or prohibition must be (1) State practice – evidenced by long-term, wide spread compliance by many states; and (2) *Opinio Juris* – States' belief that compliance with a standard is not merely

---

[169] *Ibid.*

[170] *Ibid.* See *The Assylum Case*, ICJ, 1950, 266., 171LR, 280. See also *The Right of Passage Over Indian Territory Case*, ICT Reports [1960], 6, 31 ILR, 23.

[171] Per Brierly, in his *The Law of Nations* (6th ed.) Waldoct, 1963, 41-42, 68-76 as Quoted in Harris, D.J, *Cases and Materials on International Law* (6th ed.), London, Sweet & Maxwell, 2004, 3.

[172] Garner, *Op.cit*, 835.

desired, but required by international law.[173] In other words, States are bound by customary international law norms, unless they have persistently objected to them. In 1900, the U.S Supreme Court's decision in the *Paquete Habana case*[174] underlined this fact, when it stated that customary international law is 'part of our law, and must be ascertained and administered by the Courts of Justice of appropriate jurisdiction'. The court went on to state that law could be ascertained by works of jurists commentators when there was no controlling treaty or other law.[175]

Thus, it must be observed that only widespread rather than unanimous acquiescence is needed for a practice to ripen into a customary international norm. In this regard, the *Restatement of the Foreign Relations law* of the United States has indicated that there is no precise formula to indicate how widespread a practice must be, but stated that it should reflect wide acceptance among states particularly involved in the relevant activity.[176] States' acceptance of principles in international agreements as well as their own laws, including works of jurists and commentators could presently be equated to the so-called general principles of law recognized by states. This acceptance of principles would include 'government policy statements and opinions by legal officers as part of the

---

[173] Connie de la Vega, 'Customary International Law', Forsythe, D. P., (ed.) *Encyclopedia of Human Rights* (Vol. 1), Oxford, Oxford University Press, 2009, 451. Customary International Law is that law that applies to States, while Customary Law applies to the indigenous practices in many nations, including many African countries.

[174] 175 U.S. 677.

[175] *Supra.*

[176] Connie de la Vega, *Op.cit.*, 45 – 452.

increasing practice of negotiating, and approving international instrument'.[177] It would also include 'legal briefs endorsed by states, as well as national judicial opinions'.[178] So also have, the widespread negotiation, promulgation, and acceptance of human rights treaties, declarations, resolutions, and other instruments, been recognized as indicative of state practice, as well as, of the *opinion juris* requirement. However, there is often disagreement on when a practice or rule has ripened into a customary international norm, but consensus has been reached on some human rights.[179]

It now remains to state that for a long time, the private individual was barely a 'subject' of international law. For instance, the positivist school, that dominated the field of international law from the late eighteenth century, defined international law as governing principally relations between states with individuals usually at best third-party beneficiaries.[180] *The Black's Law Dictionary* reflects this, and the fact that only recently does the law embrace, such participants as international organizations and individuals. Jessup's definition quoted *infra*, from which presumably, the dictionary draws its inspiration notes that such interrelationships of

---

[177] *Ibid.*, 451.

[178] *Ibid.*

[179] *Ibid.*, 452. The list of such human rights upon which consensus has been reached include: genocide; slavery or slave trade; murder or the causing of the disappearance of individuals; torture or other cruel, inhuman or degrading treatment or punishment; prolonged arbitrary detention; systematic racial discrimination; the application of the death penalty and life without parole sentences for offenders under eighteen years of age; and consistent patterns of gross violations of internationally recognized human rights.

[180] Ratner, S. R., *et.al., Accountability for Human Rights Atrocities in International Law: Beyond the Nuremberg Legacy* (3rd ed.) Oxford, Oxford University Press, 2009, 4.

individuals must involve matters of international concern for them to be covered by international law.

Post World War II has seen increasing protection of individuals under international law. Since then international law has explicitly provided for individual criminality or required States to make an act a crime under domestic law, or both, as does the *Genocide Convention*.[181] Ratner has also observed that it obligates 'states or an international court to carryout prosecutions or punishment as with the *Genocide Convention* or the *Geneva Conventions* or to extradite or prosecute offenders, as with the *Torture Convention*'.[182] He further observes: 'it can simply allow States or international courts to try and punish individuals for certain acts, irrespective of normal jurisdictional limits'.[183]

The foregoing spirit of the law has been given effect, in recent times, by international criminal tribunals, the International Criminal Court, and some national or domestic courts. In all these, the following three areas of international law overlap, that is, International Humanitarian Law, International Human Rights Law, and International Criminal Law.

International Humanitarian Law: International Humanitarian Law (IHL) hitherto known as the Law of War has been defined as:

The branch of international law limiting the use of violence in armed conflicts by: a) Sparing those who do not or no longer directly participate in hostilities; b) Restricting it to the amount necessary to

---

[181] *Ibid.*

[182] *Ibid.*

[183] *Ibid.*

achieve the aim of the conflict, which – independently of the causes fought for can only be to weaken the military potential of the enemy.[184] In other words, International Humanitarian Law is applicable only in times of armed conflict[185] and protects persons not or no longer taking a direct part in hostilities; and regulates permissible means and methods of warfare.[186] Flowing from the foregoing definition are the following basic principles of International Humanitarian Law: i) The principle of distinction between civilians and combatants; ii) The principle prohibiting attacks on those *hors de combat*; iii) The principle prohibiting the infliction of unnecessary suffering; iv) The principle of necessity; and v) The principle of proportionality

On the other hand, the following inherent limits of International Humanitarian Law have been acknowledged: i) It does not prohibit the use of violence; ii) It cannot protect all those affected by armed conflict; iii) It makes no distinction based on the purpose of the conflict; It does not bar a party from overcoming the enemy; iv) It presupposes that the parties to an armed conflict have rational aims

---

[184] Sassoli, M, and others, A., *How Does Law Protect in War?: Cases, documents and Teaching Materials on contemporary practice in International Humanitarian Law Vol. 1* (3rd ed.), ICRC, Geneva 2011, 93.

[185] As established in *Prosecutor v Tadic (IT-94-1-A)* May, 1997, an armed conflict is said to exist 'whenever there is a resort to armed forces between states or protracted armed violence between governmental authorities and organized armed groups or between such groups within a state'. Treaty law does not define the term; it merely regulates permissible means and methods of warfare.

[186] Sassoli, M and Bouvier, A.A., *How Does Law Protect in War?* Vol. 1 (2nd ed.), ICRC, Geneva 2006, 81. See also, Ibezim, E.C; 'Contemporary Challenges to International Humanitarian Law: the Private Military Companies' [2009/2010], *African year Book on International Humanitarian Law*, Cape Town, Juta & Co Ltd., 87.

and that those aims as such do not contradict International Humanitarian Law.[187]

International Humanitarian Law has also been conceived to include all those rules that for humanitarian reasons limit the resort to force in an armed conflict between states or in an intrastate conflict situation. Those rules are said to limit the right of parties to an armed conflict to choose methods or means of warfare, and emphasized that they prohibit the use of force against persons who are not or who are no longer taking part in hostile acts, as the civilian population and individual civilian, military and civilian prisoners or detainees described as 'protected persons', and against civilian property, described as 'protected objects'.[188] Furthermore, International Humanitarian Law is said to impose on a party to the conflict the obligation to provide, if necessary, assistance to persons under its control or to allow relief operations to be undertaken by third parties, including non-governmental humanitarian organizations.[189]

However, the International Committee of the Red Cross (ICRC) defines International Humanitarian Law as:

> International rules established by treaties or custom, which are specially intended to solve humanitarian problems directly arising from international or non-international armed conflicts and which , for humanitarian reasons, limit the right of parties to a conflict to use the methods, and

---

[187] *Ibid.*, 94.

[188] Gasser, H., 'Humanitarian Law', [2009], *Encyclopedia of Human Rights* (Vol. 2), 462. See also, Gasser, H., *International Humanitarian Law: An Introduction*, Haupt, Henry Dunant Institute, 1993, 15-20.

[189] *Ibid.*

means of warfare of their choice, or protect persons and property that are, or may be, affected by conflict.[190]

International Humanitarian Law comprises two regimes, namely, the law applicable in international armed conflict, or conflicts between States; and the rules designed to apply in non-international armed conflict, or conflicts within the territory of a State. However, the former is more developed than the latter, though the underlying principles are the same. On the whole, International Humanitarian Law has been viewed as comprising two bodies of law, namely Geneva Law and Hague Law. While Geneva law comprises the rules protecting individual persons from violence, Hague Law limits the right to use certain methods or means of warfare.[191]

The fundamental principles of International Humanitarian Law may be summarized as follows:

a) **Humanity:** The overall goal of the law is to preserve humanity, even under the worst conditions that a human being can ever encounter.

b) **Military necessity:** The Law must take into account and acknowledge the reality of warfare. Yet any military operation must pass the test of necessity: is the act of violence really necessary for achieving the (legitimate) goal?

c) **Proportionality:** A military operation must not create victims among the civilian population, nor damage and destruction among civilian goods, which would be excessive compared

---

[190] Pictet, J., *et.al* (eds.), *Commentary on the Additional Protocols of 8 June* (1997) *to the Geneva Convention of 12 August, 1949*, Geneva, ICRC, 1987, xxvii.

[191] *Ibid.,* 114.

to the expected (legitimate) military advantage gained by the operation.

d) **Incompatibility with total war:** Humanitarian Law is an unequivocal negation of total war.[192]

The fundamental principles include those of distinction (distinction between civilians and combatants)[193] prohibition on causing unnecessary suffering;[194] and independence of *jus in bello* from *jus ad bellum* (i.e. legality of the use of force and humanitarian rules to be respected in warfare, respectively).[195]

International Human Rights Law: Defining 'International Human Rights Law' may not be an easy task. However, a convenient and necessary starting point would be an examination of the concept of 'Human Rights'. Eze observes that any inquiry into the concept of human rights is bound to generate controversy as to its exact meaning, its material scope and its relevance to social organization and change.[196] This observation underlines the hackneyed notion that it is difficult to arrive at a comprehensive and generally acceptable definition of human rights.[197]

Weston graphically re-echoes this notion when he states:

---

[192] *Ibid*, 463.

[193] Sassoli, M., Bourveir, A. A. *et.al. op cit*, 163.

[194] *Ibid.*, 283.

[195] *Ibid.*, 114.

[196] Eze, O.C; 'Africa, New World Order, Human Rights and Democracy', *Inaugural Lecture*, Abia State University, Uturu 1992, 9.

[197] Ibezim, E.C. 'The Beijing Conference and the Human rights Protection of Women: A Critical Review' (An LL.M Dissertation presented to the Faculty of Law and the faculty of Post Graduate Studies, Abia State University, Uturu, 2000.

To say that there is widespread acceptance of the principle of human rights on the domestic and international planes is not to say that there is complete agreement about the nature of such rights or their definition. Some of the most basic questions have yet to receive conclusive answers. Whether human rights are to be viewed as divine, moral or legal entitlements; whether they are to be broad or limited in number and content and kindred issues are matters of ongoing debate and likely to remain so as long as there exist contending approaches to public order and societies among resources.[198]

In the face of the avowed lack of unanimity in the definition of 'human rights', it becomes absolutely necessary to consider a number of definitions or statements by learned authors, and a couple of lexicographers. Certainly, this approach shall present a spectrum of insights into the meaning of the concept, and serve to give the reader a creative rein, by indulging his critical mind to the end of a better understanding of the concept.

The Black's Law Dictionary defines 'human rights' as: '[t]he freedoms, immunities, and benefits that, according to modern values (especially at an international level), all human beings should be able to claim as a matter of right in the society in which they live.'[199] Furthermore, the dictionary refers us to the *Universal Declaration of Human Rights*,[200] presumably as the historical starting point of

---

[198] Weston, B., 'Human Rights', 20 New Encyclopedia Britannica (15th ed.)(1992) at 656 as reproduced in Steiner, H. J., and Alston, P., *International Human Rights in Context: Law, Politics Morals* (Text and Materials), New York, Oxford University Press Inc., 1996, 167.

[199] Garner, B.A., *Op.cit*, 758.

[200] The Universal Declaration of Human Rights was adopted on December 10, 1948 following General Assembly Resolution 217 (III), Un Doc. A/810 AT 71, 1948.

international protection of human rights. On the other hand, the *Oxford dictionary of Law* defines 'Human Rights' as 'Rights and freedom to which every human being is entitled'.[201] Among other things, it went further to state as follows:

> Protection against breaches of these rights committed by a state (including the state of which the victim is a national) may in some cases be enforced in international law. It is sometimes suggested that human rights (or some of them) are so fundamental that they form part of natural law, but most of them are best regarded as forming part of treaty law. The United Nations Universal Declaration of Human Rights (1948) spells out most of the main rights that must be protected but it is not binding in international law. There are two international covenants, however, that bind the parties who have ratified them: the 1966 International Covenant on Civil and political Rights and International Covenant on Economic, Social and Cultural Rights.[202]

It is noteworthy that the two dictionaries under reference view "human rights" as "freedoms", "rights" and "entitlements" or "benefits", "immunities" or "protection", which every human being is entitled to or may be able to claim as a matter of right. Both dictionaries acknowledge the *Universal Declaration of Human Rights* as the principal or foremost instrument on human rights.

Many learned authors have also proffered their definitions of human rights. For Osita Eze: 'Human rights represents demands or claims which individuals or groups make on society, some of which are protected by law and have become part of *lex lata* while others

---

[201] Martin, *Op.cit.*, 237.
[202] *Ibid*.

remain aspirations to be attained in the future.'[203] He goes on to justify his view of human rights as being in part, claims (*lex farranda*), by asserting that by presenting rights as moral or social claims on society, they lay the foundation for social and political action that more often than not lead to their transmutation into legal rights.[204] In the same vein, Umozurike posits:

> Human rights are thus claims, which are invariably supported by ethics and which should be supported by law, made on society, especially on its official managers by individuals or groups on the basis of their humanity. They apply regardless of race, colour, sex or other distinction and may not be withdrawn or denied by governments, people or individuals. They may also be defined in terms of individual self-interest. They are those rights which every individual claims and aspires to enjoy irrespective of his colour, race, religion, status in life, etc.[205]

Okoronye defines it by reference to it's divine source, thereby re-stating the age-long concept of natural law and natural rights as its character. He states:

> The concept of human rights has its origin from the concept of natural law and natural rights as expounded by the Greek and Roman Philosophers as well as the classical philosophers of the 17th and 18th centuries. Human rights are therefore rights given to man by God on creation. In other words, they

---

[203] Eze, O.C., *Human Rights in Africa: Some Selected Problems*, Lagos, Nigeria Institute of International Affairs,

(AIIA), 1984, 5.

[204] Eze, O.C; 'Africa, New World Order, Human Rights and Democracy', *op. cit.*

[205] Umozurike, U. O., *The African, Charter on Human and Peoples' Rights,* The Hague/Boston/London, Martinus

Nijhoff Publishers, 1997, 5.

are inherent rights which man enjoys by virtue of his humanity. Being inherent, human rights are therefore universal and inalienable.[206]

Clearly, Okoronye joins such learned authors as Sidorsky in asserting that human rights has its roots in ancient ideas of universal justice and in medieval notions of natural law and natural rights. Like them, he views the idea of human rights as affirming 'that all individuals, solely by virtue of being human, have moral rights which no society or state should deny'.[207]

Many national constitutions and specific domestic laws had for a long time provided for the human rights of individuals, while in a broader sense, aspects of human rights had been the subject of international concern from times earlier than the *Universal Declaration*, through treaty provisions protecting minorities or refugees and through the work of the International Labour Organization, for example.[208] However, the *Universal Declaration* had a wider aim – that of providing a universal list of rights.[209] But, effective protection of human rights demands more than simply listing the rights. It also demands the legal machinery to interpret, adjudicate and order enforcement.[210] Such machinery had mostly been limited to the States' legal system within the municipal law.

---

[206] Okoronye, I., *Terrorism in International Law*, Okigwe, Whytem Publishers Nigeria, 2013, 61.

[207] Sidorsky, D., 'Contemporary Reinterpretations of the concept of Human Rights', Sidorsky, D., (ed.), *Essays on Human Rights* 88, 1979, 98.

[208] Gardiner, R. K., *International Law*, London, Pearson (Longman) Education Ltd., 2003, 272.

[209] *Ibid.*

[210] *Ibid.*

Any outside interference had traditionally been viewed as a breach of State sovereignty under international law, as a State's relations with its own nationals had been viewed as exclusively within the realm of the State's internal affairs. Moreover, most States strongly oppose such interference on the ground that the collective interest of the State justifies suppression of purely individual interests.[211]

However, developments in international protection of human rights have gradually transformed this principle, but the enduring effect of the traditional view has continued to stall the rapid development of human rights activities internationally and at the United Nations. Thus, it is only hesitantly that direct access has been afforded individuals to international courts and tribunals having specific competence to consider human rights.[212] Even though States have increasingly incorporated international human rights provisions in their domestic law, in many cases it is only the application of international procedures which guarantees an objective means which enables international law to regulate relations between the individuals and the State.[213] This argument has been raised in relation to the *European Convention on Human Rights*.[214] In interpreting and applying the Convention, the European Court held, in the case of *Swedish Engine Driver Union v Sweden*,[215] that 'neither Article 13 nor the Convention in general lays down for the contracting States any given manner for ensuring within their internal law the effective implementation of any provisions of the

---

[211] *Ibid.*, 273.

[212] *Ibid.*

[213] *Ibid.*, 273 – 274.

[214] *Ibid.*, 278.

[215] (1976), IEHRR 617, at 631, para. 50.

Convention'. Thus, while 'it is undoubtedly an advantage that national courts should have express regard to the terms of the Convention, the real purpose and safeguard of the Convention lies in having an international guarantee.'[216] This justifies the current rapid development of international human rights law.

Ratner defines International Human Rights Law as:

The body of international law aimed at protecting the human dignity of the individual. Developed in largest part since World War II, it principally seeks to guarantee the rights of persons vis-à-vis their own government, but also protects them to various degrees against other actors in the international community that might violate those rights, whether guerilla groups, business entities, or terrorists.[217]

Erugo conceptualizes it as: 'The law that deals with the protection of guaranteed rights and with the promotion of these rights. The crux of international human rights law is to afford legal protection of human rights, far and above municipal law and practice.'[218] He acknowledges its recent origins or development in relation to the older 'articulations and developments within the context of municipalities and nations'.[219] He goes on to acknowledge its treaty-based character by tracing its development to the *United*

---

[216] *Op.cit.*

[217] Ratner, S. R, *Accountability for Human Rights Atrocities in International Law: Beyond the Nuremberg Legacy*, Oxford, Oxford University Press, 2009, 10.

[218] Erugo, S., 'Progressive Enforcement of International Human Rights Norms in Nigeria: The Question of Access to Justice', Ngwakwe, E. C., *et.al.*, (eds.), *Human Rights, Democracy and Development Revisited: Legal Essays in Honour of Professor Osita C. Eze*, Aba, KDVE – Publishers, 2012, 89.

[219] *Ibid.*

Nations Charter,[220] and the 1948 *Universal Declaration of Human Rights* (UDHR).

Having considered the foregoing definitions by dictionaries and learned authors, for the purposes of this work, International Human Rights Law could be defined as the body of law, including case law, that is generated by the principles enunciated in the *United Nations Charter,*[221] the *Universal Declaration of Human Rights*, and subsequent international and regional treaties on the human rights protection of individuals and groups. Together, the Charter and the Declaration, two foremost international legal instruments constitute the enduring 'foundations of a new legal order that is based on certain fundamental purposes and principles'.[222] With the adoption of the Declaration, the rather terse references to 'human rights and fundamental freedoms' in the Charter acquires an authoritative stature.[223] Though the Declaration recognizes civil, cultural,

---

[220] *The 1945 United Nations Charter* (as amended) was adopted on June 26, 1945, and entered into force on October 24, 1945.

[221] See, the Preamble to the Charter wherein for the first time the United Nations reaffirmed 'faith in fundamental human rights, in the dignity and worth of the human person, in the equal rights of men and women and of nations large and small, and to establish conditions under which justice and respect for the obligations arising from treaties and other sources of the international law can be maintained, and to promote social progress and better standards of life in larger freedom...'. Moreover, the Charter was the first international legal instrument to impose obligations upon member States towards the realization of protection of human rights, which it made one of the objects of the United Nation.

[222] See *Human Rights in the Administration of Justice (A manual on Human Rights for Judges, Prosecutors and Lawyers), Professional Training Series* N0. 9 published by the United Nations at chapter 1, 2.

[223] *Ibid.*, other charter provisions containing references to human rights are: Article 13(1)(b), 55(c), 62(2), 68, and 76(c). Read conjunctively, Articles 56 and 55(c) of the Charter, which place a legal obligation on United Nations Member State's 'to take

economic, political and social rights, it is not a legally binding document *per se*, since it was adopted by a resolution of the General Assembly. However, the principles contained therein are now considered to be legally binding on States either as customary international law, general principles of law, or as fundamental principles of humanity. For instance, in the *Case Concerning the Hostages in Tehran*, the International Court of Justice clearly invokes 'the fundamental principles enunciated in the Declaration' as being legally binding on Iran in particular with regard to the wrongful deprivation of liberty and the imposition of 'physical constraint in conditions of hardship'.[224]

International Criminal Law: As has been widely acknowledged, formulating the definition of International Criminal Law is not an easy task.[225] This is because of the number of the controversial definitional issues[226] that have been generated by scholars in their

---

joint and separate action in co-operation with the Organization for the achievement of 'universal respect for, and observance of, human rights and fundamental freedoms for all without distinction as to race, sex, language, or religion.

[224] *See United States Diplomatic and Consular Staff in Tehran (United States of America v Iran), Judgment,* ICJ Reports 1980, 42, para. 91, *as cited in Professional Training Series N0. 9: Human Rights in the Administration of Justice (A manual on Human Rights for Judges, Prosecutors and Lawyers, published by the United Nations.*

[225] See, Than, C. and Shorts, E., International Criminal Law and Human Rights, London, Sweet & Maxwell, 2003, 13; Sjocrona, J.M., and Orie, A.A.M., International Criminal Law, Devenver, Strafrecht, 2002, 1-10; and Ratner, S.R *et.al., Op.cit,* 10.

[226] Such issues include the scope of international criminal law, and the hybrid nature of the field-a combination of international law and criminal law involves the inculpation of individuals, but is developed and enforced by the actions of state. This includes the fact that tribunals, courts and procedure to secure compliance by individuals as are required by criminal Law have only just begun

attempt to define the concept. Be that as it may, considering the definitions proffered by certain learned authors becomes necessary.

According to Ratner and his co-authors, 'the term refers broadly to the international law assigning criminal responsibility for certain particularly serious violations of international law?'[227] They went on to observe that although some scholars limit it to responsibility for violations of human rights and humanitarian law, its scope is in fact, far wider, and includes, for instance, drug crimes and terrorism offenses. They however caution that beyond their seemingly straight forward definitions is 'a core difficulty in clarifying the nature of both international criminal law and an international crime namely, what does it mean to say that international law assigns criminal responsibility?'[228]

To answer this question, the learned authors insist that three subsidiary issues that essentially correspond to different strategies for providing international criminal responsibility must be examined, namely:

i). To what extent does international law directly provide for individual (or other) culpability or responsibility?

ii). To what extent does international law obligate some or all States or the global community at large to try and punish, or otherwise sanction, offenders?

---

to evolve. Moreover, many authors argue that a crime is not an international crime unless it may be prosecuted in an international criminal tribunal whether permanent or *ad hoc*, but that definition would exclude some of the oldest international crimes with the most accepted status, including piracy.

[227] Ratner, *Ibid*.

[228] *Ibid*., 11.

iii). To what extent does international law authorize these same actors to try and punish, or otherwise sanction, offenders?[229]

In other words, they acknowledge the fact that jurisdictional limits must be recognized, in any consideration of international criminal responsibility.[230]

However, they went on to state the possible scope of international criminal law by observing that international law can explicitly provide for individual criminality or require states to make an act a crime under domestic law, or both, as does the Genocide Convention.[231] They, further observe that it can obligate States or an international court to carry out prosecutions or punishment, as with the *Genocide Convention or the Geneva Conventions*, or to extradite or prosecute offenders, as with the *Torture Convention*.[232] They also further observe that it can simply allow States or international courts to try and punish individuals for certain acts, irrespective of normal jurisdictional limits[233]. In concluding, they declared that the foregoing strategies have been combined to a certain extent in the Security Council's statutes for the ad hoc tribunals for Yugoslavia

---

[229] *Ibid.*

[230] See Noritz, J.H., (ed.), *Pirates, Terrorists, and Warlords: The History, Influence, and future of Armed Groups Around the World,* New York, Skyhorse Publishing, 2009, 101.

[231] *Op.cit.*

[232] *Ibid.*

[233] *Ibid.*

and Rwanda, and the Rome statute of the International Criminal Court.[234]

However, these strategies which derive from the wide–ranging scope of the Law reflect the fact that International Criminal Law is capable of multifarious meanings. Chukwumaeze notes the six senses in which the term has been used, as identified by Schwarzenberger.[235] They are as follows: (1) a State domestic law rule laying down the ambit or spatial scope, of its criminal law; (2) internationally prescribed and (3) internationally authorized criminal law, that is, when a customary or treaty based rule obliges or empowers a State to enact a crime in its domestic criminal law and to punish offenders; (4) offences under domestic law which are common to all States, for example, murder (probably) the loosest sense in which the term has been used; (5) bilateral and multilateral treaties relating to international cooperation in criminal matters; (6) international criminal law in the 'material' sense, that is a body of international law proscribing those acts which strike at the roots of international society.[236] He goes on to state that basically, international criminal law encompasses both the criminal aspects of international law and the international aspects of domestic criminal law and observes as follows:

International Criminal law in the first sense involves inter-alia, internationally prescribed and internationally

---

[234] See, Security Council Resolution 827, para.2 (1993) wherein it was stated that the tribunal's purpose is 'prosecution of persons responsible for serious violations of international humanitarian law'. See also *Rome Statute of International Criminal Court*, article 1 ('jurisdiction over'), and 17 (rules on admissibility).

[235] Chukwumaeze, U. U., *Op.cit*, 292.

[236] *Ibid.*, 292 – 293.

authorized criminal law, that is where a customary or treaty based rule obliges or empowers a State to enact a crime in its domestic criminal law, and to punish offenders, as well as bilateral and multilateral treaties relating to international co-operation in criminal matters. In the second sense, international criminal law encompass a States laws laying down the ambit or spatial scope, of its criminal law and the competence of its court as well [as] other forms of mutual assistance in criminal matters.[237] It further includes extradition and co-operation in gathering evidence between the police, prosecution and courts in different countries. Mutual assistance in relating to the recognition and enforcement of foreign judgments in criminal matters, transfer of prosecution and transfer of convicted prisoners,[238]

By the foregoing observations, Chukwumaeze points to the sources of international criminal law, and the fact that international criminal law depends essentially on the political will and the cooperation of the individual States, in matters of crime; its repression, adjudication and law enforcement. More importantly, he defines international criminal law as:

A body of international rules designed both to prescribe international crimes and to impose upon states, the obligation to prosecute and punish at least some offenders of those crimes. It also regulates international proceedings for prosecuting and trying persons accused of such crimes.[239]

He describes the first limb of the definition as consisting of the substantive law, while the second limb consists of procedural law,

---

[237] *Ibid.*, 293.

[238] *Ibid.*

[239] *Ibid.*

which governs the action by prosecuting authorities and the various stages of international trials.[240]

At the centre of international criminal law lies the doctrine of individual criminal responsibility,[241] a concept that was, hitherto scarcely known to international law as the individual was not a subject of international law. However, at the aftermath of World War II, a theory and practice on individual criminal responsibility in international law emerged. Even though the concept had been formulated before the outbreak of the war, in a number of international legal documents,[242] It was Article 6 of the *Charter of the Nuremberg Tribunal* and the judgment itself that really triggered its development.[243]

Gender:

The term "sex" and "gender" have sometimes been used interchangeably as synonyms. However, language and gender theorists have generally made a distinction between sex as physiological, and gender as a cultural or social construct.[244]

---

[240] *Ibid.*

[241] The doctrine or principle was established in Nuremberg and Tokyo and was affirmed in subsequent national and International proceedings, including at the *Ad hoc* Tribunals and the International Criminal Court.

[242] See for an overview, Malekian, F., 'International Criminal Responsibility', Bassiouni 1999, 157, footnote 32.

[243] Sliedregt, E. V., *The Criminal Responsibility of Individuals for Violations of International Humanitarian Law*, The Hague, T. M. C. Asser Press, 2003, 31.

[244] Litosseliti, L. *Gender & language: Theory and Practice*, Hodder Arnold Education, London, 2006, 10.

Gender could therefore be seen as a broader, more encompassing and complex term, as it may better account for the many different life experiences of women and men than biological differences between the sexes.[245] Social constructions of these biological differences have often been used to 'justify male privileges or reassert traditional family and gender roles, for example, women's so-called "natural" role as mothers and nurturers.'[246] Indeed, this may have been the case when Aristotle observes as follows:

> ...Nature has made the one sex stronger, the other weaker, that the latter through fear may be more cautious, while the former by its courage is better able to ward off attacks; and that the one may acquire possessions outside the house, the other preserve those within. In the performance of work, she made one sex able to lead a sedentary life and not strong enough to endure exposure, the other less adapted for quiet pursuits but well constituted for outdoor activities; and in relation to offspring she has made both share in the procreation of children, but each render its peculiar service towards them, the women by nurturing, the man by educating them.[247]

Today, gender has come to be viewed as a useful vehicle for the analysis of law. 'What it does is to demonstrate how the law creates and reinforces a certain type of gender differentiation.'[248] It has been

---

[245] *Ibid*, 11.

[246] *Ibid*.

[247] Barnes, J. (ed.), *The complete works of Aristotle* vol. 2 Rev. Oxford ed. 1984, 1999, at 2131, as cited in Bartlett, K.T., *Op.cit.*, 34.

[248] See Reports of the expert Group Meeting, 'Promoting Women's Enjoyment of their Economic and Social Rights,' Abo/Turku, Finland, UN Doc EGM/WESR/1997/Report(Dec1997).

noted that examining international humanitarian law from the perspective of gender, and how it constructs the category of "woman" avoids the trap of assuming a pre-existing category of woman. Thus, those who do not fit the model are not automatically rendered invisible in the process.[249]

Women:

According to the *World Book Dictionary*,[250] the word 'woman' (singular form of 'women') denotes 'a female human being... a girl grown up... member of the feminine sex' while 'Female' means member of the feminine sex, irrespective of age and social status, and more particularly emphasizes "sex" and is largely confined to science and statistics.[251] However, the meaning of "women" not being purely indexical goes beyond its sexual denotation to encompass gender. Whereas "sex" denotes only the biological basis[252] of womanhood, "gender" connotes the socio-cultural aspects of the male-female dichotomy- a dichotomy which ascribes certain qualities, behaviors and roles to either men or women in different societies. Thus, "Men" and "Women" stand in contra-distinction, while at the same time, correlating each other.[253] This fact is borne

---

[249] *Ibid*.

[250] Barnhart, C.L. *et.al*, *Op.cit*, 2402.

[251] *Ibid*. see also Ibezim, E.C. 'The Beijing Conference and the Human Rights Protection of Women: A critical Review', *Op.cit*.

[252] See Gender Equity Reports, vol. 23, No. 2, July 1995 where a brief definition of gender was given in a call for entries for the fifth Award on Gender, Health and Technology.

[253] The distinction is made in the *Oxford Advanced Learner's Dictionary* definition of women as, 'an adult female human being physically weaker than the man...' and

out by Ogwu's definition of 'Women' as the 'Feminine component of the human species who, apart from serving as a vehicle for nurturing human life, is also a producer, a consumer and an equally endowed agent for fostering a wholesome political, social and economic development in society.'[254]

Regrettably, the history of women as subjects of Law is rather very short. Until the end of the nineteenth century, women were in legal terms, and in public life, "non-persons".[255] However, the legal categorization of women as non-persons was challenged through a series of cases in which women sought recognition as legal persons, and equal entitlement to participate alongside men in the public sphere.[256] These cases concerned the right to vote in local and national elections, to participate in government, to receive education and to gain admission to the professions.[257] The courts were therefore called upon to consider 'whether women who had the qualifications required by legislation to participate in various aspects of public life could do so unless parliament had expressly excluded them, or whether they were excluded and could only be permitted to participate, if expressly allowed to do so by legislation. In short, where legislation permitted a "man" or "persons" with specified

---

the *Blacks' Law Dictionary* (5thedn.) which describes 'female' as: 'The sex which conceives and gives birth to young'.

[254] Ogwu, J., "Women in Development: Options and Dilemmas in the Human rights Equation", Kalu, A. & Osinbajo, Y. (ed.), *Perspectives on human Rights*, Lagos Federal Ministry of Justice, 1992, 7. Ogwu's definition is more or less based on a gender rather than, a sexist perspective.

[255] Bridgman, J. and Millns, S., *Feminist Perspectives on Law: Law's Engagement with the Female Body*, London, Sweet and Maxwell, 1998, 11.

[256] *Ibid*. See *Charlton v Lings* (1868) L.R.4C.374.

[257] *Ibid*.

qualifications to hold office or in some way participate in public life, were women with those qualifications entitled to do the same?[258]

For instance, in *Charlton v Lings*,[259] one Mary Abbott claimed that, following the extension of franchise by the *Representation of the People Act 1867*, she was entitled to be included on the electoral register. The court held that what Parliament intended was, to alter the qualifications upon which someone became eligible to vote, but not the 'description of persons who were to vote.' Bovill C.J. asserted that 'man' as used in the Act 'was intentionally used, in order to designate expressly the male sex; and it amounts to an express enactment and provision that every man, as distinguished from women possessing the qualification, is to have the franchise'[260].

Finally, in recent times gender-based violence has become a dominant discourse in International humanitarian law. The *Convention on the Elimination of All forms of Discrimination Against Women* (CEDAW) committee has in its General Recommendation on violence against women stated: 'The definition of gender –based violence…include acts that inflict physical, mental or sexual harm or suffering, threats of such acts, coercion and other deprivations of liberty'.[261]

---

[258] *Ibid*, 11-12.

[259] (1868) L.R.4C. 374.

[260] *Supra*, at 387.

[261] This definition of discrimination was upheld in *Christian lawyers Association of South Africa & Others v Minister of Health &S Others* (1999) 3LRC 2003; and *Doe v Boulton* (2000) 410 U.S.179.

Feminism:

"Feminism" has been defined as 'the doctrine that favors more rights and activities for women in their economic, social, political, and private lives'.[262] It has also been defined as a movement to secure these rights.[263] In other words, it is a principle that seeks to enhance the rights and the status of women in their economic, social, political and private lives. It does this by promoting the rights of women, and advocating for the protection of such rights. On the other hand, rather than define "feminism", the *Black's Law Dictionary* defines "feminist jurisprudence".[264] It defines it as a branch of jurisprudence that examines the relationship between women and law, including the history of legal and social biases in modern law, and the enhancement of women's legal rights and recognition in society.[265] It traces the origin of the phrase to Professor Ann Scale, who first used it, in 1978, in her article titled, 'Toward a Feminist Jurisprudence'.[266]

Armed Conflict:

"Armed Conflict" is a relatively new concept in International Humanitarian Law. In fact, it is an interventionist concept. Before

---

[262] Barnhart, C. L. and Barnhart, R. K., *The World Book Dictionary (vol.1)*, Chicago, Field Educational Corporation,
1970, 784.

[263] *Ibid*.

[264] Perhaps, this is because the term 'feminism' is more or less a neutral term for the promotion of womanhood, while 'feminist jurisprudence' more succinctly locates the concept within the discipline of law.

[265] Garner, B. A. (ed.), *Black's Law Dictionary (8th ed.)*, St. Paul, A. Thomson Business, 2004, 872.

[266] *Ibid*.

1949, such situations which otherwise would have been regulated by Treaty laws of war, or International Humanitarian Law were denied such regulations even in the face of impunity, and grave violations of the *Geneva Conventions* in the absence of formal declarations of war. To remedy this mischief, *the Four Geneva Conventions* of 1949 and the *Additional Protocols* 'introduced the concept of armed conflict into this legal regime for the first time'.[267] Before then, the term "war" was generally employed.[268]

According to Pictet:

The substitution of this much more general expression ('armed conflict') for the word 'war' was deliberate. One may argue almost endlessly about the legal definition of 'war'. A state can always pretend, when it commits a hostile act against another State, that it is not making war, but merely engaging in a police action, or acting in legitimate self-defence. The expression 'armed conflict' makes such arguments less easy. Any difference arising between two states and leading to the intervention of armed forces is an armed conflict, even if one of the Parties denies the existence of a state of war…[269]

This commentary on the meaning of 'armed conflict' is important for proffering for the very first time, a definition for 'armed conflict', for apart for referring to it in Common Articles 2 and 3, the 1949

---

[267] *Ibid.*, 27.

[268] Cassese, A., (ed.) *International Criminal Justice,* Oxford, Oxford University Press, 2009, 247

[269] Pictet, J.S., *Commentary on the first Geneva Convention for the Amelioration of the Condition of the Wounded and sick in Armed Forces in the Field,* Geneva, ICRC, 1952, 32.

Geneva Conventions did not define the notion.[270] Common article 2 provides:

> In addition to the provision which shall be implemented in peace time, the present Convention shall apply to all cases of declared war or of any other armed conflict which may arise between two or more of the High Contracting Parties, even if the state of war is not recognized by one of them...[271]

On the other hand, article 3 makes reference to "armed conflict" as follows: 'In the case of armed conflict not of an international character occurring in the territory of one of the High Contracting Parties, each party to the conflict shall be bound to apply, as a minimum, the following provisions...'[272]

Clearly, the use, of this new phraseology is practically significant. Following the ban on 'war' by the International Community as embodied in the *Briand Kellog Pact* of 1928, the United Nations balked at the use of the word, 'war' preferring instead, the phrase 'use of force'.[273] Thus, the *UN Charter* employs the term or

---

[270] *Op.cit.*

[271] See G.CI, Art.2. Italics supplied.

[272] G.C.I, Art 3.

[273] See, *Legality of the Threat or use of nuclear Weapons case (ICJ), Nuclear Weapons Advisory Opinion, Reports 1996,* ss 105; Advisory Opinion (1997) 35 I.L.M. 809 and 1343 where the court appraised the *United Nations Charter* provisions relating to the threat or use of force, and observed that even though there is a general prohibition on the use of force under Article 2(4), the charter recognizes the inherent right of individual or collective self-defence. The court further observes that the charter also provides for lawful use of force under Article 42, whereby the Security Council may take military enforcement measures in keeping with chapter VII of the charter.

phrase "use of force" instead of "war".[274] However, the term "armed conflict" has been so controversial 'with conflicting views being propounded by scholars as to its concrete content.'[275]

Interestingly though, the International Committee of the Red Cross Commentary to the 1949 *Geneva Conventions* explains that the term "armed conflict" was deliberately left undefined by the Conventions as the States parties' intention was to rely on a *de facto* standard rather than on legal technicalities.[276] It further explains that what was meant to count is objective rather than subjective criteria (i.e. the existence of *animus bellandi).*[277]

Ascertaining the existence or otherwise of an armed conflict, in given situations, is decisive in the choice of applicable law. This is because the *Geneva Conventions* and the treaties on the conduct of hostilities 'apply solely if the armed conflict threshold has been attained'.[278] *Article 1 (2) of the Additional Protocol II to the Geneva Conventions* defines only the lower threshold as consisting in 'situations of internal disturbances and tensions, such as riots, isolated and sporadic acts of violence and other acts of similar nature'.[279] In the circumstances, a learned author observes:

---

[274] Cassese, A. (ed.) *Op.cit.*

[275] *Ibid.*

[276] Cassese, A. (ed.) *Op.cit.*

[277] *Ibid.* Subsequent treaties that use the same terminology, such as the 1954 *Convention for the Protection of Cultural Property in the event of Armed Conflict,* did not define the term "armed conflict" or indicate the criteria for identifying the existence of an armed conflict.

[278] Cassese, *Op.cit.,* 248.

[279] The same threshold is adopted in Article 8 (2) (f) of the Rome Statute of the International Criminal Court Statute.

The lack of precise legal standards coupled with the absence of an impartial authority mandated to establish the existence of an armed conflict in each case has led to abuses by the Parties to a conflict who, in order to avoid the application of international legal restraints, have often denied that the armed conflict threshold was overstepped in a specific context.[280]

However, recent case law has attempted to define "armed conflict". The Internation Criminal Tribunal for the former Yugoslavia has attempted to define the notion in the case of *Prosecutor v Tadic*.[281] It held that an armed conflict exists 'whenever there is a resort to armed force between States or protracted armed violence between governmental authorities and organized armed groups or between such groups within a state'. This definition has been applied repeatedly by the *Ad hoc* Criminal Tribunals.[282] The Criminal Tribunal for Former Yugoslavia has also indicated that an armed conflict may also exist if the act that is the object of an indictment has been committed in an area where no actual military combat was taking place, on condition that an armed conflict existed, at the relevant time, 'across the entire territory under the control of the warring parties'.[283]

Furthermore, the International Criminal Tribunal for Former Yugoslavia is said to have specified two elements that are required

---

[280] Cassese, *Op.cit.*

[281] Decision on the Defence Motion for Interlocutory Appeal on Jurisdiction, Tadic (IT-94-1), October 1995, S 70.

[282] See Judgment, *Furundzija* (IT-95-17/1-T), TC, 10 December 1998 $ 59; Judgment, *Kunarac* and others (IT-96-23),

AC, 12 June 2002, $56.

[283] See *Kunarac (Supra)*, AJ$64 and *Blastic* TJ, & 64.

for a conflict between governmental authorities and non-state armed groups to become an armed conflict, namely, that the non-state actor should be well-organized and have a hierarchal structure, and that the conflict should reach a certain level of intensity.[284] Thus, 'a non-state armed group that does not fulfill these two conditions is not subject to International Humanitarian Law and their activities may be dealt with under domestic law as banditry, terrorist actions or unorganized or short-lived insurrections'.[285] However, Munir observes that these two elements are not clearly defined by the Tribunal, but acknowledged that it had in a subsequent case[286] stated that 'what matters is whether the acts are perpetrated in isolation or as a part of a protracted campaign that entails the engagement of both parties in hostilities'.[287] He further observes that if the above criteria are applied, many Muslim jihadi groups may be excluded

---

[284] Munir, M., 'The Layha for the Mujahideen: an analysis of the code of conduct for the Taliban fighters under Islamic Law', [2011], *International Review of the Red Cross (IRRC)*, (Vol. 93, No 881), 82. Note that the International Court of Justice (ICJ) has on many occasions given its opinion on the criterion of intensity with respect to armed attacks. The court discussed it for the first time in the *Nicaragua case* (para.191) and later in the *Oil Platform case* (Para;64). In both of these cases, the ICJ underlined the distinction of armed attacks from other attacks by referring to the criterion of intensity.

[285] Munir, *Ibid*, 82-83. see also ICTY, *Prosecutor v Tadic*, ICTY Case No.IT-94-T, Judgment (Trial Chamber), 7

May 1997, para.562.

[286] See, ICTY, *Prosecutor v Boskoski et al, ICTY Case No. IT-04-82-T, Judgment (Trial Chamber), 10 July* [2008],

para.185.

[287] *Supra. Inter- American Commission on Human Rights, Juan Carlos Abella v Argentina*,11.137, IACHR Reports N0.55/97,30, Oct.1997 held that there could be situations where a much lower level of violence that is not protracted is seen as armed conflict for the purposes of humanitarian law.

from the definition of 'non-state actor' under International Humanitarian Law.[288] Having reasonably established the meaning of armed conflict, the typology of armed conflicts should be examined, while acknowledging that generally, armed conflicts have been classified into international and non-international. However, a third category has recently been delineated as internationalized non-International armed conflict. Even more recently less acknowledged and less clearly defined categories have burgeoned. But in reality, armed conflicts are not as clearly defined as these legal categories. Paulus and Vashakmedze capture the gravity of this situation thus: 'indeed, one of the glaring gaps in International Humanitarian Law concerns its very foundation – namely the question of the definition of war, or rather "armed conflict" … .' To this end, McCoubrey and White note that the 'grey area' of categorization remains an issue of serious potential concern.[289]

An international armed conflict usually refers to a conflict between two or more states.[290] The International Committee of the Red Cross Commentary on Common Article 2 of the Geneva Conventions explains:

> Any difference arising between two States and leading to the intervention of members of the armed forces is an armed conflict within the meaning of Article 2, even if one of the parties denies the existence of a State of war. It makes no

---

[288] Munir listed many small Muslim *Jihadi* groups, such as *Harakat al-Ansar, Harakat ul-Mujahidin, Al-Umar*.

[289] McCoubry, H. and White, N.D, *International Law and Armed Conflict*, Aldershot, Dartmouth Publishing Company

Ltd., 1992, 318.

[290] See Common Article 2 of the *Geneva Conventions*.

difference how long the conflict lasts, or how much slaughter takes place. The respect due to the human person is not measured by the number of victims.

It is thus generally agreed that a single incident involving the armed forces of two states may be sufficient to be considered an international armed conflict.[291] It may remain doubtful as to whether the threshold may ever be reached in cases of insignificant bother clashes.[292]

However, an armed conflict which otherwise is confined geographically to the territory of a single state can be qualified as international, if a foreign State intervenes with its armed forces on the side of the rebels that are fighting against government forces.[293] If the intervention of the foreign State is on the side of the State or government, in a non-international armed conflict, this does not internationalize the conflict or change the qualification of the conflict.[294]

It is doubtful whether foreign military intervention in an armed conflict which would otherwise be a non-international conflict triggers the internationalization of the entire conflict or only the conflict between the two states.[295] This author aligns with the better view, which is that there are two different types of conflict taking

---

[291] RULAC, *Ibid*, 1.

[292] *Ibid*.

[293] Chelimo, G. C., 'Defining Armed Conflict in International Humanitarian Law', available at <*http://www.student pulse.com/a?id=508*>(accessed April 8, 2017, at 1 of 7).

[294] *Ibid*.

[295] *Ibid*.

place at the same time, namely, international and non-international armed conflict.[296]

The Rule of Law in Armed Conflicts (RULAC) report also draws attention to the situation where a state intervenes indirectly without the use of its armed forces in a non-international armed conflict on the side of the rebels. The report pointed to the decision of the International Criminal Tribunal in the *Tadic case* which concluded that "overall control" of a rebel group would be sufficient to internationalize the conflict.[297] Thus, the standard set by the Tribunal does not require the 'issuing of specific orders by the State, or its direction of each individual operation'; it is sufficient that a state 'has a role, in organizing, coordinating or planning the military actions of a given non-state armed group'.[298]

International Armed Conflict: In stating that the *Geneva Conventions* apply to 'all cases of declared war or of any other armed conflict which may arise between two or more of the High Contracting Parties, even if the state of war is not recognized by one of them', article 2 Common to the *Geneva Conventions* refers to those armed conflicts that are international. Thus, it is safe to define International armed conflict as that armed conflict which may arise between two or more of the High Contracting Parties that is States,

---

[296] *Ibid.*

[297] *Ibid.*, See also Judgment of 15 July 1995, $ 131, 137. For criticism of the Tribunal's decision, see for example, Moir, L, *The law of Internal Armed Conflict: Cambridge Studies in International and Comparative Law,* Cambridge, Cambridge University Press, 2002, 49-50. Cf: ICJ, *Military and Paramilitary Activities in and against Nicaragua (Nicaragua v United States of America)* Judgment, Merits, ICJ Reports, 1986.

[298] *Tadic-case, Supra.*

even if the State of war is not recognized by one of them. In buttressing and expatiating this, the ICRC Commentary on the *Geneva Conventions* states:

> Any difference arising between two States and leading to the intervention of members of the armed forces is an armed conflict within the meaning of Article 2... it makes no difference how long the conflict lasts, or how much slaughter takes place, or how numerous are the participating forces, it suffices for the armed forces of one power to have captured adversaries falling within the scope of Article 4. Even if there has been no fighting, the fact, that persons covered by the Convention are detained is sufficient for its application.[299]

Notwithstanding the fore-going provisions, there is yet no precise definition for 'International armed conflict'. Some scholars have argued that 'in practice, it would seem that the absence of a precise definition of 'International Armed Conflict' has not proven harmful, but has favoured a very flexible and liberal interpretation of the notion, and thereby ensured a wide application of humanitarian law'.[300] It has thus been noted that in most cases, it is easy to ascertain the existence of an international armed conflict within the meaning of International Humanitarian Law.[301] This is so, because, the threshold for violence to qualify as international armed conflict is relatively low. Therefore, even short-lived cross-border armed clashes may trigger the existence of an international armed conflict.[302] However, recent state practice suggests that mere

---

[299] Pictet, J.S. *op.cit.*, 23.

[300] Paulus, A. and Vashakmadze, M., 'Asymmetrical war and the notion of armed conflict: a tentative conceptualization', [2009], IRRC, (vol. 91, No 873), 101.

[301] *Ibid.*

[302] *Ibid.*

incidents, in particular isolated confrontations of little impact between members of different armed forces, do not qualify as international armed conflict.[303]

Non-International Armed Conflict: This type of armed conflict is that between a State and dissident groups within it. It is therefore necessarily internal in nature. However, not all internal armed conflicts are classified as non-International, as *Protocol* 1 extends the range of its application to include 'armed conflicts in which peoples are fighting... and against racist regimes in the exercise of their right to self-determination',[304] as happened in South Africa. The closest International Humanitarian Law came to defining 'non-International armed conflict' is in the descriptive marginal note in *Common Article* 3 of the *Geneva Conventions*. The note describes 'non-international armed conflict' as 'conflicts not of an international character'. This note begs the question of what is 'conflicts not of an international character'. Perhaps the drafters of *Common Article* 3 are mindful of the inherent dangers in providing a precise definition of 'Non-International armed conflict'. For instance some authors have argued that no definition would be capable of capturing the factual

---

[303] This was the case with the occasional skirmishes between Nigeria and Cameroon at the Bakassi borders. For an outline of prevailing legal opinion, see 'International Committee of the Red Cross (ICRC) Opinion Paper 'on how is the term "armed conflict" defined in International Humanitarian Law?' Opinion Paper of, March 2008, available at *www.icrc.org./web/eng/siteengOnsf/html/aa/armed-conflict*. pd. (last visited 7 May 2016). See also the International Law Association Committee on the Use of force, 'Initial report on the meaning of armed conflict in International Law, 2008, available at *www.ilahq.org/en/committee/index.cfm/cid/1022* (last visited 28 April 2016); O' Connell, 'Defining armed conflict', [2009], Journal of Conflict and Security Law, (vol. 13), 393-400.

[304] See Protocol 1, Article1 (4).

situations that reality throws up and that a definition would thus risk undermining the protective ambit of humanitarian law.[305] In the first place, it has been argued that it is not clear what level of violence must be reached and how protracted the hostilities must be for it to constitute an armed conflict.[306] Furthermore, it has also been argued that internal situations with a very high level of violence have often been regarded, on the one hand, mainly for political reasons, as banditry, not reaching the threshold of armed conflict,[307] while on the other hand, there have been situations where a much lower level of violence that is not protracted has been seen as armed conflict for the purposes of humanitarian law.[308]

Another issue that has been raised is the problem of assessing the ability of armed groups to implement international humanitarian law, and whether that should be one of the criteria for qualifying them as parties to the conflict.[309] With the adoption of *Additional Protocol* II, the law of non-international armed conflict was enhanced

---

[305] Pejic, J., 'Status of armed conflicts', Wilmshurst, E. and Breau, S. (eds.), *Perspectives on the ICRC study on Customary International Humanitarian Law*, Cambridge, Cambridge University Press, 2007, 85.

[306] Paulus, A. and Vashakmadze, M., *Op.cit.*

[307] See Abresch, W., 'A human rights law of internal armed conflict: The European Court of Human Rights in

Chechnya', [2005], European Journal of international Law, (Vol. 16), 754, as cited in Paulus, *Ibid*.

[308] See, Inter-American Commission on Human Rights, Juan Carlos Abella v Argentina, case 11.13 7, IACHR Reports, *No. 55/97,30 October (1999)*, again as cited in Paulus, A. and Vashakmadze, M., *Ibid*; see also Zegveld, L., 'The Inter-American Commission on Human Rights and International Humanitarian Law: A comment on the *Tablada case'*, *[September, 1998]*, International Review of the Red Cross, (No.324), 505-511.

[309] Paulus, A. and Vashakmadze, M., *Ibid*.

beyond the limited concepts outlined in *Common Article 3*. Moreover, the instrument unwittingly accentuates the definition of non-international armed conflict when it states that its provisions apply to all armed conflicts not covered by Article I of *Protocol* I and which take place in the territory of a High Contracting Party between its armed forces and dissident armed forces or other organized armed groups which, under responsible command, exercise such control over a party on its territory as to enable them carry out sustained and concerted military operations and to implement this Protocol.[310] Thus, the Commentary on protocol II aptly states: 'To understand the scope of the Protocol, one should indeed always bear in mind the fact that this instrument supplements and develops *common Article 3*; it is an extension of it, and is based on the same structure.'[311]

In acknowledging the importance of the Protocol, Emily Crawford[312] enthuses:

> For the first time, a treaty regarding non-international armed conflict outlines provisions on permissible methods of armed conflict. These include provisions on the protection of the civilian population, prohibiting attacks on objects indispensable to the survival of the civilian population[313] and to works and installation containing dangerous forces, such as dams or nuclear power stations.[314] There are more detailed provisions regarding the protection of the wounded, sick,

---

[310] See Article 1 (1) of *Additional Protocol II*.

[311] AP Commentary on Ad*ditional Protocol* 11 at 1343, Para. 4437

[312] Crawford, E., *The Treatment of Combatants and Insurgents under the Law of Armed Conflict*, Oxford, Oxford University Press, 2010, 26-27.

[313] *Article* 14.

[314] *Article* 15.

and shipwrecked,[315] and more detailed provisions for
persons deprived of their liberty,[316] including more specific
judicial guarantees.[317]

It is noteworthy that the *Rome statute*, apart from criminalizing
the violation of Common Article 3,[318] added the minimum threshold
of *Protocol* II to this requirement for the existence of an armed
conflict. Judicial effect has been given to these requirements in the
Tadic definition of non-international armed conflict as the existence
of 'an armed conflict that takes place in the territory of a State when
there is protracted armed conflict between governmental authorities
and organized armed groups or between such groups.'[319]

However some criticisms have been made against this definition
for its apparent limitation of the scope of non-international armed
conflict[320] and because the reference to the length of the conflict
would exclude isolated war-like acts, thereby rendering early
identification of an armed conflict impossible. Expanding the scope
of non-international armed conflict would mean including
additional war crimes in the law of non-international armed conflict.
On the other hand, the requirement that the acts of violence be
'protracted' can, according to Paulus and others, be accommodated

---

[315] *Article 7-12.*

[316] *Article 4-6.*

[317] *Article 6.*

[318] See *Article 8 (2) (c) of the Rome Statute of International Criminal Court, 1998.*

[319] See, ICTY, *Prosecutor v Tadic,* Interlocutory Appeal on Jurisdiction (IT-94-1).

[320] See, in particular Dieter, F (ed.), *The Hand Book of International Humanitarian Law,* Oxford University Press, Oxford, 2008, 611, para. 1201 (5) (c) ; see also Claus, K., "War Crimes Committee in Non-International Armed Conflict and the Emerging System of International Criminal Justice," [2000], Israel Year Book on Human Rights, (Vol.30), 117-20.

by a contextual interpretation of the 'protracted' character of an armed conflict that also takes the intensity of a conflict into account.

It is necessary at this point to consider the question of internationalized non-international armed conflict; whether and what level of foreign intervention may engender this type of armed conflict.

Internationalized Armed Conflict: Generally, non-international armed conflict may be internationalized when military support is rendered to armed groups in their fight against a *dejure* government.[321] In that case, military support offered to the government in question does not internationalize such armed

---

[321] Paulus, A. and Vashakmadze, M., *op. cit.* on the level of military support required to attribute an armed group's conduct to a State thereby internationalizing the conflict, see ICJ, *Military and Paramilitary Activities in and against Nicaragua (Nicaragua v United States of America)*, Judgment, ICJ Reports 1986, Para. 115 (where the state was required to have 'effective control' over the group-financing, organizing, training, supplying and equipping of the group, the selection of targets and planning of its operations were insufficient to constitute this). Cf. ICTY, *Prosecutor v Tadic*, Case No. IT-94-I-A, Judgment (Appeals Chamber), 15 July 1999, paras. 120, 145, where it was held that the standard was 'overall control' by the State, which does not require the issuance of specific instructions or orders. See however, ICJ, *Application of the Genocide Convention (Bosnia-Herzegovina v Yugoslavia)*, Judgment, ICJ Reports 2007, where the ICJ separated the issues of attributing internationally wrongful acts to a State and the classification of a conflict. It held that for the former, the armed group must be in a relationship of complete dependence on the State (Para. 392), or else that the State must have had 'effective control' over the group and actually exercised this by giving instructions in respect of specific operations (Para. 404). It however held that for the separate issue of classifying a conflict, *Tadic's* standard of 'overall control' may well be appropriate (Para. 404). For a more incisive analysis, see also, Ibezim, E.C., 'Contemporary Challenges to International Humanitarian Law: The Private Military Companies', [2009/2010], *African Year Book on International Humanitarian Law* (AYIHL), 102-106.

conflict as long as the government maintains control of the situation.[322] However, a fascinating controversy rages as to whether a State engagement with transnational terrorist armed group can amount to international or internationalized armed conflict.

On this issue, the Israeli Supreme Court maintains:

In today's reality, a terrorist organization is likely to have considerable military capabilities. At times they have military capabilities that exceed those of States. Confrontation with those dangers cannot be restricted within the state and its penal law. Confronting the dangers of terrorism constitutes a part of the international law dealing with armed conflicts of international character.[323]

But the present state of International Humanitarian Law seems not to support this assertion by the Israeli Supreme Court. According to Common Article 2, an international armed conflict has inter-State character. Thus, a conflict between a State and a non-State group like terrorist groups is only internationalized when the military action of such groups is clearly attributable to a host State or other State.[324]

The armed conflict in Afghanistan comes close to presenting such a scenario. Clearly, the US-led attacks against the Taliban on 6 October, 2001 constituted an international armed conflict governed by applicable customary and treaty rules. However, 'whether operations against *Al Qaeda* during that conflict could be considered as part of that international armed conflict or whether they

---

[322] Paulus, A. and Vashakmadze, M., *Ibid*.

[323] *Supreme Court of Israel, Public Committee Against Torture v Israel, Judgment,* HCJ 769/02, 13 December, 2006, *Para.* 21. Here, the court applied Art. 51 of *Protocol I* to targeted killings of alleged terrorists regardless of the classification of the conflict.

[324] Paulus, A. and Vashakmadze, M., *op. cit*, 102.

represented separate non-international armed conflict is moot.'[325] Of course, it has been observed that the decision by the US Supreme Court in *Hamdan v Rumsfeld*[326] suggests that it could be the later.[327]

Terrorism:

The concept of terrorism is controversial. Many have viewed its use as often subjective and pejorative, as it is meant to convey condemnation of an adversary.[328] Thus, its use is believed to be mostly subjective, as one man's terrorist may be another man's freedom fighter or human rights fighter.[329] In this regard, Wardlaw observes that it is difficult to generate a definition which is both 'precise enough to provide a meaningful analytical device yet

---

[325] Bella, A. *et al.* 'International Law and armed non-state actors in Afghanistan', [March, 2011], *International Review of the Red Cross*, (IRRC), (Vol. 93 N0. 881), 51-52.

[326] See US Supreme Court, *Hamdan v Rumsfeld, Secretary of Defence et al.*, 29 June 2006, 6, esp. (d) (ii), available at: *http://www.supremecourt.gov/opinions/05pdf/05-184.pdf* (last visited 18 January, 2017). For a criticism of the decision in *Hamdan*, see Din S. Y., *The Conduct of Hostilities under the law of International Armed Conflict*, Cambridge, Cambridge University Press, 2004, 56-57, Paras. 129-130. For a general review of the application of international humanitarian Law to *Al Qaeda*, see Sassoli, M., 'Transnational armed groups and international humanitarian law', [Winter 2006], Program on Humanitarian Policy and Conflict Research, Harvard University, Occasional Paper Series, (No. 6).

[327] Bella, A., *Op.cit.*, 52 at fn.23.

[328] Noritz, J. H. (ed.), *Pirates, Terrorists, and Warlords: The History, Influence, and Future of Armed Groups Around the World*, New York, Skyhorse Publishing, 2009, 402.

[329] Ludwikowski, R., 'Aspects of Terrorism', [2003], Nigerian Journal of International Affairs, (Vol. 29, N0. 12), 284, cited in Okoronye, I., *Terrorism in International Law*, Okigwe, Whytem Publishers Nigeria, 2013, 7.

general enough to obtain agreement from all participants'[330] because terrorism engenders such extreme emotions, partly as a reaction to the horrors associated with it and partly because of its ideological context.[331] On the other hand, Laquer attributes the difficulty in defining terrorism to the fact that the character of terrorism has changed greatly over the years. For him:

> Terrorism is not an ideology but an insurrectional strategy that can be used by people of very different political convictions… it is not merely a technique… its philosophy transcends the traditional dividing lines between political doctrines. It is truly all-purposed and value-free.[332]

At this point, it may be necessary to outline a number of definitions of terrorism before any further discussion on the difficulty of arriving at a generally acceptable definition of the concept. The World Book Dictionary renders the meaning of 'terrorism' as:

1. The act of terrorizing; use of terror, especially the systematic use of terror by a government or other authority against particular persons or groups.
2. A condition of fear and submission produced by frightening people.
3. A method of opposing a government internally through the use of terror.[333]

---

[330] Wardlaw, G., *Political Terrorism*, Cambridge, Cambridge University Press, as cited in Okoronye, I., *Ibid*.

[331] *Ibid*.

[332] *Ibid*., 8.

[333] Barnhart, C. L. and Barnhart, R. K. (eds.), *The World Book Dictionary*, Vol. 2, Chicago, Field Educational Corporation, 1976, 2167.

The dictionary goes on to describe a person who uses or favours terrorism as a "terrorist". *The Oxford Dictionary of Law* defines "terrorism" as 'the use or threat of violence for political ends, including putting the public in fear.[334] The dictionary alludes to the *English Terrorism Act* 2000 and reproduces the definition of the *Act* as follows:

(a) The use or threat of action that involves serious violence against a person or serious damage to property, endangers a person's life, creates a serious risk to the health or safety of the public or a section of the public, or is designed to interfere with or disrupt an electronic system, or

(b) The use or threat of violence designed to influence the government or intimidate the public or a section of the public in both cases, the use or threat of such action or violence is made for the purpose of advancing a political, religious, or ideological cause ... .[335]

Black's Law Dictionary definition of terrorism is not much different from that of the *Oxford Dictionary of Law*, except that it went further to define such typologies of terrorism as cyber-terrorism, domestic terrorism and international terrorism.[336]

---

[334] Martin, E. A., *A Dictionary of Law* (5th edn.) Oxford, Oxford University Press, 2003, 495.

[335] *Ibid.*, 495 – 496.

[336] Garner, B. A. (ed.), *Black's Law Dictionary* (8th edn.), St. Paul, MN., West, a Thompson business, 2004, 1512-1513.

Other definitions of terrorism that were outlined by Okoronye[337] include:

1. Terrorism is the threat of violence, individual acts of violence, or a campaign of violence designed primarily to instill fear to terrorize;[338]

2. Terrorism is the resort to violence for political ends by unauthorized, non-governmental actors in breach of accepted codes of behavior regarding the expression of dissatisfaction with dissent from or opposition to the pursuit of political goals by the legitimate government authorities of the state whom they regard as unresponsive to the needs of certain groups of people.[339]

3. Acts of terrorism are criminal acts directed against a state or intended to create a state of terror in the minds of particular persons or a group of persons or the general public.[340]

4. Act of terrorism means an activity that (a) involves a violent act or an act dangerous to human life that is a violation of the criminal laws of the United States or any state or that would be a criminal violation if committed within jurisdiction of the United States or of any State and (b) to intimidate or coerce a civilian population; (ii) to

---

[337] Okoronye, I., *Op.cit.*, 8 – 11.

[338] Jenkins, B., *International Terrorism: A New Code of Conflict*, Los Angeles, Crescent Publishers, 1975, 1, as cited in Okoronye, I., *Op.cit.*

[339] Juliet, L (ed) *Terrorism: A Challenge to the State*, Oxford, Martin Robertson, 1981, 5, as cited in Okoronye, I., *Op.cit.*

[340] League of Nations *Convention for the prevention and Punishment of Terrorism* 1937. The Convention never entered into force because of the onset of the Second World War.

influence the policy of a government by assassination or kidnapping.[341]

5. The threat or use of force to achieve political objectives without the full-scale commitment of resources.[342]

6. The use or threat of use of anxiety inducing extra normal violence for political purposes by an individual or group whether acting for or in opposition to established governmental authority when such action is intended to influence the attitudes and behavior of a target group wider than the immediate victims and when, through the nationality or foreign ties of its perpetrators, its location, the nature or its institutional or human victims, or the mechanics of its resolution its ramification transcends national boundaries.[343]

7. Terrorism means (a) any act which is a violation of the *Criminal* code or the *Penal* Code and of freedom of, or cause serious injury or death to any person, any number of group of persons or causes or may cause damage to public property, natural resources, environmental or cultural heritage and is calculated or intended to (i) intimate, put in fear, force, coerce or induce any government, body, institution, the general public or any segment thereof, to do or abstain from doing any act or to adopt or abandon a particular standpoint, or to act according to certain principles or (ii) Create general insurrection in a state, (b) any promotion, sponsorship of,

---

[341] Official United States Code, 'Congressional and Administrative News' Oct. 19, 1984, Vol. 2 paragraph 3077.

[342] Kupperman, K. 'Low Intensity Conflict' cited in Klare, M. and Kornbluh, P. (ed.), *Low Intensity Warfare,* Pantheon, 1988, 67, 147, as cited in Okoronye, I., *Op.cit.*

[343] Mickolus, E., "Trends in Transnational Terrorism", Livinston, M. H. (ed.), *International Terrorism in the Contemporary world* London, Greenwood Press, 1978, 44, as cited in Okoronye, I., *Op.cit.*

contribution to, command, aid, incitement, encouragement, attempt, threat, conspiracy, organization or procurement of any person with the intent to commit any act referred to in paragraph (9)(i)(ii) and (iii).[344]

8. The unlawful use or threatened use of force or violence by a person or an organized group against a people or property with the intention of intimidating or coercing societies or governments, often for ideological or political reasons;[345]

9. The use or threat of violence to intimidate or cause panic especially as a means of affecting political conduct.[346]

10. The use or threat of action designed to influence the government or intimidate the public or a section of the public in order to advance a political, religious or ideological cause.[347]

11. The use of or threat of using unlawful force or violence for political ends.[348]

12. The use of a terror as a symbolic act designed to influence political behavior by extra normal means, entailing the use or threat of violence.[349]

13. Any act or threat of violence whatever its motives or purposes, that occurs in the advancement of an

---

[344] Section 40, Economic and Financial Crimes Commission (Establishment) Act No. 5 of 2002.

[345] *The American Heritage Dictionary of the English Language,* cited in *Awake,* [2006] Journal, 4.

[346] Garner, B. A. (ed.), *Op.cit.* , 1512-1513.

[347] Sheila, B. (ed.), *Osborn's Concise Law Dictionary,* (9th edn.), London, Sweet and Maxwell, 2001, 376, as cited in Okoronye, I., *Op.cit.*

[348] Sulaiman, I. N., *The Nigerian Law Dictionary,* Green World Publishing Co., 518, as cited in Okoronye, I., *Op.cit.*

[349] Wardlaw, G., *Political Terrorism: Theory, Tactics and Counter-Measures, Op.cit.,* 9.

individual or collective criminal agenda and seeking to sow panic among people, causing fear by harming them or placing their lives, liberty or security in danger or seeking to cause damage to the environment or to public or private installations or property or to occupying or seizing them or seeking to jeopardize a national resources.[350] (sic)

However, the United Nations Security Council defines terrorism as:

Criminal acts, including against civilians, committed with the intent to cause death or serious bodily injury, or taking of hostages, with the purpose to provoke a state of terror in the general public or in a group of persons or particular persons, intimidate a population or compel a government or an international organization to do or to abstain from doing any act.[351]

Insurgency:

The Black's Law Dictionary describes an 'insurgent' as a person who, for political purposes, engages in armed hostility against an established government, while denoting 'insurgency' as the adjective of an insurgent.[352] Thus, it could be inferred that 'insurgency' is the state of engaging in armed hostility against an established government for political reasons or purposes. Typically,

---

[350] Article 1 (2) of the Arab 'Convention for the suppression of Terrorism' adopted by the Council of Arab Ministers of Interior and the Arab Ministers of Justice in Cairo Egypt, 1998. As cited in Okoronye, I., Op.cit.

[351] See UN Doc. S/RES/1566,2004, para.3.

[352] Garner, B. A., Op.cit., 823.

insurgent movements often use terrorism as a tactic, among several other tactics; and to be described as a "terrorist" carries with it, an important legal connotation that is different from mere membership in an insurgent group.[353] Maybe, herein lay the primary difference between "terrorism" and "insurgency" – a functional distinction.

David Kilcullen characterizes the difference by observing that "terrorism" involves 'a relatively small number of people that may have an extreme ideology, perhaps so extreme that the majority of the populations are unlikely to ever support it.'[354] He points out that a group like that cannot, and does not rely on the support of a mass population base to get its objectives, but relies on using violence to provoke a government response, or to highlight its objectives, and to get people to think differently about an issue.[355] On the other hand, he describes insurgency as 'a group which is actually riding a mass social wave',[356] by responding to widely held grievances and issues within a much broader population base. He further asserts that it may have hundreds of thousands of people in it that are responding to a mass population base of millions of people.

However, most insurgents use terrorism, but they try to avoid the opprobrium of being labeled as terrorists, just as most terrorists do not like to be labeled as terrorists.[357] The most important thing is that the terrorists use terrorism to generate a political effect in order to highlight issues and to advance ideologies, while insurgent

[353] Bernard, V. (ed.), "Interview with David Kilcullen" on Engaging Armed Groups', [2011], *International Review of the Red Cross*, (Vol. 93, No. 883), 590.
[354] *Ibid.*
[355] *Ibid.*
[356] *Ibid.*
[357] *Ibid.*, 591.

movements use terror mainly against its own population and to generate control over that population. It is therefore almost like an abusive relationship between the insurgent group and the population that it seeks to exploit.[358] In this sense, an insurgent group is barely different from an organized crime protection racket, or an urban gang, or a communitarian or sectarian militia in a civil war – all feed off a population group and use terror to enforce support.

Armed Groups:

There does not seem to have been any definition of "armed group" under any Treaty Law.[359] However, the International Committee of Red Cross has described them as ranging from those that are highly centralized (with a strong hierarchy, effective chain of command, communication capacities, etc.) to those that are decentralized (with semi-autonomous or splinter factions operating under an ill-defined leadership structure). They acknowledge that the groups may also differ in the extent of their territorial control, their capacity to train members, and the disciplinary or punitive measures that are taken against member who violate humanitarian law.

According to Rondeau, this description meets the general requirements of the definition of 'non-state armed groups' as proposed by the United Nations' Office for the Coordination of Humanitarian Affairs (OCHA) in its Manual on Humanitarian

---

[358] *Ibid.*

[359] Rondeau, S., 'Participation of armed groups in the development of the law applicable to armed conflicts', [2011], *International Review of the Red Cross*, (Vol. 93, No. 883), 650.

Negotiations with Armed Groups. The Manual defines 'armed groups' as:

> Groups that: have the potential to employ arms in the use of force to achieve political, ideological or economic objectives; are not within the formal military structures of States, state-alliances or intergovernmental organizations; and are not under the control of the State(s) in which they operate.[360]

In other words, the critical distinguishing factor, according to this definition is that armed groups fall outside the ambit of State control.

On the other hand, Allen opines that the term "armed group" can refer to 'organized' armed groups that operate under a responsible commander and are linked to a State party to an armed conflict, to similarly organized groups that are not affiliated with any State, or to groups that fail to meet the test for an 'organized' armed group.[361] He states that armed groups might be assisting the State in its defense against another State, an occupying force (a 'resistance' movement) or another armed group; or they may be attempting to overthrow the existing government of the State (opposition groups) or to secede from the State and form a new State (perhaps invoking some version of self-determination).[362] Allen's definition or explanation seem to have implied that even though armed groups may be outside the ambit of State control, they may have links or

---

[360] *Ibid.*, See also, Michelle, M., 'Increasing Respect for International Humanitarian Law in Non-International Armed Conflicts,' [2008], Geneva, ICRC, 11, available at *http://www.icrc.org/eng/resources/ documents/publications/po923.htm* (last visited 11, April 2017).

[361] Norwitz, J. H., *Op.cit*, 99.

[362] *Ibid.*, 99 – 100.

relationships to State parties to an armed conflict or other armed groups. Thus, there is no gain-saying the fact that armed groups are complex in nature.

Combatants:

The first attempt to formulate an internationally accepted definition of combatant status was made during the Brussels Conference of 1874, when the conference annunciated its project of an *International Declaration concerning the Laws and customs of War*.[363] The Declaration states:

> The laws, rights and duties of war apply not only to armies but also to militia and volunteer corps fulfilling the following conditions:
>
> 1.   That they be commanded by a person responsible for his subordinates.
> 2.   That they have a fixed distinctive emblem recognizable at a distance.
> 3.   That they carry arms openly.
> 4.   That they conduct their operations in accordance with the laws and customs of war.[364]

However, this Declaration was amended in 1880, by the *Oxford Manual on the Laws of War*, to define an armed force to include:

1.   The army properly so-called, including the militia.

---

[363] Crawford, E., *The Treatment of Combatants and Insurgents under the Law of Armed Conflict*, Oxford, Oxford University Press, 2010, 49.

[364] Article 9 of the *Declaration*.

2. The national guards, landstrum, free corps and any other body which fulfils the requirements of:

   (a) Responsible command

   (b) The wearing of uniform or a fixed distinctive emblem recognizable at a distance.

   (c) That they carry arms openly.

1. Naval crews.

2. *Levee en masse.*

The foregoing definitions, in the *Brussels Declaration* and the *Oxford Manual*, respectively formed the basis of the definition of combatants that was accepted in the *Hague Regulations* of 1899 and 1907.[365] Under the *Hague Regulations*, "belligerents" meaning combatants must fulfill the following criteria:

1. be commanded by a person responsible for his subordinates.

2. have a fixed distinctive emblem recognizable at a distance.

3. carry arms openly, and

4. conduct their operations in accordance with the laws and customs of war.[366]

It is therefore clear that the starting point for the definition of "combatant" is *Article* 1 of *Hague Regulations* IV and Article 4 of the third *Geneva Convention* (which addresses treatment of prisoners of war). The definition is important because the Law of armed conflict

---

[365] See Arts 1-2 of the *Hague Regulations Respecting the Law and Customs of War on Land.*

[366] See Article 1 of the *Regulations.*

distinguishes between civilians and combatants, so as to properly assign applicable laws, rights and obligations or duties. Thus, the third *Geneva Convention* provides a definition of those persons who are entitled to prisoner of war status as combatants to include *inter alia*:

1. Members of the armed forces of a party to the conflict as well as members of militias or volunteer corps forming part of such armed forces.

2. Members of other militias and members of other volunteer corps, including those of organized resistance movements, belonging to a party to the conflict and operating in or outside their own territory, even if this territory is occupied, provided that such militias or volunteer corps including such organized resistance movements fulfill the following conditions:

3. That of being commanded by a person responsible for his subordinates;

4. That of having a fixed distinctive sign recognizable at a distance.

5. That of carrying arms openly;

6. That of conducting their operations in accordance with the laws and customs of war.

7. Members of regular armed forces who profess allegiance to a government or an authority not recognized by the Detaining Power.

8. Persons who accompany the armed forces without actually being members thereof, such as civilian members of military aircraft crews, war correspondents, supply contractors, members of labor units or of services responsible for the welfare of the armed forces, provided that they have received authorization from the armed

forces which they accompany, who shall provide them for that purpose with an identity card similar to the annexed model ....

9. Inhabitants of a non-occupied territory who on the approach of the enemy spontaneously take up arms to resist the invading forces, without having had time to form themselves into regular armed units, provided they carry arms openly and respect the laws and customs of war.[367]

However, *Additional Protocol* 1 provides an alternative definition which seems to have 'muddied' up, the definition of a combatant,[368] and engendered some confusion.[369] Article 43 provides:

1. The armed forces of a party to a conflict consist of all organized armed forces, groups and units which are under a command responsible to that party for the conduct of its subordinates, even if that party is represented by a government or an authority not recognized by an adverse party. Such armed forces shall be subject to an internal disciplinary system which, *inter alia*, shall enforce compliance with the rules of international law applicable in armed conflict.

---

[367] See *Geneva Convention III*, Art. 4. Article 5 provides: 'The present Convention shall apply to the persons referred to in Article 4 from the time they fall into the power of the enemy and until their final release and repatriation. Should any doubt arise as to whether persons, having committed a belligerent act and having fallen into the hands of the enemy, belong to any of the categories enumerated in Article 4, such persons shall enjoy the protection of the present Convention until such time as their status has been determined by a competent tribunal.

[368] Norwitz, J., *Op.cit.*, 108.

[369] Ibezim, E. C., 'Contemporary Challenges to International Humanitarian Law: The Private Military Companies',*Op.cit,98*.

2. Members of the armed forces of a party to a conflict (other than medical personnel and chaplains covered by Article 33 of the *Third Convention)* are combatants, that is to say, they have the right to participate directly in hostilities.

3. Whenever a party to a conflict incorporates a paramilitary or armed law enforcement agency into its armed forces it shall so notify the other parties to the conflict;

A closer scrutiny of the definitions may show that they are not irreconcilable. Whereas the third *Geneva Convention* provisions in *Article* 4 is concerned with persons that should be accorded Prisoners of War status, and thus rather inclusive of persons who may not traditionally or even be considered as combatants, *Article* 43 of *Additional Protocol* 1 contemplates combatants *strictu sensu*. Thus, the latter provision, other than the former is constitutive of the definition of "combatant", under the *Geneva Conventions*.

Genocide:

The World Book Dictionary[370] renders the meaning of 'genocide' as "the systematic extermination of a cultural or racial group, whose theoretical basis existed in the corroding Nazi doctrine of race, as expressed by Victor H. Benstein. It further observes that the word was coined in 1944 by R. Lemkin who combined the Greek 'genos' meaning race and the English 'cide' meaning killing to produce the word 'genocide'. On the other hand, the Black's Law Dictionary denotes it as 'An international crime involving acts causing serious physical and mental harm with the intent to destroy, partially or

---

[370] Barnhart, C.L, and Barnhart, R.K, *Op.cit*, 890

entirely, a national, ethnic, racial or religious group'[371]. Furthermore, the Oxford Companion to International Criminal Justice provides: 'Genocide is the perpetration of one of five well-specified categories of conduct with intent to destroy, in whole or in part, a national, ethnical, racial or religious group as such'[372], and observes that there is a widespread tendency to use the term loosely to indicate mass killing[373]. Particularly, it emphasizes that such loose perception overlooks that the term covers some specific actions if accompanied by the special intent to destroy a group, as such. It is however noteworthy, that the crime was first envisaged merely as a subcategory of the crimes against humanity.[374] The Oxford Companion to International Criminal Justice observes:

> Neither Art 6 (c) IMT Charter nor Art 11 (1) (c) CCL. No.10 explicitly envisaged genocide as a separate category of these crimes. However, the wording of the relevant provisions clearly shows that those crimes encompassed genocide (for instance Art. 6 (c)IMT Charter referred to 'murder, extermination, enslavement, deportation and other inhuman acts committed against any civilian population' as well as 'persecutions on political, racial or religious grounds).[375]

It goes on to state that though the International Military Tribunals did not explicitly mention genocide in their judgements, they mostly referred to the crime of persecution in dealing with the

---

[371] Garner B.A, *Op.cit*, 707

[372] Cassese, A(ed.), *The Oxford Companion to International Criminal Justice,* New York, Oxford University Press, 2009, 332.

[373] *Ibid*.

[374] *Ibid*.

[375] *Ibid*.

extermination of Jews and other ethnic or religious groups.[376] However, genocide was discussed in a few other cases, which include Hoess[377], and Greifelt and others[378], which were decided in 1948 by a Polish Court and a US Military Tribunal, respectively. Apparently, these discussions reflected the difficulties in determining situations that qualify as genocide, when judged against the general notion of genocide as 'the intentional annihilation of a specific group or groups' – a notion that is 'neither definitive or demonstrably effective'[379] enough to represent the meaning of genocide.

Fortunately, the 1948 *Convention on the Prevention and Punishment of the Crime of Genocide*[380] has cured this mischief by carefully setting down a definition of the crime. It provides:

> In the present convention, genocide means any of the following acts committed with intent to destroy, in whole or in part, a national, ethnical, racial or religious group, as such:
> (a) killing members of the group;
> (b) causing serious bodily or mental harm to members of the group;
> (c) deliberately inflicting on the group conditions of life calculated to bring about its physical destruction in whole or in part;

---

[376] *Ibid.*

[377] (1948) 7LRTWC II (Supreme National Tribunal of Poland)

[378] *The RuSHa Case* Nuremberg, 10 March 1948, TWC, Vol. 5, 88 – 173.

[379] De Than, C. and Shorts, E., *International Criminal Law and Human Rights,* London, Sweet and Maxwell, 2003, 66.

[380] The Convention was adopted by the United Nations General Assembly on December 9, 1948 and entered into force on January 12, 1951.

(d) imposing measures intended to prevent births within the group;

(e) forcibly transferring children of the group to another group.[381]

This definition of genocide seems to have been adopted with identical wordings by subsequent international statutes.[382] A line of cases which have been tried under these statutes have attempted to elucidate the meaning of the concept of genocide. They include *The Prosecutor v Jean-Paul Akayesu*[383]; *Kayishema and Ruzindana*[384]; *Prosecutor v Jelisic*[385], *Prosecutor v Ruzzio*[386] and *Prosecutor v Krstic*[387].

Principle of Non-Discrimination:

The principle of non-discrimination contemplates equality before the law and prohibits discrimination based on a variety of arbitrary socio-economic and legal factors. Thus, the principle or doctrine of non-discrimination is a reaction against discrimination[388],

---

[381]See Article 2 of the *Genocide Convention*.

[382] See Article 4(2) of the *Statute for International Criminal Tribunal for the former Yugoslavia*; Article 2(2) of the *ICTR Statute*; and Article 6 of *ICC Statute*.

[383] (Judgment September 2, 1998, para.523)

[384] (Judgment May 21, 1999, para.527)

[385] (IT – 95 – 10) Appeals Chambers, July n5, 2001.

[386] ICTR-97-31-1

[387] ICTY Trial Chamber, November 2, 2001.

[388] The Human Rights Committee states its belief that the term "discrimination" as used in the *International Covenant on Civil and Political Rights* should be understood to imply any distinction, exclusion, restriction or preference which is based on any ground such as race, colour, sex, language, religion, political or other opinion, national or social origin, property, birth or other status, and which has the purpose

whereas, Black's Law Dictionary defines "discrimination" as 'The effect of a law or established practice that confers privileges on a certain class or that denies privileges to a certain class because of race, age, sex, nationality, religion or handicap.'[389] It implicitly describes the principle of non-discrimination as contemplative of bodies of law that are prohibitive of discrimination based on any one of those characteristics.[390] They include relevant universal and regional legal instruments on the right to equality and non-discrimination in the administration of justice.[391]

It is noteworthy that the right to equality before the law and to non-discrimination must, in principle be respected in all

---

or effect of nullifying or impairing the recognition, enjoyment or exercise by all persons, on an equal footing, of all rights and freedoms. (See General Comments No.18, in United Nations Compilation of General Comments, 134, para. 1)

[389] Garner, B. A., (ed.),*Op.cit*, , 500.

[390] *Ibid*. It also defines discrimination as "Differential treatment; esp., a failure to treat all persons equally when no reasonable distinction can be found between those favoured and those not favoured.

[391] United Nations, Human Rights in the Administration of Justice (A Manual on Human Rights for Judges, Prosecutors and Lawyers), Professional Training Series No. 9, at Chapter 13, 1. Examples of such universal legal instruments that are based on the principle of non-discrimination include *Charter of the United Nations*, 1945, *International Covenant on Civil and Political Rights*, 1966; *International Covenant on Economic, Social and Cultural Rights*, 1966; *International Convention on the Elimination of All Forms of Racial Discrimination*, 1965; *Convention on the Rights of a child*, 1989; the Four *Geneva Conventions* of 12 August, 1949; the *1977 Protocols Additional to the Geneva Conventions* of 12 August, 1949 etcetera. On the other hand, examples of such regional instruments include, *African Charter on Human and People's Rights*, 1981; *African Charter on the Rights and Welfare of the child*, 1990; *American Convention on Human Rights*, 1969; *Inter-American Convention on the Prevention Punishment, and Eradication of Violence against Women*, 1994; *Framework Convention for the Protection of National Minorities*, 1995 etcetera.

circumstances, including in public emergencies and in times of international and non-international armed conflicts.[392] For instance, the principle runs through the four *Geneva Conventions* and their *Additional Protocols* of 1977.[393]

---

[392] *Ibid.*, 20.

[393] See inter alia, Common Articles 3 of the Four *Geneva Convention* III, 1949; Article 27 of *Geneva Convention* IV, 1949; Articles 9(1) and 75(1) of *Additional Protocol* I; and Articles 2(1) 4(1) and 7(2) of *Protocol* II

CHAPTER THREE

Historical Evolution of The Impact of War on Women

∽

The history of women's involvement in armed conflicts and their impact on them can be traced through pre-historic times to the modern times. Pre-historic warfare refers to wars that were conducted in the era before writing and before establishment of large social entities social entities like the State,[1] while the Ancient-Medieval era covers the period from about 500A.D to about 1450A.D. of course, the Modern era covers the contemporary times.

Pre-historic Era: Although not much is known about women's involvement in warfare or armed conflict in prehistoric times, it does appear that warfare took place requently during the Paleolithic[2] and the Mesolithic[3] periods. For instance, 'of the tribal societies still in existence today some lead life of great violence, frequently raiding neighboring groups and seizing territory, women and goods from others by force'.[4] However, there are some other tribes like, the

---

[1] See 'Endemic warfare', available at en.wikepedia.org/wiki/prehistoric-warfare # (last visited on 8-6-2017).

[2] By Paleolithic man, anthropologists refer to any of the men of the early Stone Age, including, in addition to Homo Sapiens, various species now extinct.

[3] Again according to anthropologists, the Mesolithic man was of, or had to do with the middle part of the Stone Age, transitional between the Neolithic and Paleolithic periods.

[4] Keely, L., *Op.cit*, 28.

Bushmen of the Kalahari who live in societies with no warfare and very few murders.[5]

Those societies that frequently engage in raids or warfare are said to be involved in endemic warfare- a situation characterized with taboos and highly ritualized practices that limit the number of casualties and the duration of a conflict.[6]

While data are available on women warriors from the Neolithic era, such as the Sauro-sarmation 'warrior-women' tomb complexes described by Davis-Kimball, comparable data do not seem to be available from earlier prehistory.[7] As for the Mesolithic era, 'images of figures apparently pierced by spears are shown from cave and rock art in Italy and France, painted over 20,000 years ago.'[8] Mesolithic remains of humans apparently killed by spears and arrows are also cited from many sites,[9] but, the first archaeological record of what could be a prehistoric battle is of a Mesolithic site known as Cemetery117. The record states:

> It was determined to be about 14,340 to 13,140 years old and located on the Nile near the Egypt- Sudan border. It contains a large number of bodies, many with arrow heads embedded in their skeletons, which indicates that they may have been

---

[5] *Ibid*, 29.

[6] *Ibid*.

[7] See David-Kimball, J., 'Warrior Women of Eurasia', [1997], Abstracts, (Vol. 50, N0. 1). available at *www.Culture–of-peace. info/books/history/pre-neolithic.html.* (Accessed on 8-6-2017)

[8] *Ibid*.

[9] *Ibid*. Note that such sites were found in Romania, France, Algeria, Denmark, Sweden, Russia, Ukraine and India.

the casualties of a battle...10 Nearly half of the bodies are female...[11]

The fact that nearly half of the bodies were female could be indicative that women were equally represented in the ranks of warriors at the time.[12] However, it is not known at precisely what point in prehistory, that warfare became monopolized by men.[13] But scholars have observed that the inequality between men and women was aggravated with the origin of the State in which war played decisive role.[14]

Women were not only involved in warfare as warriors in prehistoric times; they were also involved as targeted victims. McLennan deduces this fact from a form of marriage in which the bridegroom, alone or accompanied by friends has to feign to carry off the bride from her relatives by force.[15] He opines that this custom must be the survival of a previous custom, whereby the men of one tribe acquired their wives from outside their tribes, by actually

---

[10] *Ibid*.

[11] It has however been observed that some have questioned the conclusion that the bodies were casualties of a battle by arguing that the bodies may have accumulated over many decades, and may even be evidence of the murder of trespassers rather than actual battle. This argument does not seem tenable.

[12] *Op.cit.*

[13] The fact that nearly half of the bodies were female have also caused some scholars to question the argument for large - scale warfare. This may be because they were ignorant of a period in human history when women were assigned a higher status than men or of equal status with men. They were ignorant of the era of Bachofen and Morgan's "Mother-right" gens.

[14] See, 'Why there are so Few Women Warriors', (1983), available at www.Culture-of-peace. info/books/history/male-domination.html (accessed 29th May, 2018).

[15] *Ibid*.

abducting them by force. Thus, 'accordingly, exogamous tribes may procure their wives only from other tribes; and in the state of permanent intertribal warfare that is characterized by abduction.'[16]

However, in discussing warfare during the Mesolithic era, Davis-Kimball asserts:

Although the declared objectives of their wars are to capture women and to show other groups that they are ready to defend their sovereignty by force, nevertheless, the demonstrable result, apart from the capture of women and the gain in prestige, is that the winner often exterminates the losers, or force them to abandon territory.[17]

Arguably, this state of affairs demonstrates that even during prehistory, women were affected disproportionately in wars, in relation to men. This is completely in agreement with *Letetia vander Poll's* assertion, that the deliberate and systematic targeting of women as a practice of war dates back to time immemorial.[18] We also agree with the learned author that the idea of women as property and spoils of war has endured for centuries, thereby rendering the sexual abuse and exploitation of women 'an almost natural (and thus unavoidable) consequence of war.'[19]

---

[16] Engel, *Op.cit.* 12.

[17] *Ibid*,13.

[18] Poll, L., 'The Emerging Jurisprudence on sexual violence perpetrated against Women during Armed Conflict', [2007], *African year Book of International Humanitarian Law*, 2.

[19] *Ibid*.

Ancient – Medieval Era:

This era covers women and wars in earlier periods of world history and the period from about 500 to about 1450 A.D. Hereunder, this author portrays the historical victimization of women during wars in ancient times, before showing that women have also been combatants from ancient times.

In ancient wars, women were commonly subjected to mass rape, sexual slavery and even massacres.[20] The ancient Greeks, Persians and Romans were known to have consistently raped and enslaved women after they had conquered a city. For them, war rape of women was 'socially acceptable behavior well within the rules of warfare' and warriors considered the conquered women 'legitimate booty, useful as wives, concubines, slave labour, or battle camp trophy.'[21] In fact, to seize or carry away the riches and property[22] of an enemy was considered in itself, a legitimate reason for war.[23] Thus women were sometimes considered as legitimate reason for going to war being part of a man's property.[24]

The word 'rape' (Latin, *rapere*) meant to seize or carry off. Thus warring tribes abducted women who then became the spoils of war.

---

[20] *Ibid.*

[21] 'Rape in warfare' available at http://en.wikipedia.org/wiki/history-of-rape# In warfare, (last visited on 4-7-2017).

[22] *Ibid.*

[23] Women were included in 'property' since they were considered to be under the lawful ownership of man, whether a father, husband, slave master, or guardian. Thus, the rape of a woman was considered a property crime committed against the man who owned the woman.

[24] *op. cit.*; 'Rape in warfare', available at http://en.wekipedia.org/wiki/history of rape# In warfare (sourced on 4-7-2018).

Emmanuel Chinweike Ibezim, Ph.D

Marauding conquerors, such as the Vikings were also known to rape and violate women as an insult and challenge to the men who 'owned' the women.[25]

The Bible (Hebrew or Jewish scripture) which dates back to ancient times also records the phenomenon of war rape of women of conquered tribes. It records the practice of marauding conquerors carrying off women and even young boys as spoils of war, ostensibly to be raped, among other exploitations. For instance the only war that Abraham fought was to rescue his brother Lot, other captives, and all his property, including women, from King Chedorloamer and other four kings who allied with him.[26] King David and his men were confronted with the same dilemma when the Amalekites invaded Ziklag and carried away their women:

> And it came to pass, when David and his men were come to Ziklag on the third day, that the Amalekites had invaded the south, and Ziklag, and burned it with fire; and had taken the women captives, that were therein: they slew not any, either great or small, but carried them away, and went on their way.[27]

However, that war rape was socially acceptable at the time did not mean that it was totally legal. Some traditions and ancient legal codes prohibited war rape as much as peace-time rape. For instance, the military codices of Richard II and Henry V (1385-1419 A.D) prohibited war rape.[28] These laws formed the basis for convicting

---

[25] The notorious case of Helen of Troy readily comes to mind.

[26] See Genesis 14:12-16.

[27] See I Samuel 30:1-2.

[28] Ibid. 'Rape in warfare', available at http://en.wikipedia.org/wiki/History-of-rape# In warfare. (Accessed on 4-7-18)

and executing rapists during the Hundred Years war (1337-1453 A.D).[29] Napoleon Bonaparte also found rape committed by soldiers particularly distasteful. It is on record that he declared, during his Egyptian expedition: 'everywhere the rapist is a monster' and ordered, 'any one guilty of rape would be shot.'[30] On the other hand, Cicero made one of the earliest references to the 'laws of war' or 'traditions of war', when he urged soldiers to observe the rules of war, since obeying the regulations separated the 'men' from 'brutes'.[31] Thus, for him, it was a brutish thing to rape women.

As had been observed earlier, women had also been involved in wars or armed conflicts as combatants. Herrmann and Palmieri cited the example of the Germanic army which included female warriors, who according to the Roman Chronicles were fiercer than their male counter parts, during the Cimbrian War (113-101BC).[32] The ancient Celts are another people of classical times who have captured our modern thoughts. Images of naked barbarians charging the Roman legions, with their women fighting beside the men, and even leading armies are what come to mind when we think of the Celts.[33] These

---

[29] *Ibid.*

[30] *Ibid.*

[31] *Ibid.* see also Christopher, P., *The Ethics of war and peace: An Introduction to Legal and Moral Issues*, (3rd ed.),

New Jersey, Pearson Education Inc., 2004, 12-14.

[32] Herrmann, I., and Palmieri, D., *Op.cit.*, 22.

[33] 'War, Women and Druids: Eye witness Reports and Early Accounts of the Ancients Celts', (2010), available at

www.womenhistory.about.com/od/boundicea/p/boundicen.htm (Accessed on 3-7-2018).

images are mainly based on the descriptions handed down to us by the Greek and Roman writers.[34]

For instance Boudicca (Boadicea), a British Celtic warrior queen, led a revolt against Roman occupation about 6ICE.[35] She led about one hundred thousand strong British army in the attack of *Camulodunum* (now Colchester), where the Romans had their first centre of rule, driving out the Romans, and Procurator Decianus. Her troop burnt down *Camulodunum* and turned to the largest city in the British Isles, *Londinium* (London) also burning it down and massacring the twenty-five thousand inhabitants who had not fled.[36] However, she was ultimately defeated by the Roman troop after having terrorized them for a spell of time.

Queen Ahhotep 1 of Egypt is said to have led her troops into battle against the Hyksos invaders even before Boudicca's time, while Caesar cites a large number of examples, in his *Gallic Wars,* of women directly participating in battle.[37] However, no other story of women warriors captivates the modern mind as much as that of the Amazons. According to Hermann, they possessed the warrior attributes to which men alone were entitled until then.[38] Though

[34] The earliest Source on Celtic Warfare is the Greek historian, Xenophon who wrote circa 360BC.

[35] Available at www.womenhistory.about.com /od/boudicca/p/boudicca.htm (visited 3-7-2018).

[36] Archaeological evidence of a layer of burned ash has been cited as showing the extent of the destruction.

[37] Herrmann, I., and Palmieri D., *Op.cit.*

[38] *Ibid*, 20.

ancient Greek authors recorded women warriors known as Amazons, they were long thought to be creatures of myth.[39]

However, the most substantiated claim in living memory to the Amazons are the *Gbeto*, black Dahomey women warriors of the Gulf of Guinea (present day Benin Republic) who survived into the 19th Century. The Dahomey, Amazons or the Mino[40] were a Fon all-female military regiment of the Kingdom of Dahomey.[41] They are said to have originally been formed by the third King of Dahomey, King Houegbadja (who ruled from 1645 to 1685), and as a corps of elephant hunters called the Gbeto.[42]

Under king Agadja, Houegbadja's son, who ruled from 1708 to 1732, the corps metamorphosed into an all-female bodyguard, armed with muskets. Subsequently, according to tradition, Agadja further developed this corps of bodyguards into a powerful militia, which he successfully used in defending the neighboring Kingdom of Savi in 1727.[43] However, from the time of king Ghezo, who ruled from 1818 to 1858, Dahomey became increasingly militaristic. Ghezo was said to have placed great importance on the army, increasing its budget and formalizing its structure from ceremonial to a serious military formation. Thus, under him, the Amazons were rigorously

---

[39] Davis-Kimball, J., *Op.cit.*

[40] "Mino" in Fon language means "our Mothers". They were fondly referred to as such by the male army. While European narratives refer to the women soldiers as "Amazons", they called themselves 'ahosi', (King's wives).

[41] 'Dahomey Amazons', available at en.m.wikipedia.org/wiki/Dahomey Amazons, (accessed on 10-7-2018).

[42] *Ibid.*

[43] *Ibid.*

trained, clad in uniforms, and equipped with Danish guns, which were obtained through the slave trade.

By the mid 19th century, the Amazons of Dahomey numbered between one thousand to six thousand women, which constituted about a third of the entire Dahomey army.[44] Even though the women soldiers suffered several defeats, they were consistently judged to be superior to their male counterpart in effectiveness and bravery. Thus, they were armed with Winchester rifles, clubs and knives, and commanded each of the army units, towards the end of the nineteenth century.[45]

However, the Franco-Dahomean war proved decisive for the Amazons. Initially, France suffered many casualties, but the ultimate defeat of the Dahomean army came when the French Foreign Legion joined the fray, armed with superior weaponry, including machine guns and fought alongside their Calvary and Marine infantry, inflicting great casualties upon the Dahomean side. Consequently, the French army prevailed, after several battles.[46]

Acknowledging the military prowess of this female corps, the legionaries are said to have written about the incredible courage and audacity of the Amazons.[47] The last surviving Amazon of Dahomey is thought to be a woman named Nawi, who died in 1979.[48]

The historical importance of knighthood and chivalric traditions to the status and the protection of women under International

---

[44] Davis-Kimball, *Op.cit.*, 38.

[45] *Ibid.*

[46] *Ibid.*

[47] *Ibid.*

[48] *Ibid.*

Humanitarian Law would be considered at this point. But before then, it is necessary to determine who the knight is.

The Knight is a clear-cut historical figure, which is usually associated with the period of the Middle Ages (500-1500 AD).[49] The Equities of Ancient Rome are often considered to be the precursors of the Knight.[50] Usually, Knights were recruited from 'the nobility and ministeriality of the time' and constituted the warrior caste of the Middle Ages.[51] The knight has been described as the 'armoured warrior riding into combat'.[52]

Beyond this militaristic image, the knightly caste represented a role model for the nobility throughout Europe, and shaped life at court, while reaching out to the well-suited Parisian families of the 'medieval city'.[53] The "Code of honour" of the medieval knighthood, which thus developed, came to be known as chivalry- a concept which according to Mader should be counted among the intellectual roots of present day humanitarian law.[54] For instance, chivalric principles contributed much to the so-called metaphorical 'honour'

---

[49] Carreirars, H. and Kummel, G., (eds.), *Women in the Military and in Armed conflict*, Vs Verlag fur Sozial wissenschaften, Wiesbaden, 2008, 185.

[50] *Ibid*.

[51] *Ibid*. Knights were recruited from the nobility and ministeriality of the time because only members of well-to-do, and rich families could afford the equipment consisting of well-trained horses, armor weapons, squires and servants which required substantial financial resources.

[52] *Ibid*. Different orders of knights emerged at the time of the Crusades from the late 11th century until the middle of the 15th century. They included the Teutonic Order, the Order of the knights of St. John of Jerusalem, the Order of the Knights of Malta, and the famous Order of the Knights Templar.

[53] *Ibid*.

[54] *Ibid*., 188.

of women in modern day International Humanitarian Law.[55] Citing Painter, Gardam and Jarvis observe:

> In chivalric tradition, women were at the centre of the highly elaborate precepts of romantic chivalry. In this scheme, knights were the 'natural' protectors of women who, in a portrayal that continues today in modern International Humanitarian Law, were weak, modest, docile, incapable of looking after themselves, and thus condemned to a highly stylized inferior role in society. One commentator describes the 'protector-protected' relationship between knights and the demeaned 'other' women that was used to perpetuate chivalric dominance. The chastity of women was particularly valued and in theory protected so as to ensure the purity of the male heir.[56]

Incidentally, this idealistic picture of shelter and protection does not in reality represent the experiences of women in the medieval times.[57] The romanticism that it portrayed had its class overtones, as 'the ordinary peasant woman was not the object of knightly protection.'[58] Part of this protector/protected relationship is said to

---

[55] Gardam, J.G. and Jarvis, M.J, *Women, Armed Conflict and International Law,* The Hague, Kluwer Law International, 2001, 108. Many other writers have expressed their views on the influence of chivalry in modern International Humanitarian Law. They all agree that the prohibition of dishonorable methods of combat is derived from chivalric standards. See for example, Green, L., *The Contemporary Law of Armed Conflict (2nded.),* Manchester, Manchester University Press, 1998, 122; *Roberts, A.et.al, Documents on the Laws of War (2nd ed.),* Clarendon, Oxford, 1989, 5; Meron, T, *Bloody Constraints: War and Chivalry in Shakespeare,* Oxford, Oxford University Press, 1997, 11-15. e.t.c.

[56] *Ibid.* see also Painter, S, *French chivalry chivalric Ideas and practices in Medieval France,* Cornell, Cornell University Press, 1957, 97-100.

[57] Gardam, *Ibid.*

[58] *Ibid.*

have depended on the exclusion of women from combat on the basis of their lack of physical strength to handle the weaponry of the time.[59] Beyond this assumed lack of physical capacity, it was a taboo for women to use objects of war. For example, Joan of Arc was sentenced to be burnt at the stake, because she adopted men's clothing (including armour) in order to participate in combat or warfare.[60]

Though rape in warfare seems to have been consistently unlawful over the centuries, there was no evidence that the law was ever taken seriously. Thus, in medieval times also, rape continued to be 'regarded as part of the spoils of war, and was a major incentive for continued fighting, especially in siege situations.'[61]

Modern Era:

The modern era could be said to have been characterized by the advent of gun powder and canons, which progressively evolved, following technological advancements, into machine guns, shells and sundry explosives (including nuclear bombs). Besides this evolution in weaponry, this era has witnessed an increasing involvement of women in warfare,[62] both as combatants and

---

[59] *Ibid.*, 111.

[60] *Ibid.*, 21. See also Georges and André Duby, *Les process de Jeanne d'Arc*, Gallimard, Folio Histoire, Paris, (1995).

[61] Gardam, *Ibid*, 112.

[62] See, Sjoberg, L., 'Women Fighters and the "beautiful soul" narrative', [2010], *International Review of the Red Cross*, (Vol. 92, No. 877), 58, where Sjoberg observes that there was substantial participation by women fighters in the American Revolution, the American Civil War, the Mexican Revolution, World War I, the

otherwise. For a long time, women's direct participation in combat operations,[63] and such examples of female troops as has been seen earlier, remained relatively scarce and far between until the two world wars.

The Second World War, particularly, witnessed a 'feminization of the armed forces and an impressive upsurge in the number of female fighters.'[64] During the First World War, Russia, under the Kerernsky government, sent a unit of women soldiers known as the Battalion of Death, consisting of two thousand volunteers to fight on the front with Germany. As from 1941, during the Great Patriotic War (the Second World War) large numbers of women joined the ranks of the Soviet Army.[65] It has, however, been estimated that there were one million female soldiers in the Soviet Army, constituting 8% of the total armed forces.[66] Half of these soldiers were said to have served on the front line, either in support jobs or in actual combat, during the Second World War.[67]

Russian Civil War, World War II, the Korean War, the Vietnam War, the Afghan Civil War, the Iran- Iraq War, the Rwandan Genocide, Sierra Leone Civil War etc.

[63] Under Treaty IHL, any individual conduct that constitutes part of the hostilities id described as direct participation in hostilities, regardless of whether the individual is a victim or member of the armed forces. See API, Arts. 34(2), 45(1) and (3), 51(3), 67(1)(e) and AP II, Art. 13(3).

[64] Herrmann, I. and Palmieri, D., *Op.cit.*, 22.

[65] *Ibid.*

[66] *Ibid.* See also Reynaud, *Les Femmes la violence et l'armee, Foundation pour les estudes de defense national*, Paris, 1988.

[67] *Ibid.*

Presently, in the United States, women account for about 15% of soldiers serving in active duty.[68] One in ten American soldiers was a woman in Iraq where more American women have fought and died than in all wars fought since World War II.[69]

Most of the non- State Armed Groups feature significant number of female fighters. For instance, in Nepal, one third of the Maoist fighting forces are women.[70] So also do women make up about 15% to one-third of the Tamil Armed group's core fighters (particularly, the Liberation Tigers of Tamil Eelam (LTTE) in Sri Lanka).[71] The Sudan People Liberation Army also parades a strong contingent of women soldiers; just as women accounted for between 10-30% of the fighting forces in the conflict in Sierra Leone.[72]

Women also took an active part during wars of national liberation. For instance in Vietnam several hundred thousand women engaged in combat between 1946 and 1975, first against the French occupying forces and then against the American and South Vietnamese troops.[73] Furthermore, the Zimbabwe African National

---

[68] See 'Statistics on Women in the Military, Women in Military Service for America Memorial Foundation Inc'.,

available at: http://www. Women's memorial .org/PDFs/ station WIM.pdf (last visited 1 October 2016).

[69] *Ibid*.

[70]Fontanella-Khan, 'Women fighters in Nepal', in Financial Times, 26 September 2009, available at http://www.ft.com/cms/s/2/57c05a/a-a719-11de-bd14-00144feabdcO,dwp-uuid=a712eb94-dc2b-11da-890d- 0000779e2340.html (Last Visited 30 October 2016).

[71] Hermann, I. and Palmieri, D. *Op.cit*.

[72] *Ibid*., 110 – 111.

[73] *Ibid*., 23.

Liberation Army guerrillas who fought the racist regime in Salisbury, included about four thousand women soldiers, accounting for six percent of the movement's forces.[74] In Nigeria, *Boko Haram* has been known to recruit women who have fought as suicide bombers.

The upsurge in the direct participation of women as combatants in armed conflicts is due largely to the changing nature of present day armed conflicts which emphasizes technology rather than physical strength. Joshua Goldstein acknowledges this, when he states:

Modern warfare with its emphasis on the speed and mobility of mechanized vehicles (tanks, fighter aircrafts, etc.), differs from ancient hand-to-hand combat. Success and survival now depend much more on the ability to execute rapid sequences of small motions, and much less on upper-body strength.[75]

Besides, the proliferation of light weapons makes it easier for women, who otherwise would have found it difficult to bear heavy weapons like men, to engage in combat operations.

Granted that rape has been a corollary of war, since ancient times, it has assumed a more pervasive dimension since modern times. From the mass rapes, committed before and during World War II[76] to those perpetrated during more recent conflicts in Bosnia-

---

[74] *Ibid*. See also. Goldstein, J.S., *War and Gender*, Cambridge, Cambridge University Press, 2001, 60- 64.

[75] Goldstein, J.S., *Ibid*, 309.

[76] See Beevor, A, *Berlin: The Down fall*, Viking, London, 2002, 414, where Anthony Beevor estimates that two million German women were raped by the Soviet army at the fall of the Third Reich in April 1945.

Herzegovina, Cyprus, Rwanda, Darfur, Democratic Republic of Congo etcetera, rape has become a weapon of modern warfare. Fortunately, the law seems to have risen to the occasion in the face of recent historical convictions of rape as war crime, crime against humanity, and as an act of genocide,[77] (where it constitutes an 'act committed with intent to destroy in whole or part of a national, ethnical, racial or religious group').[78]

---

[77] See *Prosecutor v Jean Paul Akayesu*, International Criminal Tribunal for Rwanda, Case N0.1CTR-96-4-T 2 September, [1998].

[78] *Supra*, Para. 494.

CHAPTER FOUR

Protective Laws and Institutions for Women Victims of Armed Conflicts in Africa

$\sim$

Protective laws and institutions are available for the protection of women in situations of armed conflicts. They constitute the legal and institutional frameworks for protecting women in armed conflicts. In this chapter, such laws and institutions shall be discussed with particular reference to Nigeria, DR Congo and Sierra-Leone.

4.1 Legal Framework for the Protection of Women in Armed Conflicts

4.1.1. General Protective Laws for Victims of Armed Conflict

The laws governing armed conflicts and the rights which they confer should be viewed from two closely related but different arms of the law, namely, International Criminal Law and International Humanitarian Law.[1] However, International Human Rights Law is also relevant, as it operates both at peacetime and in war. Tracing developments in these regimes of Law would therefore provide a

---

[1] Chukwumaeze, U. U., "Protecting the Rights of Women in Armed Conflict: A Legal Perspective", Njoku, S. A. (ed.), *Essays on Contemporary Issues of Law*, Owerri, Peacewise Systems, 2010, 292.

necessary background to understanding the legal frameworks for the protection of women in armed conflicts.

(i) International Criminal Law: Contemporary developments of International Criminal Law with regard to victims of armed conflicts could be traced to the establishment of the International Military Tribunal (IMT) for the Prosecution and Punishment of the major World War II criminals of European Axis. This tribunal was established pursuant to the London Charter of August 8, 1945[2] and sequel to the defeat of the two main Axis powers, namely, Germany and Japan in World War II. For the purposes of placing some of the major Nazi and Japanese war criminals on trial, the governments of the victorious Allied nations agreed to establish special international courts at Nuremberg and Tokyo.[3]

The Nuremberg trials have been described as historically unique, having been prompted by 'the grotesque nature of the crimes committed' during world war II.[4] Rosenbaum further describes the emergent jurisprudence as 'a blend of universal moral standards with an evolving body of international law inspired by the moral

---

[2] Rosenbaum, A. S., *Prosecuting Nazi War Criminals*, Boulder-Sanfancisco-Oxford, Westview Press, 1993, 19. *The London Charter* was part of the agreement reached by the Allies in 1945 specifying the powers and duties of the IMT. The IMT was presided over by judges from the United States, the Soviet Union, Great Britain, and France.

[3] *Ibid*.

[4] *Ibid*. In any case, according to Rosenbaum, the Nuremberg location was selected, among other reasons, for the earlier Nuremberg Laws for the 'racial purification of the greater Reich'. For the grotesque and dastardly nature of the crimes committed, see Weber, L., *The Holocaust Chronicle: A History in Words and Pictures*, Lincolnwood, Publications International Ltd., 2000.

outrage felt by the international community ....'[5] Notably, the "Nuremberg trials" consists of four different proceedings against twenty-four high-ranking Nazis who were indicted and brought to Nuremberg to stand trials before the International Military Tribunal (IMT).

The first trial is said to have taken place between October, 18, 1945, and October 1, 1946. Ultimately, only twenty-two defendants were tried in this first instance, because one was too ill to stand trial and the other committed suicide.[6] Those that were docked were some of the surviving leaders of Nazi Germany. Each was selected because he was the most important surviving principal in his domain of responsibilities and activities for the Third Reich.[7] This first wave of trials 'resulted in a guilty verdict for nineteen defendants, with a variety of sentences ranging from prison terms to death, and in three acquittals'.[8]

The second set of trials also took place in Nuremberg, pursuant to *Control Council Law No. 10* of December 20, 1945'[9]. A number of persons which included personnel of the secret services (Sicherheits-dienst (SD), Gestapo, SA), industrialists, civil servants, physicians, and members of other groups or organizations alleged to have been of a criminal character were put on trial. The third set of Nuremberg trials took place in Tokyo. The East Asian Tribunal situated in Tokyo, otherwise described as the International Military Tribunal for the Far

---

[5] *Ibid.*

[6] *Ibid.*

[7] *Ibid.*

[8] *Ibid.*, 21.

[9] *Ibid.*, 20.

East, was composed of a multinational panel of eleven judges, while the fourth Nuremberg trial consisted of a series of judicial proceedings held either in proximity to the scenes of the crimes, in liberated areas, or in former Axis territory controlled by the victorious Allies.[10]

It is noteworthy that despite all the atrocities which were committed against women, which ranged from rape, sexual violence and sexual slavery, not even one person was charged with any of such crimes during the trials.[11] This is not withstanding the fact that the charter of the International Military Tribunal for Far East criminalized 'violations of Laws and customs of War'[12] as war crimes and as crimes against humanity[13], a situation that would have paved way for the prosecution of sexual atrocities and violence against women.

The Tribunal failed to try Japanese soldiers for their notorious violence against the "comfort women".[14] Curiously, none of the

---

[10] *Ibid*.

[11]Tachou-Sipowo, A., 'The Security Council on Women in War: between peace building and humanitarian protection', [2010], *International Review of the Red Cross* (IRRC) (Vol. 92, No. 877), 200.

[12] *Ibid*. See also *International Military Tribunal for the Far East (IMTFE) Charter*, Article 5(b).

[13]*Ibid*, *Article 5(c)*which includes murder, extermination, enslavement, deportation and other inhumane acts committed against any civilian population

[14] See Askin, K., 'Comfort women shifting shame and stigma from victims to victimizers', [2001], *International Criminal Law Review*, (Vol. 1, Nos 1-2), 5-22 as cited in Tachou-Sipowo, A., *Ibid*. Tachou-Sipowo notes that the recommendation of a 1998 UN Report on Contemporary Forms of Slavery was aimed at redeeming the memory of victims and survivors of the "Comfort Women Stations". He observes that for the first time, the liability of the Japanese government for "Comfort Women Stations" was established by Ms Gay J. McDougall, Special

judgments rendered by the Tribunal acknowledged the atrocities perpetrated against women. Even the national courts setup to try Nazi war criminals, whose charters provided for rape as a war crime never prosecuted any rape case in spite of glaring evidence.[15] So, also did the rape of Berlin, for which the Soviet liberating forces were held responsible, go unpunished.[16]

However, at the end of the day, certain principles of international law were acknowledged in both the Charter and the Judgment of the Nuremberg Tribunal. In fact, the United Nations General Assembly affirmed the principles of International Law recognized by the *Charter of Nuremberg* in one of its first resolutions.[17] The principles were formulated by the International Law Commission (ILC), in the framework of a code of offence against the peace and security of mankind. The Commission completed its formulation of the Nuremberg principles in 1950, at its second session, and submitted them to the General Assembly.[18] A summary of the principles are as follows:

Rapporteur for the commission on Human Rights, Contemporary Forms of Slavery: systematic rape, sexual slavery and slavery-like practices during armed conflict.

[15] Tachou-Sipowo, A., *Ibid.*, 201.

[16] *Ibid.*

[17] See UN General Assembly Resolution 95(1) of 11 December, 1946.

[18] Formulation of Nuremberg Principles, 1950 UN GAOR, 5th Sess. Supp. No. 12(A/1316); ILC Report in YBILL, Vol. II (1950). Although the General Assembly did not formally adopt these principles, they are generally regarded as a recognition of the rule that individuals can be held criminally responsible directly under international law.

Principle 1: Any person who commits an act which constitutes a crime under international law is responsible therefore and liable to punishment.

Principle II: The fact that international law does not impose a penalty for an act which constitutes a crime under international law does not relieve the person who committed the act from responsibility under international law.

Principle III: The fact that a person who committed an act which constitutes a crime under international law acted as Head of State or responsible government official does not relieve him from responsibility under international law.

Principle IV: The fact that a person acted pursuant to order of his government or of a superior does not relieve him from responsibility under international law, provided a moral choice was in fact possible for him.

Principle V: Any person charged with a crime under international law has the right to a fair trial on the fact and law;

Principle VI: The crimes hereinafter set out are punishable as crimes under international law:

a) Crimes against peace:

    i). Planning, preparation, initiation or waging of a war in violation of international treaties agreements or assurances;

    ii). Participation in a common plan or conspiracy for the accomplishment of any of the acts mentioned under (i).

b) War Crimes: Violations of the laws or customs of war which include, but are not limited to, murder, ill treatment, or deportation to slave labour or for any other purpose of civilian population of or in occupied territory, murder or ill treatment of prisoners of war or persons on the seas, killing of hostages, plunder of public or private property, wanton destruction of cities, towns, or villages, or devastation not justified by military necessity.

c) Crimes against humanity: Murder, extermination, enslavement, deportation and other inhumane acts done against any civilian population, or persecutions on political or racial or religious grounds, when such acts are done or such persecutions are carried on execution of or in connexion with any crime against peace or any war crime;

Principle VII: Complicity in the commission of a crime against peace, a war crime, or a crime against humanity as set forth in Principle VI is a crime under international law[19].

Granted that the indictments did not specifically identify what had happened to the Jews or to other civilian populations targeted by the Nazis and their collaborators, Article six of the *International Military Tribunal Charter* did define Crimes against humanity to include 'murder, extermination, enslavement, deportation, and other inhumane acts committed against any civilian population, before or during the war, or persecutions on political, racial or religious grounds'.[20] The German High Command, consisting mostly of Generals and Admirals, who directed Nazi Germany's military conquests and atrocities against European Jews and other civilians were tried under *the Charter*.[21] Twenty four of the most

---

[19] *Ibid.*, 22.

[20] Weber, *Ibid.*, 640.

[21] See, for example, *In Re Goering, Annual Digest, 13 (1946, No. 92);* Justice Trial, LRTWC, Peleus trial, LRTWC, Vol. 1, 1947; *US v Alfried Krupp von Bohlen*

significant Nazi leaders were indicted, while on October 1, 1946, nineteen of the defendants were found guilty. This included Martin Bormann, head of the Nazi Party Chancellery, who was tried in absentia.[22] Three of the defendants were acquitted.[23]

Seven defendants were sentenced to terms of imprisonment which ranged from ten years to life, while twelve were condemned to death by hanging. Hermann Goring, the commander-in-chief of the *Luftwaffe* committed suicide shortly before he was to be hanged. However, the pursuit of justice at Nuremberg did not end when the International Military Tribunal concluded its trials in the autumn of 1946.[24] So many other Nazi war crimes trials took place in numerous countries before and after those conducted by the International Military Tribunal.[25] Subsequent proceedings began in December 1946, and ended in April 1949. They were made up of twelve trials under American jurisdiction.[26]

UndHalbach, Jan. 21, 1948; The Justice Case, at Nuremberg, in Appleman, Military Tribunals, Case No. 3, 157-162.

[22] *Ibid.,* 639-640.

[23] Those acquitted included Hjalmar Schacht, former minister of economics; Franz von Papen, first vice Chancellor of the Nazi government; and Hansfritzsche, chief of the Propaganda Ministry's Radio Division.

[24] *Op.cit.,* 640.

[25] See, for instance, *Attorney General (Israel) v Eichmann, (1961), L.L.R, Vol. 36, No. 5, Eichmann v. Att. Gen.* (Israel)(1962) I.L.R, 277; *Demjanjuk, in the Matter of Extradition of, 475 US. 1061 (1986); the Case of Treatment of Polish Nationals in upper Danzig,* PCIJ series, AIB. No. 44, 23-25. (1932) and U.S v Lebb, Nuremberg Trials, vol. II, 1950.

[26] See for example *Ohlendorf, Re (Einsatzgruppen Trial),* US Military Tribunal at Nuremberg, April 10, 1948, 15 I.L.R 656 (1948), US v *Alfried Krupp von Bohlen UndHalbach,* Jan. 21, 1948., *USA v Wilhelm List,* Volume XI, Trials of War Criminals, p. 757, *Von Leeb, Re,* United States Military Tribunal At Nuremberg, Oct. 28, 1948, 15 ILR 376 (1949), etc.

Ultimately, the proceedings 'focused on one hundred and eighty-five Nazi doctors, jurists, industrialists, military and State Security (SS) leaders and other professionals and government officials'.[27]

However, the Nuremberg trials and judgments thereto have been criticized as "Victor's Justice", on the basis mainly that they were based on *ex post facto* laws and principles, and on preconceived ideas of guilt. In answer to this charge, Rosenbaum observes that the fact that the first wave of Nuremberg trials resulted in a guilty verdict for nineteen defendants, with a variety of sentences ranging from prison terms to death, and in three acquittals indicates that the Tribunal did not merely impose penalties based on preconceived ideas of guilt, as the detractor's charge of "Victor's Justice" implies.[28] He further argues that whatever procedural shortcomings may have plagued the proceedings, 'rudimentary sanctions by a state are probably better than a situation where war criminals feel themselves exempt from any future prosecution.'[29]

The question of "Victor's Justice" may have persisted, but it has been observed that the following response made by the Pulitzer Prizewinning philosopher, R. B. Perry must be given:

> Had those responsible for the aggressions and inhumanities of the Nazi regime been allowed to go unpunished, mankind would have lost a supreme opportunity to crystallize in legal form a recognized and pressing moral necessity. The time

---

[27] Weber, *op.cit.*; See the following cases: *Hostage Trial, LRTWC, Vol. viii, 1949; Justice Trial*, LRTWC, *Peleus Trial*, LRTWC, Vol. 1, 1947 and *Krupp Trial*, LRTWC.

[28] Rosenbaum, *Op.cit.*, 21.

[29] *Ibid*. See also De Lupis, *The Law of War*, Cambridge, Cambridge University Press, 1987, 352-355, as cited in Rosenbaum.

was ripe to step across the line from conscience to a legal order, and to create a legal precedent for future time. Those who have preferred exoneration, or assassination, or summary execution, were not the friends of law in principle, but the defenders of outmoded law or of the perpetuation of lawlessness.[30]

It is against the background of this response that the contributions of the Nuremberg trials to the jurisprudence of International Criminal Law against impunity in the event of armed conflicts would be outlined.

Indeed, the principles and trials 'step(ped) across the line from conscience to a legal order, ... to create a legal precedent for future time.'[31] They established the doctrine of individual criminal responsibility to which the defence of superior order does not avail; Head of State criminal responsibility, to which diplomatic immunity is not a defense; the principles of command responsibility and universal jurisdiction over crimes against peace, War Crimes and Crimes against Humanity. Three of the Nuremberg principles will always be relevant to any discussion on individual criminal responsibility. They are: 'any person who commits an act which constitutes a crime under international law is responsible therefor and liable to punishment' (Principle 1);[32] 'participation in a common plan or conspiracy to commit an act constituting a crime against peace is punishable'[33]; and 'complicity in the commission of a crime

---

[30] *Op.cit.*, 37.

[31] *Ibid.*

[32]See Principle1 of the *Nuremberg Charter*.

[33] See Principle Vi[a][ii] of the *Nuremberg Charter*.

against peace, is a war crime under international law'[34]. This is to say that direct perpetration, conspiracy and complicity (participation) were accepted as modes of individual criminal responsibility.[35] Thus was the foundation for a theory of individual criminal responsibility laid in international law.[36] The principle was also affirmed by the *Genocide Convention*.[37] The Convention provides that the following acts shall be punishable: a) Genocide; b) Conspiracy to commit genocide; c) Direct and public incitement to commit genocide; d) Attempt to commit genocide; e) Complicity in Genocide.[38]

Here conspiracy to commit genocide is listed as a punishable act. Sliedregt observes that this is the inchoate, Anglo-American type of conspiracy that caused so much problems at Nuremberg, but states that the drafters of the *Genocide Convention* seemed to have had less problems with the concept of conspiracy.[39] He points to Schabas' submission that by its very nature, the crime of genocide will inevitably involve conspiracy and conspirators.[40] He further observes that incitement to commit genocide is like conspiracy, an inchoate crime, which can also be construed as complicity, ("abetting") pursuant to Article III (e).[41] However, as the *Genocide*

---

[34] See Principle vii of the *Nuremberg Charter*.

[35] Sliedregt, E. V., *The Criminal Responsibility of Individuals for Violations of International Humanitarian Law*, The Hague, T.M.C, Asser Press, 2003, 32.

[36] *Ibid.*

[37] *Convention on the Prevention and Punishment of the Crime of Genocide*, 78 UNTS 277 (1948).

[38] See, Article III.

[39] Sliedregt, *Op.cit.*

[40] Schbas, W.A., *Genocide in International Law*, Cambridge, Cambridge University Press, 2000, 259, as cited in Sliedregt, *Ibid.*

[41] *Ibid.*

Convention lacks a provision for command or superior responsibility, the criminal responsibility of those who did not themselves 'wield machine guns or machetes', but ordered, organized, directed or otherwise encouraged genocide are subsumed under Article III (e). This, Sliedregt views as 'somewhat unsatisfactory', and goes back to the earlier observation that, since war crimes criminality generates a certain class of perpetrators, general law concepts, such as complicity, do not suffice as the basis of liability of major war criminals.[42] He thus endorses Schabas' view that even though complicity is sometimes described as secondary participation, there's nothing 'secondary' about it when applied to genocide, where the 'accomplice' is often the real villain, and the 'principal offender' a small cog in the machine'.[43]

The *Convention against Torture and other cruel, Inhuman or Degrading Treatment* is another source of international law that provides for individual criminal responsibility. It provides:

1. Each State Party shall ensure that all acts of torture are offences under its criminal law. The same shall apply to an attempt to commit torture and to an act by any person which constitutes complicity or participation in torture.
2. Each State Party shall make these offences punishable by appropriate penalties which take into account their grave nature.[44]

---

[42] Schabas, *Op.cit.*, 286.

[43] *Ibid.*, 33.

[44] See, Article 4 of the *United Nations Convention against Torture* (1984).

By this provision, State Parties are empowered to penalize the commission of, or participation in, acts of torture.[45] The International Criminal Tribunal for the Former Yugoslavia (ICTY) and the International Criminal Tribunal for Rwanda (ICTR), and subsequent *adhoc* international tribunals and hybrid or mixed courts that have been established by the Security Council of the United Nations, after about fifty years post Nuremberg trials, have also been empowered following the Nuremberg precedent, to invoke individual criminal responsibility over war crimes and crimes against humanity. In addressing the issue of individual criminal responsibility, the Secretary General of the United Nations, clarifies that the principle of individual criminal responsibility is not limited to those who actually committed crimes.[46] The fact 'that international crimes like genocide, war crimes, and crimes against humanity are rarely committed in isolation, by an individual on his own account is reflected in the provisions on individual criminal responsibility at both Tribunals.[47] For instance, Articles 7(1) and 6(1) of the *Statutes of International Criminal Tribunal for the Former Yugoslavia* and the *International Criminal Tribunal for Rwanda*, respectively provide as follows: 'A person who planned, instigated, ordered, committed or otherwise aided and abetted in the planning, preparation or

---

[45] See Burgers, J. W. and Danelius, H., *The United Nations Convention against Torture: A Handbook on the Convention against Torture and other Cruel, Inhuman or Degrading Treatment or Punishment*, Dordrecht, 1998, as cited in Sliedregt, *Op.cit.*, 34.

[46] See, Report of the Secretary General, para 54, in Dixon, R., and Khan, K., et al. (eds.), *Archbold International Criminal Courts: Practice, Procedure & Evidence*, London, Sweet & Maxwell, 2003, B2-010, 776.

[47] Sliedregt, *Op.cit.*

execution of a crime referred to in article 2 to 5 of the present Statute, shall be individually responsible for crime'.[48]

Articles 2 to 5 outlines the classes of the crimes as follows: "Grave breaches of the *Geneva Conventions* of 1949",[49] "Violations of the Laws or Customs of war,"[50] "Genocide",[51] and "Crime against Humanity".[52] Thus, the *Statute of the International Criminal Tribunal for the Former Yugoslavia* combines the provisions of the Geneva Law, the Hague Law, the *Genocide Convention* and those of the *Statute of the International Military Tribunal* or the *Nuremberg Charter*, on Crimes against Humanity.

Besides providing for individual criminal responsibility, the *statute of the International Criminal Tribunal for the former Yugoslavia* provides for personal jurisdiction, which emphasizes the Tribunal's jurisdiction over natural persons, irrespective of their official positions[53] or whether they are subordinates who were merely carrying out the orders of their superior.[54] On the other hand such a superior may not be relieved of criminal responsibility, 'if he knew or had reason to know that the subordinate was about to commit such acts or punish the perpetrators thereof '.[55] So also does Article

---

[48] Article 6 of the ICTR Statute reproduces *mutatis mutandis* Article 7 of the ICTY Statute.

[49] See Article 2, ICTY Statute.

[50] See Article 3, ICTY Statute.

[51] See Article 4, ICTY Statute.

[52] See Article 5, ICTY Statute.

[53] That is whether their official position be that of Head of State or any other responsible Government officials.

[54] See Article 6 and 7(1) and (2).

[55] See Article 7(3).

7(4) ensure that the fact that an accused person acted pursuant to an order of a Government or a superior shall not relieve him of criminal responsibility, but may, as in other circumstances, be considered in mitigation of punishment.[56]

Irrelevance of official capacity also featured in Article VII of the *Nuremberg Charter*, Article VI of the *Tokyo Tribunal Charter*, and Article 4 of *Control Council Law No. 10*, and of course as already stated, in Articles 7 and 6 of the *Statutes of International Criminal Tribunal for the Former Yugoslavia and Rwanda* respectively.[57] Presently, it is also embodied in Article 27 of the *Rome Statute of International Criminal Court.*

The Nuremberg Tribunal expressly affirmed individual criminal responsibility for state officials pursuant to Article VII of the Nuremberg Charter, in the case of In Re Goering.[58] Thus, in *Prosecutor v Jean Kambanda*,[59] the Prime Minister of the Interim Government of Rwanda, 'with *de jure* authority and *de facto* control over members of his government'[60] was tried on a six count indictment of genocide, and crimes against humanity.[61] He was held

---

[56] See Article 7(4).

[57] Khan, K. A. A. and Dixon, R., *Archbold International Criminal Courts: Practice, Procedure & Evidence*, (2nd edition) London, Sweet & Maxwell, 2005, 772.

[58] Annual Digest, 13 (1946, No. 92).

[59] Case No ICTR-97-23-5.

[60] *Op.cit.*

[61] *Prosecutor v Jean Kambanda*, Case No. ICTR – 97 – 23 – 5. See also *Prosecutor v Hissene Habre*, SCS/CAE, 2016, Reported in DailySun News Paper, May 31, 2016, Vol. 10, No. 3417; *Prosecutor v. Bashir Idriss Abu Garda*, (Darfur, Sudan), ICC Trial Chamber I, 2009; Prosecutor v. Omar Hassan Ahmad Al Bashir, ICC Trial Chamber IV, 2014; Prosecutor v. Omar Hassan Ahmad Al Bashir, ("Omar Al

accountable under Article 6 of International Criminal Tribunal for Rwanda which provides for individual criminal responsibility, irrespective of the fact that one is a Head of State or holds Government positions.

The facts of the case are as follows: Jean Kambanda was the Prime Minister of the Interim Government of Rwanda from 8 April, 1994 to 17 July, 1994. As Prime Minister, he was the Head of a 20 member Council of ministers and exercised *de jure* authority and control over the members of his government and the armed forces. He actually directed national policy.[62]

During his trial, he admitted that there was widespread attack on the Tutsi population aimed at exterminating them. He also acknowledged that he took part in the meetings of the Council of Ministers in which the massacres were monitored and encouraged. In fact, he also admitted to having issued directives to the Civil Defence mass killings, and trained Hutu youths on how to use arms and armed them to kill the Tutsi. Finally, he also admitted to the Tribunal that he instigated, aided and abetted the Prefects, Bourgmestres and members of the Hutu population to massacre and kill the civilian population, including moderate Hutus.[63] He was found guilty of all the counts of the indictment, and sentenced to life

---

Bashir"), No.: ICC-02/05-01/09, March 2009, Pre-Trial Chamber I, International Criminal Court. *Prosecutor v Francis Kirimi Muthaura*, Uhuru

Muigai Kenyatta and Mohammed Hussein Ali, ICC-01/09/02/11 and Prosecutor v Slobadan Miloevic (Decision on review of Indictment – November 22, 2001).

[62] Khan and Dixon, *Op.cit*. See also, Unegbu, M. O., *From Nuremberg Charter to Rome Statute: Judicial Enforcement of International Humanitarian Law*, Enugu, SNAAP Press Ltd., 2015, 149.

[63] Unegbu, M. O., *Ibid*.

imprisonment. He was sentenced to life imprisonment despite his plea of guilty, his remorse and cooperation with the prosecutor; because the Tribunal decided that the aggravating circumstances in the case outweighed the mitigating ones.[64] Many of his Ministers were also indicted and tried. They included Jerome Bicamumpaka, Minister of Foreign Affairs, Casimir Bizimungu, Minister of Health and Eliezer Niyitegeka,[65] Minister of Information. *The case of Jean Kambanda* is important for being the first conviction ever, of a former head of government for genocide.[66] However, the first judicial interpretation of the crime of genocide was made in the *case of Jean Paul Akayesu.*[67]

The case proved to be the most celebrated in the International Criminal Tribunal for Rwanda. A fifteen count indictment was filed against Jean-Paul Akayesu, the *Bourgmestre* (Mayor) of Taba Commune (an administrative district) from April 1993 to June, 1994. His responsibilities as *Bourgmestre* included the maintenance of law and order in the commune, but he did nothing when about two thousand Tutsis were killed in the commune during the ethnic conflict between the Hutus and the Tutsis.[68]

The *statute of the International Criminal Tribunal for Rwanda (ICTR)* provides that a person who planned, instigated, ordered, committed or otherwise aided and abetted in the planning, preparation or execution of a crime referred to in Articles 2 to 4 is individually

---

[64] *Ibid.*, 150. See Prosecutor v Eliezer Niyitegaka, ICTR-96-14-T, Judgment and sentence (16 may2003) paras 462,303,312,462.

[65] *Op.cit.*

[66] *Ibid.*, 146.

[67] See *Prosecutor v Jean-Paul Akayesu*, Case No. ICTR-96-4-5 of 2/11/98.

[68] Unegbu, M. O., *Op.cit*, 149.

responsible for such a crime. The statute also states that the official capacity of a suspect or superior order of government does not relieve the suspect of responsibility, if it is proved that he or she knew or had reason to know that the prohibited acts were being committed, and he took no reasonable measures to stop them.

Akayesu pleaded not guilty to the counts of indictment, contending that the massacres were widespread, and thus difficult for him to stop. Moreover, he contended that the ten communal police men under his command were helpless in the circumstances. On the count on sexual violence, the accused denied knowledge of any such thing, or even being involved. He was however found guilty of genocide, crimes against humanity (extermination, murder, torture, and rape), direct and public incitement to commit genocide. Particularly, he was found guilty in nine out of the fifteen counts indictment and sentenced to life imprisonment.[69]

Another celebrated case which involved government officials and which was also decided by the International Criminal Tribunal for Rwanda was the case that became known as the *Butare Case*.[70] The accused persons were highly placed government officials of Hutu origin, who participated in the planning of systematic extermination of Tutsis, the training of ethnic militias for that purpose and the distribution of arms to them. They were also alleged to have drafted the lists of people to be eliminated, and also engaged in direct and public incitement against the Tutsis. They ultimately ordered and

---

[69] *Ibid*.

[70] Nyiramashuko Case No. ICTR-97-21.

participated in the massacre.[71] They even ordered the killing of moderate Hutus who were opposed to their plan.

The following persons were indicted in the *Butare trial*:[72]

1. Pauline Nyiramasuhuko (Minister for Family and Women Development).
2. Arsene Shallow (Pauline Nyiramasuhuko's son and leader of a militia group).
3. Joseph Kanyabashi (Mayor of Ngoma).
4. Sylvain Nsabimana (Prefect of Butare) and,
5. Elie Ntuyambaje (Mayor of Muganza).

It is generally believed that the success recorded by the *Ad hoc* tribunals for the Former Yugoslavia and that for Rwanda encouraged the establishment of the Special Court for Sierra Leone.[73] The establishment of the Special Court and the trials thereunder shall be considered later.

(ii) International Humanitarian Law: Individual criminal responsibility is also generated by "grave breaches" of international humanitarian law, otherwise known as "war crimes".[74] The 1949 *Geneva Conventions* and the 1977 First *Additional Protocol* (API) embody rules on the punishment of violations of grave breaches of

---

[71] *Op.cit.*, 150.

[72] *Prosecutor v Nyiramasuhuko and Others, ICTR, Indictment, Case No ICTR – 97 – 2.*

[73] *Ibid.*, 151.

[74] Article 85(5) *Additional Protocol* 1 states: 'without prejudice to the application of the Conventions and of this Protocol, grave breaches of these instruments shall be regarded as war crimes'.

the Convention and the Protocol.[75] The provisions on grave breaches oblige every State Party to the Convention and the Additional Protocol to 'enact any legislation necessary to provide effective penal sanctions for persons committing, or ordering to be committed' any of the grave breaches and to search for those persons in order to either bring them before its own courts or hand them over for trial to another State Party. In other words, the maxim or principle of *'aut dedere aut judicare'* (meaning extradite or prosecute) applies to these crimes. Two facts can be deduced from the foregoing provision: 'Firstly, that, while relying on national jurisdictions, the *Geneva Conventions* and the (API) *Additional Protocol* 1 implemented a system of individual criminal responsibility for international crimes'. 'Secondly, that Geneva law is not restricted to those who perpetrate war crimes; it also applies to those who ordered them'.[76]

Article 86 of *Additional Protocol* 1 makes a separate provision for superior responsibilities. Under it, the executors of orders and those who ordered those crimes are criminally responsible for committing war crimes.[77] However, the Commentary to the Additional Protocol I explains that those who are criminally responsible are, not only those who directly took part as principal actors in physically committing the crime which amounts to a grave breach, but also

---

[75] The following articles constitute the "grave breaches provisions": Article 50 of *Geneva Convention* I; Article 51 of *Geneva Convention* III; Article 147 of *Geneva Convention* IV; and Article 85 of *Additional Protocol* 1.

[76] Sliedregt, *Op.cit.*, 33.

[77] *Ibid.*

those who have helped the offender or joint offenders in preparing or perpetuating the breach, and thus have incidentally co-operated.[78]

It may however be stated at this point, that a number of International Humanitarian Law instruments have provided general protective rights for victims of armed conflicts irrespective of their sex. Such instruments include *the 1949 Geneva Conventions*[79] and *their Additional Protocols*[80], the *Statutes of International Criminal Tribunal for the former Yugoslavia (ICTY)*[81], the *International Criminal Tribunal for Rwanda (ICTR)*[82], the *Special Court for Sierra Leone (SCSL)*[83], and the *Rome Statute of International Criminal Court* (1998)[84]. Be that as it may, this work is particularly interested in the instruments' specific rights provisions for women victims of armed conflict.

(iii) International Human Rights Law: Under this law, it is necessary to draw attention to some of the provisions of the three foremost human rights instruments which apply both in war and peace time, to protect the civilian population namely, the 1948

---

[78] Pilloud, C. et al., *Commentary on the Additional Protocols of 8 June 1997 to the Geneva Convention of 12 August 1949*, Geneva 1987, 979, available at *<http://www.icrc.org.>* as cited in Sliedregt, *Ibid.*, footnote 102.

[79] *Geneva Convention I, Articles 12 – 18;and Articles 49 – 50; Geneva Convention II, Articles 12 – 21; and Articles50 – 51; Geneva Convention III, Articles 12 – 16, Articles 89 – 99; Geneva Convention IV, Articles 13 – 26, and Articles 27 – 34 etc.*

[80] *Additional Protocol I, Articles 13 – 20; Additional Protocol II, Articles 7 – 18 and Additional Protocol III, generally*

[81] *Articles 2,3,4,and 5 of the Statute of the International Tribunal for the Former Yugoslavia (1993).*

[82] *Articles 2,3,and 4 of the Statute of the International Criminal Tribunal for Rwanda (1994)*

[83] *Articles 2,3,4, and 5 of the Statute of the Special Court for Sierra Leone (2002)*

[84] *Rome Statute of International Criminal Court (1998), Articles 6,7,and 8*

Universal Declaration of Human Rights(UDHR),[85] 1966 *International Covenant on Civil and Political Rights(ICCPR),*[86] and *International Covenant on Economic, Social and Cultural Rights(ICESCR).* Granted that the *Universal Declaration of Human Rights (UDHR)* is not a binding legal instrument, it is 'a common standard of achievement for all people and all nations'.[87] It, among other things, contemplates the equal rights of men and women, while recognizing the fact that human rights should be protected by the rule of law.[88] The first eleven articles of the *Declaration* leave no one in doubt of the object of the *Declaration* which has inspired the constitutions of most nations and their penal provisions.

The articles state as follows: "All human beings are born free and equal in dignity and rights. They are endowed with reason and conscience and should act towards one another in a spirit of brotherhood".[89]

They go on to further state:

Everyone is entitled, to all the rights and freedoms set forth in this Declaration, without distinction of any kind, such as race, colour, sex, language, religion, political or other opinion, national or social origin, property, birth or other

---

[85] The *Universal Declaration of Human Rights* was adopted by United Nations General Assembly Resolution 217A(III), dated 10 December 1948, available at *www.un.org/overview/rights.html.*

[86] The *International Covenant on Civil and Political Rights* (ICCPR) was adopted on 16 December, 1966 and came into force on 23 March, 1976. See Evans, M. D., *Blackstone's International Law Documents* (9th edn.), Oxford, Oxford University Press, 2009. 116.

[87] See Preamble to the *UDHR.*

[88] *Ibid.*

[89] Article 1 of *UDHR.*

status. Furthermore, no distinction shall be made on the basis of the political, jurisdictional or international status of the country or territory to which a person belongs, whether it be independent, trust, non-self-governing or under any other limitation of sovereignty.

Everyone has the right to life, liberty and the security of person. No one shall be held in slavery or servitude; slavery and the slave trade shall be prohibited in all their forms.

No one shall be subjected to torture or to cruel, inhuman or degrading treatment or punishment.

Everyone has the right to recognition everywhere as a person before the law.

All are equal before the law and are entitled without any discrimination in violation of this Declaration and against any incitement to such discrimination.

Everyone has the right to an effective remedy by the competent national tribunals for acts violating the fundamental rights granted him by the constitution or by law.

No one shall be subjected to arbitrary arrest, detention or exile.

Everyone is entitled in full equality to a fair and public hearing by an independent and impartial tribunal, in the determination of his rights and obligations and of any criminal charge against him.

They conclude by declaring:

1. Everyone charged with a penal offence has the right to be presumed innocent until proved guilty according to law in a public trial at which he has had all the guarantees necessary for his defence.

2. No one shall be held guilty of any penal offence on account of any act or omission which did not constitute a penal offence, under national or international law, at the time when it was committed. Nor shall a heavier penalty be imposed than the one that was applicable at the time the penal offence was committed.[90]

Even in times of war, the law protects the general well-being of the individual and the family unit by guaranteeing to them certain socio-cultural rights[91]. For instance, the *International Covenant on Economic, Social and Cultural Rights* of 1966 enjoins State Parties to the present *Covenant* to recognize that the widest possible protection and assistance should be accorded to the family, which is the natural and fundamental group unit of society.[92] The Covenant specifically provides for special protection to be accorded mothers during a reasonable period before and after childbirth.[93] Special measures of protection and assistance are also to be taken on behalf of all children and young persons without any discrimination for reasons of parentage or other conditions. They should also, according to the provisions of the covenant, be protected from economic and social

---

[90] See Articles 2 to 11, *International Covenant on Civil and Political Rights (ICCPR)*.

[91] *The principle that International Human Rights Law applies in times of armed conflicts alongside IHL was firmly reinforced in 1968 by the unanimous adoption of the U.N. General Assembly Resolution on Respect for Human Rights in Periods of Armed Conflict (see U.N. Doc. G.A.Res.2444(xxIII) of 19 Dec. 1968; see also U.N. Doc. G.A.Res.2675(xxV) of 9 Dec. 1970) which recognized the importance of minimum standards of conduct and certain fundamental human rights norms applicable in all armed conflicts.*

[92] See *Article* 10(1), International Covenant on Economic, Social and Cultural Rights (ICESCR)(1966).

[93] See *Article* 10(2).

exploitation. Thus, the law provides among other things that employing them in any work that is harmful to their morals or health or dangerous to life or likely to hamper their normal development should be punishable by law.[94] The right to adequate standard of living, including that of the highest attainable standard of physical and mental health is also recognized.[95] So are many other socio-economic rights recognized and protected under the covenant.[96]

4.1.2 Specific Rights Provisions for Women Victims of Armed Conflict

Both International Humanitarian Law and International Human Rights law have made specific provisions for the protection of women's rights in times of armed conflicts[97] and peacetime. They have provided for women's right to personal safety, which 'encompasses safety from dangers, acts of violence or threats thereof against members of the civilian population not or no longer taking a direct part in hostilities'.[98] Violence, which has been observed to include physical and mental harm, includes killing, summary and arbitrary execution, torture and mutilation, cruel, inhuman and degrading treatment, rape and violations specifically directed against women such as forced impregnation, forced pregnancy,

---

[94] *Article* 10(3).

[95] *Articles* 11 and 12.

[96] See the provisions of the *Covenant* generally.

[97] The first set of rules designed to protect women in war appears to be found in the *Lieber code*. (See Gardam, J., 'Women, human rights and international humanitarian law', [1998], *International Review of the Red Cross (IRRC)* (No. 324), 423 as cited in Tachou-Sipowo, 'The Security Council on women in war: between peace building and humanitarian protection', [2010], *IRRC*, (Vol. 92, No. 877), 200.

[98] Lindsey-Curtet, C., et al, *Addressing the Needs of Women Affected by Armed Conflict: An ICRC Guidance Document*, Geneva, ICRC, 2004, 17.

forced termination of pregnancy, enforced sterilization and other forms of sexual assault.[99] For instance, as early as 1863, the Lieber Code[100] provides:

> The United States acknowledge and protect, in hostile countries occupied by them, religion and morality; and the persons of the inhabitants especially those of women; and the sacredness of domestic relations. Offences to the contrary shall be vigorously punished.[101]

(i) Specific Rights Provisions under the *Geneva Conventions/ Additional Protocols*: The *Geneva Conventions* are not generally gender-sensitive. However, they embody specific provisions on the treatment of women in special circumstances.[102] For instance, Article 27 of the Fourth *Geneva Convention* provides *inter alia* as follows:

> Protected persons are entitled, in all circumstances, to respect for their persons, their honour, their family rights, their religious convictions and practices, and their manners and

---

[99] See for example, the specific prohibitions on sexual violence against women in Article 27 of the Fourth *Geneva Convention; Article 7 6, Additional Protocol 1; Article* 4(2) (d) and (e), and 5(c)(g) and (i) of *the Statute of the International Criminal Tribunal for Former Yugoslavia* (1993); Articles 3 and 4 of the *Statute of the International Criminal Tribunal for Rwanda (ICTR)* (1994); *Article* 2 of the *Statute* of the *Special Court for Sierra Leone and Articles 7(1)(g),* 7(2)(c) and 7(2)(f), especially of the *Rome Statute of the International Criminal Court (ICC)*(1998).

[100] See The *Lieber Code* (General Orders 100) War Dept. Classification No. 1.12, Oct. 8, 1863, as cited in Askin, K.D. and Koenig, D., Women National Publishers, Inc. 2001, 291.

[101] Order 20(Winfield Scott 1847), reprinted in William E. Birkheimer, *Military Government and Marital Law* 581 (2ded. 1904) as cited in Askin, K.D. and Koenig, D., *Ibid.*

[102] For instance, *Geneva Conventions* I and II specify in Article 12 that women "shall be treated with all consideration due to their sex.

customs. They shall at all times be humanely treated, and shall be protected especially against all acts of violence or threats thereof and against insults and public curiosity.

Women shall be especially protected against any attack on their honour, in particular against rape, enforced prostitution, or any form of indecent assault.[103]

Historically, the term "honour" is a carryover from knightly and chivalric traditions. It has thus been criticized as archaic and semantically vague, but 'it does create a binding legal norm that prohibits such attacks upon women'.[104] Besides, the term is elastic enough to accommodate any conceivable sexual offence against women, as exemplified in the last paragraph of the fore-going quotation, which listed rape, enforced prostitution, or any form of indecent assault as particulars of offences against 'honour'. However, some feminists have viewed the special circumstances where the Law ostensibly protects women as those circumstances which involve the interests of third parties, namely, the interests of the foetus/ child (in pregnancy); dependent children (as mother); and interest of the husband (as wife).

On the other hand, *Additional Protocol 1* specifically provides for the protection of women under the heading 'Protection of Women' as follows:

1. Women shall be the object of special respect and shall be protected in particular against rape, forced prostitution and any other form of indecent assault.

---

[103] *Article* 27 of the Fourth *Geneva Convention (GCIV).*

[104] Durham, H. and Gurd, T. (eds.), *Listening to the Silences: Women and War*, Boston, Martinus Nijhoff Publishers, 2005, 98.

2. Pregnant women and mothers having dependent infants who are arrested, detained or interned for reason related to the armed conflict, shall have their cases considered with the utmost priority.

3. To the maximum extent feasible, the parties to the conflict shall endeavor to avoid the pronouncement of the death penalty on pregnant women or mothers having dependent infants, for an offence related to the armed conflict. The death penalty for such offences shall not be executed on such women.[105]

The foregoing article repeats some of the provisions embodied in the *Four Geneva Conventions,* but refrains from using the term "honour".[106]

Additional Protocol II which applies in non-international armed conflicts requires humane treatment of all persons not, or no longer taking direct part in hostilities irrespective of whether they are detained or not, and without any adverse distinction.[107] Particularly, *Article* 4(2)(e) prohibits the range of crimes provided in *Article* 75(2)(b) of *Additional Protocol 1,* which are mostly committed against women, namely: 'outrages upon personal dignity, *in particular humiliating and degrading treatment, rape, enforced prostitution* and any other form of indecent assault'. [108]

Common *Article* 3 of the Four *Geneva Conventions* (the only provision in the Conventions devoted to the protection of victims of

---

[105] *Additional protocol* 1 of 1977, Article 76.

[106] Durham, *Op.cit.*

[107] *Ibid.*

[108] *Ibid.* See Article 3(1)(c), *Geneva Convention* IV.

non-international armed conflict) also forbids 'outrages upon personal dignity, in particular humiliating and degrading treatment', but it does not specifically mention rape.[109] So also do the provisions in the *Geneva Conventions* dealing with "grave breaches" not specifically mention rape or sexual violence. As unfortunate as that may be, such crimes are implicitly covered in such terms as 'inhuman treatment, willfully causing great suffering or serious injury to body or health'.[110] Humane treatment includes freedom from 'violence to life and person, in particular murder of all kinds, mutilation, cruel treatment and torture.[111] Women may not be held hostage,[112] they must be given all procedural rights recognized as indispensable by civilized peoples'.[113]

However, prosecutors have in recent times, successfully convicted individuals for sexual violence and rape under such omnibus provisions and terms. The law also seeks to ameliorate the sufferings of pregnant women and mothers of young children in times of war. *The Geneva Convention IV* states that pregnant women and mothers of children under seven years old, who are aliens in the territory of a party to the conflict, shall be granted preferential treatment, that is to the same extent of the nationals of the State concerned.[114] Particularly, Article 50 enjoins the occupying power

---

[109] *Ibid*.

[110] See, Provisions on *Grave Breaches*: Article 50 *Geneva Convention 1, Article 51 Geneva Convention II, Article 130 Geneva Convention III and Article 147 Geneva Convention IV.*

[111] *Article 3 (1)(a), Geneva Convention IV*

[112] *Article 3 (1)(b), Geneva Convention IV*

[113] *Article 3 (1)(d), Geneva Convention IV*

[114] *Article 38(1) – (5), Geneva Convention IV.*

with the co-operation of the national and local authorities, to facilitate the proper working of all institutions that are devoted to the care and education of children. Under this article, the occupying power is also forbidden to 'hinder the application of any preferential measures in regard to food, medical care and protection against the effects of war, which may have been adopted prior to the occupation in favour of children under fifteen years, expectant mothers, and mothers of children under seven years'.[115] The *International Covenant on Economic, Social and Cultural Rights* (1966) also provides specifically for special protection to be accorded mothers during a reasonable period before and after childbirth.[116]

Hospitals, safety zones and localities are also provided, for the protection of expectant mothers, and mothers of children under seven years, among others.[117] Such hospitals, and safety zones and localities may be recognized by mutual agreement between the parties to the conflict, while the Protecting Powers and the International Committee of the Red Cross may assist in facilitating the institution and recognition of such hospitals, safety zones and localities.[118]

Furthermore, the *Additional Protocol* I affirms and complements the Convention by including pregnant women and mothers of young children in its general protection of 'wounded' and 'sick'. *Article* 8 states that the terms 'wounded' and 'sick' 'also cover

---

[115] *See, Article 50, Geneva Convention* IV.

[116] See *Article* 10(2), *International Convenant on Economic, Social and Cultural Rights* (1966).

[117] See *Article* 14, *Geneva Convention* IV.

[118] *Ibid.*

maternity cases, new born babies and other persons who may be in need of immediate medical assistance or care, such as the infirm or expectant mothers, and who refrain from any act of hostility.[119]

Besides affording protection for pregnant women and mothers of young children, the *Geneva Conventions* and the *Additional Protocols* also provide specific protections for women as civilian internees[120] and also as prisoners of war.[121] For instance, women prisoners of war and internees are entitled, where feasible, to separate quarters, sanitary conveniences and supervision by women.[122] In addition to these provisions, the Model Assignment concerning Direct Repatriation and Accommodation in Neutral Countries of wounded and sick Prisoners of War who are pregnant or mother with children should be eligible for accommodation in a neutral country.[123]

(ii) Specific Provisions under the *Rome Statute of International Criminal Court*: Most of the war crimes that could be committed against women are covered under *Article 7* of the *Rome Statute of International Criminal Court* as crimes against Humanity. They include Murder, Extermination, Enslavement, Deportation or forcible transfer of population; imprisonment or other severe deprivation of physical liberty in violation of fundamental rules of international law, torture, rape; sexual slavery, enforced prostitution, forced prostitution, forced pregnancy, enforced

---

[119] *Article* 8(a), *Additional Protocol* 1.

[120] See *Article* 75(5) of *Additional Protocol* 1; and *Articles* 85, 97, 119 of *Geneva Convention* IV.

[121] See *Articles* 14,16,25, 29, 14, 49, 88, 97 and 108 of *Geneva Convention* III.

[122] *Articles* 103 and 108, *Geneva Convention* III.

[123] *Geneva Convention* III, Annex I.

sterilization, or other forms of sexual violence of comparable gravity.[124]

Article 8 titled "War Crimes", and especially under 'other serious violations of the laws and customs applicable in international armed conflict, within the established framework of international law' contain provisions that have implications for gender, and particularly women.[125] More or less, they refer back to the foregoing Article 7 crimes.[126]

(iii) Specific Provisions under *the Statutes of International Criminal Tribunal for Former Yugoslavia; International Criminal Tribunal for Rwanda and Special Court for Sierra-*

*Leone***:** The *Statute of International Criminal Tribunal for the former Yugoslavia* (ICTY) also provides for crimes against humanity in its *Article* 5 and this includes "enslavement" and "rape", which are mostly directed against women.[127] Similarly, under the *Statute of International Criminal Tribunal for Rwanda*, rape is criminalized as a crime against humanity.[128] However, the differences between the wording of the relevant articles of the Statutes have been noted as largely due to the different nature of each conflict.[129] Moreover, though both Tribunals have jurisdiction over grave breaches of the

---

[124] *Article* 7(1)(a) – (k). See also Paragraphs 2(a) – (i) and 3 for the purposes of defining the crimes in paragraph 1 and the meaning of gender, respectively

[125] *Article* 8 (1)(b)(xxi) and (xxii); 8(c)(ii) and (iii); and 8(e)(vi).

[126] Than, C.D., and Shorts, FC; International Criminal Law and Human Rights, London, Sweet & Maxwell, 2003, 430 – 431.

[127] *Article* 5 (c) and (g), *Statute of the International Tribunal for the Former Yugoslavia* (1993).

[128] *Article* 3 (g), *Statute of the International Criminal Tribunal for Rwanda*, (1994).

[129] Than, C.D. and Shorts, FC., *Op.cit.*, 355.

Geneva Conventions, including Common *Article* 3, *Article* 4 of the *Statute of International Criminal Tribunal for Rwanda* makes explicit provisions for sexual violence.[130]

(iv) Specific Provisions under the *Statute of the Special Court for Sierra-Leone*: The *Statute of the Special Court for Sierra Leone* (SCSL) made specific provisions for crimes which are more relevant to women in *Article* 2 under crimes against humanity. They include: rape, sexual slavery, enforced prostitution, forced pregnancy, and other forms of sexual violence.[131] Based on the special and hybrid nature of the court, the Statute also incorporates relevant crimes under Sierra Leonean Law, as follows:

(a) Offences relating to the abuse of girls under the *Prevention of Cruelty to Children Act,* 1926 (Cap.31), namely:

   i). Abusing a girl under 13 years of age, contrary to *section* 6;

   ii). Abusing a girl under 13 and 14 years of age, contrary to *section* 7;

   iii). Abduction of a girl for immoral purposes contrary to *section* 12.

(v) Specific United Nations Declarations and Conventions on Women in Armed Conflicts: At this point in time, it is necessary to consider the United Nations Actions aimed at promoting the rights of women in peace time and in wartime. The issue of women and children in emergency and conflict situations was first discussed in detail at the 23rd session of the Commission on the Status of Women

---

[130] *Ibid.*

[131] *Article* 2 (a) – (i) of the Statute of the *Special Court for Sierra Leone* (SCSL).

(CSW) in 1970, and subsequently in 1972 and 1974. The Commission had earlier on adopted a *Resolution on the protection of women and children in emergency or war time*.[132] Subsequently, the General Assembly adopted the 1974 *Declaration on the protection of women and children in Emergency and Armed Conflict*.[133]

The Declaration emphasizes the need to accord women special protection on account of the special role they play in society.[134] It thus criminalizes cruel and inhuman treatment of women and children, including imprisonment, torture, shooting, mass arrests, collective punishment, destruction of dwellings and forcible eviction, committed by belligerents in the course of military operation or in occupied territories.[135] Furthermore, it reaffirms the rights of women and children to: 'shelter, food, medical aid or other inalienable rights, in accordance with the provisions of the *Universal Declaration of Human Rights*, the *International Covenant on Economic, Social and Cultural Rights*, instruments under international law'.[136]

---

[132] Resolution 4 (XXII) or 3 Feb., 1969 on the *Protection of Women and Children in Emergency or Wartime, Fighting for Peace, National Liberation and Independence*; ECOSOC 64th Session, 66 (27 Jan. – 12 Feb. 1969, UN Docs E/CN.6/527, E/4619.

[133] Gardam, J. G. and Jarvis, M. J., 'Women, Armed Conflict and International Law', Kluwer Law International, the Hague, 2001, 137-138. See also CSW Res XIII of 1974 included in a draft Declaration for consideration by the ECOSOC. ECOSOC Res 1861 (LVI) of 16 May 1974 recommended that the GA adopt a *Declaration on the Protection of Women and Children in Emergency and Armed Conflict*. The GA considered the ECOSOC recommendation and adopted the *Declaration on the Protection of Women and Children in Emergency and Armed Conflict* in GA Res 3318 of (hereinafter 1974 GA *Declaration*).

[134] Gardam, *Ibid.*, 140. See also 1974 GA *Declaration, Supra*.

[135] 1974 *Declaration, Supra*, at para 5.

[136] *Ibid.*

Clearly, the foregoing provisions are vague, but they have been acclaimed as raising, for the first time, some of the broader issues facing women as a result of armed conflict. However, 'given the reality of armed conflict for women, it is clear that the 1974 *General Assembly Declaration* is inadequate in identifying and responding to the distinctive impact of armed conflict for women.[137] For instance, the *Declaration* does not explicitly make provisions against sexual violence. It merely encourages States to take steps to prohibit, *inter alia*, 'degrading treatment'. Granted that historically this type of language had been used to refer to sexual violence, the *Declaration* made strong statements to the effect that rape and other similar abuses were crimes of violence and violations of the human rights of women.[138] Notwithstanding the aforesaid limitations, and the fact that the *Declaration* is not a binding instrument, the *Declaration* is significant for being the very first time the United Nations identified the issue of women and armed conflict, and made some effort to improve the situation of women.

The starting point for improving the situation of women seems to be the elimination of discrimination against women. Thus the United Nations General Assembly adopted the *Convention on the Elimination of All Forms of Discrimination Against Women* (CEDAW) on 18th December, 1979. The *Convention* which entered into force as a binding treaty, on the 3rd of September 1981 encourages the application of equality norms in different countries and legal systems of the world.[139] It is easily the foremost international human

---

[137] *Op.cit.*, 142.

[138] *Ibid.*, 141.

[139] For the full text of the Convention, see Gandi, S. (ed.), *Blackstone's International Human Rights Documents (6th ed.)*, Oxford University Press, Oxford, 2008, 62-70.

rights instrument that establishes international standards of equality between men and women.[140]

The Convention recognizes that discrimination against women violates the principle of equality of rights and respect for human rights,[141] and notes that such discrimination affects the participation of women on equal terms with men in the political, social as well as cultural life of their countries, thereby militating against development.[142] It thus went on to encourage State parties to prevent every kind of discrimination against women by embodying principles of equality of the sexes in their national constitutions and other legislations.[143] The State Parties were also enjoined to modify or abolish existing laws, regulations, customs and practices which amount to discrimination against women.[144]

The Convention outlines certain specific prohibitions which include traffic in women for prostitution and other forms of exploitation, but regrettably, it has no specific provision on violence

---

[140] Ibezim, E. C., *The Beijing Conference and the Human Rights Protection of Women: A Critical Review, Op.cit.*

[141] See Preamble to the *Convention on the Elimination of all Forms of Discrimination Against Women* (CEDAW).

[142] *Ibid.,* In *Article* 1, the Convention defines "discrimination against women" as any distinction, exclusion or restriction made on the basis of sex which has the effect or purpose of impairing or nullifying the recognition, enjoyment or exercise by women, irrespective of their marital status, on a basis of equality of men and women, of human rights and fundamental freedom in the political, economic, social, cultural, civil or any other field.

[143] See *Article* 2(a), *Convention on the Elimination of all Forms of Discrimination Against Women* (CEDAW)

[144] *Article* 2(f), *Convention on the Elimination of all Forms of Discrimination Against Women* (CEDAW.)

against women.[145] However, in 1993, the *Committee on the Elimination of All Forms of Discrimination Against Women*, the monitoring body of the *Convention on the Elimination of All Forms of Discrimination Against Women* adopted a general recommendation on violence against women.[146] This may have been as a result of reports of the widespread sexual violence committed during the armed conflict in the Former Yugoslavia.[147] Nearly a decade earlier, the United Nations had also identified reducing violence against women as a basic strategy for addressing the issue of peace. This was under the Nairobi Forward-Looking Strategies for the Advancement of Women. The instrument is an outcome document of the World Conference to review and appraise the achievement of the United Nations Decade for Women: Equality, Development and Peace, held in Nairobi in 1985. While the conference acknowledged the prevalence of violence against women,[148] and urged governments to respond to the problem, it did not expressly recognize violence against women as a human rights issue. However, the Nairobi Forward-Looking Strategies identified reducing violence against women as a basic strategy for addressing the issue of peace and

---

[145] Gardam and Jarvis, *Op.cit.*, 146.

[146] See UN Committee on the Elimination of All Forms of Discrimination Against Women (CEDAW), Eleventh Session, General Recommendation 19, UN Doc CEDAW/C/1992/L.1/

[147] See for example, reports in the Miami Herald (18 Dec. 1992)., and Die Welt (1 Oct.), cited in Mackinnon C.A, 'Crimes of War, Crimes of Peace', Shute, S., and Hurley, S. (eds.), *on Human Rights*: The Oxford Amnesty Lecturer, 1993, 83.

[148] Gardam, *Op.cit.*, See also Report of the World Conference to Review and Appraise the Achievement of the United Nations Decade for Women: Equality, Development and Peace, Nairobi, 15-26 July, 1985.

focused on rape and domestic violence in the family, while merely showing concern about state and military violence.[149]

The fact that women in conflict situations are especially vulnerable to violence did not escape the attention of the United Nations Commission. Thus, it recommended the formulation of an international instrument on violence against women as an imperative.[150] Consequently, the *Declaration on the Elimination of Violence against Women* was drafted and unanimously adopted by the United Nations General Assembly in 1994.

Wallace describes the *Declaration* as a step forward, but observes that the fulfillment of the objectives contained therein remains the responsibility of all states, and not only that of contracting parties as in the case of the *Convention on the Elimination of All Forms of Discrimination Against Women*.[151] In other words, granted that the *Declaration* has no binding force, it does have the moral strength of world consensus.[152]

The *Declaration* is comprehensive in its coverage, and defines violence against women broadly to include physical, sexual, and

---

[149] Forsyth, D. P., *Encyclopedia of Human Rights (Vol. 2)*, Oxford, Oxford University Press, 2009, 289.

[150] The commission made the recommendation to the economic and social council. It recommended that the instrument be prepared in conjunction with the 'Committee on the Elimination of Discrimination against Women' and the 'United Nations Committee on Crime Prevention and Control'.

[151] Wallace, R. M. M. et al., *International Human Rights Text and Materials (2nd ed.)*, London, Sweet & Maxwell, 2001, 38.

[152] Merry, S. E. 'Gender Violence', Forsyth, D. P., *Op.cit*, 228. See also, Ibezim, E. C., 'Gender-Based Domestic Violence in Nigeria: A Socio-legal Perspective', Azinge, E., and Uche, L., *Law of Domestic Violence*, Lagos, Nigerian Institute of Advanced Legal Studies, 2012, 185.

psychological harm or threats of harm in public or private life,[153] and named gender based violence as a violation of human rights, and an instance of sex discrimination and inequality.[154] It explicitly attributes the roots of gender violence to historically unequal power relations between men and women, and argues that it is socially constructed and historically justified, rather than natural. The *Declaration*, however, prohibits the invocation of custom, tradition, or religious consideration to avoid its obligations and urges States to exercise due diligence to prevent, investigate and punish acts of violence against women, whether perpetrated by the State or by private individuals.[155]

The 1993 United Nations Conference on Human Rights held in Vienna marks a turning point in the recognition of women's rights, especially in the question of violence against women.[156] For the first time, violence against women was recognized as a human rights issue.[157] The *Declaration* specifically acknowledges the vulnerability of women to sexual violence during armed conflict, and condemns it as a human rights violation requiring a 'particular effective response'.[158] That response came in the appointment by the United

---

[153] See *Article* 1, *Declaration on the Elimination of Violence Against Women* (1993).

[154] *Op.cit.*

[155] See *Article* 4, *Declaration on the Elimination of Violence Against Women* (1993).

[156] See Enloe, C., "Afterword: Have the Bosnian Rapes Opened a New Era of Feminist Consciousness?", Stiglmayer, A. (ed.), *Mass Rape: The War Against Women in Bosnia-Herzegovina,* 1994.

[157] See *Vienna Declaration and Programme of Action* adopted by the World Conference on Human Rights held in Vienna from 14 to 25 June 1993, UN Doc A/Conf.157/24(13 Oct.1993) (hereinafter Vienna Declaration).

[158] Vienna Declaration, *Ibid,* para 38 and paras 28, and 29 as cited in Gardam and Jarvis, *Op.cit,* 147.

Nations of Special Rapporteurs on Thematic Issues Related to Sexual Violence during Armed Conflict.

The Final Report of the Special Rapporteur examines the legal framework for prosecuting sexual slavery and sexual violence under international law, and also 'focuses significant attention on the issue of redress (including compensation), for women who have been subjected to systematic sexual violence, and finds that "under customary international law, the Government of Japan must provide redress for the atrocities perpetrated against the "comfort women".'[159] This may take the form of compensation paid directly to each of the surviving women, or their governments, who should in turn ensure that the payment gets to the women concerned.[160] Of course, among other things, the Special Rapporteur also recommends that the United Nations should work towards prosecuting the persons responsible for the crimes committed against the "comfort women".[161]

By mid-1990s, though sexual violence remained a central focus, international concern had begun to expand to include other consequences of armed conflict for women.[162] For instance, women and armed conflict was identified as one of the twelve critical areas of concern at the Beijing Conference which were to be addressed by Member States, the international community and civil society.[163]

---

[159] McDougall, Final Report, UN Doc E/CN.4/Sub.2/1998/13(22 June 1998) (hereinafter McDougall 1998 Final Report, Appendix *para* 31.

[160] *Ibid*.

[161] *Ibid*., Appendix para 63.

[162] Gardam and Jarvis, *Op.cit*, 163.

[163] See Report on Fourth World Conference on Women, Action for Equality Development and Peace, *Beijing Declaration and Platform for Action*, UN Doc

Thus, the *Platform for Action* enjoins 'governments, the international community and civil society, including non-governmental organizations and the private sector... to take strategic action' in relation to the 'effects of armed or other kinds of conflict on women, including those living under foreign occupation'.[164]

Gardam and Jarvis observe that the Beijing Platform for Action places the issue of armed conflict in a broader framework, thereby linking the general vulnerability of women to the adverse effects of armed conflicts to the discrimination and disadvantage they are subjected to in many areas of life.[165] This, they also observe is underlined by the Platform for Action's acknowledgment that while entire community suffer the consequences of armed conflict and terrorism, women and girls are particularly affected because of their sex.[166]

The Platform for Action also acknowledges that civilian casualties often outnumber military casualties in contemporary armed conflicts, with women and children accounting for a significant number of the victims.[167] It re-affirms that rape is a crime notwithstanding the fact that it is common during armed conflicts. It observes that under certain circumstances, it could be an act of genocide, and condemns 'ethnic cleansing' and rape as strategies of

---

A/Conf.177/20 (1995) [hereinafter *Beijing Declaration, and Beijing Platform for Action*].

[164] *Ibid*, at *para* 44.

[165] Gardam and Jarvis, *Op.cit.*

[166] *Op.cit.*, at *para* 135.

[167] *Ibid.*, at *para* 135.

war which must be stopped.[168] To this end, it recommends that governments take the following actions: (i) adopt and implement legislations to end violence against women; (ii) work actively to ratify and implement all international agreements related to violence against women, including the United Nations *Convention on the Elimination of All Forms of Discrimination Against Women*; (iii) provide shelter, legal aids and other services for girls and women at risk, and provide counseling and rehabilitation for perpetrators of violence against women; and (iv) setup national and international cooperation to dismantle networks engaged in trafficking in women.[169]

(vi) Specific UNITED NATIONS Security Council Resolutions On Women and Armed Conflicts: Besides the foregoing human rights instruments that were adopted under the aegis of the United Nations, the United Nations Security Council has since 1999 adopted a number of resolutions which are intended specifically for the protection of women in the event of armed conflict.[170] This intervention was on the basis 'that massive human rights violations in armed conflicts constitute a threat to peace and women are the most severely affected by the scourge of war'.[171] The resolutions have been acknowledged for contributing to the development of

---

[168] See Ibezim, E. C., 'The Beijing Conference and the Human Rights Protection of Women: A Critical Review', *Op.cit*, 43.

[169] See *Beijing Declaration and the Platform for Action* produced and published by the United Nations Development Fund for Women (UNIFEM) and the United Nations Information Centre, Nigeria (UNIC).

[170] Tachou-Sipowo, A., 'The Security Council on Women in War: between peace building and humanitarian protection', [March 2010], *International Review of the Red Cross (IRRC)*, (Vol. 92, No. 877), 197.

[171] *Ibid*.

humanitarian law applicable to women, and for underscoring the value of active participation of women in peace efforts.[172]

However, the thematic and declaratory resolutions on which the law is largely based are not binding, but they have been acknowledged as relatively effective with regards to the provisions that are directed at the United Nations bodies.[173] Therefore, it has been suggested 'that the Council's role could be better accomplished through situational resolutions than through resolutions declaratory of international law'.[174] So far, the Security Council has adopted, *inter alia*, the following resolutions that are aimed at specifically protecting women during armed conflicts: *Resolution 1265* (1999); *Resolution 1325* (2000); *Resolution 1889* (2009); and *Resolution 1820* (2008).

Resolution 1265 which the Security Council adopted on 17 September, 1999 addresses the protection of civilians in war generally, while:

> evidencing a grave preoccupation with the status of women in war and formulating various recommendations; it expressed its concern at the fact that the vast majority of victims in conflicts are civilians, particularly women, children and other vulnerable groups, and acknowledged the direct impact of conflict on women.[175]

It also encourages an acknowledgement of the need for gender specific humanitarian aid and a recognition of the violence women

---

[172] *Ibid.*

[173] *Ibid.*

[174] *Ibid.*

[175] Tachou-Sipowo, *Op.cit.*, 213.

suffer. It therefore advocates the incorporation of special protective provisions for vulnerable groups, including women and children, into peacekeeping mandates,[176] and calls upon States to ratify instruments of international humanitarian law, human rights and refugee law.[177] This Resolution is also important, for in it, the Security Council, provides for the first time, 'the possibility of intervening in situations of armed conflict where civilians are being targeted or humanitarian assistance to civilians are being deliberately obstructed.[178]

Tachou-Sipowo observes that in *Resolution* 1325 (2000), 'the Security Council highlights that the threat to women in war is distinct from that facing the civilian population, as a whole, as it had previously done in the case of children'.[179] According to him, this resolution:

> expands on the provisions relating to women contained within Resolution 1265 (1999),180 and points out that women are being increasingly targeted during armed conflict and stresses the importance of full respect for international law relative to protecting women from gender-based violence – particularly rape and other forms of sexual abuse – and all other forms of violence in situations of armed conflict, and

---

[176] *Ibid.*, See *Security Council Resolution* 1265 (1999), *para.* 13. *Resolution.*

[177] *Ibid.*, para. 5.

[178] *Ibid.*, 213-214. See also *para.* 10, *Ibid.*

[179] *Ibid.*, 214. See *UN Security Council Resolutions on Children and armed conflicts: Resolutions 1261 (1999); Resolution* 1314 (2000); 1379 (2001); 1460 (2003); 1539 (2004); 1612 (2005); and 1882 (2009).

[180] Tachou-Sipowo, *Ibid.*

calls upon states to take special measures to protect women.[181]

He further points out that the *Resolution* stipulates that those crimes cannot be included in any amnesty provision, and that states have a responsibility to prosecute any perpetrators of such acts. He went on to note that the Council also urges, in the same *Resolution*, that the gender-specificity of needs be taken into account in mine clearance and mine awareness programmes,[182] disarmament, demobilization and reintegration, while men and women should be equally represented among peacekeeping operations personnel, and receive training on gender issues. According to him, the *Resolution* also states that a gender perspective should be adopted when negotiating peace agreements.[183] Finally, he acknowledges the fact that the '*Resolution* breaks new ground, not only in the area of protection, but also in promoting women both as the solution to their own suffering and as active and valuable participants in the restoration of peace and security',[184] and listed measures set forth by the Council to that effect as follows:

1. Increased representation of women at all decision-making levels in national, regional and international institutions and mechanisms for the prevention, management, and resolution of conflict;

2. Increased participation of women at decision-making levels in conflict resolution and peace processes;

---

[181] *Ibid*. See *Resolution* 1325 (2000), preamble and *paras* 9-10.

[182] *Ibid*. preamble.

[183] *Ibid*. See *para*. 8 of *Resolution 1325* (2000)

[184] *Ibid*.

3. The appointment of more women as special representatives and envoys to pursue good offices on behalf of the UN Secretary- General, and the creation of a roster of female candidates for this role;

4. Expansion of the role and contribution of women in United Nations field-based operations, and especially among military observers, civilian police, human rights and humanitarian personnel;

5. Incorporation of a gender perspective and gender component into peace-keeping operations;

6. Training by and guidelines for Member States on the rights and particular needs of women, as well as on the importance of involving women in all peacekeeping and peace-building measures.[185]

The Security Council has concerned itself with a comprehensive assessment of the implementation of these recommendations relating to the promotion of women as agents of peace. *Resolution 1889* (2009) reports the result of the assessment, which has been described as mixed.[186] It is reported to have welcomed some achievements such as the efforts of States to implement *Resolution 1325* (2000) at the national level through action plans,[187] the efforts of the Secretary-General to boost more women to senior United Nations positions, and the establishment of a United Nations Steering Committee on *Resolution 1325* (2000).[188] On the other hand, 'the Council remained concerned about the under-representation of women at all stages of peace processes, and the persistence of

---

[185] *Ibid.*, 214-215. See also paras. 1-6 of *Resolution 1325* (2000)

[186] *Ibid.*, 215.

[187] See *Resolution 1889* (2009), 5 October 2009, 1.

[188] *Ibid.*, 2 – 3.

obstacles to their participation, such as violence and intimidation, insecurity and lack of rule of law, cultural discrimination and stigmatization, lack of access to education, marginalization and lack of funds for efforts to rehabilitate women'.[189]

However, *Resolution 1820* (2008) *on women, peace and security,* besides showing concern about the general situation of women in war and the obstacles to their participation in the promotion of peace, emphasizes on rape and other acts of sexual violence against them during armed conflict.[190] This situation of violence against women, the resolution acknowledges as having intensified since 2000 in the majority of conflicts all over the world.[191]

It has been observed that this phenomenon 'is especially prevalent in Africa, in the bloody conflicts of the DRC, Uganda, the Central African Republic, Sierra Leone, Liberia and Sudan/Darfur'.[192] The Council recognizes that in these conflicts, women and girls are particularly targeted for sexual violence 'including as a tactic of war to humiliate, dominate, instill fear in, disperse and/or forcibly relocate civilian members of a community or ethnic group.'[193] The Council further 'stresses that sexual violence against women can exacerbate armed conflicts and may impede the restoration of peace, and reaffirms its readiness to adopt appropriate measures to address widespread or systematic sexual violence on a

---

[189] *Ibid.,* 2.

[190] Tachou-Sipowo, A-G., *Op.cit.,* 215.

[191] *Ibid.*

[192] *Ibid.*

[193] *Ibid.,* See *Resolution 1820* (2008), 19 June 2008, Preamble

case-by-case basis.'[194] Finally, *Resolution* 1820 (2008) recommends both short and long term action to be taken by the United Nations.

In the short term, 'the Council can condemn all forms of sexual violence committed in armed conflicts,[195] demand their immediate cessation,[196] and take targeted measures against parties to conflicts who commit these crimes'.[197] Longer term measures include 'promoting activities to prevent and address rape and sexual violence, protective action by states in accordance with their obligations, and punishment of the perpetrators of sexual crimes.'

4.2 Legal Framework for the Protection of Women in the Armed Conflicts in Nigeria, DR Congo and Sierra Leone

In this sub-chapter, the nature of the legal frame-work for the protection of women in the armed conflicts in Nigeria, DR Congo and Sierra Leone shall be analyzed and appraised. How the respective countries have responded to the rules of international law which are applicable in times of armed conflict and especially those that are protective of women shall also be considered. This includes a consideration of their accession or ratification, implementation and enforcement of such rules.

In order to determine the applicable law at any material time during the foregoing armed conflicts, it shall be necessary to make a finding or acknowledge the findings of relevant authorities

---

[194] *Ibid.*, See also *Para 1, Ibid.*

[195] See preamble to *Resolution 1820* (2008), *Ibid.*

[196] *Ibid.*, para. 2.

[197] *Op.cit.*, 216.

(including the courts) with regard to whether or not the state of armed conflict exists or existed, and if so, also classify or characterize the armed conflict, in terms of whether it be international, non-international or internationalized. By so doing, we would be determining the relevant legal and institutional frame-work for the protection of women in the respective armed conflicts.

Nigeria

(i) **International Legal Frame-work:** Here relevant treaties that were acceded to or ratified by Nigeria shall be considered. However, before considering Nigeria's commitment to implementing and enforcing relevant international law obligations, it is necessary to review her status in terms of subscription to international law rules or treaties that regulate armed Conflicts, including related human rights instruments. For instance, Nigeria has signed and ratified or acceded to a number of international Legal Instruments that regulate armed conflicts and those that seek to protect women, especially in times of armed conflicts. They include the following:[198] *Geneva Conventions* I – IV, 1949;[199] *Additional Protocol* I, 1977;[200] *Additional*

---

[198] The list covers ratifications as at 30 may, 2013

[199] Ratified 20-06-1961. See *Geneva Convention for the Amelioration of the Condition of the wounded and Sick in Armed forces in the field* of August 12,1949 (*Geneva Convention I).' Geneva Convention. For the Amelioration of the Condition of wounded, Sick and Shipwrecked Members of Armed forces at see* of 12 August 1949 (*Geneva Convention II).' Geneva Convention Relative to the Treatment of Prisoners of war* of 12 August 1949 (*Geneva Convention* III); and *Geneva Convention Relative to the Protection of Civilian Persons in Time of War* of 12 August 1949.

[200] *Protocol Additional to the Geneva Conventions of 12 August, 1949 and Relating to the Protection of Victims of International Armed Conflicts (Protocol I)* of 8 June 1977. Ratified 10-10-1988.

Protocol II, 1977[201] *Additional Protocol I, Article 90,*[202] *Additional Protocol III,2005*[203]; *Child Rights Convention, 1989;* [204] *Optional Protocol to the Child Rights Convention, 2000*[205]; *Rome Statute of the International Criminal Court, 1998;*[206] The *Hague Convention Relative to the Protection of Cultural Property 1954;*[207] *Protocol to the Hague Convention, 1954;*[208] *Protocol to the Hague Convention, 1999;*[209] *Environmental Modification Convention, 1976;*[210] *Convention Relative to the Status of Refugees, 1951, Convention on the Elimination of All Forms of Discrimination Against Women* (CEDAW), *1979;*[211] and *Optional Protocol to the Convention on the Elimination of all Forms of Discrimination Against Women* (CEDAW), *1999*[212].

However, besides these instruments, Nigeria also ratified the following instruments among others on the regulation of weapons: *Geneva Gas protocol, 1925; Bacteriological Weapons Convention (BWC), 1972; Chemical Weapons Convention (CWC),1993;* and *Additional*

---

[201] *Protocol Additional to the Geneva Conventions of August 1949 and Relating to the Protection of Victims of Non- International Armed Conflicts (Protocol II), of 8 June,* 1977. Ratified 10-101988.

[202] Not yet ratified.

[203] Not yet ratified.

[204] United Nations *Convention on the Rights of the Child,* 1989 ratified on 19-04-1991.

[205] Ratified 20-09-2012.

[206] Ratified 27-09-2001

[207] Ratified 5-6-1961

[208] Ratified 5-6-1961.

[209] Ratified 21-10-2005.

[210] Not ratified yet.

[211] Ratified 13-6-1985.

[212] Ratified 2004.

Protocol,(AP) Mine Ban Convention, 1977.[213] She also ratified a plethora of African regional human rights instruments that may have implications for the protection of victims of armed conflict. They include the following: *Treaty Establishing the African Economic Community* (1991/1999)[214]; *Constitutive Act of the African Union* (2000/2001);[215] *Protocol on Pan African Parliament* (2001/2003);[216] *Protocol on the Peace and Security Council* (2002/2003);[217] *African Charter on Human and Peoples Rights* (1981/1986);[218] *Protocol on the African Human Rights Court* (1998/2004);[219] *Protocol on the Africa Charter on Human and Peoples Rights on Women* (2003/2004);[220] *OAU Refugee Convention* (1969/1974);[221] *African Cultural Charter* (1976/1990);[222] *African Children Charter* (1990/1999);[223]

OAU Convention on Nature (1969/1974).[224]

No doubt, the foregoing list of treaties and international legal instruments, which Nigeria has signed, ratified or acceded to, is impressive, but relatively few of them have been domesticated by

---

[213] She has also most recently signed the Cluster munitions Convention by June, 2017, and the Anti-Nuclear weapons convention, by September 2017.

[214] Ratified 31-12-1991

[215] Ratified 29-03-2003.

[216] Ratified 23-12-2003.

[217] Ratified 23-12-2003

[218] Ratified 22-06-1983.

[219] Ratified 20-05-2004

[220] Ratified 16-12-2004

[221] Ratified 23-05-1986

[222] Ratified 24-09-1986

[223] Ratified 23-07-2001

[224] Ratified 02-04-1974

any form of legislation. This has the effect of limiting their application in Nigeria, as implementing the rights so promoted goes beyond the obligation to respect them, which is inherent in the fact of accession or ratification. It encompasses mechanisms for their enforcement in Nigeria, which entails domestic legislation to incorporate them into the *juris corpus* of Nigeria in line with the country's dualist approach to international law.

(ii) National (Domestic) Legal Frame-work: So far, only few of the international instruments ratified by Nigeria have been domesticated accordingly, and they include: the *Geneva Conventions I-IV of 1949*, which have been implemented by domestication as the *Geneva Conventions Act, 1961*[225] (the *Additional Protocols I and II to the Geneva Conventions,* though ratified since 1988, are yet to be domesticated); the *Nigeria Red Cross and Red Crescent Act, 1961*[226] is clearly a domestication legislation for the *International Red Cross treaties,* while the *African Charter on Human and People's Rights* has been implemented by the enactment of the *African Union Charter on Human and People's Right (Ratification and Enforcement) Act.*[227] The *African Charter Act* clearly states that it is a domesticating legislation for *the African Charter on Human and People's Right* and went on to annex the instrument, However unlike it, the *Child Rights Act,* 2003, does not explicitly indicate on its face that it purports to domesticate the United Nations *Convention on the Rights of the Child (CRC),* and *the African Union Charter on the Rights and Welfare of the Child*

---

[225] Cap. G3, *Laws of the federation of Nigeria,* 2004.

[226]Cap. N13, *Laws of the federation of Nigeria,* 2004.

[227] Cap. A9, *Laws of the federation of Nigeria,* 2004.

(*ACRWC*).[228] But a perusal of the *Child Rights Act*, 2003 reveals that in reality, it is intended to implement those conventions since, to a large extent, it conforms to them.[229] In spite of this, in 2005, the United Nations Committee on the Rights of the Child expressed their concern that existing legislations at federal, state and local government levels, in particular the religious and customary laws, did not fully comply with the principles and provisions of the *Convention on the Rights of the Child*.[230]

However, Nigeria cannot be said to have performed well in terms of the number of international instruments which has been domesticated by local legislations. This poor performance may be traced to her dualist approach to domestication of treaties, an approach or system that is currently enshrined under Section 12 of the *1999 Constitution of the Federal Republic of Nigeria*.[231] Section 12 of the 1999 *constitution* provides: 'No treaty between the Federation and any other country shall have the force of law except to the extent to which any such treaty has been enacted into law by the National Assembly.'[232] By this provision, the National Assembly, which is the

---

[228] The two instruments, United Nations *Convention on the Rights of the Child* (CRC), 1989, and the *African Charter on the Rights and Welfare of the Child (ACRWC)*, 1999 were ratified by Nigeria on 19 April 1991, and July, 2001, respectively.

[229] According to the Honorable Minister of Women Affairs, 'The Act gives legal effect to the commitment made by Nigeria under the UN Convention on the Rights of the Child: Egede, *Op.cit*; 269.

[230] Amnesty International, *Nigeria-50 Years of Independence: Making Human Rights a Reality*, London, Amnesty international Publications, 2010, 16.

[231] See Section 1 (2) of the *Constitution (Promulgation) Act*.

[232] The 1999 *Constitution* came into force on 29 May, 1999 with the swearing in of the democratic government of President Olusegun Obasanjo. Previous constitutions of Nigeria contain similar provisions. See Section 69 of the 1960

federal legislative arm of government, is empowered generally to enact legislations for the purpose of implementing treaties. However, for matters outside the Exclusive legislative List, a bill to implement a treaty shall not be presented to the President for his assent, nor shall it be enacted, unless it is ratified by two-third majority of all the legislative houses of the states in the federation.[233] This legislative stricture seems to be one of the reasons for the poor performance of Nigeria in the implementation of international Law standards. Regrettably, it is nothing but 'a mere historical incidence and a colonial relic'.[234] Thus, in the Supreme Court of Nigeria case of *Ibidapo v Lufthansa Airlines,* Wali JSC explained: 'Nigeria like any other common wealth country, inherited the English Common Law rules governing, the municipal application of international law'.[235]

The status and effect of Section 12 (1) of the *Constitution* was examined by the Supreme Court of Nigeria in relation to the *African Charter on Human and Peoples' Rights (the African Charter)* in the case of *Abacha v Fawehinimi (the Abacha* Case).[236] In that case, the applicants filed an application in court against the respondents for among other things, unlawful arrest and detention contrary to the provision of the 1979 *Constitution* (which at the time of his arrest was

---

Constitution; Section 74 of the 1963 Constitution; Section 12 and 13 of the 1979 and 1989 Constitutions, respectively.

[233] See Section 12 (1) of the 1999 Constitution of the Federation of Nigeria; and Egede, E, 'Bringing. Human Rights Home: An Examination of the Domestication of Human Rights Treaties in Nigeria, [October 2007]*Journal of African Law,* [October. 2007], (Vol.51, No2), available at http://journals.Cambridge.Org/abstract 5002 185530700290, 249-284, at 250-251.

[234] *Ibid.*

[235] *Ibidapo v Lufthansa Airli*[1997] 4 NWLRC

[236] [2000] 6NWLR (part 660) 228.

the existing Constitution) and also the provisions of the *African Charter on Human and peoples' Rights (Ratification and Enforcement) Act.*[237] On the other hand, the respondents filed a preliminary objection challenging the jurisdiction of the court to hear the case. They argued that various decrees of the then military government had ousted the jurisdiction of the court to hear the case, while the applicant argued that the provisions of the relevant decrees were inferior to the provisions of the *African Charter* under which he was seeking relief. After hearing the arguments, the trial Judge held that the jurisdiction of the court was ousted and struck out the suit, whereupon the applicant appealed to the Court of Appeal.

The Court of Appeal held *inter alia* that having been enacted into Nigerian domestic law, the *African Charter* had assumed a superior position to all other municipal laws by virtue of its international flavour.[238] Consequently, this decision was followed in several other Court of Appeal cases that dealt with the *African Charter.*[239] Even the Economic Community of West African States (ECOWAS) court supports this view.[240]

---

[237] Cap 10, *Laws of the Federation of Nigeria, 1990. The African Charter on Human Peoples' Rights was domesticated as the African Charter on Human and Peoples' Rights (Ratification and Enforcement) Act (the African Charter Act.)*

[238] *Fawehinmi v Abacha* [1996] 9 NWLR (Part 475) 710 at 747, Per the lead Judgment of Mustapher, JCA.

[239] See for example *Comptroller of Nigeria Prisons & 2 Ors. V Adekanye & 26 Ors* [1999], 10NWLR (Part 623) 400 and *Ubani v Director of State Security Services* [1999] 11 NWRL (Part 625), 129.

[240] In *Socio-Economic Rights and Accountability Project (SERAP) v Federal Republic of Nigeria and Anor.*suit No.ECW/CCJ/APP/08/08,the ECOWAS Court held that the right to education, among others, embodied in chapter2 of the *Constitution of the Federal Republic of Nigeria,* which is non-justiciable, by virtue of Section 6(6)(c) of

The decisions may have been motivated by the well intentioned desire, not only to protect citizens from human rights abuses, by the then military government, but also to ensure that Nigeria honours its international obligations in the human rights treaties it has ratified.[241] However, not being satisfied, the respondents in the *Abacha Case* appealed to the Supreme Court. Like the trial court and the Court of Appeal, the Supreme Court examined *section* 12 1979 *Constitution*, which is identical to the present *section* 12(1) of the 1999 *Constitution* and unanimously confirmed the dualist effect of the section.

The Supreme Court had, in the earlier case of *African Reinsurance Corporation v Abata Fantay*,[242] endorsed the dualist position of the application of treaties in Nigeria, under Section 12 (1) of the Constitution. The case concerned a non- human rights treaty, and the Supreme Court emphatically held that the treaty, though ratified by Nigeria, did not have any force of law because it had not been enacted into law by the federal legislative body. Curiously, even though this case was relevant to the *Abacha case*, the Supreme Court never referred to it.

The judgment of the Supreme Court confirmed that the constitutional requirement of *Section* 12 (1) has the effect of excluding Nigeria's international law obligations from domestic application, by denying them force of law and justiciability. In other words, the

---

the constitution, but which rights are guaranteed by Articles 1,2,17,21 and 22 of the *African Charter on Human and People's Rights* can be enforced in Nigeria as the *African Charter* is assumed to be superior to the *Constitution* by virtue of its international status.

[241] Egede, E. *Op.cit*, 253.

[242] [1986] 3 NWLR (Part 32), 811.

Nigerian people are at the mercy of the legislature, which might deliberately or perhaps unwittingly fail to enact such international standards into domestic legislations. The preposterous and unwarranted oddity of this position is captured by 'the rather disturbing statement of one of the Supreme Court justices' as follows:

> It is therefore manifest that no matter how beneficial to the country or the citizenry an international treaty to which Nigeria has become a signatory may be, it remains unenforceable, if it is not enacted into law of the Country by the National Assembly.[243]

Granted that the judgment of the Supreme Court seems inequitable and unfair, we agree with Egede that to hold otherwise would have resulted in the judicial absurdity of declaring the *African Charter* supreme to the *Constitution* in spite of the clear provision of the *Constitution* which declares the *Constitution* to be the supreme law of the land.[244] There is therefore the need to cure this mischief by amending *section* 12 of the *Constitution* in such a way that it would permit direct application of treaties in Nigeria. After all, under the *Constitution of the United States of America,* on which the 1999 *Constitution* of Nigeria was modeled, 'all treaties made or which

---

[243] *Abacha's Case, Supra,* at 356-357.

[244] *Section* 1 (1) and (3) of the 1999 *Constitution* which is identical to the same section in the 1979 *Constitution* declares: 'This constitution is Supreme and its provision shall have binding force on all authorities and persons throughout the Federal Republic of Nigeria. If any other law is inconsistent with the provisions of the constitution, this constitution shall prevail and that other law shall to the extent of the inconsistency be void'. However, whenever there was military intervention in Nigeria, they usually repeal these provisions of the constitution, and give a supreme status to their legislations in form of decrees.

shall be made, under the authority of the United States, shall be the supreme law of the land; and the judges in every State shall be bound thereby, anything in the *constitution* or laws of any State to the contrary notwithstanding'.[245] However, there has been some difficulty for the American Courts in interpreting *Article* VI, *Clause* 2 of the *American Constitution* which embodies this provision. 'The US Courts have over the years, distinguished between self-executing treaties (having automatic domestic application) and non self executing treaties (requiring implementing domestic legislation)'.[246] Paust had argued that this distinction is a judicial invention which is rather subjective in its application.[247] The lack of 'Clear-cut and objective rules' has resulted in uncertainty in the law, as the United States courts seem to have arbitrarily held treaties to be self-executing, on some occasions, and not to be self executing on some others. This, it has been submitted creates a problem in respect of direct domestic application of certain ratified human rights treaties.[248]

However, it has been suggested that the monistic model which has been applied by most continental European countries may be a

---

[245] See *Article* VI, *Clause* 2 of the US *Constitution*. See also, *Trans world Airlines, Inc. v Franklin Mint Corp.* 466 Us 243 at 252 (1984); *Weinberger v Rossi* 456 US 25 at 32 (1983); *Washington v Washington State commercial passenger Fishing Vessel Association* 443 US 5658 at 690 (1979).

[246] See Forster v Nelson 27 Us (2 Pet) 253 at 254; *Cook v United States* 288 US 102 at 119 (1933); Frolova v USSR 761 f. 2d 370 at 373 (7th Cir. 1985); *People of Saipan v US Department of Interior* 502 F. 2d 90 at 97 (9th Cir. 1974); 420 US 1003 (1975). (All the Foregoing Cases were cited in Egede, E *op. cit*, 279.

[247] Paust, J. J, *International law as law of the United States*, Durham NC, Carolina Academic Press, 1996, 51 as cited in Egede, E, *Ibid*.

[248] Egede, E., *Ibid*.

preferable option for Nigeria rather than the full dualist model of most common law countries or the partial dualist model of the United States of America.[249] It may be noted here that certain African States have adopted the automatic domestic application of treaties in their constitutions. The 1992 *Constitution of Cape Verde* readily comes to mind. It provides:

> International Treaties and Agreements validly approved and ratified shall be in force in the Cape Verdian Judicial system after the official publication as long as they are in force in the international legal system. Rules, principles of international law, validly approved and ratified internationally and internally, and in force, shall take precedence over all laws and regulations below the constitutional level.[250]

The 1992 *Ghanaian Constitution* is another example of a monist system. That of Sierra Leone may also be considered as another, as we may see later in this work.

At this point, it must be noted that though Nigeria is yet to domesticate any of the treaties and international standards on the rights of women, many State Houses of Assembly have passed laws

---

[249] It has been observed that the *Constitutions* of most continental European Countries recognize that treaties ratified by the State, including human rights treaties automatically become part of the law of the land, without any distinction between self executing and non self executing treaties. For example, art. 55 of the 1958 *French Constitution* provides that treaties duly ratified published shall operate as laws within the municipal setting and States: 'Treaties or agreement duly ratified or approved shall upon their application, have an authority superior to that of laws, subject for each agreement or treaty to its application by the other party'.

[250] Egede, E., *op cit*. Also available at <http: //capeverde–islands. Com/ cv constitution. htm1# P1t2> (last accessed 17 May 2017).

which seem to have been inspired by the provisions of such international treaties on women which Nigeria had ratified. This may be construed as an indirect means of implementing such instruments. Such laws that have been passed by the State Houses of Assembly in Nigeria, which have implications for the rights of women include: *Cross River State law to prohibit Domestic Violence Against Women and Maltreatment;*[251] *Lagos State Protection Against Domestic Violence and Connected Purposes Law;*[252] *Enugu State infringement of widows' and widowers' Right Law of 2001; Edo State, Inhuman Treatment of widows (Prohibition) law,* 2003; *Ekiti State Law Against Gender-Based Violence,* 2001;[253] *Female Circumcision and Genital Mutilation (Prohibition law)* 1999 of Edo State; *Law to Prohibit Girl-Child Marriages and Female Circumcision,* 2000 of Cross River State and *Child Rights laws.*[254] Besides the foregoing indirect ways of implementing non-domesticated human rights treaties, the Courts can also apply non-domesticated human rights treaties by relying on them in the interpretation of similar provisions in the constitution and other municipal or national legislation. In the *Abacha case,* one of

---

[251] Law No.1 of 2004, of Cross River State.

[252] Law No. C 131, 2007.

[253] This law is the first of its kind in the country. It is comprehensive and omnibus in its coverage. Its coverage goes beyond domestic violence to encompass violence within the public sphere.

[254] *Child Rights laws* have been passed in not less than 23 States of the federation, including Lagos, Anambra, Imo, Ebonyi, Nassarawa, Plateau, Ogun, Ekiti, Abia, Rivers, Taraba e.t.c (see Uche, O.L., "Effects of Domestic Violence on Children: A Nigerian Syndrome", Azinge, E. and Uche, L., *Law of Domestic Violence in Nigeria,* Lagos, N.I.A.LS, 2012, 258. It should however be noted that the *Child Rights Laws* derive from the *Child Rights* Act, which is a domestication of the *Convention on the Rights of the Child,* 1989, at the Federal Government level. This is so as the issue of children's welfare is not on the Exclusive Legislative List.

the Justices of the Supreme Court of Nigeria recognized the importance of international human rights instruments in interpreting Local laws.[255] While acknowledging that a treaty not incorporated into national law cannot be enforced, the learned Justice said: 'However, it is also pertinent to observe that the provisions of an unincorporated (sic) treaty might have indirect effect upon the construction of statutes or might give rise to a legitimate expectation by citizens' that the government, in its acts affecting them, would observe the terms of the treaty.[256]

On rare occasions, Nigerian judges have been known to refer to non-domesticated treaties that have been ratified by Nigeria, as persuasive authorities, in aid of interpretation of Nigerian laws. The example of Niki Tobi, JCA (as he then was) readily comes to mind. The learned Justice of the Court of Appeal alluded to the *Beijing Conference and its Platform for Action* and the *Convention on the Elimination of All Forms of Discrimination against Women* in arriving at his decision in *Mojekwu v Ejikeme,* that the Nrachi Nwanyi custom of Nnewi was repugnant and ought to be struck out.[257] He did the same thing at the lower court in the case of *Mojekwu v Mojekwu*.[258]Another way in which human rights treaties can be applied in Nigeria without having first been domesticated by legislation, is if the provisions of the treaty have crystallized into rules of customary international law. This is so, as in Nigeria and most other common law countries, Customary international law applies automatically without the provisions having been enacted into domestic

---

[255] Egede, E, *op. cit.,* 275.

[256] *Abacha case, Supra* at 342.

[257] [2000] 5NWLR, 402.

[258] (1997) 7 NWLR (Pt. 512), 238.

legislations. It is enough that they have become part of *ius congens* and thus assumed the status of customary international law by virtue of widespread usage. In this vein, the International Court of Justice (ICJ) declared as follows, in *Federal Republic of Germany v Denmark and Netherlands* (the North Sea continental shelf cases):[259]

> With respect to the other elements usually regarded as necessary before a conventional rule can be considered to have become a general rule of international law, it might be that, even without the passage of any considerable period of time, a very widespread and representative participation in the convention might suffice of itself, provided it included that of the States whose interests were specially affected.[260]

Most of the human rights and international humanitarian law treaties have been adopted widely by most countries in the world, including Nigeria.[261] It is therefore surprising that the Supreme Court of Nigeria did not consider the possibility of the *African Charter* having crystallized into customary international norm, in the

---

[259] 8 ILM 340 (1960). See also *Military and Paramilitary Activities and Against Nicaragua (Nicaragua v United States of America) (Merits) case [1986] ICJ Rep. 14*

[260] *Federal Republic of Germany v Denmark and Netherlands, Supra.*

[261] gede, E., *op.cit.*, 277, where we have the following record cited as example 'as at 24 April 2017, the number of States parties to the following human rights [instruments] were: *Convention on the Prevention and Punishments of the Crime of Genocide* -140 parties; *Convention on the Elimination of All Forms of Racial Discrimination* -173 parties; *International Covenant on Economic, Social and Cultural Rights* -156 parties; *International Covenant on Civic and Political Rights*-160 parties; *Convention on the Elimination of All Forms of Discrimination Against Women*-185 parties; *Convention of the Rights of the Child*- 193 parties; and *Convention Against Torture and other Cruel, Inhuman or Degrading Treatment or Punishment*-144 parties. This statistics is available at < http://www.ohch.org/english/countries/ ratification/index htm> (last accessed 24 April 2017).

Abacha Case.[262] It is however hoped that the courts in Nigeria would be more activist and pragmatic enough to deploy, as customary international law, most of those international norms, which the country has ratified, in protecting the human rights of individuals, both in peace and in war times. It is equally against this background that the legal framework for the protection of women in the armed conflicts in Nigeria, namely, the Nigerian Civil War and Boko Haram insurgency could be considered.

Without any doubts, Common *Article* 3 to the 1949 *Geneva Conventions* would be applicable to the Nigeria – Biafra armed conflict, the *Conventions* having been acceded to, ratified and domesticated in 1961,[263] shortly after Nigeria's independence. Besides, the Common *Article* 3 to the *Conventions*, the rest of the four *Geneva Conventions* would not apply, as the conflict was an armed conflict of non-international character. If the armed conflict had taken place after 10th October 1988, the *Additional Protocol* II to the *Geneva Conventions* may have applied, as Nigeria ratified that Protocol on 10th October, 1988. Human rights law, especially international human rights law would also apply. So also may the national laws of Nigeria, especially the Criminal and the *Penal Codes* apply in relevant circumstances.

Common *Article* 3 to the four Geneva Conventions enjoins parties to an armed conflict to treat persons taking no active part in the hostilities humanely, in all circumstances, without any adverse distinction founded on race, colour, religion or faith, sex, birth or

---

[262] *Supra.*

[263] See The *Geneva Conventions* Act, Cap G3, *Laws of the Federation of Nigeria,* 2004.

wealth or any similar criteria.[264] It went on to prohibit the following acts as constituting inhumane treatment:

1. Violence to life and person, in particular murder of all kinds, mutilation, cruel treatment and torture;
2. Taking of hostages;
3. Outrages upon personal dignity, in particular humiliating and degrading treatment;
4. The passing of sentences and the carrying out of executions without previous judgment pronounced by a regularly constituted court, affording all the judicial guarantees which are recognized as indispensable by civilized peoples.[265]

Nonetheless, the details of humane treatment were not fully specified unlike we have in the provisions for international armed conflicts.[266] This, as has also been observed by Unegbu, 'necessitated the subsequent adoption of *Additional Protocol* II in 1977, the aim of which was, as much as possible, to fill the gap between the law on international and non-international armed conflicts.[267] Obviously, the provisions of *Additional Protocol* II[268] are more comprehensive and thus better protective than those of *Article* 3 Common to the

---

[264] See *Article* 3(1) common to the *Geneva Conventions* of 1949. See also, Unegbu, M. O., *From Nuremberg Charter to Rome Statute: Judicial Enforcement of International Humanitarian Law*, Enugu, SNAAP Press Ltd., 2015, 242.

[265] *Article* 3 (1)(a) – (d) Common to the *Geneva Conventions*.

[266] Unegbu, *Op.cit.*, 244.

[267] *Ibid.*,244 – 245.

[268] *Protocol Additional to the Geneva Conventions of 12 August 1949, and Relating to the Protection of Victims of Non-International Armed Conflict* (Protocol II).

Geneva Conventions, which could be applicable to the Biafra – Nigeria conflict.

Unegbu seems to have agreed with Umozurike,[269] that the Nigerian Civil War transformed into an international armed conflict when other states or countries intervened on the side of both parties with military and other material assistance, but observes that the exact point in time when the conflict became internationalized may not be easily determined.[270] He therefore endorses Umozurike's view which he quotes thus:

> The Nigerian civil war was complicated by the trappings of recognition for Biafra from Tanzania, Zambia, Gabon, Ivory Coast and Haiti; arms flowed to the federal side from USSR and Britain while Egyptian pilots manned the federal air offensives. Battles were fought on land, sea and in the air. There must have been an indeterminate moment of transition from a civil to an international war.[271]

However, the factual situation does not seem to support the claim of internationalization. A non-international armed conflict or a civil war could be said to have become internationalized when one or more states intervene militarily, either by supplying weapons or by planning and controlling the military activities of the non-state actors[272]. In the Nigerian civil war nothing of the sort happened in

---

[269] See Umozurike, U. O, 'Application of IHL to Civil Conflicts', , [1992], *African Journal of International and Comparative Law* (Vol. 4, pt. 2), 493-505, at, 497 as cited in Unegbu, *Op.cit.*, 245.

[270] Unegbu, *Ibid.*

[271] *Ibid.* 8

[272] See *ICJ Military and Paramilitary Activities case (Nicaragua v USA,* ICJ Reports 1986 at 14; and case1 T-94-1, *Proescutor v Tadic* (1999) ILM vol 38, 15 18 at 1541, para 11.

favour of Biafra. The military interventions by state actors like Britain and Russia were on the side of Nigeria. The countries that recognized Biafra did not seem to have got involved militarily. However, if they did, their action would have actually internationalized the conflict, thereby making the 1949 *Geneva Conventions*, and the *Additional Protocol* I applicable to the conflict. On the contrary, there are no concrete evidence to show that any of the countries that recognized Biafra intervened on her side militarily either by training her forces, supplying arms or fighting alongside her army. Thus, it is here submitted that the Nigerian Civil War remained a non-international armed conflict, which was governed by common *Article* 3 to the *Geneva Conventions* only. *Additional Protocol* II would not apply, as Nigeria was yet to domesticate it. However, the provisions of the four *Geneva Conventions* may also apply as Customary International Law. Definitely, Nigerian Domestic Laws especially Criminal Laws and Human Right Laws would apply.

Democratic Republic of Congo (DR Congo):

(i) **International Legal Frame-work:** DR Congo has ratified a number of International Humanitarian Law treaties.[273] They include the *Rome Statute of International Criminal Court, 1998;*[274] the four *Geneva Conventions;*[275] *Additional Protocols* I and II to the *Geneva*

---

[273] The ratified listed herein are as at 30th may 2013.

[274] Ratified 11th April, 2002.

[275] *Geneva Conventions* 1-IV. Ratified 24th February, 1961.

Conventions;[276] *Convention on the Rights of the child,* 1989;[277] *Optional Protocol to the Convention on the Rights of the child, on the involvement of Children in Armed Conflict,* 2002;[278] *Protocol III, Additional to the Geneva Conventions,* 2005;[279] *Protocol I, Additional to the Rome Statute;*[280] *Amendments to the Rome Statute;*[281] the *Hague Conventions,* 1954;[282] *Protocol I to the Hague Conventions* 1954;[283] and *Protocol II to the Hague Conventions,*1999.[284] Besides the foregoing instruments, DR Congo has also ratified many United Nations *Human Rights Conventions* and has thus made binding international commitments to adhere to the standards laid down in them.[285] However, it is important to emphasize that she also ratified *the Convention on the Elimination of*

---

[276] Ratified 3rd June, 1982 and 12th December, 2002 respectively.

[277] Ratified 27th September, 1990.

[278] Ratified 11th April, 2002.

[279] Not yet ratified.

[280] Ratified 3rd July, 2007.

[281] None has been ratified yet.

[282] Ratified 18th April, 1961

[283] Ratified 18th April, 1961

[284] Not ratified yet.

[285] Such conventions include the *International Covenant on Civil and Political Rights* (ICCPR), 1966 (Ratified 1976), (Last State report, 2005, and Last Concluding Observations, 2006); *International Covenant on Economic, Social and Cultural Rights* (ICESCR) (Ratified 1976), (Last State Report, 2009, and Last Concluding Observation, 2009); *International Convention on the Elimination of All Forms of Racial Discrimination,* 1965 (Ratified 1976) (Last State Report 2006, and Last Concluding Observation 1996); and the *Convention on the Elimination of All Forms of Discrimination Against Women,* 1979 signed and ratified 1980 and 1986, respectively) (Last State Report, 2004) (Last Concluding Observation, 2006). The DR Congo has also ratified the *Convention Against Torture and other Cruel, Inhuman or Degrading Treatment or Punishment,* 1984 (Ratified 1996) (Last State Report, 2005 and Last Concluding Observation, 2006).

All form of Discriminations Against Women and its African regional counterpart, the *Protocol to the African Charter on the Rights of Women in Africa*.[286] This is so as those instruments are gender specific to women and thus aimed at specific protection for women in times of peace and armed conflicts.

(ii) National (Domestic) Legal Frame-work: The primary legislative measure that has been undertaken by the DR Congo is the drafting and subsequent adoption of the *Congolese Constitution* (2006).[287] This constitution enshrines a monistic approach to international law by authorizing 'civil and military courts [to] implement duly ratified international treaties', and by providing that 'duly concluded treaties and international agreements ... have superior authority to that of laws'.[288] Before this development and shortly after DR Congo ratified the *Rome Statute of International Criminal Court*, the Congolese Parliament amended the country's military codes, and granted military courts exclusive jurisdiction over international crimes.[289] However, the draft *law on the domestic implementation of the Rome Statute* (2008) which has been before the Congolese National Assembly proposes to transfer the exclusive jurisdiction over international crimes to the civilian court system.[290] Meanwhile, Congolese Military Courts have been applying the

---

[286] The two instruments were ratified in 1986, and 2009, respectively.

[287] See Constitution of DR Congo (18 February, 2006), available at <*http://www.wipo.Int/wipo.ex/en/text.jsp?fileid=193575*> accessed on 5th March, 2011 (hereinafter: 'DRC Constitution of 2006').

[288] See Articles 153 and 215 of the DRC Constitution of 2006 which provide a legal basis for directly applying international treaty provisions in national cases.

[289] See *DR Congo Military Criminal Code*, Article 161. See also Horovitz, *Op.cit.*, 28.

[290] Horovitz, *Ibid*, 15.

provisions of the *Rome Statute of the International Criminal Court* directly on the basis of the aforementioned constitutional provisions.[291] Unfortunately, 'while the preamble to the revised *Military code* acknowledged that the DR Congo had ratified the *Rome Statute*, of International *Criminal Court*, it did not adopt the statute's definitions of genocide, war crimes, and crimes against humanity, instead the 'Code proposed alternate, unclear definitions'.[292]

Nevertheless, the statute has directly been invoked by the military courts of the country in different provinces, in accordance with the country's monist system.[293] Furthermore, the courts have in addition to referring to the *Rome Statute*, also referred at times to the *'Elements of Crimes' document*.[294] The military courts have also been known to refer to the jurisprudence of the International Tribunals for the Former Yugoslavia and Rwanda.[295]

In the *Songo Mboyo* case,[296] for instance, the courts applied the *Rome Statute* for the first time to convict soldiers of mass rape and sexual violence as crimes against humanity. (It is proposed to consider the military court trials in more details under National Judicial Response later). This means that the courts could as well in

---

[291] *Ibid*, 43.

[292] Adjami, M., and Mushiata, G., 'DR Congo: Impact of the Rome Statute and the International Criminal Court', [May 2010], 27.

[293] In Monist legal systems, an international treaty once ratified is considered incorporated into domestic law.

[294] The *'Elements of Crimes' document* was adopted by the States Parties pursuant to Article 9 of the Rome Statute in order to assist the ICC in interpreting and applying the Rome Statute definitions of international crimes.

[295] Horovitz, *Op.cit.*, 30.

[296] *Mbandaka Military Garrison Court, Songo Mboyo Case*, RPA615/2006 (April 12, 2006)(on file with ICTJ).

the spirit of the country's monist constitution, automatically or directly apply any of the international law instruments and other related treaties which the DR Congo has ratified.[297] The same thing applies to the international instruments on women's right that the DR Congo has ratified, namely, the *Convention on the Elimination of All Forms Of Discrimination against Women* (CEDAW)[298] (otherwise known as *Women Convention*), and The *Protocol to the African Charter on Human and Peoples' Rights on the Rights of Women in Africa* (the Maputo Protocol).[299]

To this end, *Article* 14 of the 2006 Congolese Constitution is salutary as it provides:

> The public authorities see to the elimination of all forms of discrimination against women and ensure the protection and promotion of their rights. They take in all areas, and most notably in the civil, political, economic, social and cultural areas, all appropriate measures in order to ensure the full realization of the potential of women and their full participation in the development of the nation. They take measures in order to fight all forms of violence against women in their public and private life. Women are entitled to equitable representation in national, provincial and local institutions.

The State guarantees the achievement of parity between men and women in said institutions. The law determines the conditions for the application of these rights.

---

[297] See the country's ratification table on International Humanitarian Law Treaties and other treaties infra.

[298] The *Convention* was ratified in 1986.

[299] The *Protocol* was ratified, in February, 2009.

Clearly, this article seeks by necessary implications, to invoke and legislatively implement the letters and the spirit of international women's conventions, and relevant international human rights instruments to which DR Congo has acceded. This resolve is reinforced by *Article* 15 which states:

> The public authorities are responsible for the elimination of sexual violence. International treaties and agreements notwithstanding, any sexual violence committed against any person with the intention to destabilize or to displace a family and to make a whole people disappear is established as a crime against humanity punishable by law.

Besides, the country has adopted or amended a number of laws also in her bid to reinforce the legal status of women. They include: *Law on the Prohibition of Sexual Repression,* 2006; *Equality Law* (yet in the process of being adopted by Parliament as at 2013); Amendments to the *Family Code* and Amendments to the *Labour Code.*[300] However, the fact that the country has neither signed nor ratified the *Protocol to the Women's Convention* is a delimiting factor. This is exacerbated by the lack of implementation measures which translates into the under-representation of women in both public and political life. For instance, in 2010, women made up only 8.4% of members of the National Assembly and 4.6% of Senators.

There was no law or policy to ensure the application of the principles of fair representation and non-discrimination against women, as provided for by *Article* 14 of the *Congolese Constitution.*[301]

---

[300] See Report on Violence against Women in North and South Kivu, in the DR Congo: Alternative report for the Committee on the Elimination of All Forms of Discrimination Against Women presented to the 55th Session, July 8-26, 2013, 2.

[301] *Ibid.*

The electoral law does not set minimum quotas, but merely calls for the representation of women to be taken into account in the compiling of electoral lists.[302]

Legally speaking, the persistence of violations of women's rights is encouraged by the existence of discriminatory legislations. For instance, the country's *Family Code* contains provisions that are particularly discriminatory against women. Article 352 sets a minimum age of marriage for women that is different from that for men (18 for men, 15 for women). Article 355 states that 'women may not remarry until a period of 300 days had passed from the time of dissolution or annulment of the previous marriage. This period ends in the event of child birth'.[303]

Other provisions of the Code have the effect of subjugating women in marriage. *Article* 444 provides that the husband is the head of the household and owes his wife protection, while his wife must obey him. *Article* 445, on the other hand, states that the married couples contribute to the moral and material management of the household under the leadership of the husband. Under article 450 with certain exceptions:

> the wife cannot appear in court on civil matters, acquire, sell, or undertake commitments without the authorization of her husband. If the husband refuses to authorize his wife, authorization may be given by a judge. The husband can give

---

[302] See 'CEDAW Committee Recommendations, August 2006; FIDH, DR Congo: Breaking Impunity', available at www.fidh.org; and Inter parliamentary Union, available at www.ipu.org; for more information on women's rights and the campaign in DR Congo, see: *www.africa4womensrights.org* (cites accessed on 15-12-2016).

[303] *Ibid.*

general authorization, but he still retains the right to revoke it.

Under *Article* 454, only the husband has the right to establish the marital home or residence, while *Article* 467 'establishes discrimination in the area of adultery, as it penalizes adultery by the husband only, in certain circumstances, while adultery by the wife is punishable in all circumstances'.[304] Even the *Congolese Nationality Law*[305] discriminates against women by forbidding their retaining their Congolese Nationality if they married a foreigner.[306] However, *Article* 5 of this law permits women to pass on their Congolese nationality to their descendants in the same way as men. These discriminatory laws presents a conducive background to all manner of violence against women during the armed conflicts in DR Congo, and act as a foil to whatever national implementation mechanism that may be put in place.

Thus, the adoption in July 2006 of two laws on sexual violence,[307] and in January 2009 of a *Child Protection Law*[308] have failed to stem the tide of rape in DR Congo, where rape has been acknowledged as a weapon of war, which has been 'deployed systematically and on a huge scale'.[309] Clearly, with this climate of discriminatory laws and violence, it has not been easy to effectively implement the laws,

---

[304] *Ibid.*

[305] See Law No. 004/24 of 2004.

[306] Article 30.

[307] See Laws No. 06/018 and 06/019, 2006.

[308] See Laws No. 09/001, 2009.

[309] *Convention on the Elimination of All forms of Discrimination Against Women Committee Recommendations*, August 2006, *Ibid.*

while such crimes are also being committed in zones of relative stability.

Sierra Leone

(i) **International Legal Frame-work:** Sierra Leone subscribed to international obligations aimed at implementing and enforcing the following international legal instruments which are relevant to the promotion and protection of women's rights in times of armed conflicts and on the dates indicated herein: The *Geneva Conventions I-IV, 1949;*[310] *Protocol I,* Additional to the *Geneva Conventions, 1977*[311]; *Protocol II Additional to the Geneva Conventions, 1977*[312] ; *Convention on the Rights of the Child* (CRC) 1989[313]; *Optional Protocol on the Convention on the Rights of the Child, 2000*[314]; *Rome Statute of the International Criminal Court* (ICC), 1998;[315] *International Convention of the Elimination of All forms of Racial Discrimination, 1965;*[316] and *International Covenant on Economic, and Socio-Cultural Rights (ICESCR) 1966; and International Covenant on Civil and Political Rights (ICCPR), 1966.*[317] The Country also ratified the following instruments: The *Convention on the Elimination of All Forms of Discrimination Against Women, 1979;*[318] *Convention Against Torture*

---

[310] The Country ratified the Convention on 10-6-1965.

[311] Ratified on 21-10-1986.

[312] Ratified on 21-10-1986.

[313] Ratified on 18-10-1986.

[314] Ratified on 15-05-2002.

[315] Both instruments and their optional Protocol were ratified in 1996.

[316] Ratified 15-09-2000.

[317] Ratified 1967.

[318] Ratified 1988.

(CAT), 1984;[319] *Convention on the Sale of Children, Child Prostitution and child Pornography;*[320] and *Convention on the Rights of Persons with Disability* (CRPD).[321]

Of all these instruments, only the *Convention on the Elimination of All Forms of Discrimination against Women* and the *Protocol to the African Charter on Human and Peoples' Rights on the Rights of Women in Africa* are gender specific. However, all the instruments are relevant to the promotion and the protection of the rights of men and women both in times of peace and in times of armed conflict. For instance, the definition of discrimination under *Article* 1 of the *Convention on the Elimination of All Forms of Discrimination Against Women* (CEDAW) is deemed to include 'gender-based violence precisely because gender-based violence has the effect or purpose of impairing or nullifying the enjoyment by women of human rights' on a basis of equality with men.[322] So also does the kind of sexual violence witnessed in the armed conflict in Sierra Leone violate women's right to be free from discrimination on the basis of sex as provided for under the *International Covenant on Civil and Political*

---

[319] For the above ratification table. See Human Rigts Commission of Sierra Leone Submission to the First Report to Universal Periodic Review Mechansim established by the UN Human Rights Council Resolution 5/1 dated 18 June. 2007 and submitted on the 28th of November. 2010.

[320] Ratified 2011.

[321] Ratfied 2010. For more information on the ratified status of Sierra Leone, See Human Rights Commission of Sierra Leone submission to the first Report to universal Periodic Review Mechanism established by the UN *Human Rights Council Resolution* 5/1 dated 18 June, 2007 and submissitted on the 28th of November, 2010

[322] Women, Law and Development International, *Gender Violence: The Hidden War Crimes*, Washington D.C., Women, Law and Development International, 1998, 37, as cited in Human Rights Watch, *Op.cit.*, 57.

Rights, 1966.[323] Even the *Convention on the Rights of the Child* affords protection to the Sierra Leonean children victims of the armed conflict, especially the girl-child by providing for freedom from discrimination on the basis of gender,[324] and the right to enjoyment of the highest attainable standard of health.[325] Furthermore, states are enjoined to take all appropriate measures to promote physical and psychological recovery and social integration of a child victim of any form of neglect, exploitation, or abuse; torture or any other form of cruel, inhuman or degrading treatment or punishment; or armed conflicts. The Convention also enjoins states to provide special protection and assistance to a child 'temporarily or permanently deprived of his or her family environment.'[326]

International Covenant on Civil and Political Rights and the *Convention on the Elimination of All Forms of Discrimination against Women* forbid slavery and forced prostitution in times of armed conflict as witnessed in Sierra Leone, as it constitutes a basic violation of the right to liberty and security of persons.[327] *Article* 8 of *International Covenant on Civil and Political Rights* which prohibits slavery, which is a *jus cogens* norm from which no derogation is

---

[323] See *Articles* 2(1) and 26, *International Convention on Civil and Political Rights* (ICCPR).

[324] See *Articles* 2, *Child Right Convention.* (CRC).

[325] See *Articles* 24, *Child Right Convention.* (CRC).

[326] *Article* 20(1) of the *Child Right Convention.* (CRC.)

[327] *Article* 9 of the *International Convention on Civil and Political Rights (ICCPR)* provides for the freedom from arbitrary arrest, detention or exile, whilst Article 23 prohibits forced marriage. Under Article 6 of *Convention on the Elimination of Discrimination Against Women* (CEDAW), States are required to take all appropriate measures, including legislation, to suppress all forms of traffic in women and exploitation of prostitution of women.

permitted, also prohibits forced labour.[328] Finally, the *African Charter on Human and Peoples Rights*, to which Sierra Leone is a party, guarantees the 'elimination of every discrimination against women… and protection of the rights of the woman and the child'.[329]

The country also ratified the *Maputo Protocol*, that is, the *Protocol to the African Charter on Human and Peoples' Rights on the Rights of Women in Africa*. However, it is yet to ratify a number of international human rights treaties, which include the *Optional Protocol to the Convention on the Elimination of All forms of Discrimination Against Women and the Optional Protocol to the Convention Against Torture and Other Cruel, Inhuman and Degrading Treatment or Punishment*.[330]

(ii) National (Domestic) Legal Frame-work: The government of Sierra Leone has domesticated some of the foregoing international legal instruments discussed or mentioned earlier. For instance, those legal instruments that provided for the right to freedom from slavery and any form of torture or any punishment or other treatment, which is inhuman or degrading have been domesticated by express incorporation into the *Sierra Leonean Constitution*. The *Constitution* provides, in *section* 19(1), for the right to freedom from slavery.[331] It

---

[328] Human Rights Watch, *Op.cit.*, 58. See also *United Nations, Slavery Convention of 1926*, Treaty Series, Vol. 212, July 7, 1955, 17.

[329] *Article* 3 of the *African Charter on Human and Peoples Rights,* adopted June 27, 1981 (Organization of African Unity Doc. CAB/LEG/67/3 rev. s, 21 I.L.M 58, 1982. Sierra Leone signed and ratified this treaty on August 27, 1981 and September 21, 1993, respectively.

[330] Amnesty International, Sierra Leone: Submission to the UN Universal Periodic Review, 24th Session of the UPR working Group, January 2016, 2.

[331] See The *Constitution of Sierra Leone* (1991, chapter III – The Recognition and Protection of Fundamental Human Rights and Freedoms of the Individual, S. 19(1).

also prohibits 'any form of torture or any punishment or other treatment which is inhuman or degrading'.[332]

Sierra Leone has also domesticated the *Convention on the Elimination of All Forms of Discrimination against Women* in 2007. This resulted in the enactment of a number of Gender Acts, namely: *Domestic Violence Act*, 2007; the *Child Rights Act*, 2007; the *Legal Aid Act*, 2012; the *Convention on the Elimination of All Forms of Discrimination Against Women Act*, 2007 and the *Sexual Offences Act*, 2012. Other relevant domestic legislations include the *Anti Human Trafficking Act*, 2005; the *Right to Access Information Act*, 2013 and the *Correction Act*, 2014.

Until the passage of the new *Sexual Offences Act*, 2012, the formal legal protection accorded to women in Sierra Leone was based on the outdated *Offences against the Persons Act*, 1861, and the *Christian Marriage Act*, 1960.[333] However, despite the enactment of the new Acts, the Human Rights Commission of Sierra Leone observes that the rate of violence against women has remained high, as shown by the volume of complaints it receives.[334] It therefore urges the Sierra Leonean government to take more hostile and aggressive steps in dealing with perpetrators of gender-based violence, as it considers violence against women as inhuman and degrading.[335]

The Commission further observes that the practice of female genital cutting or mutilation (FGM) has remained prevalent in Sierra

---

[332] *Ibid.*, S. 20(1).

[333] Cap 95 of the *Revised Law of Sierra Leone*, 1960. See also Human Rights Watch, *Op.cit.*, 57.

[334] *Ibid.*

[335] *Ibid.*

Leone in spite of the provisions against harmful traditional practices against children in the *Child Rights Act* (CRA), 2007.[336] It blames this on government's failure to take actions that would demonstrate the political will to address the phenomenon which has continued to undermine and violate the right to liberty and security of persons.

However, traditional, political and family interventions have continued to pose a challenge in addressing issues of female genital mutilation to the extent that the clause that prohibits female genital mutilation in the 2007 *Child Rights Act* has been deleted due to pressure. Thus, the practice is no longer explicitly prohibited by law.

On the whole, it remains to be observed that as a non-international armed conflict, the applicable laws are Common *Article 3* to the *Geneva Conventions*; *Protocol* II, Additional to the *Geneva Conventions*; Human rights law; and Sierra Leonean domestic or national laws. Customary International Law and International Criminal Law, particularly, the *Rome Statute*, may also apply. Most of these laws, especially Common Article 3 apply to the conflict through their prohibition of 'outrages upon personal dignity, in particular humiliating and degrading treatment'. Moreover, Common *Article* 3 implicitly condemns sexual violence.

Article 4 of *Protocol* II also applies to this conflict in Sierra Leone, and expressly forbids 'violence to life, health and physical or mental well-being of persons, in particular murder, as well as, cruel treatment, such as torture, mutilation or any form of corporal punishment' and 'outrages upon personal dignity in particular humiliating and degrading treatment, rape and enforced prostitution and any form of indecent assault' as well as 'slavery and

---

[336] *Ibid.*

the slave trade in all their forms.[337] The foregoing provision 'reaffirms and supplements Common *Article* 3… [because] it became clear that it was necessary to strengthen … the protection of women … who may also be the victims of rape, enforced prostitution or indecent assault'.[338] Unfortunately, the provision is couched in such language that mis-characterizes crimes of sexual violence and particularly rape 'as attacks against the honour of women or an outrage on personal dignity as opposed to attacks on physical integrity'.[339] This mis-characterization has generally been viewed as diminishing the serious nature of the crime and contributing to the widespread misperception of rape as an attack on honour, which of course is an 'incidental' or 'lesser' crime than such crimes as torture or enslavement.[340] This belies the fact that rape is 'an assault on human bodily integrity as well as one that dishonours the perpetrator and not the victim'.[341]

4.3 Institutional Frame-Work for the Protection of Women in the Armed Conflicts in Nigeria, DR Congo and Sierra Leone

Many national and international organs, organizations and bodies play key roles in the protection of women's rights, in the

---

[337] *Protocol II, Article* 4(2)(a), (e) and (f).

[338] Sandoz, C., and others, (eds.), *ICRC Commentary on the Additional Protocols of June 1977 to the Geneva Conventions of 12 August 1949*, Geneva, Martinus Nijhoff, 1987, 1375, para. 4539.

[339] Human Rights Watch, *Op.cit.*

[340] *Ibid*. See also Niarchos, C. N, 'Women, War and Rape: Challenges facing the International Criminal Tribunal for the Former Yugoslavia', [1995], *Human Rights Quarterly*, (Vol. 17), 672.

[341] Human Rights Watch, *Ibid.*

event of armed conflicts. Such organs, organizations and bodies constitute the institutional framework for the protection of women in armed conflicts. They are usually judicial, quasi judicial or administrative in nature, and include international tribunals and special courts, the International Criminal Court (ICC), the International Court of Justice (ICJ), the International Committee of the Red Cross (ICRC), United Nations High Commission on Refugees (UNHCR), the United Nations and the United Nations Security Council (UNSC), United Nations High Commission on Human Rights (UNHCHR), National Committees and similar bodies on International Humanitarian Law, National Refugees Commissions, the Police, the Prisons, the Judiciary and national courts, etcetera.

It is therefore against this background that the effectiveness or otherwise of some of these international and national institutions that may be involved in the protection of women in the armed conflicts in Nigeria, DR Congo and Sierra-Leone shall be considered.

Nigeria: In Nigeria, the Army, the Police, the Prisons and the Judiciary which ought to be the basic institutional framework for the protection of citizens, and women in particular, in times of armed conflict hardly serve as such due to indiscipline and general lack of sufficient professionalism. There does not seem to be any record of these institutions having played a role in protecting women in either the Nigeria-Biafra war or the present war against *Boko Haram* insurgency. Rather Amnesty International claims to have received consistent reports that women have been raped or sexually abused by the Police in the streets, while being transferred to police stations, while in custody, or when visiting male detainees[342]. The reports further state that rape and other forms of sexual violence or the threat of torture and ill-treatment are used by the Police to extract confessions or other information; and that method include insertion of foreign objects, such as bottles into the woman's vagina.

Regrettably, there seems not to be investigations yet, into these allegations and incidents, neither has anyone been prosecuted in the country, for gender-based violence or rape in the on-going war against *Boko Haram* insurgency. However, there are indications that the International Criminal Court[343] and some foreign jurisdictions may intervene on the basis of complementary or universal jurisdiction, respectively.

The Office of the Prosecutor at the International Criminal Court has determined that there is a reasonable basis to believe that crimes against humanity have been committed in Nigeria, namely acts of

---

[342] See Amnesty International, 'Nigeria: Boko Haram and Nigerian Military committing crimes under international law in north east Nigeria' (Amnesty International written statement to the 28th session of the UN Human Rights Council) (2-27 March, 2015)

[343] The International Criminal Court was established pursuant to the *Rome Statute of the International Criminal Court*, 1998, as permanent institution which is empowered to exercise jurisdiction over persons for the most serious crimes of international concern, which are embodied in the statute. The Court is imbued with a jurisdiction that is complementary to national criminal jurisdictions. Whereas, the seat of the court is established at the Hague in the Netherlands, 'the court may sit elsewhere whenever it considers it desirable as provided in this statute', under Article 3. Furthermore, the court shall have international legal personality, and such legal capacity as be necessary for the exercise of its functions and the fulfillment of its purpose. Importantly, the jurisdiction of the court covers gendered crimes against women, which may be tried under the provisions on Genocide, crimes against humanity and war crimes.

murder and persecution which are attributed to *Boko Haram* insurgents. The Prosecutor has therefore decided that preliminary examination of the situation in Nigeria should advance to Phase 3 (Admissibility) with a view to assessing genuine proceedings in relation to those who appear to bear the greatest responsibility for such crimes and the gravity of such crimes.[344]

Unfortunately, despite apparent gender-based violence against women and other violations of International Humanitarian Law that are perpetrated by *Boko Haram,* the Nigerian judiciary and its courts have failed to prosecute suspects accordingly. The Federal High Court[345] is the proper forum for trying such violations of international humanitarian law[346], while appeals from the court shall lie with the Federal Court of Appeal, and ultimately the Supreme Court[347]. The few cases that have been tried, at the Federal High Court, were tried under the Terrorism Act, rather than under International Humanitarian Law. Clearly, this is a pointer to the poor implementation of international humanitarian law, in the country,

---

[344] See International Criminal Court (ICC), 'Situation in Nigeria, under Article 5 Report, dated 5 August, 2013. The International Criminal Court also observes that although there are allegations against Nigerian Security forces in the context of their serious human rights violations, the information available as of December 2012 does not provide a reasonable basis to believe that the alleged crimes were committed pursuant to or in furtherance of a State or Organization policy to attack the civilian population.

[345] See Section 247 of the *Constitution of the Federal Republic of Nigeria* for the Establishment and composition of the
Federal High Court.

[346] See Section 252 (8) of the *Constitution of the Federal Republic of Nigeria.*

[347] See Sections 239 and 231 of the Constitution respectively.

despite the establishment of the National Committee on International Humanitarian Law[348].

The National Committee of International Humanitarian Law of Nigeria has the mandate to serve as an important point of contact in relation to the adoption and domestic implementation of International Humanitarian Law treaties[349]. Its work is to support the national authorities in the following ways:

i). To submit advisory opinions to national authorities;

ii). To assist the government in implementing and disseminating International Humanitarian Law.

iii). To evaluate existing domestic law and make recommendations for further implementation[350].

On the whole, the work of the committee is meant to be part of the broader task of promoting respect for human rights. The committee also serves as a vehicle for building public confidence and trust in the legal process[351].

Unfortunately, the National Committee which was inaugurated on 23rd July 2010, by the Attorney General of the Federation and

---

[348] See generally, Okorie, H. S., The Role of National Committee in the Enforcement of International Humanitarian Law, 2016 (An unpublished Ph.D. Thesis) (Abia State University, Uturu).

[349] See National Committees and similar Bodies on International Humanitarian Law available at www.icrc.org/en/document/table-nationl-committees-and-other-national-bodies-international-humanitarian-law (accessed 12th September, 2018)

[350] *Ibid.*

[351] *Ibid.*

Minister of Justice, and which enjoys a broad based representation[352] was as at 31st July, 2018, yet to receive the necessary legal *imprimatur* by being enacted into law by the National Assembly. Though, the committee has met a few times, it is yet to be funded, and thus has not been able to effectively take-off. However, its work is complemented by the work of the National Human Rights Commission of Nigeria.

The National Human Rights Commission reports to the office of the High Commissioner on Human Rights. The *Office of the High Commissioner for Human Rights* (OHCHR) was established in 1993 by member states of the United Nations by a General Assembly Resolution of that year[353]. The office is mandated to promote and protect the enjoyment and full realization by all people, of all rights established in the charter of the United Nations and in international human rights laws and treaties. Its mandate also 'includes preventing human rights violations, securing respect for all human rights, promoting international cooperation to protect human rights; coordinating related activities throughout the United Nations and strengthening and streamlining the United Nations systems in the

---

[352] The Committee whose chairmanship and secretariat rests with the Solicitor General of the Federation and the Permanent Secretary in the Federal Ministry of Justice has representatives from the following parastatals and institutions: Foreign Affairs, Defence, Justice, Interior, Finance, Tourism, Culture and National Orientation, Health, Education, Women's Affairs and Social Development, Defence Headquarters, National Commission for Refugees, National Human Rights Commission, Migrants and IDPs, Office of the Secretary to the Government of the Federation, National Population Commission, Scholars, and the Secretary General of the Nigerian Red Cross Society,

[353] See 'Office of the High Commissioner on Human Rights available at www.ohchr.org/EN/About us/pages/missionstaement.aspx (accessed on 12th September, 2018)

field of human rights. The office is also known to champion efforts to integrate a human rights approach within the work of the United Nations agencies. Thus, most of the United Nations agencies or bodies rely on the office for both substantive and secretariat support in discharging their duties.

While the institution's West African Regional Office (WARO) was established in 2008, to help bridge gaps in human rights implementation at the national and regional levels, Nigeria is one of those countries where it has no presence[354]. However, Nigeria has established a National Human Rights Commission.

The National Human Rights Commission was established by the *National Human Rights Commission Act* 1995 as amended in 2010. The Commission has the mandate to deal with all matters relating to the protection of human rights in Nigeria as guaranteed by the *Nigeria Constitution,* the *African Charter on Human and Peoples Rights*, the *United Nations Charter,* the *Universal Declaration on Human Rights* and other international human rights treaties to which Nigeria is a party.[355]

The Committee on the Elimination of Discrimination against Women is the notable gender-specific institution that serves to protect women both in peace and war time. It is the body of independent experts that monitors implementation of the *Convention*

---

[354] See 'OHCHR – West Africa Regional Office (2010 –2011)' available at www. Such other countries include Benin, Burkina Faso, Cape Verde, Gambia, Ghana and Mali

[355] See Report of the National Human Rights Commission of Nigeria on State of Comphance with International Minimum standards of Human Rights by Nigeria under the Universal Periodic Review Mechanism at the 2nd Cycle, 17th Session, October, 2013.

on the Elimination of All Forms of Discrimination against Women[356]. The committee consists of 23 experts on women's rights from around the world[357].

State parties to the treaty are required to submit regular reports to the Committee on how the rights provided by the Convention are implemented in their country. The committee considers each state party's report, during its sessions, and addresses its concerns and recommendations to the state party in the form of concluding observations[358].

The committee is mandated under the *Optional Protocol to the Convention*, to: (i) receive communications from individuals or groups of individuals who submit claims of violations of rights protected under the convention to the committee and (ii) initiate inquiries into situations of grave or systematic violations of women's rights. The foregoing procedures are optional and are only available. The committee may also formulate general recommendations and suggestions. Such general recommendations are directed to States and concern articles or themes in the *Conventions*[359].

Under this procedure, the committee reviewed the implementation record of Nigeria under the *Convention* in July, 2017. This review was based on the report submitted by Women International League for Peace and Freedom (WILPF), in coalition

---

[356] See 'Committee on the Elimination of Discrimination Against Women' available at www.ohchr.org/EN/HRBodies/CEDAW/pages/introduction.aspx

[357] *Ibid.*

[358] *Ibid.*

[359] *Ibid.*

with seven women's rights organizations[360]. It highlighted the gaps in the implementation of the *Convention* in Nigeria, with specific attention to Women, Peace and Security issues[361] and 'formulates recommendations on five themes namely: conflict prevention, discrimination and gender-based violence, women's space in political and public life, the situation of rural women and the education of women and girls[362].'

Based on the foregoing report, the Committee on the Elimination of all Forms of Discrimination:

> enquired about the implementation of the Second National Action Plan on UN Security Council Resolution 1325 across all states of Nigeria; how Nigeria intended to monitor and halt the proliferation of small arms and light weapons, and Nigeria's plans to deal with the violent clashes and deadly attacks arising from the competition for natural resources between farmers and Fulani herders in many areas of the country, which have had a dramatic impact on the lives and security of girls and women.[363]

---

[360] The organizations are namely: Arike Foundation, Dorothy Njemanze Foundation (DNF), Federation of Muslim

Women Association of Nigeria (FOMWAN), Initiative For Sustainable Peace, West Africa Network for Peace Building (WANEP), Women's Right Advancement and Protection Alternative (WRAPA), Women for Skill Acquisition Development and Leadership Organization (WOSADLO).

[361] See 'Outcome of CEDAW Review of Nigeria: More Action Needed to Implement the WPS Agenda, available at //http://tbinternet.ohchr.org (accessed on 12th September, 2018)

[362] *Ibid.*

[363] *Ibid.*

In its concluding observations, the committee recommends the following actions to Nigeria:

1. On the issue of conflict prevention:

> ... to ensure the effective regulation of small arms and light weapons, to allocate an adequate budget to the implementation of the NAP on 1325, to ensure the participation of women in conflict prevention, as well as to protect women and girls that are disproportionately affected by the attacks carried out by the Fulani herdsmen. Such protection should ensure that the perpetrators of such attack including gender-based violence, are arrested, prosecuted and punished with appropriate sanctions.[364]

2. On the issue of Discrimination and gender-based violence:

> ...the Committee called on Nigeria to domesticate the Violence Against Persons Prohibition Act, Child Rights Act, and the CEDAW Convention in all states; to expedite the adoption of the Gender and Equal Opportunities Bill; and to address the root causes of trafficking of women and girls, including addressing their economic situation.

The Committee also made specific recommendations on the issue of women's inheritance rights and on child marriage; and on access to legal support and safe shelters for women survivors of violence.

---

[364] See UN Committee on the Elimination of Discrimination Against Women (CEDAW), Concluding Observations of

the Committee on the Elimination of Discrimination against Women: Nigeria, paragraph 16(e) 21 July, 2017, CEDAW/C/NGA/CO/7-8, available at: http://tbinternet.ohchr.org/-layouts/treatybodyexternal/Download.aspx?symbolno=CEDAW%2fNGA%2fCO2f7-8&Lang=en (accessed on 14/2/019)

The Federal Ministry of Women Affairs and Social Development has been the relevant institution of government that deals with matters of gender and women's rights in Nigeria, both in peace and in war time. The Ministry sponsored the adoption of a *National Gender Policy* in 2006 in a bid to implement the country's obligations with respect to international concern for gender equality, equity and justice. This policy which replaced an earlier one has been described as elaborate and practical[365]. In 2008, the country further adopted a counterpart document, 'the *Strategic Implementation Framework and Plan for the National Gender Policy*[366], sponsored by the ministry and which was meant to facilitate the implementation of the policy. The framework and plan is unique for incorporating benchmarks, goals, and a performance appraisal system.

The National Gender Policy Strategic Development Results Framework make provisions for gauges, such as outcomes,[367] indicators,[368] Responsible Agencies,[369] Timelines,[370] Outputs,[371] and

---

[365] Ibezim, E.C., "Gender-based Domestic Violence in Nigeria: A Socio-Legal Perspective", Azinge, E. and Uch, L., *Law of Domestic Violence in Nigeria,* Lagos, N.I.A.L.S, 2012, 226.

[366] See the *National Gender Policy Strategic Implementation Framework and Plan* produced by the Federal Ministry of Women Affairs and Social Development, Abuja, 2008,2.

[367] Outcomes are results that the whole country is working towards and not achieved only as a result of National Gender Policy.

[368] Indicators are those variables that would show the level of commitments made.

[369] Responsible Agencies are network of actors, institutions and agencies strategically charged with certain actions.

[370] Timelines are dates at which desired results are expected.

[371] Outputs are actual results from the implementation of National Gender Policy of 5 years.

Strategic Interventions.[372] These bench marks and gauges are what ensure that the strategies are not only practical, but indeed result-oriented.[373] The strategic framework has been 'designed to utilize prescribed and related strategies of the policy outcomes in a systematic approach that promotes coherence among the intricate network of actors, institutions and agents. [374]

The *Strategic Framework and Plan of the National Gender Policy* identified five critical areas (by synchronizing sixteen key thematic areas that cut across several sectors), namely:

i). Cultural re-orientation and sensitization to change gender perceptions and stereotypes;

ii). Promotion of women's human rights and in particular focusing on sexual and gender-based violence and in supporting new legislations that promote and protect legal rights of women;

iii). Promoting the empowerment of women and integrating gender with key sectors as highlighted within the *National Gender Policy* (agricultural/Rural Development; Environmental/ National Resources; HIV/AIDS Health and reproductive Health/Rights; Education/ Training; Labour/Employment);

iv). Women's political participation and engendered governance including gender and conflict management and;

---

[372] These are those strategic actions that are required under the Strategic Implementation Framework and Plan.

[373] Ibezim, E.C., *Op.cit*.

[374] *Ibid*.

v).   Supporting institutional development including the use of internet communication Technology (ICT) and building strategic partnerships, including identifying new partnerships with men's organizations, faith-based organizations and traditional institutions.

The office of the *United Nations High Commissioner for Refugees* (UNHCR) also known as the UN Refugee Agency is the leading organization that aids and protects people that are forced to flee their homes due to violence, conflict, persecution, war or natural disaster. In keeping with its global mandate, the organization works to safeguard the rights and well being of internally displaced persons (IDPs), refugee returnees, refugees and asylum seekers and persons of concern in the Economic Community of West African States (ECOWAS) region[375]. For instance, the office of the High Commissioner for Refugees has inspite of the challenges posed by the *Boko Harram* violence and the military counter terrorism operations 'completed a number of multi-sector and sector-specific rapid needs assessments and monitoring visits in the six states of the North East.[376]' Following these needs assessments, the United Nations Refugee Agency has striven to ensure, in collaboration with the Nigeria National Refugee Commission and other agencies, that displaced persons are granted safe refuge, including shelter, food, water, medical care and other life-saving assistance.

---

[375] See 'UNHCR in Nigeria' available at http://unhcr.ng/unhcr-in-nigeria-sitaution.php (accessed on 20/1/019)

[376] *Ibid.*

The United Nations High Commissioner for Refugees (UNHCR) has, since its formation by the United Nations General Assembly in 1950, received the Nobel Peace Prize, for helping millions of refugees restart their lives, after many debilitating armed conflicts[377].

At this point, the International Red Cross and Red Crescent Movement must be considered, as one of the major institutional actors in the protection of victims of armed conflicts, and especially women. Originally, its component parts are the International Committee of the Red Cross (ICRC), and the national societies[378].

The International Committee of the Red Cross was formally established in 1863, following Henry Dunant's account of the battle of Solferino[379]. It was established as a private association of Swiss citizens and has since then played an important role in the development and implementation of International Humanitarian Law[380]. The *Statute of the Movement* describes it as having 'a status of its own' (sui generis)[381].

---

[377] *Ibid*.

[378] Kalshoven, F., and Zegveld, L., *Constraints on the Waging of War: An Introduction to International Humanitarian Law* (4th edn.), Cambridge, Cambridge University Press, 2011, 276. The national societies are known as the Red Cross or Red Crescent and later include the Israeli Magen David Adom, or Red Shield of David and presently includes the Red Crystal.

[379] Dunant, H., A Memory of Solferino, (English Version) Geneva (1862), American Red Cross, 1939, 1959.

[380] Melzer, N., International Humanitarian Law: A Comprehensive Introduction, Geneva, ICRC, 313.

[381] *Statute of the International Red Cross and Red Crescent Movement*, adopted by the 25th International Conference of the Red Cross at Geneva in October 1986 and amended by the 26th International Conference of the Red Cross and Red Crescent.

Thus, as a private association under Swiss law, 'the ICRC is not an intergovernmental organization'[382], neither does it qualify as a typical non-governmental organization. For instance, the organization has acquired an 'international legal personality (which) enables it to sign headquarters agreements with states to provide its personnel, premises and correspondence with diplomatic protection'[383]. This notwithstanding, the ICRC's headquarters and employees in Geneva remain subject to Swiss law, while Switzerland recognizes and respects its international mandate[384]. Importantly, the fact that in 1990, the United Nations General Assembly granted it observer status has been taken as a further illustration of its *sui generis* status[385].

Generally, the International Committee of the Red Cross intervenes to protect people who are affected by armed conflicts and other situations of violence in order to alleviate their sufferings as stipulated in the *Geneva Conventions*. It does this by assuming and discharging two functions:

(a) Being present and active wherever and whenever there is armed conflict or other situations of violence to protect the people affected and to provide them assistance.

---

[382] Melzer, N., *Op.cit.*, 314

[383] *Ibid.*

[384] *Ibid.*

[385] See United Nations General Assembly Resolution 45/6 of 16 October, 1990.

(b) Promoting and helping to formulate treaties, which lessen unnecessary human loss of life while still achieving military advantage in armed conflicts[386].

It is in the context of these functions that the International Committee of the Red Cross intervened to center for war victims, including women and children in the Biafra-Nigeria Civil War (1967 – 1970) and the on-going war against *Boko Harram* insurgency.

Reminiscing on Biafra, Professor Emma Okoronta pays tribute to the International Committee of the Red Cross during the occasion of the celebration of Henry Dunant's 150-year-old legacy. He expresses his appreciation 'for the rations of corn meal, Quaker Oats, dried eggs, milk and iodine that stopped tetanus from eating up our limbs.... . For teaching our mothers to cook the sour leaves so that we could get protein...'[387] On the other hand, in the case of war against *Boko Harram* terrorist insurgency, the International Committee of the Red Cross worked to assist thousands of displaced persons and to mobilize state authorities to provide food and water. While the National Emergency Management Agency (NEMA) distributed basic food items, 'the Red Cross gave additional supplies such as cooking oil, salt, onions, tomatoes, and pepper[388]'. The Red Cross also mobilized the police and public services to begin the important task of collecting the dead from the streets, and took the lead in organizing *ad hoc* shelter for the displaced people. 'In particular, the Red Cross closely monitored the plight of kidnapped persons mostly

---

[386] Newsletter, 'Promoting International Humanitarian Law', Abuja, ICRC, March, 2010, 2.

[387] *Ibid*. 4

[388] *Ibid*., 6.

women and children – forcefully taken from different states in the north into Maiduguri, until their eventual repatriation back to their places of origin. Finally, it is important to note that in most of these activities, the International Committee of the Red Cross work together with the Nigerian Red Cross Society[389]. It however, remains to acknowledge that the organization has sponsored studies on the impact of armed conflicts on women, and worked to promote and protect their rights in the event of armed conflicts.

DR Congo: Understandably, the Congolese national justice system comprising of the Judiciary, the Police and the Prisons were thoroughly degraded by protracted armed conflict, thereby making it difficult, if not impossible to arrest, prosecute or punish violators of international humanitarian law, especially perpetrators of sexual violence.[390] There is therefore no doubt that the Congolese national justice system seriously lacks the capacity to live up to the challenges of post-conflict justice delivery. The Secretary General of the United Nations confirms this in his March 2007 report to the Security Council, and maintains that the system has never been independent, nor has it ever had the resources necessary to investigate and prosecute criminals and ensure that court decisions are implemented.[391] He goes on to report as follows:

> Low salaries have contributed to corruption and very few people have access to legal aid. Under 60% of the 180 courts of first instance that the country needs have been created,

---

[389] *Ibid.*

[390] See, The Report of International Federation of Human Rights on the DR Congo (DRC) titled 'Breaking the Cycle of Impunity'.

[391] *Ibid.*

laws are obsolete and the judicial structures, the courts and the prisons are in a state of disrepairs.

Although the military courts have recently rendered a small number of decisions on human rights violations, the reigning culture in DR Congo is one of generalised impunity.[392]

Consequently, civilian courts in DR Congo have not been able to prosecute any of the serious crimes committed during the wars, 'partly due to the fact that there is no legislation "domesticating" the *Rome Statute* which defines such crimes, which is to say that there is no law to integrate the crimes... into national law...'.[393] Thus, the Congolese national courts lack the jurisdiction to try cases involving such crimes. However, the Congolese military courts have been able to prosecute perpetrators of such serious crimes under the *Military Criminal Code of 2002*, which incorporates the crimes provided for in the *Rome Statute of International Criminal Court*. So far, they have only been able to prosecute a few of such cases. The International Criminal Court, on its part has indicted a number of suspects, but that is as far as it can go, as its mandate covers only those that bear 'the greatest responsibility' for the violations. Besides, most of the serious crimes committed in DR Congo fall outside the court's temporal jurisdiction as they were committed between 1996 and 2003, most of them before the country ratified the *Rome Statute*, and before she invited the court to investigate and prosecute certain individuals for the atrocities committed in the armed conflict.

---

[392] *Ibid*.

[393] Open Society Initiative for Southern Africa, 'The DR Congo: Military justice and human rights – An urgent need to complete reforms (A Discussion Paper),' [2009], An Open Society Institute Publication, 3.

By and large, the task of investigating and prosecuting the pervasive infractions of the law of armed conflict and of the many violations that affected women disproportionately rests on the Police and the National Courts that should champion the fight against impunity, and contribute to the building of the nation. Regrettably, the Congolese authorities have not shown the political will necessary to enforce the new law which it passed on judicial organization and competencies empowering the civil courts, including the Court of Appeal, to try international crimes. Of course, without an effective judicial system, effective implementation of the law becomes difficult. For instance, the Court of Appeal in Bukavu has only four judges as against five judges which the law provides for in cases involving international crimes.

In spite of the impunity with which sexual violence was perpetrated, national institutions 'failed to prosecute and punish perpetrators due to the weakness of the judicial system, the lack of infrastructure (particularly in rural areas) and of trained staff as well as the lack of implementation of legal decisions'[394]. Therefore, international implementation and enforcement mechanisms seem the surer avenues for securing the rights of the citizens, and especially women of DR Congo, as the country has ratified many international instruments and committed herself to some of their implementation and enforcement mechanisms. For instance, DR Congo has ratified the *Optional Protocols to the United Nations Human Rights Convention* and accepted the competence of the corresponding United Nations Treaty Bodies to entertain complaints from her

---

[394] *Ibid*

citizens.[395] Thus, the inhabitants of the DR Congo and their representatives are able to invoke their human rights through these bodies. They may also 'turn to the UN Human Rights Committee through procedure 1503, to the Special Rapporteurs for violations of specific human rights or to (ECOSOC) Economic, Culture and Social Council for women's rights violations.[396] Being 'a member state of UNESCO, its citizens may use the UNESCO procedure for human rights violations in UNESCO fields of mandate'.[397] Aggrieved women, as others, may also take advantage of the fact that "Employers" or "Workers" and certain other organizations (not individuals) of DR Congo may file complaints through the International Labour Organization (ILO) procedure in the cases of those conventions which DR Congo has ratified.[398] As a member of the African Union (AU), her citizens may also file complaints to the African Commission on Human and Peoples Rights. They may also file complaints according to the European Union guidelines (on Human Rights Defenders, Death Penalty and Torture) to Embassies of European Union Member States and the ---Delegations of the European Commission.[399] Most importantly, DR Congo, having ratified the *Rome Statute of the International Criminal Court*, may request the court to investigate and possibly prosecute offenders in cases of war crimes, genocide and crimes against humanity.

---

[395] See 'Claiming Human Rights: Guide to International Procedures Available Cases of Human Rights Violations in Africa (Claiming Human Rights in the DR Congo)', available at *http//www.claiming humanrights.org/drcongo.html* (accessed 13-1-2017).

[396] *Ibid.*

[397] *Ibid.*

[398] *Ibid.*

[399] *Ibid.*

Domestic law and customary international humanitarian laws may also apply to fill conceivable gaps in the laws.

In view of the fact that the relevant institutions totally collapsed in the course of the war, it is clear that the DR Congo government is 'unable' to bring the perpetrators of international crimes, including sexual violence against men and women, to justice. It therefore has had no choice than to 'call upon the resources of the ICC, ABA/ROLI's commitment to building the capacity of judges, lawyers, police investigators, and court personnel so as to begin to redress decades of impunity for crimes both large and small in the DRC'[400]. One can safely state that the International Criminal Court; the Congolese Military Courts, and the Gender Mobile Courts established by the American Bar Association (ABA) in collaboration with the Rule of Law Initiative (ROLI) constitute the institutional framework for judicial enforcement in DR Congo.

On the other hand, the United Nations Office of the High Commissioner on Human Rights established its presence in DR Congo in 1996. The focus of the office was on technical assistance and its overriding objective was the fight against impunity, especially with regards to sexual violence[401]. For this, a Human Rights Division was established within the United Nations Organization Mission in Congo (MONUC) with the mandate to monitor and report sexual violence in DR Congo. Subsequently, the office and the Division were integrated to create the United Nations Joint Human Rights Office (JHRO) which was tasked with

---

[400] *Ibid.*

[401] See 'Office of the High Commissioner on Human Rights' available at www.ohchr.org/EN/About us/pages/missions statement.asp (accessed 20/1/019)

improving respect for human rights in DR Congo by assisting the government and Mission in Congo in implementing the mandate. Finally, in 2010 and by the United Nations Security Council *Resolution* 1925, the Mission (MONUC) became the United Nations Organization Stabilization Mission in Congo (MONUSCO).

Unfortunately, DR Congo has yet to establish a National Committee or any similar body on International Humanitarian Law, as at 31 July, 2018.

Sierra Leone: Like what happened in DR Congo, the Sierra Leonean Judiciary, the Police and the Prisons were detrimentally affected by the armed conflict. In fact, prior to the conflict, the judiciary barely existed in the provinces and in Freetown and was only accessible to those who had sufficient funds.[402] It is, therefore, not surprising that it totally collapsed during the war, as the lawyers fled the conflict, while 'much of the infrastructure, including the law courts in Freetown, was destroyed'.[403] Moreover, the low salaries of personnel working in the judiciary predisposed the magistrates, lawyers and judges to accepting bribes and/or being intimidated.[404]

The state of the Judiciary, the Police and the Prisons was such that 'women and girls have little faith in the criminal justice system or the customary law system, which were never equipped to deal with crimes of such widespread and systematic nature'.[405] The fact that the judiciary was dominated by men and that some of its older

---

[402] *Ibid.,* 67.

[403] *Ibid.*

[404] *Ibid.*

[405] *Ibid.,* 66.

members, in particular, do not think that rape is a serious crime and believe that the victims are generally to blame, did not help matters.

As a result of this poor administrative response of the Sierra Leonean criminal justice system, it is doubtful that there was any prosecution in the Sierra Leonean national courts of any cases of conflict-related sexual violence or other human rights abuses.[406] This may also have been partly because of the amnesty provisions against national prosecutions of violations that occurred during the armed conflict. Another factor that contributed to the problem is the administrative requirement that such cases must be submitted to the High Court through the Magistrates Court, which must first determine whether sufficient evidence exists, and whether to grant bail.[407] The effect of this administrative arrangement has been summarized as follows:

> Many cases die in the magistrates' courts, as victims run out of money, patience and/or time. Cases at this stage are also frequently dismissed, if, for example, three witnesses do not show in court (after three no shows, the case can be dismissed): witnesses often decide, against appearing in court for reasons including intimidation, ignorance of the law, lack of transportation money, and the slow pace at which court cases proceed, or because they simply do not care. The requirement of corroborating evidence is often an obstacle to prosecution and violates international norms.[408]

Furthermore, the Sierra Leone police is lacking in professionalism. It had, even before the conflict, been hijacked by the

---

[406] *Ibid.*

[407] *Ibid.*

[408] *Ibid.*

politicians 'for their own purposes, and had not received any substantive training for decades.[409] Besides, the attitude of the police to domestic and sexual violence has remained insensitive, as they chastise women who report domestic violence, and as they often do not take reports of rape seriously.[410] On the whole, many problems have been associated with police investigation of rape cases in Sierra Leone. Such problems include:

i). The fact that the police lack basic investigation skills.

ii). The fact that victims must be examined by state-employed doctors, including police doctors, as only a state-employed doctor can present medical evidence in court, and they both often charge money for the examinations, which should be free of charge.

iii). Both the doctors and the police may be intimidated and/or bribed to drop the cases, or police may demand money from plaintiffs before interviewing witness and arranging their transport to court.

However, a nationwide system of Family Support Units (FSUs) has been put in place, with the support of the British –funded Commonwealth Community Safety and Security Project (CCSSP), to deal with cases of sexual and domestic violence.[411] The foregoing state of affairs in Sierra Leone necessitated the establishment of the Special Court for Sierra Leone.

---

[409] *Ibid.*, 68.

[410] *Ibid.*

[411] *Ibid.* See also McFerson, H. M., 'Women and Post-Conflict Society in Sierra Leone', [2012], *Journal of International Women's Studies*, (Vol. 13, No. 1), 60.

The Special Court for Sierra Leone was established by an agreement between the United Nations and the government of Sierra Leone, following the request of President Ahmad Tejan Kabbah of Sierra Leone to the United Nations Security Council to that effect.[412] The court came into being pursuant to *United Nations Security Council Resolution 1315* of 14 August 2000,[413] and after the Special Court Agreement and Special Court Statute had been ratified by the Parliament of Sierra Leone in March 2002.[414]

The *Statute of the Special Court for Sierra-Leone* provides as follows, on the competence of the court:

The Special Court shall, except as provided in subparagraph (2), have the power to prosecute persons who bear the greatest responsibility for serious violations of international humanitarian law and Sierra Leonean Law committed in the territory of Sierra Leone since 30 November 1996, including those leaders who, in committing such crimes, have

---

[412] See the letter dated 9th August 2000 from the Permanent Representative of Sierra Leone to the United Nations addressed to the President of the Security Council, UN Doc. No. S/2000/786, 10th August 2000, as cited in Unegbu, M. O., *From Nuremberg Charter to Rome Statute: Judicial Enforcement of International Humanitarian Law*, Enugu, SNAAP Press Ltd., 2015, 154.

[413] The *Prosecutor of the Special Court of Sierra Leone v Alex Tamba Brima, Brima Bazzy Kamara, and Santigie Borbor Kanu,* Case No. SCSL-04-16-T, 65-79, paras 156-209.

[414] See Special Court Agreement (Ratification) Act of Sierra Leone, 2002. See also, Mujuzi, J.D., 'The Special Court for Sierra Leone and its Justification of Punishment in Cases of Serious Violations of International Humanitarian Law and Human Rights Law: Reflecting on the *Prosecutor of the Special Court v Alex Tamba Brima, Brima Bazzy Kamara and Santigie Borbor Kanu* in the Light of the Philosophical Arguments on Punishment, [2007], *African YearBook on International Humanitarian Law,* 105.

threatened the establishment of and implementation of the peace process in Sierra Leone.[415]

Subparagraph 2 excludes transgressions or violations:

by peacekeepers and related personnel present in Sierra Leone pursuant to the status of Mission Agreement in force between the United Nations and the Government of Sierra Leone or agreements between Sierra Leone and other Governments or regional organizations, or, in the absence of such agreement, provided that the peacekeeping operations were undertaken with the consent of the Government of Sierra Leone. Violations by such personnel are 'within the primary jurisdiction of the sending State.[416]

The Special Court for Sierra Leone is a country specific *ad hoc* tribunal comparable to the International Criminal Tribunal for the Former Yugoslavia (ICTY) and the International Criminal Tribunal for Rwanda (ICTR). However, unlike the two prior tribunals, it was a creation of a special agreement between Sierra Leone and the United Nations Secretary General, as stated earlier, rather than a direct creation of the United Nations Security Council, as was the case of the International Criminal Tribunals for the Former Yugoslavia and Rwanda, respectively.

The reason behind this kind of arrangement is probably to avoid a repeat of objections raised against the previous tribunals with

---

[415] See paragraph 1(1) of the *Statute of the Special Court for Sierra Leone*, as reproduced in Khan, K.A.A and Dixon, R., *Archbold International Criminal Courts: Practice, Procedure & Evidence*, London, Sweet & Maxwell Limited, 2005, 82.

[416] See *Statute of the Special Court for Sierra Leone*, (2002), Article 1(2). For a full text of the statute, see Evans, M.D, (ed.), *Blackstone's International Law Documents* (9th edn.), Oxford, Oxford University Press, 2009, 584.

regard to their legality, on the ground that the *United Nations Charter* did not empower the Security Council to establish international courts by resolutions.[417] However such objections and oppositions may have easily been overruled and discountenanced, except that they may in reality, politically cast doubts on the credibility and legitimacy of the entire judicial process.[418]

Obviously, the Special Court is an independent tribunal. It is independent of the Judiciary of Sierra Leone.[419] Unlike the two earlier international tribunals for the former Yugoslavia and Rwanda, it has the unique and unprecedented power of enforcing both international law principles and municipal laws of Sierra Leone. This is what has earned it the popular epithet as a hybrid court. Besides, the Judges of both the Trial and the Appeal Chambers were either appointees of the United Nations Secretary General or of the government of Sierra Leone. It is for this reason that the United Nations Secretary General described the court as a 'treaty-based *sui generis* court of mixed jurisdiction and compositions'.[420]

The site of the court has also been lauded. Unlike the International Criminal Tribunal for the Former Yugoslavia and the International Criminal Tribunal for Rwanda which were sited at Hague and Arusha, Tanzania, respectively, the Special Court for Sierra Leone sat in Freetown, the capital of the country which witnessed the civil war and notorious atrocities and violations of

---

[417] Unegbu, *Op.cit.*, 154.

[418] *Ibid*.

[419] *Article* 11(2) of the Special Court Agreement specifically provides that the court shall not be a part of the Judiciary of Sierra Leone.

[420] Unegbu, *Op.cit.*, 155.

international humanitarian law. However, for security reasons sittings were later transferred to The Hague during the trial of Charles Taylor.[421]

Issues about the court's jurisdiction are covered by *Articles* 2 to 5 and 7 to 8 of the *Statute of Special Court for Sierra Leone*. *Article* 2 stipulates crimes against humanity, which it states that the Special Court shall have the power to prosecute persons who commit them as part of a widespread or systematic attack against any civilian population. It listed them as Murder, Extermination, Enslavement, Deportation; Imprisonment, Torture, Rape, Sexual slavery, Enforced prostitution, Forced pregnancy and other forms of sexual violence; Persecution on political, racial, ethnic or religious grounds, and other inhumane acts.[422] *Article* 3 empowers the court to prosecute violations of the *Geneva Conventions* and the *Additional Protocol* II. Such violations shall include: Violence to Life, health and physical or mental well-being of persons, in particular murder as well as cruel treatment such as torture, mutilation or any form of corporal punishment; Collective punishments; Taking of hostages; Acts of terrorism; Outrages upon personal dignity, in particular humiliating and degrading treatment, rape, enforced prostitution and any form of indecent assault; Pillage; the passing of sentences and the carrying out of executions without previous judgment pronounced by a regularly constituted court, affording all the judicial guarantees, which are recognized as indispensable by civilized people; and threat to commit any of the foregoing acts.[423] The Special Court for Sierra Leone is also empowered to prosecute persons who commit

---

[421] *Ibid.*

[422] *Articles* 2 (a) – (i).

[423] *Article* 3(a) – (h).

'other serious violations of international humanitarian law'.[424] These other violations are listed as:

(a) Intentionally directing attacks against the civilian population as such or against individual civilians not taking direct part in hostilities;

(b) Intentionally directing attacks against personnel, installations, material, units or vehicles involved in a humanitarian assistance or peace keeping mission in accordance with the Charter of the United Nations, as long as they are entitled to the protection given to civilians or civilian objects under the international law of armed conflict;

(c) Conscripting or enlisting children under the age of 15years into armed forces or groups or using them to participate actively in hostilities.[425]

The special and hybrid nature of the court is also captured by the incorporation into its jurisdiction of crimes under Sierra Leonean law. Thus, under Article 5:

The Special Court shall have the power to prosecute persons who have committed the following crimes under Sierra Leonean law:

(a) Offences relating to the abuse of girls under the *Prevention of Cruelty to Children Act*, 1926 (Cap. 31):

i). Abusing a girl under 13 years of age, contrary to section 6;

ii). Abusing a girl between 13 and 14 years of age, contrary to section 7;

---

[424] *Article* 4(a) – (c). See Evans, *Op.cit.*, 585.

[425] *Article* 5 of the *Statute of the Special Court for Sierra Leone.*

iii). Abduction of a girl for immoral purposes, contrary to section 12.

(a) Offences relating to the wanton destruction of property under the *Malicious Damages Act*, 1861:

i). Setting fire to dwelling-houses, any person being therein, contrary to section 2;

ii). Setting fire to public buildings, contrary to sections 5 and 6;

iii). Setting fire to other buildings, contrary to section 6.

However, the court lacks jurisdiction over persons of 15 years of age, even if they committed the fore-going offences. It would rather treat 'any person who was at the time of the alleged commission of the crime between 15 and 18 years of age... with dignity and a sense of worth'[426] in view of 'his or her young age and the desirability of promoting his or her rehabilitation, reintegration into and assumption of a constructive role in society, and in accordance with international human rights standards, in particular the rights of the child'.[427] Thus, in disposing such cases against a juvenile offender:

The Special Court shall order any of the following: care guidance and supervision orders, community service orders, counseling, foster care, correctional, educational and vocational training programmes, approved schools and, as appropriate, any programmes of disarmament, demobilization and reintegration of programmes of child protection agencies.[428]

---

[426] *Article 7(1).*

[427] *Ibid.*

[428] *Article 7(2).*

The Statute also provides for concurrent jurisdiction between the Special Court and the National Courts of Sierra Leone over the foregoing offences. However, the Special Court shall have primacy over the national courts of Sierra Leone. This includes the fact that the Special Court may at any stage formally request a national court to 'defer to its competence in accordance with the present Statute and the Rules of Procedure and Evidence'.[429]

Besides the Special Court, in order to promote and implement International Humanitarian Law, Sierra Leone established a National Committee for the Implementation of International Humanitarian Law, in 2011[430]. The committee was launched in 2012 with the following institutions being represented: Foreign Affairs, Defence, Justice, Education, Health and Sanitation, Small Arms Secretariat, Prison Service, Police Legal Department, Sierra Leone Institute of International Law, Civil Society Movement, Women's Forum, Human Rights Commission of Sierra Leone, Office of National Security, Special Court for Sierra Leone, International Organization for Migration, and the Sierra Leone National Society of Red Cross.

The Committee has the following mandate:

(ii)   To recommend and promote the accession to or ratification of International Humanitarian Law treaties and their implementation.

---

[429] *Article* 8(1) and (2).

[430] See National Commitees and Similar bodies on International Humanitarian Law, available at www.icrc. org/en/document/table-nationl-committees-and-other-national-bodies-international-humanitarian-law (accessed 12th September, 2018)

(iii)   To promote, develop and provide support for the dissemination of International Humanitarian Law in State Institutions

(iv)   To evaluate domestic implementation of International Humanitarian Law.

(v)   To make recommendations for establishing *ad hoc* working groups in connection with adopting the necessary implementation measures.

(vi)   To promote cooperation between the government and international organizations for strengthening respect for International Humanitarian Law.

(vii)   To promote measures that will contribute to ensuring respect for and applying International Humanitarian Law.

(viii) To serve as an advisory body to the government

(ix)   To prepare draft regulations and instructions for implementing International Humanitarian Law.

(x)   To develop, promote and coordinate a national plan of action for ensuring the promotion and application of International Humanitarian Law.

(xi)   To exchange information and experience with other bodies concerned with International Humanitarian Law.

(xii)   To draw up and present initial reports on the implementation of International Humanitarian Law.

(xiii) To carry out any other task related to the object of the committee.

CHAPTER FIVE

Judicial Enforcement of The Rights of Women in Armed Conflicts in Africa

✿

Enforcing the rights of women under international humanitarian law and other relevant bodies of law will be illusive without the adjudicative role of the judiciary. Traditionally, the judiciary has not been gender-sensitive in its adjudicative role, neither does it seem to recognize that women have specific needs for the protection of the law, because of their gender. However, in recent times, the courts are being encouraged to be sensitive to the plight of women in armed conflicts, and redress the many injuries and wrongs that are meted out to them in the course of armed conflicts. Thus, the role of the judiciary in the protection of victims of the armed conflicts under reference shall be considered here-under.

5.1 NIGERIA

Nigerian Civil War: Very few judicial responses, including courts marshal have been recorded, in respect of the Nigerian Civil War. Notable among them was the case *of Pius Nwaoga v The State.*[1] However, in spite of the targeted attacks on women and indiscriminate bombardments which resulted in disproportionate number of deaths for women, no one has been prosecuted for war

---

[1] Sc, 13 (1972); ILR, 1972, 494-497.

crimes against women in the Nigerian Civil War. Equally unfortunate is the fact that in spite of widespread sexual violence against women, in that war, no one has been prosecuted for war-time rape and sexual violence.

Sexual violence was evident during the Nigerian Civil War with the record of indiscriminate gang rapes which happened routinely in the war-zone among many more horrendous tales of mothers, who were raped in full view of their children, before being bludgeoned to death and stories of machete-wielding soldiers, who split open the bellies of pregnant women at road blocks, 'to find hidden rebels'.[2] Post war, Igbo women were targeted for sexual violence because of their gender and ethnic identity.[3] All these happened and have received no judicial response despite the Operational Code of Conduct issued to the federal armed forces in line with the *Geneva Conventions* that provide that women will be protected against any attacks on their person, honour and in particular, against rape or any form of assault.

The insensitive attitude of the Federal Government to the welfare and well-being of unexploded ordnance and explosive remnants of war victims, who are mostly women, led to the landmines victims filing a suit against the government at the sub-regional Economic Community of West African States (ECOWAS) Court of Justice, Abuja.[4]

---

[2] Ogbonna –Nwaogu, I.M, 'Civil Wars in Africa: A Gender Perspective of the cost on women,' [2005] *Journal of Social Sciences*, (Vol. 16, N03), 253.

[3] *Ibid.*

[4] See Mine *Action Victims/Survivors (Vincent Agu and others) v Federal Government of Nigeria*, Suit No ECW/CCJ/APP/06/12.

Nigeria is a state party to the *Ottawa Convention (Mine Ban Treaty)*, 2002 which prohibit the use, stockpiling, production and transfer of Anti-Personnel mines and urged their destruction. Thus, Nigeria owes the obligation of clearing, removing or destroying the mines otherwise described as Explosive Remnants of War pursuant to *Article* 3(1) of the *Convention* or *Treaty*, but failed to do so. However, while the matter was pending in court, the Nigerian government opted for out of court settlement,[5] but abandoned the process when 'overwhelmed by the unsettling revelations and quantum of evidence against the attitude of the federal government towards Nigeria's Civil War contaminated areas and victims/survivors.'[6]

Quite recently (2017) the court found in favour of the Mine Action Victims and Survivors and awarded them substantial damages.[7] However, there is nothing in the judgement of the court that suggests that it considered the disproportionate impact of the mine action on women in awarding damages to the victims, neither was it gender-sensitive in adjudicating the case.

At this point, the facts of Nwaoga's case may be considered, even though it has no direct implications for the legal protection of

---

[5] This proposition was by a letter from the Attorney General of the Federation with Reference No. MJ/CIV/ABJ/190/12, dated 11th march, 2013. Consequently, two meetings were held in the office of the Solicitor-General of the Federation, before the government discontinued with the process and engaged the services of Femi Falana and company to fight the victims in the court.

[6] Chukwukadibia, N.A; *War Without End in Nigeria: Landmines, Bombs & Explosive Remnants of War (The Law, Treaty, Conventions Practice and Procedure in ECOWAS Court)*, Owerri, Cleanbills Publishers, 2014, 113-114.

[7] Tsa, G, 'Civil war Landmines: ECOWAS court awards N88bn fine against FG', [Tuesday, October 31,2017], Daily Sun,Vol. 14, No3787,39.

women, but to show that Nigerian Courts hardly considers the implementation and the enforcement of International Humanitarian Law. Pius Nwaoga was charged alongside another defendant, for the murder of one Robert Ngwu, on 20 July 1969, at Inagwa Nike. He was convicted and sentenced to death, while the second defendant was discharged and acquitted. Nwoaga appealed against his conviction.[8]

On appeal, the Supreme Court observed as follows:

The incident which led to the killing of the deceased happened during the civil war in the country. The appellant joined the rebel forces known as Biafran Army. He joined as a private and later became a Lieutenant. He was attached to the BOFF (Biafran Organization of Freedom Fighters). He was deployed to Nike and at the time Nike was in the hands of the federal troops.

The deceased was also a soldier in the rebel forces; he and the appellant were both natives of Ibagwa Nike and well-known to each other. Before July 1969, the appellant was posted in command of a rebel company to a town called Olo, near Ibagwa Nike, with operational headquarters of his brigade at Atta. In July 1969, the appellant was summoned to Atta. There he was instructed to lead Lieutenant Ngwu and Lieutenant Ndu to Ibagwu Nike to point out the deceased to them. He was told that as he knew the area well and also knew the deceased, his duty was to identify the deceased to the Lieutenants who would eliminate him.[9]

---

[8] *Pius Nwaoga v The State*, Supra.

[9] *Supra.*

The offence of the deceased was that he was given £800 to re-open and operate the Day Spring Hotel in Enugu for the benefit of the members of the Biafran Organisation of Freedom Fighters (BOFF) but he instead diverted the money to the operation of his contract business. Indeed, he had entered into a contract with the Federal Government to carryout repairs to the Enugu Airfield which had been damaged by rebel aircraft. In reaching a decision, the Supreme Court considered the following facts:

1. That the appellant and those with him were rebel officers.
2. That the appellant was operating inside the federal territory as the evidence shows that the area was in the hands of the Federal Government and Federal Army.
3. That the appellant and those with him were operating in disguise in the Federal territory, as saboteurs.
4. That the appellant and those with him were not in the rebel army uniform but were in plain clothes, appearing to be members of the peaceful private population.

The Supreme Court opined that on these facts, if any of these rebel officers, as indeed the appellant did, committed an act which is an offence under the Criminal Code, he would be liable for punishment, just like any civilian would be, whether or not he is acting under orders.[10] The Court maintained:

> We are fortified in this view by a passage from Oppenheim's International Law, 7th edition, volume ii, at page 575, dealing with War Treason, which says: ' Enemy soldiers, in contra distinction to private enemy individuals, may only be punished for such acts when they have committed them

---

[10] *Pius Nwaoga v The State, Supra.*

during their stay within a belligerent's lines under disguise. If, for instance, two soldiers in uniform are sent to the rear of the enemy to destroy a bridge, they may not, when caught, be punished for 'war treason,' because their act was one of legitimate warfare. But if they exchanged their uniforms for plain clothes, and thereby appear to be members of the peaceful private population, they are liable to punishment.

Relying on Oppenheim's view and a case in the foot-note under the above quoted paragraph, in which two Japanese officers disguised themselves in Chinese clothes, during the Russo-Japanese War in1904, in order to destroy a railway bridge in Manchuria, but were caught, tried, found guilty and shot, the Supreme Court upheld the conviction of the appellant and dismissed the appeal. They reasoned that deliberate and intentional killing of an unarmed person living peacefully inside the Federal Territory, as in this case, is a crime against humanity, and even if committed during civil war, it is in violation of the domestic law of the country, and must be punished.

With due respect to the distinguished Justices of the Supreme Court, it is here submitted that the court should have gone beyond applying domestic criminal law, to considering or canvassing international humanitarian law. Most likely, they would have still upheld the decision of the lower courts that convicted the appellant, but it would have been an opportunity for the Supreme Court to consider the *Geneva Conventions* which the country had ratified and even domesticated. It would have been an opportunity to consider the status of the appellant (whether or not he was a combatant), and the fact that the deceased was *hors de combat*. Furthermore, the concepts of "perfidy," "military occupation," and even "armed conflict" may have been considered thereby enriching the jurisprudence of international humanitarian law, and especially in relation to the Nigerian Civil War.

Boko Haram Insurgency and Nigerian War Against Terrorism: Judicial response to *Boko Haram* insurgency and Nigerian war against terrorism has also not been satisfactory. In the first place, none of the cases arising from it seems to have been brought under international humanitarian law, which is the law of armed conflict. Secondly, it does not seem that anyone has been charged for sexual violence, or any gender-based violence for that matter, despite the fact that *Boko Haram* has been notorious for the widespread use of gender-based violence, abduction and rape of women as a weapon of war. Indeed, the government of Nigeria seems to have been unable to take prompt and effective steps to investigate and hold accountable most perpetrators of serious crimes on all sides, including *Boko Haram*, Nigerian Military forces and the Civilian Joint Task Forces (TJF).[11] Though the military alleges that it has arrested large numbers of *Boko Haram* suspects, Amnesty International believes that none of the arrested persons are linked to *Boko Haram* or have committed crimes under international law. They have also gone on to observe that few, if any, of the prosecutions appear to be of senior *Boko Haram* commanders. Besides, it seems the very few that has been charged, has been charged under domestic criminal law and the *Terrorism (Prevention) Act* 2011 as amended in 2013, and punishable under same.

---

[11] Amnesty International, 'Nigeria: Torture, Cruel inhuman and degrading treatment of detainees by Nigeria security forces', being Amnesty international's written *statement* to the 25th Session of the UN Human Rights Council (3-28 March, 2014).

In *State v Mohhammed Usman & Ors*,[12]the Federal Government had brought an 11count charge against seven suspected members of the *Boko Haram* sect, to which they all pleaded not guilty. The suspects, who were arraigned before Justice John Tsoho are Mohammed Usman (also known as Khalid Albarnawi), who was described as the leader of a *Boko Haram* splinter group, *Jamatu Asaraul Muslimina Fibiladis Sudan (datti)*, Yakubu Nuhu (also known as Bello Maishayi), Usman Abubakar (Mugiratu) and a lady, Halima Haliru. The defendants were charged, with conspiracy, hostage taking, supporting a terrorist group, illegal possession of firearms and concealing information on terrorism. They were charged with conspiracy to commit terrorism, contrary to *Section 17* of the *Terrorism (Prevention) Act* 2011, as amended in 2013, and punishable under same.

According to the charge filed by the office of the Attorney General of the Federation, the defendants in February 2013, at Ikirima *Boko Haram* camp in Sambisa forest, allegedly murdered seven internationally protected persons and buried them in a shallow grave. The court, in its ruling, granted the prosecution's application to protect witnesses that will testify by shielding witnesses that will testify in the case; and denied the accused and defendants bail, and ordered that they be remanded in Kuje Prison, pending the determination of the case. Again, in *Mohammed Yunus v the State*[13] where counsel to the applicant had prayed the court to grant his client, a *Boko Haram* suspect, bail, counsel to the respondent

---

[12] Unreported case, available at custodyvangard.ngr.com (sourced on 20 April, 2017).

[13] Unreported Case, available at custodyvanguard. ngr.com (sourced on 20 April, 2017).

(State Security Service) objected and prayed the court to refuse the bail application, on at least three grounds. The grounds included that the suspect might jeopardize investigations; that there was an existing Federal High Court order which empowered the State Security Service (SSS) to detain the applicant for 45 days in order for the State Security Service (SSS) to carry out their investigation; and that granting the applicant bail will contravene the provision of *section* 27 (I) of the *Terrorism Amendment Act* of 2013. The accused was therefore denied bail. However, in *Umar v Federal Republic of Nigeria & Ors*,[14] the Court of Appeal, Abuja Division had the opportunity of thoroughly espousing the law with regard to right to bail, for the *Boko Haram* terrorist suspects. The appeal is against the ruling of the Federal High Court, Abuja delivered on 7th day of March 2014[15].

The facts of the case are that the appellant was charged with two others for breach of several provisions of the *Terrorism (Prevention) Amendment Act*, 2013, as reflected at pages 1-3 of the Record of Appeal. The appellant (applicant at the trial court) applied to be admitted to bail pending the hearing and determination of the charge (s) against him pursuant to *Section* 34 and 35 of the *1999 Constitution* (as amended) and *Section* 118 (2) of the *Criminal Procedure Act* and under the inherent jurisdiction of the court. The trial judge, in his considered ruling refused the application, where-upon the appellant instituted this appeal. The appellant contended that the trial court 'delved into extraneous matter in refusing the appellant bail instead of relying on facts before him as required by law'. The extraneous matter complained of by the Appellant is that

---

[14] [2014] LPELR-24051 (CA), Court of Appeal Abuja Division.

[15] See *Federal Republic of Nigeria v Umar*, Charge No: FHC/ABJ/CR/13/2014.

the trial Judge took into cognizance the happenings in Borno, Yobe and Adamawa states of the North Eastern part of Nigeria, specifically, act of terrorism which is the offence with which the Appellant is charged.

The learned Justice observed that the offence with which the Appellant is charged is terrorism, a capital offence which must be taken with caution, because death sentence is the highest of all penalties, but failed to see the wrong committed by the trial judge in taking judicial notice of the terrorist acts in the North Eastern states of Nigeria, specifically Borno, Yobe and Adamawa States. This, he opined is because the court owes a duty to protect the society, and no principle of law demands that crime of terrorism should be ignored. Furthermore, the learned Justice of the Court of Appeal observed that even though bail is a constitutional right, it is not granted as a matter of course. He affirmed that there must be placed before the court, sufficient materials disclosing exceptional circumstance to warrant a grant. He also pointed out that the court is guided by certain criteria in granting or refusing bail and noted the criteria as provided by the Supreme Court in the case of *Suleiman v C.O.P*[16] as follows:

(a) The nature of the charge
(b) The strength of the evidence which supports the charge.
(c) The gravity of punishment in the event of conviction.
(d) The previous criminal record of the accused if any.
(e) The probability that the accused may not surrender himself for trial.

---

[16] (2008) 8NWLR (Pt 1089) 298 SC.

(f) The likelihood of the accused interfering with witnesses or suppressing any evidence that may incriminate him.

(g) The likelihood of further charge being brought against the accused; and

(h) The necessity to procure medical or social report pending final disposal of the case.

The court observed that the first three criteria listed above are relevant to the instant case and that bail pending trial is not normally granted *ex-debito justitia,* where the offence is a capital offence. In dismissing the appeal, the learned Justice held that it is his view that the trial court exercised its discretion judicially and judiciously, and that the case of *Suleiman v C.O.P*[17] relied on heavily by the appellant is not of any assistance to his case.

Legal skirmishes which have been here, and isolated cases of General Courts Martial, such as the one in Maiduguri, where Lance Corporal Hillary Joel was condemned to death for killing an alleged *Boko Haram* suspect,[18] are not enough to show that the Nigerian government is willing and able to take prompt and effective steps to investigate and hold accountable most perpetrators of serious crimes on all sides, including *Boko Haram,* Nigerian armed forces and the Civilian Joint Task Forces.[19] Importantly, it is pertinent to observe

---

[17] *Supra*

[18] See News Agency of Nigeria's report by Michael Olugbode, John Shiklam, and Paul Obi. The report stated that four other soldiers were found guilty of various offences bordering on violation of human rights and other operational breaches in the ongoing counter insurgency operation in the North East, tagged "Operation Lafia Dole".

[19] Emblematic cases of government's failing to investigate and prosecute crimes include government's refusal to investigate high rates of death under military

that the Nigerian government has not been sensitive to the plight of women with regard to gender- based violence and rape, despite the fact that *Boko Haram* has engaged it as a weapon of war.[20] Moreover, Amnesty International claims to have received consistent reports that women have been raped or sexually abused by the police in the street, while being transferred to police stations, while in police custody, or when visiting male detainees.[21] The reports further state that rape and other forms of sexual violence or the threat of torture and ill-treatment are used by the police to extract confessions or other information; and that method include insertion of foreign objects, such as bottles into the women's vagina.

Regrettably, there seems not to be investigations yet, into these allegations and incidents, neither has anyone been prosecuted for gender-based violence or rape in the on-going war against *Boko Haram*. However, there are indications that the International Criminal Court and foreign jurisdictions may intervene on the basis of complementarity and universal jurisdiction, respectively. The

---

custody and possibly prosecute those responsible for such deaths. Another instance is government's failure to investigate and prosecute those soldiers in Maiduguri who, on 14 March, 2014, extra-judicially executed more than 640 recaptured detainees freed by *Boko Haram* from the Giwa Barracks even after Amnesty international published video evidence of some of those executions. Granted that the government announced an internal military investigation into the allegations, no precise composition and timeline for the investigation was made public, neither has anyone been made accountable for the executions.

[20] The Chibok girls' saga is illustrative; so also is the use of female suicide bombers.

[21] See Amnesty International, 'Nigeria: Boko Haram and Nigerian Military committing crimes under international

law in north east Nigeria' (Amnesty International written statement to the 28th session of the UN Human Rights Council) (2-27 march 2015).

office of the Prosecutor, in the International Criminal Court has determined that there is a reasonable basis to believe that crimes against humanity have been committed in Nigeria, namely acts of murder and persecution attributed to *Boko Haram*. The Prosecutor has therefore decided that preliminary examination of the situation in Nigeria should advance to Phase 3 (Admissibility), with a view to assessing genuine proceedings in relation to those who appear to bear the greatest responsibility for such crimes, and the gravity of such crimes.[22] However, whether the International Criminal Court would prosecute crimes involving gender-based violence against women in the armed conflicts in Nigeria remains moot.

Interestingly, a Spanish public prosecutor has already brought charges against Abubakar Shekau (leader of *Boko Haram*), for crimes against humanity, in the Spanish High Court. The court presided over by Justice Fernando Andrew ruled that Shekau and his group would be tried under the principle of universal jurisdiction. The prosecutor describes how Shekau and his group had been responsible for the deaths of many women and children and insisted that they must answer for their acts, before the courts. The lawsuit relates specifically to a march, 2013 attack by *Boko Haram*, on the remote town of Ganye, which lies close to Nigeria's eastern border

---

[22] See International Criminal Court (ICC) 'Situated in Nigeria, under Article 5 Re-report, dated 5 August, 2013. International Criminal Court also observes that although there are allegations against Nigerian Security forces in the context of their serious human rights violations, the information available as of Decembers 2012 does not provide a reasonable basis to believe that the alleged crimes were committed pursuant to or in furtherance of a State or Organization policy to attack the civilian population.

with Cameroon.[23] *Boko Haram* is being prosecuted for allegedly abusing and harassing a Spanish nun in that attack. The nun, Maria Jesus Mayor managed to escape and will appear in court for questioning. The British Broadcasting Corporation reported at the time that at least twenty five people died during the violence.[24] The victims included nine Spanish citizens.[25] The Judge has asked the International Police (Interpol) in conjunction with the European police service to prepare a report on *Boko Haram* as part of the proceedings.[26]

There have also been reports of prosecution of *Boko Haram* suspects by Niger Republic and Chad.[27] The report states that Niger has begun the trials behind closed doors of about one thousand suspected *Boko Haram* fighters, which were either captured during combat or arrested in the course of identity checks. According to the reports, the Nigerien Chief Prosecutor, Chaibou Samna said that the trials on charges of terrorist link had begun since March, 2, 2017; and that those facing trials are from a number of countries which include Niger, Mali and Nigeria, where the deadly insurgency began in1999, before spreading abroad.[28] He said that the trials which will continue for several months entail offences, which attract 'not more than 10 Years in Prison'; and stated that many have already been convicted,

---

[23] See Gaffey, O, 'spanish judge puts Boko Haram on Trial' available at newsweek.com, (5/29/15) (Accessed on 10-3-2017)

[24] See Spanish Newspaper El Mundo (date of publication is mistakenly omitted)

[25] *Ibid*.

[26] *Ibid*.

[27] See A F P reports of March 10, 2017

[28] *Ibid*.

while a large number of suspects have been freed for lack of evidence.[29]

However, a court in Chad is reported to have sentenced ten suspected members of Nigerian-based *Boko Haram* fighters to death in connection with a double suicide bombing in June that killed thirty-eight people in the Chadian capital city, N'Djamena.[30] The defendants were accused of criminal conspiracy, murder, and willful destruction with explosives, fraud, and illegal possession of arms and ammunitions, as well as, using psychotropic substances.[31]

5.2 DR CONGO

International Criminal Court and Gender-based Violence Against Women in the Armed Conflict in DR Congo: DR Congo is a party to the *Rome Statute of International Criminal Court*, which established the International Criminal Court.[32] Based on information it had received from individuals, international organizations and Non-governmental organizations, the office of the Prosecutor decided in July 2003, to closely follow the situation in the Ituri district of DR Congo, where the violence was said to have reached catastrophic magnitude.[33] By the later part of the year, the Prosecutor expressed his intention to seek the authorization of an International

---

[29] *Ibid.*

[30] *Ibid.*

[31] *Ibid.*

[32] DR Congo ratified the *Rome Statute* on 11-04-2002, as stated *infra*.

[33] See 'ICC Press Release, Communication Received by the Office of the Prosecutor of the ICC, ICC-OTP-20030716-27 (16 July 2003), 2-4', available at <*http://www.icc-cpi.int/NR/rdonlyres/9B5B8D79-C9C2-4515-906E-125113CE6064/277680/16 July english 1.pdf*> (accessed on 9 March 2011).

Criminal Court Pre-Trial Chamber to commence an investigation in DR Congo *proprio motu* (on his own initiative). However, before he could do that, the Congolese government, on 19 April, 2004, requested the International Criminal Court to investigate crimes committed in the course of the armed conflict in DR Congo.[34]

On the basis of that request, on 23 June 2004, the Office of the Prosecutor commenced an investigation into war crimes in DR Congo.[35] That investigation was the court's very first investigation. Based on the investigation, five militia leaders were charged with various crimes that were committed in DR Congo. They were Thomas Lubanga Dyilo, Germain Katanga, Mathieu Ngudjolo Chui, Bosco Ntaganda and Callixte Mbarushimana. Besides these men, the International Criminal Court also indicted other Congolese nationals for crimes committed in the Central African Republic.

Thomas Lubanga Dyilo was convicted of committing, as co-perpetrator, war crimes consisting of:

> Enlisting and conscripting of children under the age of 15 years into the Force patriotique pour la liberation du Congo [Patriotic Force for the Liberation of Congo]. (FPLC) and using them to participate actively in hostilities in the context of an armed conflict not of an international character from 1

---

[34] Horovitz, S., *Ibid.*, 36.

[35] See ICC Press Release, 'Prosecutor receives referral of the situation in DR Congo, ICC-OTP -2004 0419-50 (19 April 2004)', available at *http://www.icccpi.int/Menus/ICC/Structure+of+the+court/office+of+the+Prosecutor/ Reports+and+Statements/Press+Releases/Press+Releases+2004/* (accessed on 9 March 2011).

September 2002 to 13 August 2003 (punishable under article 8(2)(e)(vii) of the Rome Statute).[36]

On 10 July 2012, Trial Chamber 1 sentenced him to a total term of 14 years imprisonment. On appeal, the Appeals Chamber, on 1 December, 2014 confirmed, by majority, the verdict declaring him guilty and the decision sentencing him to 14 years imprisonment. On reparations, the Trial Chamber had on 7 August 2012, also issued a decision on the principles and the process to be implemented for reparations to victims in the case, which was also subject to appeal.[37]

In the *case of Germain Katanga*,[38] the defendant was also found guilty on 7 March 2014, by Trial Chamber II, as an accessory within the meaning of *article 23(3)(d) of the Rome Statute of International Criminal Court*. He was found guilty of one count of crime against humanity (murder) and four counts of war crimes (murder, attacking a civilian population, destruction of property and pillaging) committed on 24 February, 2003, during the attack on the village of Bogoro, in the Ituri district of DR Congo. He was however acquitted of the other charges that he was facing, which included sexual slavery. The office of the Prosecutor and the Defence appealed the judgment on different grounds, but on 25 June 2014, both counsels discontinued their appeals against the judgment. The judgment is now final. Meanwhile, Trial Chamber II, by a majority

---

[36] *Prosecutor v Thomas Lubanga Dyilo, ICC-01/04-01/06* Lubanga's trial is the first in the history of the International Criminal Court. Lubanga is the alleged former leader of the Union *des Patriotes Congolaisn* (UPC) and the Forces *Patiotiques pour la Liberation du Congo* (FPLC).

[37] *Supra.*

[38] *The Prosecutor v Germain Katanga, and Mathieu Ngudjolo Chui, ICC-01/04-01/07.*

ruling, had on 23 May, 2014 sentenced Germain Katanga to a total of 12 years imprisonment.

Ngudjolo who was supposed to be Katanga's co-defendant was acquitted on 18 December 2012, following the severance of their joint charges on 21 November 2012, and released from the custody of the International Criminal Court on 21 December, 2012. The office of the Prosecutor appealed the judgment. On 27 February 2015, the Appeals Chamber confirmed, by a majority decision, Trial Chamber II judgment of 18 December 2012 acquitting Mathieu Ngudjolo Chui of charges of crimes against humanity.

The third case from DR Congo that was still pending at the time of writing concerns Bosco Ntaganda,[39] who had been at large,[40] until

---

[39] *The Prosecutor v Bosco Ntaganda, ICC-01/04-02/06.*

[40] According to Human Rights Watch 2010 World Report (n40), 104, evidence suggested that he had been appointed to a senior position in DR Congo army. The report reads 'The fight against impunity [in the DRC] was seriously undermined by the promotion of Bosco Ntaganda to the rank of general, despite an ICC arrest warrant for war crimes he committed in Ituri between 2002 and 2004'. United Nations Human Rights Commission (UNHRC) 2010 Expert Report on DR Congo (n33) para. 64 states 'In January 2009, Bosco Ntaganda was promoted to the rank of General in the context of the rapprochement with CNDP, even though nine months earlier the International Criminal Court had published an arrest warrant for war crimes against him. During the Human Rights Council's Universal Periodic Review in November and December 2009, the Government explicitly rejected the recommendation that Ntaganda should be arrested and transferred to the International Criminal Court. Despite Government assurances that Ntaganda no longer exercises command functions within FARDC, reports indicate that he remains involved in the FARDC command structure, including in the context of the Kimia II operation'. The ICC had issued its first warrant of arrest against Ntaganda: issued under seal on 22 August 2006, the said warrant was unsealed on 28 April 2008. The DRC claimed that Ntaganda was crucial to the peace progress, and therefore that his arrest at the time would be inauspicious.

his voluntary surrender to the International Criminal Court on March 22, 2013. On 9 June 2014, Pre-Trial Chamber II unanimously confirmed charges consisting of 13 counts of war crimes (murder and attempted murder; attacking civilians; rape; sexual slavery of civilians; pillaging; displacement of civilians; attacking protected objects; destroying the enemy's property; and rape, sexual slavery, enlistment and conscription of child soldiers under the age of fifteen years and using them to participate actively in hostilities) and 5 counts of crimes against humanity (murder and attempted murder, rape, sexual slavery, persecution, forcible transfer of population) against Bosco Ntaganda allegedly committed between 2002 and 2003 in the Ituri Province of DR Congo.

According to the office of the Prosecutor, Bosco Ntaganda bears individual criminal responsibility pursuant to different modes of liability namely: direct perpetration, indirect co-perpetration;[41] ordering, including[42] any other contribution to the commission or attempted commission of crimes;[43] or as a military commander for crimes committed by his subordinates.[44] On November 7, 2019, Trial Chamber IV of the International Criminal Court (ICC) unanimously sentenced Bosco Ntaganda to a total of 30years of imprisonment for war crimes and crimes against humanity. Reparation proceedings have been on against Ntaganda. On 28 February, 2020, the Registry, the Defence, the LRVs[45], the Prosecution and the TFV[46] filed their

---

[41] See article 25(3)(a) of the *Rome Statute of International Criminal Court*.

[42] Article 25(3)(b) of the *Statute*.

[43] Article 25(3)(d) of the *Statute*.

[44] Article 28(a) of the *Statute*.

[45]

[46] Trust fund for victims.

respective submissions on reparations. The defence has closed its case on 11 January, 2021 and the Trial Chamber's decision on reparation orders are being awaited as at the time of going to press.[47]

In *The Prosecutor v Callixte Mbarushimana*,[48] the Pre-Trial Chamber I decided on 16 December 2011, by a majority decision to decline confirmation in the charges brought against Mr. Mbarushimana. Consequently, he was released from the International Criminal Court's custody on 23 December 2011, upon the completion of the necessary arrangements, as ordered by Pre-Trial Chamber 1.

Mr. Mbarushimana was allegedly criminally responsible for:

1. Five counts of crimes against humanity; murder, torture, rape, inhumane acts and persecution; and
2. Eight counts of war crimes: attacks against the civilian population, murder, mutilation, torture, rape, inhuman treatment, destruction of property and pillaging.[49]

However, in the case of *Prosecutor v Jean-Pierre Bemba Gombo and others*,[50] another DR Congo national stands trial at the International

---

[47] See ICC-01/04-02/06-2634-Red 11-01-2021 4/48 EC available at icc-cpi.int.

[48] ICC-01/04-01/10. Mbarushimana, a Rwandan nationale, and alleged executive secretary of the FDLR, was charged with a number of war crimes and crimes against humanity, allegedly committed in the North and South Kivu provinces.

[49] *Prosecutor v Callixte Mbarushimana, Supra.*

[50] Jean-Pierre Bemba Gombo is the presidential candidate who ran against Joseph Kabila in DR Congo presidential elections 2006 and received 42% of the votes in the second round. It has also been noted that Bemba received more votes than Kabila in the Kinshasa region. Moreover, his supporters claim that he won the national elections and that Kabila's victory was fraudulent. See BBC news, 'Kabila

Criminal Court, but in connection with crimes committed in the Central African Republic. He was charged alongside fellow nationals, Aime Kilolo Musamba, Jean-Jacques Mangenda Kabongo and Fidele Babala Wandu, alongside a Central African national, Narcisse Arido.[51]

Bemba is allegedly criminally responsible, as military commander, for: two counts of crimes against humanity: murder (article 7(1)(a) of the Rome Statute of International Criminal Court), and rape (article 7(1)(g) of the Statute); three counts of war crime: murder (article 8(2)(c)(i) of the Statute); rape (article 8(2)(e)(vi) of the Stature); and pillaging (article 8(2)(e)(v) of the Statute).[52]

In as much as most of the accused persons have been charged with crimes of sexual violence against women, the judgments delivered so far by the International Criminal Court, show that, the office of the prosecutor was not gender-sensitive in gathering and adducing evidence of sexual violence and other gendered crimes. This can be seen in the fact that the International Criminal Court did not charge Lubanga with sexual violence crimes in spite of the fact that the armed conflict in DR Congo witnessed the highest incidents of sexual violence against women in the world, and that the forces he commanded were known to have committed widespread sexual violence against women. Many Non-Governmental organizations have complained that the International Criminal Court did not charge Lubanga with sexual violence crimes, which were

named DR Congo poll winner' (15 November, 2006) available at <http://news.bbc.co.uk /2/hi/africa/6151.598.stm> accessed on 11 January 2011.

[51] *The Prosecutor v Jean-Pierre Bemba Gombo, Aime' Kilolo Musamba, Jean-Jacques Mangenda Kabongo, Fidele Babala Wandu and Narcisse Arido, Supra.*

[52] *Supra.*

perpetrated mostly against women, in the very first case that it tried.[53] As a result, activists who were disappointed that Lubanga was not charged with sexual violence crimes advocated for the prosecution of such crimes by other means, including domestic courts.[54] Subsequent cases before the International Criminal Court did not fare any better. Katanga who was found guilty, as an accessory, of one count of crime against humanity (murder) and four counts of war crimes (murder, attacking a civilian population, destruction of property and pillaging), was acquitted of all charges of sexual violence which was mostly committed against women. Ngudjolo who was charged with three counts of crimes against humanity and seven counts of war crimes, which included sexual slavery and rape, which are gendered crimes against women was acquitted of the charges and ordered to be released immediately. The

---

[53] The Women's Initiatives for Gender Justice (WIGJ), an international women's human rights organization which advocates for the prosecution of gender-based crimes in ICC cases has been noted as one of the main NGOs that have complained that the ICC did not charge Lubanga with sexual violence crimes. See, for example, The New York Times, 'For International Criminal Court, Frustrations and Missteps in its First Trial' by Marlise Simons, 21 November 2010. That report states 'Congo has among the highest sexual violence in the world – its unfathomable that they brought no such charges [in the Lubanga trial]', said Bridgid Inder of the Women's Initiative for Gender Justice, one of the rights group that followed in the trial'.

[54] See Open Society Initiative (OSI), 'Putting Complementarity into Practice', 27 (n69), a Land mark Trial of 10 March 2009, available at <www.hrw.org/en/news/2009/03/10/dr-congo-militia-leaderguilty-landmark-trial> accessed on 31 July, 2010; *Kalonga Katamasi Case, Kilwa Case, Kipanga Case, Milobs Case (2002), Mitwaba Case, Mutins de Mbandaka Case (2006), Songo Mboyo Case (2006), and Walikale Case* (All the cases were cited in ASF 2009 study (n.61), Annex, ICTJ).

Appeals Chamber, on 27 February 2015, confirmed, by majority, the Trial Chamber II's decision acquitting him.

With the fore-going trend, it is doubtful that the International Criminal Court would be able to convict persons standing trial for sexual violence crimes against women in the few cases from DR Congo that are pending before it. Meanwhile, Le Fraper du Hellen, an International Criminal Court prosecutor claims that she and her colleagues were satisfied that they had properly emphasized sexual violence investigations and they have also succeeded in bringing representative charges.[55] Another prosecutor, Chung agrees with her assertion, stating that over all, the office of the prosecutor has done well in making sexual violence a priority and bringing charges that represent the scope of sexual violence. According to him, 'sexual violence crimes are adequately represented, and ICC cases reflect more representation (of crimes committed) than has been achieved at any of the other tribunals ....'[56]

Whichever way one looks at it, there has been the need to address the extensive number of gender violence, especially sexual in nature that had taken place (and continued to take place) in South Kivu, and in DR Congo in general. The International Criminal Court cannot be expected to achieve much in this regard, in view of its restrictive mandate. It may therefore be necessary to look to national courts for any hope of redemption, though with cautious optimism, as gender discrimination against women has remained entrenched and pervasive in DR Congo.

---

[55] Tosh, C. and Chazan, Y. (eds.), *Special Report: Sexual Violence in DR Congo*, The Hague, Institute for War & Peace Reporting, 2008, 12.
[56] *Ibid.*

National Courts and Gender Mobile Courts and the Protection of Women in the Armed Conflict in DR Congo: As has been observed earlier, it is clear that the Congolese government has been unable and/or unwilling to prosecute violators of the laws of armed conflict and those who have committed war-related atrocities, especially against women. Nevertheless, the country's military courts have been able to try a number of atrocity-related cases. The military courts have exclusive jurisdictions, under Congolese law, over war crimes, crimes against humanity and genocide, even when the defendants are civilians or rebels that fight the regular army.[57] The nation's *Military Criminal Code* of 2002 criminalizes war crimes and crimes against humanity. It defines war crimes as 'any violation of the laws of the Republic committed during the war which are not justified by the laws and customs of war';[58] and defines crimes against humanity as 'grave violations of international humanitarian law committed against civilian populations before or during the war'.[59] It also provides that crimes against humanity are not necessarily linked to the state of war.[60]

However, it has been observed that the fore-going definitions are 'somewhat ambiguous and do not fully correspond to the Rome Statute definitions of these crimes.'[61] Furthermore, it has also been observed that one reason for this inconsistency lies in the fact that

---

[57] See *DR Congo Military Justice Code*, Act No. 023-2002, 18 November 2002 (hereinafter, 'DRC Military Justice Code'), which authorizes military courts to judge civilians.

[58] See *DR Congo Military Criminal Code, Article* 161.

[59] *Ibid.,* Article 163.

[60] *Ibid.,* Article 165.

[61] Horovitz, *Op.cit.,* 20.

the Rome Statute has still not been implemented domestically in DR Congo.[62] But it is clear that Congolese Military Courts have been known to apply provisions of the Statute in their judgments.[63]

A study of some of these judgments has been published by Avocats Sans Frontiers (ASF) in 2009.[64] The study identifies thirteen atrocity-related trials which were held by the military courts between 2004 and 2009.[65] A total of one hundred and eighty-eight Congolese defendants were involved in these trials. They were personnel of the regular army and the non-state armed groups.

The *Ankoro trial* held in 2004 by the Military Court of Katanga in the city of Lubumbashi has been acclaimed by many reports, as the first atrocity-related trial in DR Congo since the Pretoria Peace Agreement was concluded in 2002.[66] According to the ICTJ, the trial

[62] It may however be noted that the *Rome Statute of International Criminal Court* does not require states to implement nationally its definitions of crime.

[63] This is based on the provisions of Articles 153 and 215 of the statute *DR Congo Constitution* of 2006 which provide a legal basis for directly applying international treaty provisions in national cases.

[64] Avocats Sans Frontiers, 'Case Study: The application of the *Rome Statute of the International Criminal Court* of DR Congo 2009, available at <*http://www.asfbe/publications/ASF Case study Rome Statute Light Page Per Page.pdf*> accessed on 4 May 2010 (hereinafter: 'ASF 2009 study').

[65] The study's main objective was to identify and access instances where the *Rome Statute* was directly applied by Congolese courts. It examines not only how the national military courts deal with definitions of international crimes, but also with principles such as command responsibility, excuses and justifications and sentencing practices. It also includes a section on the 'civil responsibility of the state', where the DRC's practices of victim participation and compensation is discussed in light of provisions of the Rome Statute.

[66] See, for example, *Bavi Case*, 2007, *ASF* 2009 Study, Annex, ICTJ, Biyoyo Case, *ASF* 2009 Study, Annex, ICTJ ASF 2009 study, *Ibid*, Annex; and ICTJ, 'A First Few Steps: The Long Road to the Just Peace in DR Congo' 2004, available at

attracted a great deal of interest as the first trial for crimes against humanity to take place since the beginning of the transition.[67] More than twenty soldiers were charged in the proceedings with atrocities committed against civilians in the town of Ankoro, in November 2002. The atrocities included the killing of more than sixty people, the burning and destruction of more than four thousand homes, and the pillaging of more than one hundred and seventy buildings.[68] In a report published before the judgment was issued, the International Center for Transitional Justice (ICTJ) observed that by holding the trial so far from Ankoro, victims and witnesses were prevented from testifying, thus creating the suspicion that the trial was being held in order to set the prisoners free.[69] The judgment seems to have confirmed the suspicion. The court acquitted about half of the defendants and sentenced others to less than two years imprisonment, and released them as they had spent over two years in pre-trial custody.[70]

The Gedeon trial, another landmark trial by the military court, also took place in Katanga province. In that case, a Mai Mai commander Kyungu Mutanga Gedeon and more than twenty Mai Mai fighters were tried for atrocities which they committed in Katanga between 2003 and 2006. These atrocities included mass rape, use of child soldiers in active hostilities, cannibalism, use of firearms, creating a

---

<*http://www.ictj.org/images/ content/1/1/115.pdf*> accessed on 28 February 2011 (hereinafter 'ICTJ, A First Few Steps'), p. 23, as cited in Horovitz, *Op.cit.,* 20.

[67] Horovitz, *Ibid.,* 30.

[68] *Ibid.*

[69] *Ibid.*

[70] *Ibid.,* 31.

rebel movement, pillaging and destruction of property.[71] The court sentenced Gedeon to death for crimes against humanity, insurgency and terrorism, alongside six others who were also convicted for crimes against humanity.[72] Most national jurisdictions have yet retained capital punishment for crimes against humanity. For instance, on 17 September 2013, the Appellate Division of the Bangladesh Supreme Court overturned the lower court judgment and sentenced Abdul Quader Molla to death for crimes committed during the country's Liberation War in 1971. Following the February 2013 amendments to the *International Crimes (Tribunal) Act* which allowed the appeal of sentencing orders, the government of Bangladesh appealed the International Crimes Tribunal – 2 (ICT-2) judgment, wherein the accused was sentenced to life imprisonment. The government of Bangladesh demanded that the Appellate Division of the Supreme Court sentence Mr. Molla to death, the highest sentence envisaged by *International Crimes (Tribunal) Act of Bangladesh.*

Molla is said to have been accused of having 'actively aided, abetted, facilitated and substantially assisted, contributed and provided moral support and encouragement in committing appalling atrocities in 1971 in the territory of Bangladesh.'[73] The

---

[71] See HRW, 'DR Congo: Militia Leader Guilty in Landmark Trial' (10 March 2009), available at <*www.hrw.org/en/news/2009/03/10/dr-congo-militia-leader-guilty-landmark-trial*> accessed on 31 July 2016, as cited, *Ibid.*

[72] *Ibid.*

[73] See *Chief Prosecutor v Abdul Quader Molla*, Criminal Appeal, Nos. 24-25 of 2013, Appellate Division of the Supreme Court of Bangladesh, as cited in Jaccard, J., 'Reports and Documents: What's new in law and case law around the world? (Biannual update on national implementation of international humanitarian law-

Appellate Division affirmed the Judgment of International Crimes Tribunal, finding Molla guilty of committing murder and rape as a part of a systematic or organized attack against civilian population in the 1971 Liberation War. After considering the gravity of the conduct and the high profile of the accused, the Appellate Division modified the sentence imposed by the tribunal and condemned him to death by hanging.[74]

DR Congo's Military Criminal Code of 2002 grants the military courts the discretion to impose the death penalty in cases of genocide and crimes against humanity, as well as in certain war crimes such as reprisals, use of prisoners as human shields, and pillage in times of war.[75] This was the basis upon which it imposed the death penalty in the *Gedeon case*.[76] However, Congolese military courts have refrained from imposing the death penalty in some of the cases that involved these crimes which carry the death penalty under national courts by giving precedence to the *Rome Statute sentencing norms, over domestic provisions. Of course, the Rome Statute excludes the death penalty.*

Thus, in the *Bongi case*,[77] the Military Court of Orientale province held:

The provisions of the Treaty of Rome are more humanizing and less severe in terms of punishment such that capital

---

July-December, 2013' [2014], *International Review of the Red Cross (IRRC)*, (Vol. 96, No. 893), 386.

[74] *Supra.*

[75] See *Articles* 65, 164, 167, 171, and 172, as cited in Horovitz, *Op.cit.*, 51.

[76] Gideon Case *Supra.*

[77] Military Court of Orientale Province, *Bongi Case, Judgment,* 4 November 2006, RPA030/06.

punishment is unrecognized, contrary to the Military Panal Code ... and for these reasons the Military Court ... decide to apply the Treaty of Rome.[78]

In the *Bongi case,* a military commander captain Blaise Bongi Massamba was charged in connection with an attack on the civilian population in the village of Tshekele in Ituri on 20 October 2005. The charges against him included looting civilian property, forcing five civilians to carry the looted goods, and subsequently killing them in the village of Bussinga. On 24 March 2006, the accused was sentenced to life imprisonment. He however escaped from Bunia prison in March 2007.

In the *Songo Mboyo trial or case,*[79] the Military Tribunal also cited, the *Rome Statute of International Criminal Court* directly in sentencing seven members of the Congolese army to life imprisonment for collective rape,[80] and for the first time, a national court in DR Congo, described collective rape as crime against humanity. The case involved twelve soldiers (including two lieutenant-colonels) who were tried in connection with a mutiny committed in the village of *Songo Mboyo* on 21 December 2003, during which the soldiers perpetrated a series of mass rapes (including against the wives of senior army officers). On 21 April 2006, the lower military court sentenced seven defendants to life imprisonment for crimes against humanity and other military offences, and acquitted five other

---

[78] *Supra,* 15 – 16.

[79] *Supra.* See also ASF 2009 study, Annex.

[80] See also *the Milobs case, Supra,* 16 – 17, where the Military Garrison Tribunal of Ituri explicitly ruled that 'substantive Congolese law introduced into its legal arsenal ... the *Statute of International Criminal Court,* [which] becomes a legal instrument that forms an integral part of Congolese penal law.'

defendants. On 7 June 2006, the Appellate Court upheld the decision of the lower court concerning six defendants and reversed the conviction of the seventh defendants.

The foregoing trials and convictions secured for crime of gender and sexual violence against women may not be enough to laud the Congolese Military Court as there was no evidence of deliberate gender-sensitive procedures in the handling of the cases. In other words, there was no evidence of the court mainstreaming gender in its jurisprudence, a fact which whittles down the juridical weight of its legacy for the protection of women against gender-based violence. This is why the importance of the Gender Justice Mobile Court project in DR Congo cannot be over-emphasized.

The Gender Justice Mobile Court's project which was designed and operated by Open Society Initiative for Southern Africa (OSISA) and Open Society Justice Initiative (OSJI) in partnership, with the American Bar Association and the Rule of Law Initiative (ABA/ROLI) is said to have boldly confronted head-on, 'the current justice crisis in DR Congo by fixing on a particular area of Eastern Congo – South Kivu province – and by focusing on the needs of a specific population, namely South Kivu's women and children'.[81] The mobile courts are distinct from other itinerant courts that have been mounted by European Union Programme for the Restoration of Justice in Eastern Congo (REJUSCO) and Non-governmental Organizations, such as Avocats Sans Frontiers (ASF) by being the only tribunal in the region whose primary business is to adjudicate

---

[81] Davis, M. M., 'Helping to Combat Impunity for Sexual Crimes in DR Congo: An Evaluation of the Gender Justice Mobile Courts', [2012], *Open Society Initiative for Southern Africa*, (Vol. 04), 13.

crimes and legal issues of particular importance to women.[82] For instance, the goals of the gender justice mobile court project, which was articulated by the Open Society Justice Initiative (OSJI) in 2008 included the following:

1. The court specializing in gender issues and specifically, in 'sexual violence related to the conflict'. But the court's jurisdiction could also extend to women issues more generally – including topics related to family law, property rights, and inheritance laws.
2. The court has jurisdiction over military as well as civilian justice issues, and is authorized to hear both civil and criminal cases.
3. The court's focus on trying crimes of sexual violence 'complements' ICC prosecutions in the Hague – given its mandate to try crimes committed against women and children in South Kivu on a massive scale related to persistent and continuing armed conflict there.
4. The court is positioned squarely within the structure of DR Congo justice system, which has long provided for itinerant courts that travel to remote communities lacking court houses of their own.

At the beginning of the project (phase 1), the Open Society Initiative for Southern Africa approved a grant of Eight Hundred and Forty-Four Thousand Dollars ($844,000.00) to American Bar Association/Rule of Law Initiative for them to 'establish a pilot project which will travel throughout remote areas of South Kivu to

---

[82] *Ibid.*

provide gender justice to women who are victims of sex crimes or who need other forms of judicial redress.'[83]

Indeed, within the pilot phase, from October 2009 to December 2010, the mobile court project made impressive achievements in line with the expressed objective of taking justice to the remote areas of South Kivu, by:

1. Holding nine sessions in hard-to-access areas of South Kivu;
2. Raising public awareness as to the importance of reporting and prosecuting crimes of sexual violence; and
3. Training various justice sector officials with respect to best practices for investigating and adjudicating gender based crimes.[84]

According to Davis' report, in the first year of the courts operation (2010):

Altogether nine sessions of the itinerant courts heard 186 cases: of these dossiers, as they are called in French, 94 resulted in convictions for rape and 41 in convictions for other offences for a grand total of 135 convictions. There were 22 acquittals in rape cases and 18 acquittals related to other offences.[85]

---

[83] See 'Terms of Grant from OSISA to ABA/ROLI,.1 (September, 2009)' cited *Ibid*, 15.

[84] *Ibid*.

[85] *Ibid*.

The report further stated that sentences imposed for rape convictions ranged from three to twenty years and that there were significant financial penalties that were accessed as well.[86]

The report also observed that six of the nine court sessions were conducted by military tribunals at Kamituga and Baraka, in July 2010, while the remaining three were held in civilian courts at Shabunda in November 2010. The courts were said to have 'generally operated on the ground for a period of two weeks at a time and on average tried 20 accused during this two week period'.[87] It may however be observed that all the rape charges were brought 'under Congolese penal law, and did not implicate international law',[88] because they were not committed during armed conflicts, even though many of the incidents occurred in so-called military 'operational zones'. It is necessary to consider three of such trials, at this point in time.

Trial of Justin Paluku (Paluku's Case):[89] The accused in this case was an officer of the Congolese national police. He was charged with attempting to rape a ten year old girl on August 10, 2010. The prosecution alleged that the young complainant, together with her two young sisters, had been in a field behind the police camp gathering grass to feed their guinea pigs when the accused approached and asked the girls to cut grass for his guinea pigs, promising to pay them 500CF. He then sent the younger sisters off to hunt for grass in a different area of the bush, and grabbed the ten-

---

[86] *Ibid.*

[87] *Ibid.*

[88] *Ibid,* 20.

[89] Gender Justice Mobile Court No.RP003/13

year-old girl, clapped his hand over her mouth, pulled down her under wear and threw her on the ground. When he removed his hand from her mouth in a bid to lower his own underwear, the girl screamed, and her sisters returned. He let them go, and they immediately reported the attempted rape to a relative.[90]

The case was brought before the tribunal or mobile court which rendered judgment a few days later. The accused was found guilty of attempted rape and was sentenced to five years in prison and a penalty of 200,000CF, in addition to the court costs, on the criminal charge. With respect to the civil action, the court decreed that the accused and DR Congo were jointly liable to the girl's father in the equivalent in Congolese Francs of US$3,000.[91]

The written judgment carefully set forth the procedural history of the case, and elucidated the facts presented at the trial. The applicable law was also analyzed, before determining that guilt had been proven conclusively in the criminal matters. With regards to the civil matter, causality had been established for the wrong inflicted on the girl's father for which the State was partially responsible. In rejecting the State's claim that it lacked responsibility for the accused's conduct, 'the court noted that the defendant was wearing his uniform at the time of the attack in the vicinity of the police camp; that he was accountable for the security of the community; and that the State should not have hired him in the first place!'[92]

---

[90] *Supra*, at 22.

[91] *Supra*.

[92] *Supra*.

Trial of Abuku Wandango (Abuku Wandango's Case):[93] The accused in this case was a sergeant from the rebel Mai Mai group. He was charged with the rape of a thirteen year old girl, who was his relative and lived in the same family compound as the victim and her guardian.[94] On the night in question, the young girl was said to have been sleeping alone 'when the accused entered her room, overpowered her, and completed the act of rape'.[95] He threatened to kill her if she reported the rape to anyone and promised to buy her some beauty cream and a skirt if she kept quiet. For several days, she did not mention the attack to anybody, until it became necessary for her to seek medical attention for vaginal pain. The nurse observed that the young girl, who was accompanied to the clinic by the accused, and her guardian, was 'unable to standup' and suffered from a 'perforation of the hymen' and 'damage to the vagina'.[96]

The counsel for the civil party cited international law when urging that the victim's statement to the judicial police made out a case of rape. Particularly, he cited *Akayesu case*[97] in support of the preposition that the accused's threat to kill the complainant, amounted to the requisite 'coercion'. He also cited *Bemba's case* to emphasize that 'a victim's failure to make a prompt outcry is not fatal to bringing a rape prosecution'.[98]

---

[93] Gender Justice Mobile Court, Case No. RMP0375.

[94] *Supra*

[95] *Supra*

[96] *Supra* at 23

[97] *Prosecutor v Akayesu, Supra.*

[98] *Prosecutor v Jean-Bemba & others (Supra).*

On the other hand, a military prosecutor argued that the accused, being a member of the Mai Mai group, worshipped fetishes and believed that he would become immortal and untouchable if he had sex with a young girl. However, this was not supported with any evidence at the trial. The defence maintained that there had been no proof of rape, as no document properly attested to the time or the fact of rape.[99]

The court convicted the accused of rape and sentenced him to twenty years in prison, and to the payment of penalty in the amount of Two Hundred Thousand Congolese Francs (200,000CF). He was also found to be individually responsible in damages and compensation in the civil case, in which the equivalent of Ten Thousand Dollars (US$10,000) was awarded against him.

The Fizi Trial (Fizi's Case):[100] Before the *Fizi trial*, all the defendants tried in mobile courts in South Kivu had been middle level officers, but this time, a commander was held accountable alongside eight of his subordinates, for widespread rape and pillaging that took place in the town of Fizi on New Year's Day, 2011. In all, eleven soldiers were brought to trial within six weeks of the attacks. One of them was acquitted of all the charges, while one of the cases was transferred to a civil court because the accused was a minor.[101]

The court charged Lt. Col. Kibibi Mutare, the commander, with ordering his troops to attack the village of Fizi in retaliation for the death of a soldier after an altercation with a local resident, and convicted him of crime against humanity and sentenced him to

---

[99] Abuku Wandango's case *(Supra)*.

[100] Gender Justice mobile Court, case No.BBM/013,24.

[101] *Supra.*

twenty years in prison. One of the victims, who, like other rape survivors gave evidence in closed sessions and under a pseudonym, testified that he had raped her for forty minutes. Thus, the commander was held accountable for committing rape himself, in addition to being convicted, under the theory of joint criminal enterprise and, 'at a minimum looking the other way while those under his control raped, pillaged, and unlawfully detained individuals who had the misfortune to find themselves in the vicinity of the rampaging soldiers.'[102]

Interestingly, the military tribunal applied international law in holding the nine accused persons accountable for 'widespread and systematic' attacks against the people of Fizi. Accordingly, the forty-three paged judgment 'thoroughly discusses the applicability of the *Rome Statute of the International Criminal Court* to the crimes at issue, noting that the DRC's constitutional framework mandates that international treaty law trump domestic legislation.' [103] Besides, the fact that the 2006 Congolese *constitution* gives precedence to international legislations which the country has ratified, and the tribunal's reliance on the *Rome Statute* is underscored by the fact that the statute's definitions of crime are more exact than the relevant domestic law provisions. It also offers more favourable protection to the rights of both the accused and the victims. For instance, it does not provide for death penalty.[104]

---

[102] *Supra* 25 – 26.

[103] *Supra* 26.

[104] *Supra.*

The court has also been acclaimed for paying particular attention to procedural rules, and for the thoroughness of its judgment.[105]

The Minova Trial (Minova's Case):[106] The Minova trial is one of the cases handled by national military courts in DR Congo. It affords a wonderful opportunity for analyzing and appraising Congolese national judicial response to grave violations of international human rights and humanitarian law. The earlier cases were mostly based on infractions outside armed conflicts.

The *Minova trial* is a fall-out of an armed conflict which erupted in eastern Congo's North Kivu province between the Congolese army and a new rebel movement called, the M23.[107] The M23 captured the eastern city of Goma on November 20, 2012. This incident led to several Congolese army battalions being ordered to retreat to Minova, a town 50 kilometers away, in order to reorganize and prepare for next steps.

While beating a retreat, soldiers committed widespread looting of homes and mass rapes of women and girls in and around communities.[108] 'Human Rights Watch documented at least 76 cases of rape of women and girls by soldiers from November 20 to

---

[105] *Supra*. Of course the judgment is not perfect. It has been criticized for containing the names of the 55 civil parties, who are identified only by number in the judgment, while being named on the title page, despite the care with which the tribunal examined the issue of witness protection by invoking Article 68 of the Rome Statute of the International Criminal Court, which provides for witnesses testifying using pseudonyms and in closed session.

[106] Case No.RP003/13 and Case No. RMPO372/BBM/013.

[107] Human Rights Watch, 'Justice on Trial: Lessons from the *Minova Rape Case* in DR Congo', October 2015, 13.

[108] *Ibid.*, 14.

November 30 in Minova and the nearby villages of Bwisha, Buganga, Mubimbi, Kishinji, Kotolo, Ruchunda, and Kalungu.'[109] The United Nations Joint Human Rights Office documented one hundred and thirty-five cases of sexual violence committed by Congolese army and M23 fighters in the same ten days, namely rapes against ninety-seven women and thirty-three girls aged six to seventeen, and five attempted rapes.[110] The report put the date in which these atrocities happened at between November 22, to 23, 2012.

Investigations were ordered, and both the South Kivu and the North Kivu military prosecutors got involved, because Minova is located at the border between the two provinces, and the 10th and 8th military regions. Thus, the crimes and the soldiers implicated in the crimes fall under the jurisdictions of both prosecutors. Led by the South Kivu prosecution office, three short investigation missions to Minova were undertaken in late December 2012 and in February, 2013 with the support of international partners. However, the General Military Prosecution Office in Kinshasa sent a general military prosecutor to take over the investigation due partly on growing international pressure on Congolese authorities.[111]

At the end of what appeared to be a shoddy investigation, the prosecutor of the North Kivu Operational Military Court (*Cour militaire operationnelle*, CMO) issued indictments on November 5,

---

[109] *Ibid.*, See also 'DR Congo: War Crimes by M23, Congolese Army', Human Rights Watch news release, February 5, 2013, available at *http://www.hrw.org/news/2013/02/05/dr.congo-war-crime-m23.congolese-army* (Accessed 5-10-2019).

[110] *Ibid.*

[111] *Ibid.*, 18.

2013 against thirty-nine accused: fourteen officers and twenty-five regular soldiers of the Congolese army. With the exception of one officer, all of them were charged with the war crimes of rape, pillage, and murder committed by troops under their control. These charges are reflective of the concept of 'command responsibility' as embodied and defined by the *Rome Statute of International Criminal Court*.[112]

In the course of the trial, thirty-nine defendants, fifteen witnesses and seventy-six victims, including fifty victims of rape and twenty-six of pillage testified.[113] Finally, the Operational Military Court gave its decision[114] on 5 May 2014, as follows:

1. Two of the defendants (rank and file soldiers) who were initially accused of rape as an ordinary crime were convicted, one for raping a girl as an ordinary crime and the other for rape as a war crime. They were sentenced to 20 years and life in prison, respectively.

2. All other regular soldiers were acquitted of the war crime of rape, but were convicted of other crimes including violating military instructions and the war crime of pillage, with sentences ranging between three and 10 years in prison[115];

---

[112] See *Article* 28 of the *Rome Statute of the International Criminal Court*, 1998. *Minova's case (Supra)*.

[113] See 'Minova Hearing Transcripts', Case No. RP003/13 and Case No. RMP0372/BBM/013, produced by the registry of the Operational Military Court, on file with Human Rights Watch.

[114] Its judgments cannot be appealed, and this is mainly why the United Nations and civil society organizations strongly resisted the use of the court for the *Minova trial*.

[115] *Minova Case, Supra*.

3. All the officers prosecuted on account of their responsibility as superiors were acquitted of all crimes; and

4. The officer accused of being a direct perpetrator was acquitted of rape but found guilty of stealing a motorbike and sentenced to five years in prison.[116]

The fore-going decision was received with widespread disappointment by victims and civil society activists. The *Minova trial* had been viewed as a test case for the Congolese justice system in terms of its ability to hold perpetrators of grave human rights abuses to account. Thus, certain observations have been made which are either salutary or critical of the trial. For instance, the Human Rights Watch noted the following positive aspects:

i). The government affirmed its commitment to justice and made funds available for the trial, during which all parties had legal representation;

ii). The military judges on the bench directed the hearing effectively;

iii). Challenges such as protecting or organizing victim and witness participation, were well addressed;

iv). Military prosecutors and judges directly applied provisions of *Rome Statute of the International Criminal Court* (ICC), notably with regard to the legal theory of command responsibility and protection measures that are not available under Congolese law; and

v). Diplomatic pressure ensured that the case went to trial: the United Nations, for example, which has supported Congolese troops in military operations, threatened to

---

[116] *Supra*, 84 – 97.

withdraw support unless those responsible for crimes were arrested and brought to justice.[117]

On the other hand, Human Rights Watch has identified three key sets of problems or challenges that bedeviled the trial. They are as follows:

i). Several prosecution offices were involved in the investigation and prosecution of the case, creating confusion. There was no investigation plan or strategy to tackle such a mass crime scene. Lack of expertise and diligence contributed to the poor quality of the investigation and a week prosecution on file;

ii). The rights of defendants to a fair and impartial trial were compromised. In particular, some rank-and-file soldiers suffered from weak legal representation and were convicted for the war crime of pillage and sentenced to up to 20 years in prison despite a lack of evidence. Congolese military law does not allow the right to appeal before the type of military courts that heard the *Minova Trial*; and

iii). The selection of accused by military prosecutors raised concerns about the political will of the armed forces to allow all those responsible for the numerous crimes in Minova to be prosecuted. Some of the officers indicted appeared to be uninvolved scape goats for other officers with genuine command roles. There did not seem to be any willingness to seriously investigate the responsibility of certain suspects beyond field commanders, notably

---

[117] Human Rights Watch, *Op.cit.*, 3.

high level officers who were present in Minova and may have had command responsibility.[118]

The above stated short-comings typify some of the main problems 'that hamper accountability for serious crimes in Congo'.[119] Human Rights Watch has observed that these problems have remained unaddressed despite years of international assistance and training of military justice officials aimed at strengthening the capacity of the national judicial system. Such training is to enable it to handle grave international crimes and promote accountability before national courts to complement the work of the International Criminal Court.

5.3 SIERRA LEONE

To date, judicial enforcement of international humanitarian law vis-à-vis the Sierra Leonean armed conflict seems to have been limited to the trials by the Special Court for Sierra Leone (SCSL). National courts of Sierra Leone have refrained from trying perpetrators of violations as the Lome Accord which ended the conflict 'still provides an absolute and free pardon for all those responsible for crimes under international law committed in Sierra Leone, such as crimes against humanity and war crimes.'[120] However, the provision was not a bar to prosecutions before the

---

[118] *Ibid.*, 3-4.

[119] *Ibid.*, 4.

[120] Amnesty International, 'Sierra Leone: Continuing human rights violations in the post conflict period' (Amnesty International Submission to the UN Universal Periodic Review, May 2011), 2010, 5.

Special Court for Sierra Leone except under Sierra Leone Law.[121] This is why in spite of the few trials by the Special Court, no other investigation or trial has been entertained by the national courts of Sierra Leone.[122]

Therefore, those trials and especially their impact on and implications for the rights of women who were targeted during the conflict, especially for sexual violence shall be considered herewith.

The Trials and their Implications for Women: On the whole thirteen men who were considered to have borne the greatest responsibility for crimes against humanity, war crimes and other violations of international humanitarian law, as well as crimes under relevant Sierra Leonean law were indicted at the Special Court for Sierra Leone. Nine out of these thirteen individuals were associated with the Civil Defence Force, the Armed Forces Revolutionary Council, and the Revolutionary United Front. However, these indictments were subsequently consolidated as three cases and have

---

[121] See decisions on *Prosecutor v Gbagbo Augustine*, Decision on Preliminary Motion on the invalidity of the Agreement between the United Nations and the Government of Sierra Leone on the Establishment of the Special Court, SCSL-2004-15-AR 72(E), May 25, 2004; *Prosecutor v Moinina Fofana*, Decision on Preliminary Motion on Lack of Jurisdiction: Illegal Delegation of Jurisdiction by Sierra Leone, SCSL, 2004-14-AR 72(E), May 25, 2004 Appeals Chamber; and *Prosecutor v Sam Hinga Norman*, No. 28, 2003 Appeals Chamber, SCSL, 2003-08-PT. These decisions have essentially held that any national amnesty granted by Sierra Leone cannot operate to exclude liability for crimes under international law which are the subject of universal jurisdiction; nor can it deprive international courts, such as the Sierra Leone hybrid tribunal of jurisdiction. The decisions are premised on article 10 of the Special Court's Statute. (Per Archbold, 767).

[122] *Ibid.*, 6.

been 'commonly referred to as the CDF, the AFRC, and the RUF trials'.[123] The cases may now be considered one after the other.

(i) *The AFRC Trial (Prosecutor v Brima, Kamara & Kanu*[124]*):* The defendants were indicted on a fourteen counts charge, including war crimes and crimes against humanity. They were senior commanders of the Armed Forces Ruling Council (AFRC). Brima was the overall commander, Kamara was the deputy, while Kanu was the Chief of Staff.[125]

Specifically, they were 'charged with the crimes against humanity of rape, sexual slavery, and any other forms of sexual violence, and forced marriage under the category of "other inhumane acts", as well as the war crimes of outrages upon personal dignity'.[126] Forced marriage has been described as 'the practice during the Sierra Leonean conflict of assigning abducted girls and women to combatants as "wives".[127] These so-called "wives" were often raped by their so-called "husbands", and sometimes forced to bear unwanted children and to undertake domestic labour such as

---

[123] Doherty, T. A., 'Developments in the Prosecution of Gender-based Crimes – The Special Court for Sierra Leone Experiences' [2008], *American University Journal of Gender, Social Policy and Law*, (Vol. 17, No. 1), 327.

[124] *Prosecutor v Alex Tamba Brima, Brima Bazzy Kamara, and Santigie Borbor Kanu* (Judgment) SCSL-2004-16-T (20, June 2007).

[125] See Akiyode-Afolabi, *'Gender justice in post-conflict societies: an assessment of Sierra Leone and Liberia,'*. (Ph.D Thesis), London, SOAS, University of London, 2013, 90, available at http://eprints.soas.ac.uk/16643 (accessed 11/5/17).

[126] Oosterveld, V., 'Lessons from the Special Court for Sierra Leone on the Prosecution of Gender-Based Crimes', [2009], *Journal of Gender, Social Policy & Law*, (Vol. 17, Issue 2), 7.

[127] *Ibid.*

cleaning, cooking, and laundry,[128] as was noted in chapter two. Besides, they are also exposed to health hazards, especially sexually transmitted diseases and Human Immunodeficiency Virus (HIV). For this reason, forced marriage has been described as 'a type of gender-based crime with sexual and numerous non-sexual aspects'.[129]

However, this conception of forced marriage was not understood or accepted by a majority of judges of the Trial Chamber in the AFRC case. Thus, they held: 'the prosecution evidence in the present case does not point to even one instance of a woman or girl having had a bogus marriage forced upon her in circumstances which did not amount to sexual slavery.'[130] According to them, 'subtract the sexual aspects of the forced marriage evidence (as these go to proof of sexual slavery) and the remaining non-sexual aspects (presumably the forced domestic labour, physical abuse, and forced child-bearing and child-rearing) do not reach the gravity required for "other inhumane acts"'.[131]

Thus, the Trial Chamber acquitted Brima and Kamara of count II (other inhumane acts as Crimes Against Humanity, and refused to consider Joint Criminal Enterprise as a mode of criminal

---

[128] *Prosecutor v Brima and others (Supra),* where Sebutide, J. concurred, noting that stereotyped perceptions of women are exacerbated during wartime, and that women are put at greater risk of abduction and violence.

[129] *Op.cit.*

[130] *Ibid.,* 8. See *Prosecutor v Brima and ors (Supra),* where majority opinion indicated that not one of the victims of sexual slavery had given evidence that their rebel captor's declaration of marriage had caused any particular physical and mental trauma.

[131] Ooasterveld, *Ibid.*

responsibility because it found it to be defectively pleaded.[132] It also dismissed count 7, which pleaded sexual slavery and other forms of sexual violence as Crimes Against Humanity, and count 8 (other inhumane acts as Crimes Against Humanity) 'as duplicative pleadings of other charges.'[133] The prosecution had argued in counts 7, 8 and 9 that forced marriages which fell under count 8 as other inhumane acts were distinct from sexual acts, but the Trial Chamber rejected this argument and found that 'the evidence did not establish a non-sexual crime of "forced marriage" independent of sexual slavery under Article 2(g) of the Statute'.[134] It therefore concluded that the crime of sexual slavery subsumes the crime of "forced marriage" in count 9, and so dismissed counts 7 and 8.

However, on appeal, the Appeals Chamber overruled the above reasoning and found that a forced marriage is not necessarily a sexual crime because 'sex is not the only incident of the forced relationship'.[135] It went on to describe forced marriage as involving 'a perpetrator compelling a person by force or threat of force, through words or conduct of the perpetrator or those associated with him into a forced conjugal association',[136] which results 'in great suffering or physical or mental injury'[137] to the victim. The Appeals Chamber also found that the count on Joint Criminal Enterprise was not defectively pleaded. However, the Chamber still went on to

---

[132] Shahram, D., 'The Sentencing Legacy of the Special Court for Sierra Leone', [2014], *Georgia Journal of International and Comparative Law*, (Vol. 42, No. 3), 640.

[133] *Ibid.*

[134] *Ibid.*, 640-641.

[135] *Ibid.*, 641.

[136] *Ibid.*

[137] *Ibid.*

affirm the sentences handed down to the defendants, in spite of the fact that it reversed the rulings of the Trial Chamber, which dismissed counts 7 and 8, and the count on Joint Criminal Enterprise mode of liability.[138]

Brima and Kanu were sentenced to fifty years imprisonment, while Kamara was sentenced to forty-five years. According to the Trial Chamber, the three accused persons were convicted of 'some of the most heinous, brutal and atrocious crimes ever recorded in human history'.[139] Brima was said to have committed atrocious crimes against 'very large number of unarmed civilians and had a catastrophic impact' on the victims and their families.[140] Specifically, Brima was directly criminally responsible for exterminations, murders, mutilations (amputations of various limbs), and terrorizing the civilian population, pursuant to *Article* 6(1) of the *Statute*.[141] He was said to have personally planned and ordered the crimes of collective punishment, recruitment and use of child soldiers, sexual enslavement, looting, murders and enslavement of civilians.[142] He was also found liable under *Article* 6(3) for crimes committed by his subordinates in various districts.

In fact, the Trial Chamber found no personal circumstances that justified mitigation in Brima's case especially as he was a

---

[138] *Ibid.*

[139] *Prosecutor v Brima, Kamara and Kanu* (Sentencing Judgment) *(Supra)*, 34.

[140] *Supra*, 40.

[141] *Article* 6(1) of the *Statute of the Special Court for Sierra Leone* states: 'A person who planned, instigated ordered, committed or otherwise aided and abetted in the planning, preparation or execution of a crime referred to in *Article* 2 to 4 of the present *Statute* shall be individually responsible for the crime.'

[142] *Prosecutor v Brima and other (Supra)* at 37.

professional soldier, with a duty to protect civilians, but failed to do so. Moreso, he carried out attacks himself, which according to the Trial Chamber aggravated his punishment.[143] It was further aggravated by the fact that Brima was the overall commander of his troops. Other aggravating factors included Brima's tactics of extreme coercion, his zealous participation in some of the crimes, and the prolonged period of time during which enslavement and attacks on places of worship were carried out.[144]

In the *Case of Kamara*, the Trial Chamber found as of fact, that he was responsible for ordering five murders of civilians, planning abduction of children for use as child soldiers, planning crimes of sexual slavery and enslavement against civilians, aiding and abetting murder and extermination of civilians, and mutilations of persons. He was therefore indicted for them all under *Article* 6(1) of the *statute of the Special Court for Sierra Leone*. He was also found liable under *Article* 6(3) of the same *statute* for crimes that were committed by his subordinates in various districts.[145] Like Brima's, his crimes were extremely brutal, they targeted 'a very large number of unarmed civilians and impacted the victims' lives in "catastrophic and irreversible" way.[146] Again, like in the *Case of Brima*, the Trial Chamber 'found that nothing in Kamara's personal circumstances warranted mitigation of his punishment'.[147] He was also a professional soldier, who instead of protecting civilians, attacked them, and gave orders that they be attacked by soldiers under his

---

[143] *Supra* at 53.

[144] *Supra* at 55.

[145] *Supra* at 71.

[146] *Supra* at 72. See also Shahram, *Op.cit.*, 643.

[147] *Supra* at 78. See also Shahram, *Ibid*.

command.[148] This, among other things, was considered to be a particularly aggravating factor.[149] The vulnerability of victims, the heinous nature of the crimes, and the fact that he was a senior government and military official with a duty to prevent or punish crimes were also considered by the Chamber as aggravating factors.[150]

With regard to Kanu, the Trial Chamber found him responsible both under *Article* 6(1) and 6(3), for direct participation in the crimes; and as a commander that failed to prevent or punish the crimes of subordinates under his control,[151] respectively. Thus, the court held that Kanu was directly responsible for the following crimes pursuant to *Article* 6(1): (a) planning abduction of children for use as child soldiers; (b) committing sexual slavery and enslavement of civilians; (c) ordering murders and mutilations; (d) personally mutilating civilians and looting civilian property; (e) instigating other murders; and (f) aiding and abetting murder and extermination of civilians.[152] The Judges were said to have rejected his claim that most of the crimes or atrocities were committed by the Revolutionary United Front, who were not under his control.[153]

The court rejected arguments for mitigation based on his personal circumstances, as it did against Kamara and Brima, and found that his position as third in command was an aggravating

---

[148] *Supra* at 73, *Ibid*.

[149] *Supra*, at 82, *Ibid*.

[150] *Supra*.

[151] *Supra*, 92-93.

[152] *Supra*, 100.

[153] *Supra*, 98.

factor. So also was the fact that he was involved in amputations and ordered people to engage in killings. Moreover, he did not express any genuine remorse in his statement to the Chamber, and thus lost the chance for a mitigated sentence.[154]

(ii) *The CDF Trial (Prosecutor v Fofana & Kondewa[155])*: The Prosecutor of the Special Court indicted three persons within the Civilian Defence Force (CDF). They were Sam Hinga Norman, The Civil Defence Force's "National Coordinator", Moinia Fofana, the "Director of War", and Allieu Kondewa, who was the "High Priest" of the militia group'.[156] Originally, the three of them were indicted separately, with Norman's indictment being approved on 7th March;[157] and those against Fofana and Kondewa being approved on 24 June, 2003.[158] The three indictments were subsequently consolidated into a single indictment on February 5, 2004.[159]

They were charged with the following offences:

murder (both as crimes against humanity) and war crimes; inhumane acts as a crime against humanity; and six counts of war crimes, including violence to life, health and physical or mental well-being of persons (in particular cruel treatment), pillaging, acts of terrorism, collective punishments, and enlisting children under the age of fifteen years into armed

---

[154] *Supra*, 139.

[155] See *Prosecutor v Fofana and Kondewa*, Case No. SCSL-04-14-T, Judgment, 1.

[156] See *Prosecutor v Norman, Fofana and Kondewa*, Case No. SCSL-03-14-I, Indictment (Feb. 5, 2004).

[157] *Prosecutor v Norman (Case No. SCSL – 03 – 08)*.

[158] *Supra*. See also Oasterveld, *Op.cit*, 7.

[159] *Ibid*.

forces or groups or using them to participate actively in hostilities.[160]

At the end, judgment was pronounced against Fofana and Kondewa, while proceedings against Norman were terminated when he died after the trial was completed but before the delivery of judgment. Fofana was found guilty of war crimes, but acquitted of all crimes against humanity. He was convicted of the following war crimes, namely: murder, cruel treatment, pillage, and collective punishment. So also did the Trial Chamber acquit Kondewa of all crimes against humanity as well as acts of terrorism as a war crime, while convicting him of the war crime of pillage. He was convicted of pillage pursuant to a theory of superior responsibility under *Article* 6(3) of the *statute*, for incidents of pillage in Moyamba and Bonthe Districts, respectively.

On appeal, the Appeals Chamber reversed Fofana's conviction on war crime of collective punishment (count 7), the Trial Chamber's acquittal on murder and inhumane acts as a crime against humanity (count 1 and 3), and unanimously held that Fofana was not guilty of acts of terrorism, and by majority, not guilty of war crimes for collective punishment and enlisting of child soldiers.[161] On the whole, the Appeals Chamber found Fofana guilty on five counts and not guilty on three counts and reversed the Trial Chamber's sentence of six years imprisonment upward and sentenced him to fifteen years.

---

[160] CDF Trial, *Supra*, 2. See also Shahram, *Op.cit.*, 645.

[161] *Supra*, at 18 (at least one appeals judge dissented on the Appeal's Chambers not guilty verdicts for collective punishment and enlisting of child soldiers). See also Shahram, *Op.cit*, 647-648.

The Appeal's Chamber also reversed Kondewa's conviction for superior responsibility for pillage committed in Moyamba on the grounds that it was not proved beyond reasonable doubt that he exercised control over the perpetrators.[162] It also set aside some other of Kondewa's convictions for lack of evidence.[163] At the end, he was acquitted on counts 6, 7, and 8, and was found guilty on counts 1, 2, 3, 4 and 5 (in part). The counts include murders as crimes against humanity and as war crimes, aiding and abetting murders, other inhumane acts, cruel treatment and pillage as war crimes. Consequently, the Appeals Chamber also reviewed his sentence upwards to twenty years imprisonment.

The trials and conviction of Fofana and Kondewa have significant implications for the protection of women and children during armed conflicts because, the court found them liable for the large scale and "particularly serious" crimes which involved extreme brutality, and targeted killing of women and children, which were committed by their subordinates. For instance Fofana was held liable for the gruesome murders of two women by subordinates under his control pursuant to superior command responsibility. His subordinates murdered these women by inserting sticks into their 'genitals until their mouths'.[164] This is not withstanding the fact that Fofana was not present at the scene of the

---

[162] CDF: *Prosecutor v Fofana and Kondewa*, Appeal Judgment, 580B.

[163] The specific conviction that were set aside or reversed were the guilty verdicts that were given against him pursuant to *Article* 6(1) for murder committed in Talia and Base zero and for enlisting children under the age of fifteen years into armed forces of groups and using them to participate actively in hostilities.

[164] CDF: *Prosecutor v Fofana and Kondewa*, Sentencing Judgment, 45.

crimes, nor did he order them or aid and abet their commission.[165] The Trial Chamber found him criminally liable only because of his failure to punish the perpetrators who were under his control.[166]

> (iii) *The RUF Trial (Prosecutor v Charles Taylor*[167]*)*: This case arose because Charles Taylor was alleged to have been the major financier and trainer of the insurgents whose target was the control of Sierra Leone's diamond mines.[168] The insurgents called themselves the Revolutionary United Front (RUF). The group engaged mainly child soldiers contrary to the law of armed conflicts, especially, the *Geneva Conventions* and the *Additional Protocols*.[169]

Clearly, 'much of the case against Charles Taylor rested upon finding him criminally responsible for the assistance he provided, including various quantities of arms and ammunitions, to the rebel groups fighting and committing war crimes' in the armed conflict in Sierra Leone.[170] These rebel groups committed many gender-based crimes, which the Special Court for Sierra Leone had found and held against Charles Taylor as accomplice liability, for aiding and abetting the crimes through his assistance, direction or control of the

---

[165] *Supra.*

[166] *Supra*, 51.

[167] Case No. SCSL-03-1-T, Judgment (Trial Chamber II) 26 April 2012; Case No. SCSL-03-1-A, Judgment (Appeals Chamber) 26 September, 2013.

[168] Unegbu, M. O. *Op.cit*, 153.

[169] *Ibid.*

[170] Darcy, S., 'Assistance, direction and control: Untangling International Judicial Opinion on individual and State responsibility for war crimes by non-State actors', [2014], *International Review of the Red Cross*, (Vol. 96, No. 893), 250.

groups. Such gender-based crimes include sexual violence against men and women, ranging from rape, sexual mutilation, sexual slavery (especially of women), and forced marriages. Prominent among the crimes for which he was indicted is the recruitment, and use of child soldiers, both boys and girls.

In determining Taylor's liability, the Special Court for Sierra Leone departed from the International Criminal Tribunal for Former Yugoslavia's decision in the case of *Perisic*,[171] concerning specific direction as an *actus reus* element of aiding and abetting.[172] The Appeals Chamber of the Tribunal had explained that aiding and abetting involves the carrying out of 'acts specifically directed to assist, encourage or lend moral support to the perpetration of a certain specific crime... and this support has a substantial effect upon the perpetration of the crime'.[173] This was in *Tadic*[174] where it held that an aider and abettor must know that his or her acts assist the commission of a specific crime.

In contradistinction to the International Criminal Tribunal for the Former Yugoslavia's Jurisprudence on aiding and abetting crimes, the Trial Chamber of the Special Court for Sierra Leone considered that Taylor's aid amounted to practical assistance to the commission of crime being indispensable to military offensives in

---

[171] ICTY, *Prosecutor v Perisic*, Case No. IT-04-81-A, Judgment (Appeals Chamber), 28 February 2013. Other noteworthy cases which followed the reasoning in *Perisic* include ICTY, *Prosecutor v Gotovina and Markac*, Case No. IT-06-90-A, Judgment (Appeals Chamber) 16 November 2012.

[172] Darcy, *Op.cit.*

[173] ICTY, *Prosecutor v Tadic*, Case No. IT-94-1-A, Judgment (Appeals Chamber), 15 July 1999, paras 172-233.

[174] *Supra.*

certain instances, and having an overall substantial effect on the commission of the crime charged.'[175] The Appeals Chamber of the Special Court emphasized that the essential requirement for aiding and abetting is that the acts of an accused have 'a substantial effect on the commission of the crime charged', and it concurred with the International Criminal Tribunal for Former Yugoslavia that it was not necessary to establish that an accused 'had any power to control those who committed offences'.[176] Thus, Charles Taylor was found guilty as charged and sentenced to fifty years in prison.[177]

At this point, how the Trial Chamber established a link between Taylor and the commission of gender-based crimes may be considered. The chamber found that 'as early as August 1997, when he became President of Liberia, Taylor was aware that RUF, AFRC, RUF-AFRC, junta and/or affiliated fighting forces were committing various forms of sexual and gender-based violence'.[178] It noted, for example, that he was given an ECOWAS report of the Committee of Four on the situation in Sierra Leone dated 26 August 1997 which described the 'massive looting of property, murder and rapes following the coup by the Revolutionary United Front and sections of the (Sierra Leone Army)' against the Sierra Leone government on

---

[175] *Op.cit.* This is reminiscent of *Nicaragua v United States. (ICJ, Military and Paramilitary Activities in and Against Nicaragua (Nicaragua v United States of America), Judgment, ICJ Reports 1986, para. 109).*

[176] SCSL, *Prosecutor v Taylor*, Case No. SCSL-03-1-A, Judgment (Appeal Chamber), 26 September, 2013.

[177] SCSL, *Prosecutor v Charles Taylor, Case No. SCSL-03-01-T, Sentencing Judgment (Spec. Ct. Sierra Leone, May 30, 2012).*

[178] SCSL, *Prosecutor v Taylor*, Case No. SCSL-03-0T, Trial Chamber II, Judgment, 6882.

May 25, 1997.[179] The Trial Chamber also found that he was aware of a speech to the nation on June 18, 1997, in which the Revolutionary United Front forces apologized for 'the atrocities they [had] committed in Sierra Leone, including killings and rapes'.[180] Thus, the Trial Chamber concluded as follows:

> the sole reasonable inference that can be drawn from this evidence is that as early as August 1997, the Accused, as President of Liberia and a member of the ECOWAS Committee of Five, was informed in detail of the crimes committed by the AFRC/RUF members during the Junta period, including murder, abduction of civilians including children, rape, amputation and looting.[181]

Therefore, Taylor was imputed with knowledge that the Armed Forces Revolutionary Council and the Revolutionary United Front would commit similar crimes in future.[182] Moreover, the chamber observed that media and international coverage of the groups' crimes grew after August 1997, such that, at the time, it was public knowledge that these groups were committing sexual violence, among other crimes'.[183] More so, he was presumed to be aware of this public knowledge, as was shown by a 1998 joint communiqué which he, Taylor and the President of Sierra Leone issued, strongly

---

[179] *Supra*, 6880.

[180] *Supra*.

[181] SCSL, *Prosecutor v Taylor*, Case No. SCSL-03-01-T, Trial Chamber II, Judgment, 6882 (May 18, 2012).

[182] *Supra*.

[183] *Supra*, 6883, n.15477 (listing United Nations, non-governmental and other reports of sexual violence in Sierra Leone in 1998). See also Oosterveld, V., 'Gender and the Charles Taylor Case at the Special Court for Sierra Leone [2012], *Williams & Mary Journal of Women and the Law* (Vol. 19, Issue 1), 31.

condemning the continuing rebel activities in Sierra Leone, as well as the horrendous atrocities that had been committed there. Therefore, to the Trial Chamber, the only logical conclusion that could be reached is that, at the time in question, Taylor 'knew of the AFRC/RUF's operational strategy and intent to commit crimes', and that he knew that included rape.[184] Thus, the Trial Chamber extrapolated that because he knew of this operational strategy, the arms and ammunition he gave to the groups and Liberian fighters 'constituted direct assistance to the commission of crimes, including sexual slavery, rape, and outrages upon personal dignity'.[185] The chamber concluded that these and other forms of assistance amounted to substantial assistance.[186] Besides, Taylor was said to have participated in a plan with the Revolutionary United Front's Sam Bockarie to invade Freetown, which included plans for other attacks.[187]

The Trial Chamber argued that since Charles Taylor knew of the operational strategies of the groups, he either 'intended that the crimes charged in counts 1 to 11 of the Indictment be committed or was aware of the substantial likelihood that the RUF/AFRC forces would commit such crimes as a result of executing the plan which he and Bockarie designed', which included sexual violence.[188] Considering all these, the Trial Chamber found that the necessary links were established between Taylor in Liberia and the crimes

---

[184] *Supra*, 6885-86.

[185] *Supra*, 6911-12. See also Oosterveld, V., *Op.cit.*

[186] See, for example, *Prosecutor v Taylor*, Case No. SCSL-03-01T, Trial Chamber II, Judgment, 6918-19, 6922-24, 6936-37, 6950, 6953 (May 18, 2012).

[187] *Supra*, 6961-62, 6968.

[188] *Supra*, 6970.

committed in Sierra Leone by the Revolutionary United Front, African Revolutionary Council and an alliance of the two groups and other fighting forces.[189]

---

[189] *Supra,* 6950- 6971.

CHAPTER SIX

Comparative Assessment of The Legal Protection of Women in The Armed Conflicts in Nigeria, Dr Congo, And Sierra Leone

❧

This chapter offers the opportunity to compare and assess performances that were adopted *vis-à-vis* implementation measures, enforcement mechanisms and strategies for the protection of women in the armed conflicts in Nigeria, DR Congo and Sierra-Leone. The quality of the international legal provisions that the countries subscribed to, either by accession or by ratification, shall also be considered in terms of whether they are gender sensitive enough to adequately secure women's right to protection in the armed conflicts or not. Besides, the countries' domestic legislations on the protection of victims of armed conflict shall also be assessed with regards to their gender sensitivity to the protection of women. To achieve this, a comparative assessment shall be undertaken under the following sub-headings: Effectiveness of Implementation Measures; Effectiveness of Enforcement Measures and Effectiveness of Strategic Activities.

6.1 Effectiveness of Implementation Measures

Before undertaking a comparative assessment of the implementation measures adopted by the countries under review, it may be necessary to assess the gender disposition of the international legal instruments which the countries ratified. With the exception of the *Rome Statute of International Criminal Court*, 1998, it's *Optional Protocol*, the *Women's Conventions* and *Declarations*,[1] none of the mainstream international legal instruments, which the three countries under review subscribed to by ratification or accession is gender-sensitive to women. Such instruments which include the *Geneva Conventions* and their *Additional Protocols*, the *Hague Convention* and its *Protocols*, the *Universal Declaration of Human Rights*, the *International Covenant on Civil and Political Rights*, the *International Covenant on Economic, Social and Cultural Rights*, the *Child Right Convention* and so on, are not couched in gender sensitive language. This, as has been observed earlier, seems to be because international law, especially International Humanitarian Law assumes a population in which there is no systematic gender inequality, and thus fails to recognize the unequal situations of men and women in society, with regard to humanitarian needs that are engendered by armed conflicts. This is what has been reflected in the language of mainstream legal instruments, which are mostly

---

[1] They include the *Convention on the Elimination of All Forms of Discrimination Against Women(CEDAW),(1979)*; *Protocol to the African Charter on Human and Peoples Rights on the Rights of Women in Africa(2003)*; the *Beijing Declaration and Platform for Action(1995)*; the *Declaration on the Elimination of Violence Against Women (DEVAW),(1994)*; *Declaration on the Protection of Women and Children in Emergency and Armed Conflicts(1974)*; and *UN Security Council Resolutions* 1325 and 1820, respectively on Women, Peace and Security.

couched in gender neutral terms, by employing such phrases as "a person", "a prisoner" and so on, but regrettably ending up using the masculine gender of pronouns, such as "he", "his", "him" and "himself", in specifying those who are covered or protected by the law.

This is exemplified by the *Geneva Conventions,* which are the primary international instruments that protect victims of armed conflict. Article 39 of the Fourth *Geneva Convention* subtitled "Means of existence", which provides for the support of those aliens, in the territory of a party to the conflict, who have lost their gainful employment, proceeds by using impersonal pronouns or noun phrases, such as "Protected Persons" and ending up specifying those covered by the provision as "his" and "himself". It states:

> …Where a party to the conflict applies to a protected person methods of control which result in his being unable to support himself, and especially if such a person is prevented for reasons of security from finding paid employment on reasonable conditions, the said Party shall ensure his support and that of his dependants…

The same thing applies to Article 42, which provides grounds for internment or assigned residence,[2] and a number of other articles.[3] It is interesting to note that on rare occasions, some provisions have referred to both genders by providing for "he or she", as we see in Article 33 and 45. Article 33 sub-titled "Individual responsibility, Collective Penalties, Pillage and Reprisals" provides: 'No protected Person may be punished for an offence he or she has not personally

---

[2] See Article 42, *Geneva Convention* IV.

[3] See for instance Article 68 and 85 of *Geneva Convention* IV.

committed[4].... On the other hand, Nuremberg with short title as "Transfer to another Power", states: In no 'circumstances shall a protected person be transferred to a country where he or she may have reason to fear persecution for his or her political opinions or religious beliefs.'[5]

Article 85 of *Geneva Convention* IV shows how tentative any thought of the instrument offering protection to women is. It provides:

> In all cases where the district in which a protected person is temporarily interned, is in an unhealthy area or has a climate which is harmful to his health, he shall be removed to a more suitable place of internment as rapidly as circumstances permit.
>
> The premises shall be fully protected from dampness...account being taken of the climate and the age, sex and state of health of the internees. Whenever it is necessary, as an exceptional and temporary measure, to accommodate women internees who are not members of a family unit in the same place of internment as men, the provision of separate sleeping quarters and sanitary conveniences for the use of such women internees shall be obligatory.

This provision is primarily protective of men as indicated by the use of "his" and "he", but could be extended to women whenever it is necessary, as an exceptional and temporary measure.[6] The argument that the masculine pronouns are used in a generic sense to

---

[4] Article 33, *Geneva Convention* IV.

[5] Article 45, *Geneva Convention* IV

[6] Article 45, *Geneva Convention* IV

cover both genders is rather untenable because whenever the rights of women are not explicitly guaranteed by specific references, they tend to remain unrecognized, un-accommodated and untenable.[7] Even when the provisions are consistently couched in gender-neutral terms as most of the *Geneva Conventions* and the *Additional Protocols* are, sexism or gender discrimination attends the enjoyment of the specific rights that are contemplated.[8] This is the case with most of the international legal instruments which Nigeria, DR Congo, and Sierra Leone ratified and, in some cases even domesticated.[9] The situation is exacerbated by the widespread gender discriminatory attitude of the societies against women.

However, with the ratification and in some cases domestication of international instruments that exclusively target women,[10] such as the *Convention on the Elimination of All forms of Discrimination* against women and the *Protocol to the African Charter on Human and Peoples Right on the Rights of Women in Africa*, the three countries have had

---

[7] Tomasevski, K., *Women and Human Rights (Women and Development Series)*, London, Zebi Books Ltd., 1993,3.

[8] *Ibid*.

[9] See Chapter Four of this work, for the countries' records of ratification and domestication of the relevant instruments.

[10] International Instruments that exclusively target women include: the *Convention on the Elimination of All Forms of Discrimination Against Women(CEDAW)*,(1979); *Convention on the political rights of Women*, 1952; *Convention on the Nationality of married Women, Convention on the Consent of Marriage, Minimum age for Marriage and Registration of Marriage, Protocol to the African Charter on Human and Peoples Rights on the Rights of Women in Africa*(2003); the *Beijing Declaration and Platform for Action*(1995); the *Declaration on the Elimination of Violence Against Women (DEVAW)*,(1994); the *Declaration on the Protection of Women and Children in Emergency and Armed Conflicts*(1974); and UN Security Council Resolutions 1325 and 1820, respectively on Women, Peace and Security.

the opportunity of implementing gender-sensitive laws for the protection of women in armed conflicts, and generally. Whereas, DR Congo and Sierra Leone seem to have seized the opportunity by incorporating such legal instruments into their domestic laws, Nigeria has failed to domesticate any of them. However, certain legislations at the level of the State Houses of Assembly seem to have been inspired by them, as has been acknowledged in Chapter Four.

Furthermore, DR Congo has undertaken a fundamental legislative measure by drafting and subsequently adopting her 2006 *Constitution*, which enshrines a monistic approach to the application of international law. This seems to be an advantage over Sierra-Leone and Nigeria, as it entails direct application of international legal instruments in DR Congo. In other words, the constitution empowers civil and military courts to implement duly ratified international treaties and provides that duly concluded treaties and international agreements have superior authority to that of domestic laws. As we had earlier observed, before this development and shortly after DR Congo ratified the *Rome Statute of International Criminal Court* of 1998, the Congolese Parliament amended the country's *military codes*, and granted military courts exclusive jurisdiction over international crimes. However, this exclusive jurisdiction over international crimes may soon be transferred to the civilian court system as the *Draft Law on the domestic implementation of the Rome Statute*, which proposes to do so, has been pending before the Congolese National Assembly.[11]

---

[11] See Article 153 and 215 of the 2006 *Congolese Constitution* which provide a legal basis for directly applying international treaty provisions in national cases.

As we had also noted in the preceding chapter, the *Rome Statute of International Criminal Court* has directly been invoked by the Military Courts of DR Congo, in different provinces, in accordance with the country's monist system. In fact, the courts have in addition to referring to the *Rome Statute of International Criminal Court*, also referred at times to the *"Elements of Crimes" document*. The Military Courts have also referred to the jurisprudence of the International Tribunals for the former Yugoslavia and Rwanda as binding authorities. This means that the Congolese Court could as well, in the spirit of the countries monist Constitution, automatically or directly apply any of the international law instruments and other related treaties which DR Congo has ratified, including the international instruments on women's right such as the *Convention on the Elimination of All Forms of Discrimination Against Women* (CEDAW) and the *Protocol to the African Charter on Human and Peoples' Rights on the Right of Women in Africa (the Maputo Protocol)*. This is clearly an advantage over Nigeria that operates a dualist Constitution with regard to the implementation of International Law.

By virtue of its 1991 *Constitution*, Sierra Leone also has an advantage over Nigeria in terms of ease of domestication of international legal instruments. It directly implemented many of the international legal instruments, which the country has ratified by expressly incorporating them into the constitution.[12] In other words, it domesticates the international instruments by express incorporation into the constitution, as we see in section 19(1) and

---

[12] See chapter III 'The Recognition and Protection of Fundamental Human Rights and Freedoms of the Individual, at section 15-20 of the 1991 *Sierra Leonean Constitution*.

20(1) which provide for the right to freedom from slavery and any form of torture or any punishment or other treatment that is inhumane or degrading.[13] In fact the rights recognized and protected under Chapter Two of the *Constitution* are directly derived from such instruments as *International Covenant on Economic, Social and Cultural Rights* (ICESCR), 1966 and *International Covenant on Civil and Political Rights* (ICCPR), 1966, etcetera, which the country ratified.[14] In order to protect women and children in the event of armed conflict, the country also domesticated the relevant international legal instruments, which it ratified by enacting the following Acts: *Domestic Violence Act, 2007; the Sexual Offences Act* 2012; the *Child Rights Act,* 2007; the *Legal Aids Act,* 2012; the *Anti-Human Trafficking Act,* 2005; the *Right to Access Information Act,* 2013; and the *Correction Act,* 2014.

Unfortunately, in contrast to DR Congo and Sierra Leone, Nigeria has not been able to domesticate any of the international legal instruments on women's right which she has ratified. This failure has been attributed to the country's dualist approach to treaty implementation, lack of political will and customary law, and traditional beliefs on the status of women in Nigeria.[15] Clearly, most of the instruments run contrary to the country's customary laws and

---

[13] This is clearly a codification of the 1984 *Convention against Torture and other Cruel, Inhumane or Degrading Treatment or Punishment* which it ratified in 2001.

[14] See Section 15-28 of the *Constitution.*

[15] We have seen female gender denigrating attitudes play out on the floor of the National Assembly of Nigeria. Most of the members of the National Assembly insist that gender equality is a western imposition which is alien to their Muslim faith. Recently, President Buhari berated his wife publicly for her public statements of opinion, insisting that the place of his wife Aisha Buhari is in the kitchen and the bedroom.

traditional beliefs on the status of women generally, and widows in particular.

For instance, in Nigeria, women have been regarded as minors. The case of *Priye Iyalla-Amadi v Director General, Nigeria Immigration Service (NIS) and Anor.*[16] illustrates this fact, which is a carryover from Nigeria's customary law and traditional beliefs. In this case, the plaintiff applied to the Nigeria Immigration Service for a re-issuance of her International Passport, which was lost. The Immigration Service included a Consent Letter from her husband among the required documents that she has to submit before her application could be processed. She sued challenging her treatment as a minor who requires the consent of his guardian husband.

In its defence, the Nigeria Immigration Service insisted that women were minors for the purpose of the issuance of International Passport and as such require consent from the head of the family. They further argued that the requirement for consent was put in place to perpetuate the authority of the man over his wife, no matter the status she had attained in society and to avoid unnecessary breakdown of the marriage institution in the country. The Presiding Judge, Justice Olotu held that the requirement was not only a violation of section (42)(1)(a) of the *Constitution* but also against Article 18(3) of the *African Charter on Human and Peoples Rights*, which disallows discrimination on grounds of sex and insisted that such obnoxious policies should have no place in the 21st Century Nigeria.

---

[16] Unreported, FHC Judgment delivered by Justice G. Olotu on 1st June 2009, and cited in Eruagu, O.O, "Inequality in Society and the Impact on Women", Azinge E and Uche, L.(eds), *Law of Domestic Violence in Nigeria*, Lagos, Nigerian Institute of Advanced Legal Studies (N.I.A.L.S.), 2012, 362.

The widows have suffered worse fate as they have even been regarded as chattels or part of the husband's inheritable estate. This reflects the intense patriarchal system which Nigeria operates and which permits customs and traditions to exclude women's property rights[17]. The widow is forbidden to inherit her deceased husband's property under customary law, whereas the husband inherits the entire deceased wife's personal property even when they jointly acquired them[18]. The case of *Suberu v Sunmonu*[19] bears eloquent testimony to this particular stance. Here Jibowu, F. J states: It is a well settled rule of native law and custom of the Yoruba people that a wife could not inherit her husband's property since she herself is like a chattel, to be inherited by a relative of her husband.

Furthermore, in *Shaibu v Bakare*,[20] the Supreme Court reaffirmed that under Yoruba customary law, where a man dies intestate, his property is transferred to his children, not his wife, who herself becomes part of the deceased inheritable estate, as was reaffirmed in *Akinnubi v Akinnubi*.[21] In fact, this position of the law has been established in a long line of cases which include those under the Igbo Customary Law.[22]

---

[17] Olomojobi, Y., *Human Rights on Gender, Sex and the Law in Nigeria*, Lagos Princeton Publishing Company,

2013, 165.

[18] *Ibid*.

[19] (1957) 2F.S.C. 31 at 33.

[20] (1983) SC. 115.

[21] (1997) 2NWLR, 144.

[22] See *Nezianya v Okagbue* (1963), All NLR 352, *Nzekwu v Nzekwu*, (1989), 2 NWLR, pt104, *Ojiogu v Ojiogu* (2009) 9 NWLR(Pt.1198)1 S.C.

Fortunately, inspired by the Women's Convention[23] and the *Beijing Declaration*[24], the courts have in certain cases, struck down some of these discriminatory customs as being repugnant to natural justice[25]. For instance, in the case of *Mojekwu v Mojekwu*[26] the Court of Appeal struck down an Igbo custom that denied the widow the right to inherit the property of her deceased husband based on the *Oli-ekpe* custom. In doing so, Niki Toby J.C.A. (as he then was) declared: 'we need not travel all the way to Beijing to know that some of our customs including, the Nnewi "Oli-Ekpe" custom relied upon by the appellant are not consistent with our civilized world...' However, unfortunately, in *Mojekwu v Iwuchukwu*[27] 'the Supreme Court reminded us about the strong roots of our patriarchal system',[28] by reversing the decision in *Mojekwu v Mojekwu*[29], and holding that the *Oli-ekpe* custom was not a repugnant custom, and hence not discriminatory against women.[30]

Incidentally, *Nnanyelugo v Nnanyelugo*,[31] 'presented the court with another opportunity for judicial intervention in the plight of

---

[23] *Convention on the Elimination of All Forms of Discrimination Against Women* (CEDAW), 1979

[24] *Beijing Declaration and Platform for Action*, 1995.

[25] See for instance, *Theresa Onwo v Nwafor Oka and 12 others* (1996) 6NWLR (Part 456); *Mojekwu v Ejikeme and others* (2000) 5NWLR (Pt 657) 402 and *Alajemba Uke and Anor v Albert Iro* (2001) 11 NWLR (Part 723), 203.

[26](1997) 7NWLR Pt.512, 238.

[27](2004) NWLR (Pt. 883).

[28] Olomojobi, *Op.cit.*, 45

[29] *Supra*.

[30] *Op.cit.* See *Mojekwu v Iwuchukwu* (2004) II N.W.L.R. (pt.883) 196

[31] (2008) All FWLR (Pt. 401), 897.

widows.'[32] The court found in favour of the first respondent, the widow and awarded her reliefs as sought. On appeal, the court affirmed as follows:

> The trial judge's perpetual injunction granted to the 1st respondent is a step in the right direction of ensuring that, justice is done to widows with their children in accordance with law. This action will go a long way to reduce the plight of dispossessed widows and their (children in relation to)... the deceased husband's property.[33]

The court also promised to henceforth 'do substantial justice and not allow repugnant traditions, customs and traditional law of inheritance or even technicalities distract them from achieving substantial justice[34].

The Nigerian courts have kept this promise as we see in the most celebrated and most recent case of *Ukeje v Ukeje*,[35]which entitles the Nigerian female child to an inheritance from her father's estate. The case arose as a result of the death of one Lazarus Ogbonnaya Ukeje, a native of Umuahia, in Imo State, who died intestate on the 27th day of Deceember,1981. He had real property in Lagos State and for most of his life was resident in Lagos State. The Ist appellant got married to the decreased on the 13th of December 1956. There are four children of the marriage. The respondent is one of the four. After Lazarus Ogbonnaya Ukeje died, the 1st and 2nd appellants (mother

---

[32] Ibezim, E.C. "Gender- Based Domestic Violence in Nigeria: A socio-legal perspective", Azinge and Uche, *Op.cit.*,213.

[33] *Nnanyelugo v Nnanyelugo (Supra)*, at 902.

[34] *Supra*, at 901.

[35] (2014) 11 NWLR (Pt. 1418), S.C. 384.

and son) obtained letter of administration for and over the deceased's estate.

On being aware of this development, the plaintiff/respondent filed an action in Court where she claimed to be the daughter of the deceased and by virtue of that fact had a right to partake in sharing of his late father's estate. Her claims before a Lagos High Court were for five (5) reliefs.

The trial Court in its judgment found that the plaintiff/respondent is a daughter of L.O, Ukeje (deceased) and proceeded to grant reliefs 2, 3 and 4. As regards relief 5, the trial Court ordered the 1st and 2nd appellants to hand over the administration of the estate to the Administrator General pending when the deceased's children would choose 3 or 4 of them to apply for fresh letters of administration.

The appellants, who were aggrieved with the judgment of the Court of Appeal, appealed to the Supreme Court, which held *inter alia* on constitutionality of Igbo customary law which disentitles the female child from partaking in her deceased father's estate:

> No matter the circumstances of the birth of a female child, she is entitled to an inheritance from her late father's estate. Consequently, the Igbo customary law which disentitles a female child from partaking in her deceased father's estate is in breach of section 42(1) and (2) of the constitutional provision guaranteed to every Nigerian. The said discriminatory customary law is void as it conflicts with section 42(1) and (2) of the Constitution.[36]

---

[36] *Supra* at 408, paras. C-E

The discriminatory treatment of women has also been reflected in the attitude of the criminal law to them, in certain circumstances, and has also led to violence against them. We have cases from certain northern states in which women were convicted for offences that involved extra marital sexual relations contrary to *Sharia* Criminal laws, while the men involved were not even prosecuted. The cases include *Amina Lawal v Katsina State*,[37] and *Safiyatu Hussaini and Anor v Commissioner of Police, Sokoto State*.[38]

Violence against women can also be traced to their demeaned status in the society. In most cases women face imminent danger of losing their lives and have been known to lose their lives, as a result of such violence. The many newspaper reports of husbands who murdered their wives or men who murdered the women in their lives attest to this grim reality.[39] For instance in *Ezwediufu v State*,[40] the appellant killed his mother in cold blood, with a machete and buried her in a shallow grave. His defence was that his mother hated him. The trial court convicted him and the Court of Appeal considered the provisions of Section 27 and 28 of the *Criminal Code* and dismissed the appeal. He further appealed to the Supreme Court which also affirmed his death sentence. In the case of *Nweke v State*[41], the appellant slashed his wife's throat because, according to him, his wife was a troublesome woman who was carrying another man's pregnancy, and had refused to carry the pregnancy to the owner.

---

[37] US/FT/CRA/1/002

[38] USC/GW/F1/10/2001., and SCA/S/2000

[39] Ibezim, E.C., *Op.cit.*, 198.

[40] (2008) vol.1 WHRC 129. See also Quadri, F.A., *Beacon of Hope: Woman's Human' Rights Cases,* Ibadan, life gate Publishing Co.Ltd., 2008,128-161

[41] See also (Quadri *Ibid.*,106-128) (2008) vol.1 WHRC 106.

The Supreme Court affirmed the judgment of the Court of Appeal, which had earlier on affirmed the death sentence passed on the appellant by the trial court.

Of course, it is not all the incidents of gender based homicides that occur in the homes that are reported and prosecuted.[42] Even the infants are not spared the orgy of violence against women.[43] In *Idowu v State*,[44] the deceased, an infant aged 4 years and 9 months was placed in the custody of the appellant, her uncle, by her parents who had traveled. The appellant 'Savagely and in a most horrendous manner pounced on the deceased, her infant niece, pulled off her pant and had carnal knowledge of her forcefully and the infant died. The appellant was found guilty of murder, convicted and sentenced to death by hanging. The Court of Appeal and the Supreme Court, respectively, affirmed the sentence of death by hanging.

In the case of *Oni v State*,[45] the appellant was charged and tried for the murder of his daughter. According to his wife (PWI), the appellant was inside the room with the baby when it cried following which she rushed in and found that his husband had poured some

---

[42] This researcher is aware of a case in his community, where following an altercation between a man and his wife, the man pursued his wife into his brother's house, whereupon his brother pulled out a gun and inadvertently shot the woman dead. He had intended to shoot his brother for spiting him. The interesting thing is that it is alleged that even though the police was invited, no arrests were made and that even the deceased woman's kinsmen were easily "appeased" because after all she was only a woman.

[43] See the National Gender Policy Strategic Implementation Framework and Plan produced by the Federal Ministry of Women Affairs and Social Development, Abuja, 2008, 2.

[44] (2008) Vol.1 WHRC 467.

[45] *Oni v State (2008) Vol. 1 WHRC 1.*

liquid, which turned out to be acid into the mouth and on the body of the baby. The doctors tried to save the baby but, it eventually died. The trial court found the appellant guilty of the offence of murder as charged, convicted him and sentenced him to death.

The Appeal and the Supreme Courts both upheld the conviction and dismissed his appeals.

The foregoing instances of gender discrimination against women and their attendant violence set the stage for the disproportionate violence against women that we have observed in the armed conflicts under reference. However, the recent development in Nigeria, whereby State Houses of Assembly have passed gender-sensitive legislations to protect women, the girl-child and widows is very commendable. It compares to the spate of gender sensitive enactments in Sierra-Leone, except that they are limited to the states, as the National Assembly of Nigeria is yet to make similar enactments.

6.2 Effectiveness of Enforcement Measures:

Despite the fact that women were targeted for sexual violence and rape in the Nigerian Civil War because of their gender and ethnic identity, Nigeria has not prosecuted any of the offenders for war crimes or crimes against humanity. This is notwithstanding the Operational Code of Conduct issued to the Armed Forces of the Federal Republic of Nigeria during the civil war which invoked the *Geneva Conventions'* provision to the effect that women will be protected against any attacks on their person, honour and in particular against rape or any form of assault. In other words, Nigeria has done nothing to protect those women whose rights were violated through attacks on their person, honour and in particular, rape and other forms of assault.

In another vein, the insensitive attitude of the Federal Government of Nigeria to the rights, welfare and well-being of victims of unexploded ordinance and explosive remnants of war, who are mostly women led to the victims filing a suit against the government at the Economic Community of West Africa States (ECOWAS) Sub-regional Court in Abuja. In 2017, the Court delivered judgment in favour of the victims, and awarded substantial damages to them for their injuries and loss of limbs. However, there is nothing in the judgment of the court that suggests that it considered the disproportionate impact of the mine action on women in awarding damages to the victims, neither did the court seem to be gender sensitive in its adjudication of the case.

On the other hand, with regard to Boko Haram insurgency, apart from a few legal actions, some of which have been discussed already, the Nigerian government does not seem to be willing and able to take prompt and effective steps to investigate and hold accountable, perpetrators of serious crimes involving Boko Haram, the Nigerian Armed Forces and the Civilian Joint Task Force. Such relevant agencies like the Nigerian Police, the Office of the Attorney General and the relevant courts have not been effective enough to investigate, prosecute and try perpetrators of war crimes and crimes against humanity. More especially, they have not been able to investigate, prosecute and try gender-based violence against women, including rape, despite the fact that Boko Haram has engaged it as a weapon of war.

Indications that the International Criminal Court and foreign courts may intervene, on the basis of complementarity and universal jurisdiction, respectively seem to have ended up as a mirage. For instance, the Office of the Prosecutor, International Criminal Court, does not seem to have indicted any one since August 2013, when it determined that there was a reasonable basis to believe that crimes against humanity have been committed in Nigeria, and decided that preliminary examination of the situation in Nigeria should advance to Phase 3 (Admissibility) with a view to assessing genuine proceedings in relation to those who appear to bear the greatest responsibility for such crimes. However, as observed earlier, a Spanish public prosecutor has already brought charges against Abubakar Shekau for crimes against humanity, in the Spanish High Court. The court has ruled that Shekau and his group would be tried for the deaths of many women and children and insisted that they must answer for their criminal acts before courts, under the principle of universal jurisdiction.

Niger Republic and Chad have also prosecuted Boko Haram suspects. In fact, a court in Chad have sentenced ten suspected members of Boko Haram to death in connection with a double suicide bombing that killed thirty-eight people in the Chadian capital of N'Djamena.

DR Congo and Sierra Leone seem to have fared better than Nigeria in terms of enforcing the rights of victims of the respective armed conflicts, and especially the rights of women. In DR Congo, the Office of the Prosecutor, International Criminal Court, investigated alleged crimes and charged five militia leaders and found some of them guilty and sentenced them to terms of imprisonment. However, one of the findings of this research is that the Office of the Prosecutor does not seem gender-sensitive enough in gathering and adducing evidence of sexual violence and other gendered crimes in DR Congo, as was demonstrated in the fact that Lubanga was not charged with sexual violence crimes inspite of the fact that DR Congo witnessed the highest incidents of sexual violence against women, the world over, and that the forces that he commanded were known to have omitted large-scale and widespread sexual violence crimes and rape against women. Further findings also show that subsequent cases handled by the International Criminal Court did not fare any better, but Congolese national military courts and the Gender Justice Mobile Courts have been able to try a number of atrocity-related cases. They have applied provisions of the *Rome Statute* in their judgments on the strength of the constitutional provision, which allows direct enforcement of ratified international legal instruments. Besides, the nation's *Military Criminal Code* of 2002 criminalizes war crimes and crimes against humanity, even though its definitions of war crimes and crimes against humanity are some what different. It also granted the military courts the discretion to impose the death penalty in cases of genocide and crimes against humanity, as well as in such crimes as reprisals, use of prisoners as human shields, and pillage in times of war. However, the Congolese Military Courts have refrained from imposing the death penalty in some of the cases that involved these crimes and preferred to give precedence to the *Rome Statute* sentencing norms.

The Gender Justice Mobile Courts, which was found to be distinct from other itinerant courts, have the advantage of focusing primarily on crimes and legal issues of particular importance to women. Its goals includes the following:

1. Specializing in gender issues and sexual violence related to the conflict in DR Congo, but the court's jurisdiction could also extend to women issues more generally, including topics related to family law, property rights, and inheritance laws.

2. Having jurisdiction over military, as well as civilian justice issues, and to hear both civil and criminal cases.

3. Focusing on trying crimes of sexual violence and complementing International Criminal Court prosecutions in the Hague, given its mandate to try crimes committed against women and children in South Kivu on a massive scale related to persistent and continuing armed conflict there; and

4. Positioning the court squarely within the structure of DR Congo justice system, which had long provided for itinerant courts that travel to remote communities and that lack court houses of their own.

In the first year of the courts operation, that is in 2010, nine sessions of the itinerant courts heard 186 cases. Of these dossiers, as they are called in French, 94 resulted in convictions for rape and 41 in convictions for other offences, making a grand total of 135 convictions. However, there were 22 acquittals in rape cases and 18 acquittals related to other offences.

Sentences imposed for rape convictions ranged from three to twenty years, including significant financial penalties. It may however be observed that all the rape charges were brought under Congolese penal law, and so did not implicate international law, because they were not committed during armed conflicts, even though many of the incidents occurred in so-called, military 'operational zones'.

The foregoing scenario contrasts with the situation in Sierra-Leone, where judicial enforcement of international humanitarian law and redress for war crimes and crimes against humanity seemed to have been limited to trials by the Special Court for Sierra-Leone. This is so as national courts of Sierra-Leone have refrained from trying perpetrators of violations, as Lome Accord, which ended the conflict has provided an absolute and free pardon for all those responsible for crimes under international law committed in Sierra-Leone, such as crimes against humanity and war crimes. This bar from prosecution does not augur well for judicial enforcement of relevant laws, as it has the effect of encouraging impunity generally, and especially against women in times of armed conflict.

However, the jurisprudence of the Special Court for Sierra-Leone has contributed so much to judicial enforcement of international humanitarian law, and even the Sierra-Leonean domestic laws, as its jurisdiction includes them. On the whole, the court tried thirteen individuals who have borne the greatest responsibility for crimes against humanity, war crimes and other violations of international humanitarian law, as well as crimes under relevant Sierra-Leonean laws.

Nine out of these thirteen individuals were associated with the Civil Defence Force, the Armed Forces Revolutionary Council and the Revolutionary United Front. The nine persons were indicted, and their cases, which are commonly referred to as CDF, the AFRC and the RUF trials.

Most of the trials and convictions have significant implications for the protection of women and children during armed conflicts. They involved the enforcement of legal provisions against gender-based crimes of violence, which included sexual violence against men and women, ranging from rape, sexual mutilation, sexual slavery (especially of women), and forced marriages. However, it remains to state that among the three countries under review, Nigeria seems to have done the least in terms of enforcing the rights of women in armed conflicts. DR Congo seems to have excelled in employing gender-sensitive enforcement mechanisms and measures, while in Sierra-Leone, the Special Court for Sierra-Leone seems to have contributed most to the jurisprudence on judicial enforcement of international humanitarian law in Africa, so far.

6.3 Effectiveness of Strategic Activities

This sub-chapter comparatively assesses the strategies[46], if any, that the respective countries under review may have deployed for the legal protection of women in the respective armed conflicts. In formulating and deploying appropriate strategies, the specific needs or problems confronting the law has to be considered. In other words, there could be as many types of strategy as there are specific problems or needs for change. This is to stay that strategies could also be seen as the different responses to a problem. Therefore, the

---

[46] According to Schuler, "Strategy" is the and art of employing the political, economic, and psychological forces of a group to afford the maximum support for adopted policies, a careful plan or method; the art of devising or employing plans toward a goal. [See Schuler, M. "Conceptualizing and Exploring Issues and Strategies of the third World Women, New York, O.E.F. International, 1991, 20. See also Ibezim, E.C., 'Strategies for the Achievement of Gender Equality under the Law' [2007/2008], AkpuruAja, A. (ed.), Millennium Journal of International Studies (MJOIS), Imo State University, 263.

type and nature of strategy to be adopted in any given situation would depend on the nature of the problem in question[47].

In the context of the present discourse, the problem in question is that women have been discriminated against in law and in practice, and in the law of armed conflict in particular. This is reflected in the fact that women's right to protection in armed conflicts had neither been effectively provided for nor effectively implemented in the domestic legislations and legal systems of Nigeria, DR Congo and Sierra-Leone. Thus, the countries have taken certain strategic actions aimed at changing the legal systems in such a way as to make them protective of women, especially in armed conflicts. Such strategic actions target the three components of the legal systems, namely, the structural, the substantive and the cultural. The structural component consists of courts, administrative and law enforcement agencies, while the substantive and the cultural components consist of the contents of the law and shared attitudes and behaviours about the law, respectively[48].

Nigeria does not seem to have established any judicial or administrative forum for specially addressing gender-based violations of the rights of women in any of its armed conflicts.

Generally, the Nigerian Courts have remained patriarchal and gender-insensitive to the rights if women. The Federal High Court of Nigeria which is the particular forum for the judicial enforcement of the law of armed conflict or international humanitarian law is no

---

[47] Ibezim, E. C., 'The Beijing Conference and the Human Rights Protection of Women: A Critical Review', 2000,134 (Unpublished Master of Laws (LL.M) dissertation)

[48] *Ibid.*, 135.

exception. Though the Nigeria Police may have established the section for domestic violence against women, it seems incapable of addressing war-time gender-based violence.

However, Nigeria has taken certain administrative measures which may also have implications for the rights of women generally. They include the establishment of the National Agency for the prohibition of traffic in persons and other Related Matters (with a mandate to combat human trafficking within and across Nigeria's borders)[49] and the adoption in 2006 of a National Gender Policy[50]. The policy which is elaborate and practical replaced an earlier one[51]. The Nigerian government further demonstrated a political will to foster equality by formulating and publishing the Strategic Implementation Framework and Plan for the National Gender Policy,[52] in 2008. The framework and plan incorporates benchmarks, goals, and a performance appraisal system[53].

The substantive and the cultural components of the Nigerian legal system have been targeted with the adoption of some relevant legislations and media campaigns. They include: the amendment of the *National Human Rights Commission Act*, 2010, which granted the commission operational and financial independence, and enhanced

---

[49] See Report of the Working Group on the Universal Periodic Review on Nigeria delivered to Human Rights Council, Twenty-Fifth Sessions, 3.

[50] See the National Gender Policy produced by the Federal Ministry of Women Affairs and Women Affairs and Social Development, Abuja, 2008,2

[51] Ibezim, E.C., "Gender Based Domestic…

[52] See National Gender Policy Strategic Implementation Framework and Plan produced by the Federal Ministry of Women Affairs and Social Development, Abuja, 2008,2.

[53] Ibezim, E. C., *Op.cit.*

its investigative and enforcement powers[54]; accession to and ratification of several international human rights instruments[55], including those on women's rights[56]; *Administration of Criminal Justice Act,* 2016; the *Legal Aid Act,* 2011, which broadened the scope of the mandate of the Legal Aid Council, empowering it to utilize paralegals for service delivery to the grass-roots level. Targeting the cultural components of the law in Nigeria, the government has launched several campaigns on violence against women and girls, at both the federal and the state levels, while several categories of legal officers, law enforcement and judicial officers have been trained on women's right protection and gender issues[57].

All the foregoing strategies should have both direct and indirect implications for the legal protection of women's right, in Nigeria, but regrettably they do not seem to be reflected in the armed conflicts in Nigeria. This may be traced to a lack of political will on the part of government, as exemplified in the non-implementation and non-enforcement of the declared 30 – 35% quota representation for women in all government activities, organs and appointments. This is further reflected in the non-prosecution of gender-bas\\ed violence in the two armed conflicts reviewed under Nigeria. Thus, there is a great need to task Nigerian government for the implementation and enforcement of measures that are gender sensitive to women.

---

[54] See Report of the Working Group on the Universal Periodic Review, *Op.cit.,*3

[55] *Ibid.*

[56] For instance, Nigeria has signed and ratified the *Convention on the Elimination of All Forms of Discrimination Against Women (CEDAW) 1989.*

[57] *Op.cit.,* 6.

Like Nigeria, DR Congo adopted the strategy of targeting the substantive component of her legal system by ratifying a number of relevant international legal instruments, namely international humanitarian law treaties, the *Rome Statute of International Criminal Court* and international human rights treaties. These include the four *Geneva Conventions* of 1949 and their *Additional Protocols* of 1977; the *Convention on the Elimination of Discrimination Against Women*, 1979; the *Convention on the Rights of the Child (CRC)*, 1989, *International Covenant on Economic, and Social-Cultural Rights (ICESCR)* 1966; *International Covenant on Civil and Political Rights* (ICCPR), 1966; the *Protocol to the African Charter on Human and Peoples' Rights on the Rights of Women in Africa*, etc.

In order to implement such international legal instruments as the foregoing, DR Congo adopted the 2006 *Congolese Constitution* which enshrined a monistic approach to international law by authorizing civil and military courts to implement duly ratified international treaties, and by providing that duly concluded treaties and international agreements have superior authority to that of laws. On the basis of this provision, DR Congo has been able to adopt and amend relevant laws in her bid to reinforce the legal status of women, and thus has done better than Nigeria in the legal protection of women.

However, discriminatory legislations against women still persist and conduce to all manner of violence against women in peace time as well as during the armed conflict. This has been a foil to whatever national implementation measures that have been put in place. Thus, the adoption in July 2006 of two laws on sexual violence, and in January of a Child Protection Law failed to stem the tide of rape in DR Congo. Clearly with this climate of discriminatory laws and violence, it has not been easy to effectively implement the gender-sensitive laws.

Furthermore, DR Congo does not seem to have done enough to change the cultural component of her legal system. This can only come about through sustained campaigns for behavioural and attitudinal change in favour of legal and social protection of women.

Having said this, DR Congo seems to have performed better than Nigeria and Sierra-Leone by targeting the structural component of her legal system through empowering military tribunals to directly implement international legal instruments.

DR Congo also increased access to justice by authorizing Military Courts to try civilians also. Unfortunately, even though the courts convicted offenders of gender-based sexual violence against women, they did not seem to have deliberately followed gender-sensitive procedures in handling the cases. This has earlier been asserted as whittling down the judicial weight of the legacy of the Military Courts in DR Congo. This is why the importance of the Gender Justice Mobile Court project, which is peculiar to DR Congo, cannot be over-emphasized. They are distinct from other itinerant courts that have been mounted by the European Union Programme for the Restoration of Justice in Eastern Congo (REJUSCO) and Non-Governmental Organizations by being the only tribunal in the region whose primary business is to adjudicate crimes and legal issues of particular importance to women.

Nigeria and Sierra-Leone have no such gender-specific courts, but the special court for Sierra-Leone was very effective in its prosecutions of gender-based crimes against women; while the Nigerian courts seem less inclined to prosecuting war crimes, and especially gender-based crimes against women. On the whole DR Congo performed better than Nigeria and Sierra-Leone because she adopted a strategy that simultaneously targeted all the components of the legal system, viz the structural, the substantive and the cultural in her bid to protect women in the armed conflict there. She did this by establishing specialized courts and tribunals to try gender-based violations of laws of armed conflict against women; incorporating international legal instruments that are specifically protective of women like the Rome Statute of the International Criminal Court *etcetera*, particularly the *Convention on the Elimination of Discrimination Against Women*; and embarking on campaigns for attitudinal and behavioural change in favour of women's right.

In terms of strategic funding, the United Nations Fund for Population Activities (UNFPA) has been involved in funding programmes for rehabilitation of Internally Displaced Persons in the Nigerian War against Boko Haram terrorists. A few countries have also been involved in funding operations aimed at ameliorating the condition of victims of the Boko Haram insurgency, which has affected women disproportionately. They include Demark. The country has made financial contributions as follows: Danish Red Cross, 879,882 USD; Danish Refugee Council, 283,691 USD; Save the Children (a Non-Governmental Organization), 99,342 USD; and CARITAS (to internally Displaced persons in Niger), 141,916 US Dollars. As at the end of 2015, Denmark had committed a total sum of 1,404,831 US Dollars.[58]

---

[58] Source: Danish ministry of Foreign Affairs: The department for Humanitarian Action, Civil Society and Personal Assistance.

DR Congo also benefitted from strategic funding by international donors and its own government. International donors assisted in the area of trials of cases, especially of gender-based violence. For instance, 'some activities - such as support to "mobile court" or trainings – have been funded by multiple donors.[59] Such international financial support was critical for the success of the *Minova Case,* which appears to have been extremely reliant on international financial and material support.[60]

The World Organization against Torture (OMCT) has also helped many women victims of sexual violence in North and South Kivu, through its fund for emergency assistance to victims of torture.[61] For instance, it provided emergency medical assistance in several cases of victims of sexual violence. On the other hand, the Gender Justice Mobile Court, which is distinct from other itinerant courts in DR Congo is funded by the Open Society Initiative for Southern Africa (OSISA). At the beginning of the project (phase1), the Open Society Initiative for Southern Africa approved a grant of Eight Hundred and Forty-four Thousand Dollars ($844,000.00) to the American Bar Association's Rule of Law Initiative to 'establish a pilot project which will travel throughout remote areas of South Kivu to provide gender justice to women who are victims of sex

[59] Human Rights Watch, 'Justice on Trial,' October 2015, 9, available at www.hrw.org. (accessed on 23-6-2018)

[60] *Ibid*; 100.

[61] See Report on Violence against Women in North and South Kivu, in DR Congo (Alternative report for the Committee on the Elimination of all forms of Discrimination Against Women) submitted at the 55th session of the Committee July 8-26,2013,6.

crimes or who need other forms of judicial redress'.[62] The European Union through its programme for the Restoration of Justice in Eastern Congo (REJUSCO) and some Non-governmental organizations, such as *Avocats Sans Frontiers* (ASF) funded and mounted other itinerant courts. However, there appears to be disproportionate funding available to prosecute sexual violence crimes, when compared to other grave international crimes. Other aspects of justice delivery seem either to be neglected or so inadequately funded.[63] While dedicating specific support for justice for the worst crimes in Congo, which include crimes of sexual violence has been lauded, there is yet the need to strengthen this support in the future, in a number of ways. This includes diversifying the types of criminal justice projects that should be sponsored by donors. Ultimately, the Congolese government should be encouraged to sustain strategic funding of justice by developing a national strategy for sustainable funding.

In Sierra Leone, 'little to no funding was allocated to the protection need of abducted women and children and only a small number of programs that provide education, skills training and counseling were established'[64] for them, within the Disarmament, Demobilization and Reintegration programme. Donors were therefore called upon to learn from their failure in Sierra Leone and

---

[62] Davis, M. M ; 'Helping to Combat Impunity for Sexual Crimes in DR Congo: An Evaluation of Gender Justice Mobile Courts' [2012], Open Society Initiative for Southern Africa , (Vol. 04),13. See also, Terms of Grant from OSISA to ABA/ROLI (September 2009), 1.

[63] Human Rights watch, *Op.cit*; 99.

[64] Human Rights watch; 'Sierra Leone: "We'll Kill You if You Cry"- Sexual Violence in the Sierra Leone Conflict' [2003], *Human Rights Watch Report*, (Vol.15,No.1(A)), 69

ensure that subsequent Disarmament, Demobilization and Reintegration programmes, in other countries, where large numbers of women and girls have been abducted by the fighting forces, such as DR Congo and Nigeria, integrate the protection needs of such abducted women and girls.[65]

The United Kingdom has been the biggest donor in Sierra Leone.[66] In 2002, it contributed €50millon (approximately U.S $145millon) of which about €50million (approximately U.S $73million) was disbursed through its development agency, the Department for International development (DFID).[67] It funded programmes aimed at strengthening the protection and promotion of women's human rights.[68]It also funded the Commonwealth Community Safety and Security project (CCSSP), which has worked to establish a nationwide system of Family Support Units (FSUS) to deal with cases of sexual and domestic violence.[69] The Department for International Development has also provided €2.5million (about U.S $3.5million) for a three year programme that will establish sexual and physical assault referral centers across the country.[70] The United Kingdom also contributed a total of over U.S $500,000 to the operation of the Truth and Reconciliation Commission (TRC) and its secretariat. On the whole, the country committed at least U.S

---

[65] *Ibid.*

[66] *Ibid.*

[67] *Ibid.*

[68] *Ibid*; 69-70.

[69] *Ibid*; 70

[70] *Ibid.*

$9.110,000 over a period of three years, to the Special Court of Sierra Leone.[71]

The United States of America and the European Union also contributed their own quota. 'The United States has funded several women's programs, notably in the field of health, including the provision of obstetric surgery and HIV/AIDS education, a sexual and gender-based violence program, a program aimed at promoting women in politics, and micro-finance schemes for women.'[72] Besides, the Senate's Foreign Relation Committee of the country recommended that the United States Agency for International Development (USAID) expand services to rape victims and fund a public education programme on women's rights. The country has also contributed about US $15million in support of the Special Court of Sierra Leone, and $500,000 to the Truth and Reconciliation Commission. On the other hand, the European Union also contributed funds to human rights-related programmes, and women rights issues.

---

[71] *Ibid.*

[72] *Ibid.*

CHAPTER SEVEN

Summary, Conclusions and Recommendations

⌒⌒⌒

This last chapter summarizes findings, draws conclusions and makes necessary recommendations for the legal protection of women in armed conflicts generally, and particularly armed conflicts in Nigeria, DR Congo and Sierra Leone.

7.1 Summary

Women are one of the most vulnerable groups in the event of armed conflicts. They are discriminated against and disproportionately targeted as objects of gender-based sexual violence. Their attackers or the perpetrators operate with impunity in spite of elaborate provisions of international law, (especially international humanitarian law) against such violations, as we see in the armed conflicts in Nigeria, DR Congo and Sierra Leone.

Despite widespread ratifications of relevant treaties and consequent enactment of appropriate laws, the rate of violence against women has remained high, as exemplified in the foregoing countries under review. This has been found to be as a result of: a lack of the political will required to implement the laws and punish perpetrators of gender-based violence; negative influences of patriarchal, cultural and traditional beliefs on the status of women, which invokes cultural relativism in order to deny women's rights;

the insensitive attitude of the Police and the Judiciary to domestic and sexual violence against women; and the gender-insensitive language of the law.

The language of mainstream legal instruments is mostly couched in gender-masculine pronouns like "he", "his", "him", "himself", or such neutral or impersonal noun phrases as, "a person", "a prisoner", and so on. Even when it employs gender-neutral terms, it ends up using the masculine gender pronouns, such as "he", "his", "him", "himself", in specifying those who are covered or protected by the law. Moreover, even when the provisions are consistently couched in gender-neutral terms, as most of the *Geneva Conventions* and the *Additional Protocols* and other mainstream legal instruments are, sexism or gender discrimination attends the enjoyment of the specific rights. Furthermore, the argument that the masculine pronouns are used in the generic sense to cover both genders is rather untenable, because whenever the rights of women are not explicitly guaranteed by specific references, they tend to remain unrecognized and unaccommodated. Consequently, the law assumes certain characteristics of men and women, as a basis of its construction and has only just recently begun to acknowledge the impact of gender in the analysis of International Law and International Humanitarian Law, in particular.

Although a number of feminist legal scholars have acknowledged the need for an integration of a gender perspective in the relevant laws, hardly any of them has recommended strategies for achieving gender-mainstreaming in the law. This constitutes a gap in the existing literature. Besides, none of the scholars seems to have advocated the formulation of fresh gender-sensitive legislations and treaties, or consequential amendments, which might involve a re-engineering of the language of the law, or if possible, a total deconstruction of the law, so as to evolve a legal regime that would be equally protective of women.

However, the United Nations Security Council has intervened by adopting a number of Resolutions specifically intended for the protection of women. The intervention has been on the basis 'that massive human rights violations in armed conflicts constitute a threat to peace and women are the most severely affected by the scourge of war.'[1] The resolutions have been acknowledged for contributing to the development of humanitarian law applicable to women, and underscoring the value of active participation of women in peace efforts. However, the thematic and declaratory resolutions on which the law is largely based are not binding, but they have been acknowledged as relatively effective with regards to the provisions that are directed at the United Nations bodies. These Resolutions have not only been relevant, but also helpful in the armed conflicts in DR Congo, and Sierra Leone.

The conflicts in DR Congo alternated between non-international and international armed conflicts, while those in Sierra Leone and Nigeria remained non-international. Consequently, while International Humanitarian Law and International Human Rights Law may apply to the conflict in DR Congo during those internationalized phases, Common Article 3 to the *Geneva Conventions*; *Additional Protocol* II to the *Geneva Conventions*; International Human Rights Law and domestic or national laws may

---

[1] Tachou-Spiowo, A., 'The Security Council on Women in War: between peace building and humanitarian protection', (March 2010), *International Review of the Red Cross* (IRRC), (Vol.92, No.877), 197.

also apply to it, in its non-international phases. So also may they apply to the non-international armed conflicts in Sierra Leone and Nigeria.

The judiciaries in both DR Congo and Sierra Leone broke down during the respective armed conflicts, while that in Nigeria collapsed in the parts of the country that have been directly involved in the armed conflicts. Thus, the Congolese national institutions failed to prosecute and punish perpetrators due to the weakness of the judicial system, the lack of infrastructure (particularly in the rural areas) and of trained staff as well as the lack of implementation or enforcement of legal decisions. The Congolese government was therefore 'unable' and 'unwilling' to bring the perpetrators of international crimes, including sexual violence against men and women to justice. This necessitated the intervention of the International Criminal Court and the American Bar Association and the Rule of Law Initiative (ABA/ROLI).

The International Criminal Court has undertaken the trial of those that bear the greatest responsibility for the crimes, while the American Bar Association and the Rule of Law Initiative (ABA/ROLI) organized and funded mobile military courts for the trial of perpetrators of war crimes and crimes against humanity. Besides these trials, they also have committed themselves to building the capacity of judges, lawyers, police investigators and court personnel, so as to enable DR Congo to redress decades of impunity. Interestingly, in addition to this, the Open Society Justice Initiative (OSJI) established Gender Justice Mobile Courts with a mandate which includes specializing in cases involving gender issues and specifically, sexual violence in relation to the conflict. A number of cases on sexual and gender-based violence were tried by these mobile courts, in conjunction with mobile military courts of DR Congo.

On the other hand, the judicial responses to violations of International Humanitarian Law that occurred during the armed conflict in Sierra Leone were basically limited to the trials by the Special Court of Sierra Leone (SCSL). The court is an independent tribunal, which was independent of the Judiciary of Sierra Leone; unlike the earlier international tribunals for the former Yugoslavia and Rwanda, it has the unique and unprecedented power of enforcing both international law principles and municipal laws of Sierra Leone. This is one of the things that has earned it the popular epithet of a hybrid court. Besides, the Judges of both the Trial and the Appeal Chambers are either appointees of the United Nations Secretary General or of the government of Sierra Leone. Thus, the United Nations Secretary General describes it as 'a treaty-based, sui generis court of mixed jurisdiction and compositions'.

Finally, while there was hardly any judicial response to violations of international humanitarian law that occurred during the Nigeria-Biafra war, the few judicial interventions that have been witnessed in relation to Nigeria's war against Boko Haram terrorists are unsatisfactory. For instance, none of the cases arising from the Boko Haram Insurgency or Nigerian War against Terrorism seems to have been brought under international humanitarian law. It also does not seem that anyone has been charged for sexual violence or any gender-based violence, despite the fact that Boko Haram fighters have been notorious for widespread use of gender-based violence, abduction of women, rape as a weapon of war, and forced marriages.

The government does not seem willing and able to take prompt and effective steps to investigate and hold accountable, perpetrators of serious crimes on all sides of the conflict, that is Boko Haram fighters, Nigerian Military Forces, the Police Force and the Civilian Joint Task Forces. The few prosecutions appear to be of senior Boko Haram fighters only. They have also been charged only under domestic criminal law, and the *Terrorism (Prevention) Act* 2011 (as amended in 2013), and punished under same to the exclusion of International Humanitarian Law, even when they have committed crimes against humanity, war crimes and other violations of international humanitarian law. In other words, none of the suspects have been tried under international law. It may well be that the prosecutors and the lawyers lack expertise in international humanitarian law and gender jurisprudence.

7.2 Conclusions

In the course of this research, a number of assumptions have been interrogated and resolved.

In the first instance, it is abundantly clear that women's rights are not adequately secured by existing legal provisions on armed conflicts despite the fact that some of the provisions are specific to them. This is so, because the relevant protective laws, especially, International Humanitarian Law is not gender-sensitive to women, and this is reflected in the language of the law. The law is mostly couched in gender-masculine or gender-neutral terms and this has had the overall effect of excluding women in its protective ambit. In other words, the psycho-linguistic effect of proceeding from impersonal noun phrases like "a prisoner" and so on, and ending up with masculine pronouns like "he", "his", "him", and "himself", is to exclude women from the protective effect of the law, for whenever the rights of women are not explicitly guaranteed by specific references, they tend to remain untenable, unrecognized and unaccommodated.

Even when the law makes specific provisions for the protection of women, as it has done in a number of instruments,[2] it proceeds from the male perspective of what it is to be a woman and what it is about women that warrants protection.[3] Thus, 'International Humanitarian Law perpetuates and further constructs a particular vision of men and women.'[4] This has been seen in its conception of "honour" as a natural construction, which characterizes men as brave, strong and self-reliant, while women are chaste, modest, frail and dependent. Consequently, the rules of International Humanitarian Law are founded on these assumed characteristics, and historically accord preference to the characteristics that represent the masculine. This inures to structures of systematic inequality and discrimination against women, even in those special circumstances when the law ostensibly seeks to protect them. For instance, it has been noted that the focus in those circumstances is more on the interests of third parties, namely, the interests of the

---

[2] See Article 27, *Geneva Convention* IV; Article 76, *Additional Protocol* I, Articles 4(2)(d) and (e), and 5(c) and (i) of the *Statute of the International Criminal Tribunal for Former Yugoslavia (ICTY)*(1993), Article 3 and 4 of the Statute of the International Criminal Tribunal for Rwanda (ICTR)(1994); and Article 7 (1)(c)(g)(h)(f)(k) etc of the *Rome Statute of the International Criminal Court* (1998).

[3] See Reports of the Expert Group Meeting, 'Promoting Women's Enjoyment of their Economic and Social Rights, Abo/Turku, Finland, UN Doc EGM/WESR/1997/Report (Dec.1997).

[4] *Ibid.*

foetus or the infant (when the woman is pregnant or nursing) or those of dependent children and husbands.

Secondly, the existing rules that specifically target the protection of women in situations of armed conflict are not discriminatory of men or the male gender, as they indirectly serve the interests of men as well. Beyond this, it is clear that the constitutional and normative principles of equality aim at, as far as possible, removing discriminations and injustices against men and women, including other minority groups. It aims at creating equality of rights, responsibilities and opportunities, by stating that such rights must accrue to individuals, without any adverse distinctions that are based on sex, etcetera. We have however come to the conclusion that this stance of the law generally perpetuates existing injustices against women, by insisting on equal treatment and opportunity for all, notwithstanding differences in sex or circumstances. In other words, the constitutional or normative principles of equality do not take antecedent nature or nurture or assumed or biological roles into account. This produces unfair results, as 'no one deserves his greater natural capacity or merits a more favourable starting place in the society.[5] Thus, for any fair equality of opportunity to be attained, the different nature and circumstances of women should receive differential or preferential treatments.[6] This is to say that they must

---

[5] Nnam, M.N., *Anglo-American and Nigerian Jurisprudence: A Comparison and Contrast in Legal Reasoning and Concept of Law,* Enugu, Fourth Dimension Publishing Co. Ltd., 1989, 138.

[6] There is the tendency to consider preferential quotas as unconstitutional when considered from the point of view of "equality of opportunity" principle. But American Courts have endorsed preferential quota in cases such as *University of California v Bakke* 438 U.S.268Ct273357L2d750 (1978) and *Swann v Charlotte-Mecklenburg Board of Education* 402 U.S.I., 915Ct.1267.28L.Fed.2d544 (1971).

admit of some discriminations aimed at redressing past inequities, or accommodating their distinctive circumstances. This kind of discrimination which has been described as Reverse Discrimination is fair and therefore permissible in law.[7] Thus, it is upon this basis that we have concluded that the existing rules of International Humanitarian Law that specifically target the protection of women, in situations of armed conflict are not discriminatory of men or the male gender.

It remains to state that the countries, whose armed conflicts have been reviewed in this book, namely, Nigeria, DR Congo and Sierra Leone, have failed, in varying degrees, to adequately provide for the rights of women, particularly in armed conflicts. This is so even though they have signed and ratified or acceded to a number of international legal instruments that regulate armed conflicts and those that specifically seek to protect women, in times of peace and in times of armed conflicts. Most of such instruments have been found to be gender-insensitive to women, as international law, especially International Humanitarian Law seems to assume a population in which there is no systematic gender inequality, and thus fails to recognize the unequal situations of men and women in society.

Even when such instruments are gender-sensitive, as in the case of those that specifically target the protection of women, lack of proper implementation measures, and formidable conflicting

---

[7] Professor Hardy Jones of the University of Nebraska, United States of America defines "Reverse Discrimination" as an important way of compensating victims of injustice by preferring them over and above beneficiaries of justice and defended it as fair because it gives more benefits to those who have been treated unjustly, thereby seeking to "even the score"

customary and traditional laws, including negative cultural attitudes ensure failure in their application. For instance, whereas DR Congo and Sierra Leone seem to have incorporated such legal instruments that are gender-sensitive to women into their domestic laws, Nigeria has failed to domesticate any of them. However, this is not to say that women's right are adequately secured in DR Congo and Sierra Leone, as traditional beliefs and cultural attitudes have tended to deny them the rights in terms of practical applications. Nigeria seems to have fared even worse.

7.3 Recommendations

Having summarized findings, and drawn necessary and valid conclusions, it remains to make certain recommendations for improved or adequate legal protection of women in the event of armed conflict. There are many conceivable recommendations that could be made, but the following recommendations would suffice:

1. Governments should repeal all legislations that discriminate against women and enact legislations that are gender-sensitive to women, in conformity with the principles and recommendations of international legal instruments on women such as the *Convention on the Elimination of all forms of Discrimination Against Women (CEDAW)*, and the *Protocol on the African Charter on the Rights of Women in Africa* (the Maputo Protocol). They should not only be encouraged to ratify such international instruments, including the relevant treaties on the law of armed conflict, but also be encouraged to domesticate them, and make them applicable in their various countries.

2. Governments and Non-Governmental Organisations should take all necessary measures to ensure access of women to justice by prosecuting and punishing perpetrators of sexual and gender-based violence, particularly by training judges, lawyers, public prosecutors and police officers on the content of national and international instruments and legislations aimed at protecting women's rights; simplifying and disseminating the texts of these instruments so as to make them accessible and comprehensible to the whole population, including in rural areas; and creating legal aid and financial assistance structures to enable victims of violence and discrimination to go to court, notwithstanding any lapse of time, or provisions of amnesty, as in the cases of Nigeria-Biafra War, DR Congo and Sierra Leone wars, as lapse of time and amnesty should not translate to general amnesia.[8]

3. A total deconstruction of the law of armed conflict, aimed at integrating a gender perspective, in such a way as to accommodate the female or feminine norms is not only desirable, but also recommended to the extent that is feasible, and this would entail engaging not only in new legislative actions, and consequential amendments to existing legislations, but also engaging strategies for changing the law and negative attitudes and responses to it, especially with respect to women's rights, by targeting its cultural component with sustained enlightenment campaigns, etcetera.

---

[8] *See Convention on the Non-applicability of Statutory Limitation to War Crimes and Crimes against Humanity, 1968.*

4. Particularly, the three countries under review should be encouraged to implement, domesticate, and enforce relevant treaties, like the *Rome Statute of International Criminal Court*; the *Protocol to the African Charter on Human and Peoples Right on the Rights of Women in Africa* (The Maputo Protocol); and the International Humanitarian Law Treaties, which they have ratified. To this end, Nigeria should adopt a monistic approach to the implementation of International law treaties; she should also investigate and prosecute alleged war crimes in the Nigerian armed conflicts, but where she is unwilling or unable, the International Criminal Court should investigate and prosecute alleged perpetrators of such war crimes. Finally, the judiciaries of the respective countries should be strengthened for more effective judicial interventions by appointing the requisite number of judges at the various levels of adjudication and subjecting them to continuing and regular training.

Bibliography

BOOKS

Abraham G., and Strydom, H., *African Year Book on International Law Claremont, Juta and Company*, 2014, 219.

Achebe, C., There was a Country: A personal History of Biafra, London, Penguinn Group, 2012.

Ajala A. and Sagay I. E., *Implementation of International Humanitarian Law in Nigeria*, Lagos, International Committee of the Red Cross, 1997.

Alabi-Isama G., *The Tragedy of Victory: On-the spot Account of the Nigeria–Biafra War in the Atlantic Theatre*, Ibadan, Spectrum Books Ltd., 2013.

Allen M. J. and Copper S., *Elliott & Wood's Cases and Materials on Criminal Law (9th ed.)* London, Sweet and Maxwell Ltd., 2006.

Amnesty International, Nigeria – 50 years of Independence: Making Human Rights a Reality, London, Amnesty International Publications, 2010.

Appel M. et al., Advancing *Women's Status: Women and Men together? (Gender, Society and Development) (Critical Reviews and Annoted bibliographies series)* Amsterdam, Royal Tropical Institute Kit Press, (1995).

Appignanesi R. and Garratt C., *Postmodernism For Beginners*, 1995.

Askin K. D. and Koenig D. M. (ed.), *Women and International Human Rights Law (Vol.1) (Introduction to Women's Human Rights Issues)*, New York, Transnational Publishers, Inc., 1999.

Askin K. D. and Koenig D. M. (ed.), *Women and International Human Rights Law (Vol.2) (International Courts, Instruments and Organization and Selected Required Issues Affecting Women)*, New York, Transnational Publishers, Inc., 2000.

Askin K D. and Koenig D. M. (ed.), *Women and International Human Rights Law (Vol.3) (Towards Empowerment)*, New York, Transnational Publishers. Inc., 2001.

Ayua I. A. et al (ed.), *Nigeria: Issues in the 1999 Constitution*, Lagos, Nigerian Institute of Advanced Legal Studies, 2000.

Azinge E. and Uche L., *Law of Domestic Violence in Nigeria*, Lagos, NIALS, 2012.

Barnes J. (ed.), *The Complete Works of Aristotle*, (Vol. 2), Rev. Oxford (ed.), 1984.

Baaz M. E. and Stern M., *The Complexity of Violence: A Critical Analysis of Sexual Violence in the Democratic Republic of Congo*, Sweden: Nordsika Afrikainstitutet and Sida, 2010.

Bantekas I., *Public International Law (2002/03): Sweet and Maxwell's Status Series, (1st ed.)* London, Sweet and Maxwell, 2002.

Barnhart C. L. and Barnhart R. K. (ed.), *The World Book Dictionary (vol. 1)*, Chicago, Field Enterprises Educational Corporation, *1976.*

Barnhart C. L. and Barnhart, R. K., (ed.), *The World book Dictionary Vol. (ll)*, Chicago, Field Enterprises educational corporation, 1976.

Bartlett K. T., *Gender and Law: Theory, Doctrine, Commentary*, Boston/ New York, Little Brown and Company, 1993.

Beevor A., *Berlin: The Down fall*, London, Viking, 2002.

Behabid S. et al., *Feminist Contentions: A Philosophical Exchange*, New York, Routledge, 1995.

Beigbeder Y., *Judging War Crimes and Torture: French Justice and International Criminal Tribunals and Commissions (1940-2005)*, Netherlands, Martinus Nijhoff Publishers, 2006.

Bello E., *African Customary Law*, Geneva, 1980.

Berger L. P. and Luckman T., *The Social Construction of Reality: Everything that passes for knowledge in Society,* Allen Lane, *The* Penguin Press, 1966.

Best S. G. (ed.), *Introduction to Peace and Conflict Studies in West Africa*, Ibadan, Spectrum Books Limited, 2006.

Bix B., *Jurisprudence: Theory and Context,* London, Sweet and Maxwell, 2006.

Bossier P., *History of the International Committee of the Red Cross: From Solferino to Tsushima*, Geneva, New York, 1985.

Bothe M., and Kondoch B. (ed.), *International Peace Keeping: The Year Book of International* Peace Operations (Vol. 7), The Hague, Kluwer Law international, 2002.

Bridgman J. and Millns, *Feminist Perspectives on Law: Law's Engagement with the Female Body*, London, Sweet and Maxwell, 1998.

Brierly, *The Law of Nations (6thed.)*, Waldoct, 1963.

Briggs J., *Innocents Lost: When Child soldiers Go to war*, New York, Basic Books, 2005.

Bull R. (ed.), *Children and the Law: The Essential Readings*, Malden/Oxford, 2001.

Burgers J. W. and Danelius H., *The United Nations Conventions against Torture: A Handbook on the Convention against Torture and other Cruel Inhuman, or Degrading Treatment or Punishment*, Dordrecht, 1998.

Butler J., *Gender Trouble*, 1990.

Cameron I. A., *The Protective Principles of International Criminal Jurisdiction*, Aldershot, Darmouth Publishing Company Ltd., 1994.

Carabine J. (ed.), *Sexualities: Personal Lives and Social Policy*, Milton Keynes/Bristol, The Policy Press, 2004.

Carey J., et al. (ed.), *International Humanitarian Law: Origin,* New York, Transnational Publishers Inc., 2003.

Carey J. et al., (ed.), *International Humanitarian Law: challenges,* New York Transnational Publishers Inc, 2004.

Carey J. et al., (ed.), *International Humanitarian Law: Prospects,* New York, Transnational Publishers Inc, 2006.

Carreirars H. and Kummel, G. (eds.), *Women in the Military and in Armed Conflicts,* vs Verlag fur sozial wissen schaften wiesanden, 2008.

Carroll J. A. et al., *Prentice Hall Writing and Grammar: Communication in Action (Diamond Level),* Upper Saddle River, Prentice Hall Inc., 2001.

Cassese A., (ed.) *International Criminal Justice,* Oxford University Press 2008.

Chinweizu, *Anatomy of Female Power,* Lagos, Pero Press, 1990.

Christopher P., *The Ethics of War and Peace: An Introduction to Legal and Moral Issues (3rd ed.),* New Jersey, Pearson Education, Inc., (2004).

Chukwukadibia N. A., *War Without End in Nigeria: Landmines, Bombs & Explosive Remnants of War (The Law, Treaty, Conventions, Practice and Procedure in ECOWAS Court),* Owerri, Cleanbills Publishers, 2014.

Chukwumaeze U. et al. *Law, Social Justice and Development: A Festschrift for Professor Uba Nnabue,* Owerri, Imo State University Press, 2013.

Chukkol K. S., *The Law of Crimes in Nigeria,* Kaduna, Ahmadu Bello University Press, 2010.

Clastres P., *Archeologie de la violence: La guerre dan les societies primitives,* Edition dal' Aube, la Tour d' Aigues, 2005.

Convreur P. (ed.), *International Court of Justice Year Book, (2000-2001), (No. 55),* The Hague, 2001.

Convreur P. (ed.) *International Court of Justice Year Book (2005-2006), (No. 60),* The Hague, 2006.

Coulter C., *Bush Wives and Girl Soldiers: Women's Lives Through War and Peace in Sierra Leone,* New York, Cornell University Press, 2009.

Crawford E., *The Treatment of Combatants and Insurgents under the Law of Armed Conflict,* University Press, Oxford, 2010.

Crawford J. et al., *The British Year Book of International Law 2005,* Oxford, Oxford University Press, 2006.

Crawford J. et al., *The British Year Book of International Law 2006,* Oxford, Oxford University Press 2007.

Crawford J. et al. *The British Year Book of International Law 2007,* Oxford, Oxford University Press, 2008.

Crawford J. et al., *The British Year Book of International Law 2008*, Oxford, Oxford University Press, 2009.

Cullen, A., *The Concept of Non-International Armed Conflict in International Humanitarian Law* (Unpublished Ph.D Thesis, 2007, accepted for publication in 2009 by Cambridge University Press).

Dake F. J. (ed.), *Dake's Annotated Reference Bible: The Holy Bible*, Lawrenceville, Dake Publishing, Inc., 2005.

De Lupis, *The Law of War*, Cambridge, Cambridge University Press, 1987, 352-355.

Democracy in Nigeria: Continuing Dialogue(s) for National-Building (Capacity- Building series 10), Stockholm, and International Institution for Democracy and Electoral Assistance (International/DEA, 2000).

De Lupis, The Law of War, Cambridge, Cambridge University Press, 1987.

Dieter F. (ed.), *The Hand Book of International Humanitarian Law*, Oxford, Oxford University Press, 2008.

Dike, P.C. (ed.), *The Women's Revolt of 1929: Proceedings of National Symposium to mark the 60th Anniversary of the Women's Uprising in South-Eastern Nigeria, Lagos, Nelag & Co. Ltd, 1995*

Din S. Y., *The Conduct of Hostilities Under The Law of International Armed Conflict*, Cambridge, Cambridge University Press, 2004.

Dixon R. et al., (eds.), *Archbold International Criminal Courts:* Practice, Procedure and Evidence, London, Sweet and Maxwell, 2003, b2-010, 776.

Donovan O., *The Just War, Revisited,* Cambridge, Cambridge University Press, 2003.

Dougals E. and Edlin (ed.), *Common Law Theory: Studies in Philosophy and Law,* Cambridge, University Press, 2007.

Drobak J. N., (ed.) *Norms and the Law,* Cambridge, Cambridge University Press 2006.

Dunant H., *A Memory of Solferino,* Geneva, ICRC, (1862), (English Version), American Red Cross, 1939, 1959.

Durham H. and Gurd T. (ed.), *Listening to the Silences: Women and War,* Leiden/Boston, Martinus Nijhoff Publishers, 2005.

Engles F., *The Origins of the Family, Private Property and the State,* Moscow, Progress Publishers, 1884. (reprinted 1985).

Evans M. D., *Blackstone's International Law Documents (9th Edition),* Oxford, Oxford University Press, 2009.

Eze O., *Human Rights in Africa: Some selected Problems,* Lagos, Nigeria Institute of International Affairs/Macmillan Publishers, 1984.

Ezeani E., *In Biafra Africa Died: The Diplomatic Plot (2nd ed.),* London Veritas Lumen Publishers, 2013.

Federal Ministry of Women Affairs and Social Development, National Gender Policy, Abuja, Federal Ministry of Women Affairs and Social Dev., 2006

Federal Ministry of Women Affairs and Social Development, *National Gender Policy Strategic Implementation Framework*, Abuja, Federal Ministry of Women Affairs, 2008

Ferretti A., *International Rules of Warfare and Command Responsibility*, Bankok, ICRC Regional Delegation for East Asia, 1998.

Ferme M. C., *The underneath of Things: Violence, History, and the Everyday in Sierra Leone*, Berkeley, the University of California Press, 2001.

Festman C. et al. (ed.), *Reparations for Victims of Genocide, War Crimes and Crimes against Humanity: Systems in Place and Systems in the making*, Leiden/Boston, Martinus Nijoff 2009.

Freeman J., *Women: A Feminist Perspective (4th Edition)*, Mountain View, Mayfield Publishing Company, 1989.

Freeman M. D. A, Lloyd's *Introduction to Jurisprudence (7th Edition)*, London, Sweet and Maxwell Ltd., 2001.

Forsythe D. P. (ed.), *Encyclopedia of Human Rights (Vol.1)*, Oxford, Oxford University Press, 2009.

Forsythe D. P. (ed.), *Encyclopedia of Human Rights (Vol.2)* Oxford, Oxford University press, 2009.

Forsythe D. P. (ed.), *Encyclopedia of Human Rights (Vol.3)*, Oxford, Oxford University Press, 2009.

Forsythe D. P. (ed.), *Encyclopedia of Human Rights (vol.4)*, Oxford, Oxford University Press, 2009.

Forsythe D. P. (ed.) *Encyclopedia of Human Rights (vol.5)*, Oxford, Oxford University press, 2009.

Gardam J. and Jarvis M., *Women, Armed Conflict and International Law*, The Hague, Kluwer Law Intl., 2001.

Gardiner R. K., *International Law*, London, Pearson Education Ltd., 2003.

Garner B. A., (ed.), *Black's Law Dictionary (8th Edition)*, St Paul's MN, West, a Thomson Business, 2004.

Gasser H., *International Humanitarian Law: An Introduction*, Haupt, Henry Dunant Institute, 1993.

Gasiokwu M. O. U., *Human Rights: History, Ideology & Law*, Jos, Fab Arieh (Nigeria) Ltd., 2003.

Georges and Andre' Duby, *Les process de Jeanne d'Arc, Gallimard*, Folio Histoire Paris, 1995.

Ghandhi S., (ed.), *Blackstone's International Human Rights Documents (6th edition)*, Oxford, Oxford University Press, 2008.

Glahn G. V., *Law Among Nations: An Introduction to Public International Law*, New York, Macmillan Publishers, 1976.

Goldsterin J. S., *War and Gender*, Cambridge, Cambridge University Press, 2001.

Green L., *The Contemporary Law of Armed Conflict (2nd edition)*, Manchester, Manchester University Press, 1998.

Green W., *Current Law: Monthly Digest*, Scotland, Sweet and Maxwell Publisher. 2000.

Guilain J. and Zammit Le Sentier de la Guerre: *Visages da la violence pre historique*, Paris, le Seuil, 2000.

Hall R. et al, *The State of the World's Refuges: In search of solutions*, New York Oxford University Press, 1995.

Haralambos M. and Holborn M., *Sociology: Themes and Perspectives, (7th edn.)*, London, Harper Collins Publishers Ltd., 2008.

Harris D. J., *Cases and Materials on International Law*, London, Sweet and Maxwell Publishers, 2004.

Henckaerts J. and Doswald –Beck L., *Customary International Humanitarian Law (vol.1): Rules*, Cambridge, Cambridge University Press, 2005.

Heyns C., *Compendium of key Human Rights Documents of the African Union*, Pretoria, Pretoria University Law Press, 2005.

Holborn M., and Haralambos, M., *Sociology: Themes and Perspectives (7th edition)*, London, Harper Collins Publishers Ltd., 2008.

Holzgrefe J. L. & Keohane, R. O., *Humanitarian Intervention: Ethical. Legal and Political Dilemmas*, Cambridge, Cambridge University Press, 2003.

International Law concerning the Conduct Of Hostilities: Collection Of Hague Conventions And Some Other International Instruments, Geneva, (1949).

Jagger A. M. and Struhl P. R., *Feminist Frameworks, Alternative Theoretical Accounts of the Relations between Women and Men*, New York, Mc Graw-hill Books Company, 1978.

Jenkins B., *International Terrorism: A New Code of Conflict*, Los Angeles, Crescent Publishers, 1975.

Juliet I., *Terrorism: A Challenge to the State*, Oxford, Martin Robertson, 1991.

Jurdi N. N., *The International Criminal Court and National Courts: A Contentious Relationship*, Surrey, Ashgate Publishing Ltd., 2011.

Kalshoven F. and Zegveld L., *Constraints on the Waging of War: An Introduction to International Humanitarian Law, (4ᵗʰ edition)*, Cambridge, Cambridge University Press 2011.

Kalu A. and Osinbajo Y. (ed.) *Perspectives on Human Rights*, Lagos, Federal Ministry of Justice, 1992.

Kaiffman L. and Blackwell B., (ed.), *Gender & The Dialogues in Feminist Criticism*, New York, Bantan Books, 1989.

Keely L., *War Before Civilization: The Myth of the Peaceful Savage,* Oxford, Oxford University Press, 1996.

Khaiarallah,D.L., Insurrection under International Law: With Emphasis on the Rights and Duties of Insurgent, Beirut, Lebanese University, 1973.

Khan K. A. A, et al., *Archbold: International Criminal Courts: Practice, Procedure and Evidence,* (2nd ed.) London, Sweet and Maxwell, Ltd., 2005.

Kirgis F. L., *International Organizations in their Legal setting (settled Documents),* St. Paul West Publishing Co., 1993.

Kristof N. D. and Wudum S., *Half of the Sky: Turning Oppression into Opportunity for Women Worldwide,* New York Vintage Books, 2010.

Ladan M. T., *Introduction to International Human Rights and Humanitarian Law,* Zaria. Ahmadu Bello University Press Limited 1999.

Ladan M. T., *Materials and Cases on Public International Law,* Zaria. Ahmadu Bello University Press Limited, 2007.

Lee R. S., *The International Criminal Court: The making of the Rome statute: Issues, Negotiations, Results,* The Hague, London, Kluwer Law International, 1999.

Lenaerts K. et al, (ed.), *Procedural Law of the European Union,* London, Sweet and Maxwell Publishers, 2006.

Lia L., *Gender & Language: Theory and Practice*, New York. Oxford, Oxford University Press, 2006.

Litosseliti L., *Gender & language: Theory and Practice*, Hodder Arnold Education, London, 2006.

Lijinzaad L. et al *Making the Voice of Humanity Heard: Essays on Humanitarian Assistance and International Humanitarian Law in Honour of HRM Princess Margriet of the Netherlands,* Leiden /Boston, Martinus Nijhoff Publishers, 2004.

Lindsey- Curtet, C. et al, *Addressing the Needs of Women Affected by Armed Conflict: An ICRC Guidance Document,* Geneva, ICRC, 2004.

Lindsey C., *Women Facing War,* Geneva, ICRC, 2001.

Madiebo A. A., *The Nigerian Revolution and the Biafra War,* Enugu, Fourth Dimension Publishing Co., Ltd., 1980.

Martin E. A. (ed.), A *Dictionary of Law (5th edition),* Oxford, Oxford University Press, 2003.

Martin M., *The State of Africa: A History of the Continent Since Independence, New Delh. / Sydney, Simon & Schuster, 2011.*

May L., *War Crimes and Just war,* Cambridge, Cambridge University Press, 2007.

McCormack T. L. H. and McDonald A., *A Year Book of International Humanitarian Law (Vol.7) (2004),* The Hague, T.M.C Asser Press, 2006.

McCoubry H. and White N. D., *International Law and Armed conflict,* Aider Shot, Dartmouth Publishing Company Limited, 1992.

Melzer, N., *Interpretive Guidance on the Notion of Direct Participation in Hostilities under International Humanitarian Law,* Geneva, ICRC, 2009.

Moir, L., *The Law of Internal Armed Conflict: Cambridge Studies in International and Comparative Law,* Cambridge, Cambridge University Press, 2002.

Murphy J. B. et al (ed.), *The Nature of Customary Law: Legal, Historical and Philosophical Perspectives,* Cambridge, Cambridge University Press, 2007.

N. I. O. and D. L. B., *Boko Haram: Between Myth and Reality.*

Ngwakwe E. C. et al, *Human Rights, Democracy and Development Revisited: Legal Essays in Honour of Professor Osita C. Eze,* Aba, KDV E Publishers, 2012.

Njoku S. A. (ed.), *Essays on Contemporary Issues of Law,* Owerri, Peacewise System, 2010.

Nnachi R. O., *Explorations in Sex and Gender Issues: A Psychobiogical Guide for Critical Learning,* Owerri, Hudson-Jude publishers 2011.

Nnam,M.N., Anglo-American and Nigerian Jurisprudence: A Comparison and Contrast in Legal Reasoning and Concept of Law, Enugu, Fourth Dimension Publishing Co. Ltd., 1989.

Noritz J. H., (ed.), *Pirates, Terrorists, Warlords: The History, Influence, and Future of Armed Groups Around the World*, New York, Skyhorse Publishing, (2009).

Nwauche E. S. and Asogwah F. I. (ed.), *Essays in Honour of Professor C.O. Okonkwo (SAN)*, Port-Harcourt, Jite Books Publishers, 2000.

Oakley A., *Gender, Women and Social Science*, Bristol, Policy Press University of Bristol, (2005).

Odumegwu-Ojukwu,E., Because I am Involved, Ibadan, Spectrum Books Limited, 1989.

Ogundipe-Leslie M., *Re-Creating Ourselves: African Women and Critical Transformations*, Trenton, N. J., Africa World PR., 1994.

Ojukwu C. O., *Biafra: Selected Speeches with Journals of Events*, New York, Harper and Row Publishers, 1969.

Okocha E., *Blood on the Niger: The First Black-on-black Genocide*, New York/Lagos/Abuja, Gomsian Books, 220.

Okoronye I., *Terrorism in International Law*, Okigwe, Whytem Publishers Nigeria, 2013.

Olomojobi Y., *Human Rights (on Gender, Sex, and the Law)*, Nigeria, Lagos, Princeton Publishing Company, 2015.

Onyekpere E., *Economic, Social and Cultural Rights*, Lagos, Shelter Rights Initiatives, 2001.

Oppenheim,L., *International Law: A Treatise, (Vol. II), War and Neutrality*, London, Longman, Green and Co., 1906.

Orucu E., *The Enigma of Comparative Law: Variations on a Theme for the Twenty-First Century*, Leiden/Boston, Martinus Nijhoff Publishers, 2004.

Painter S., *French chivalric Ideas and Practices in Medieval France*, Cornell, Cornell University Press, 1957.

Paust,J.J., International Law as Law of United States, Durham NC, Carolina Academic Press, 1996.

Pictet J. et al, *Commentary on the Additional Protocol of 8 June(1997) to the Geneva Convention of 12 August, 1949*, Geneva, ICRC, 1960.

Pictet J. S., *Commentary: III Geneva Convention: Relative to the Treatment of Prisoners of War*, Geneva, International Committee of the Red Cross, 1960.

Pictet J. S., *Commentary: IV Geneva Convention Relative to the Protection of Civilian Persons in Time of War*, Geneva, International Committee of the Red Cross, 1958.

Pilloud C. et al., *Commentary on the Additional Protocols of 8 June 1997 to the Geneva Convention of 12 August 1949*, Geneva, 1987.

Pinsof W. M. and Lebow J. L., *Family Psychology*, Oxford, Oxford University Press, 2005

Prunier, G., *Africa's World War: Congo, the Rwandan Genocide, and the making of a Continental Catastrophe*, Oxford, Oxford University Press, 2010.

Quadri,F.A., *Beacon of Hope: Women's Human Rights Cases*, Ibadan, Lifegate Publishing Company Ltd., 2008.

Ratner S. R. et al, *Accountability for Human Rights Atrocities in International Law: Beyond the Nuremberg Legacy (3rd edition)*, Oxford, Oxford University Press, 2009.

Reynaud, *Les Femmes la Violence et Frame*, Paris, Foundation Pour les Estudes de Defense National, 1998.

Roberts A. et al, *Documents on the Laws of War (2nd edition)*, Oxford, Clarendon, 1989.

Robertson G. N. and Col A., *England*, Sweet and Maxwell Publisher, 2002.

Rombauer M. D., *Legal Problem Solving: Analysis Research and Writing*, Washington, West Publishing Company, 1973.

Rosenbaum A. S., *Prosecuting Nazi War Criminals*, Boulder/Sanfrancisco, West View Press, 1993.

Rosenau, J.N., *International Aspect of Civil Strife*, Princeton University Press, 1964.

Rover C., *To Serve and to Protect*, Geneva, International Committee of the Red Cross, 1998.

Sandoz, C., and others, (eds), *ICRC, Commentary on the Additional Protocols of June 1977 to the Geneva Conventions* of 12th August 1949, Geneva, Martinus Nijhoff, 1987.

Sassoil M. and Bouvier A. A., *How does Law protect in War?: Cases Documents and Teaching Materials on Contemporary, Practice in International Humanitarian Law* (Vol.1) (1st edition), Geneva, ICRC, 2000.

Sassoli M. and Bouvier A. A., *How Does Law Protect in War?: Cases, Documents and Teaching Materials on Contemporary Practice in International Humanitarian Law* (Vol. 1)(2nd edition), Geneva, ICRC, 2006.

Sassoli M. and Bouvier A. A., *How Does Law Protect in War?: Cases, Documents and Teaching Materials on Contemporary Practice in International Humanitarian Law* (Vol. ll) (2nd edition), Geneva, ICRC, 2006.

Sassoli M. et al., *How Does Law Protect in War? Cases, Documents and Teaching Materials on Contemporary Practice in International Humanitarian Law,* Vol. 1 (3rd edition), ICRC, 2011.

Sassoli, M. et al., *How Does Law Protect in War? Cases, Documents and Teaching Materials on Contemporary Practice in International Humanitarian Law,* Vol. ll (3rd edition), ICRC, 2011.

Sassoli M. et al., *How Does Law Protect in War? Cases, Documents and Teaching Materials on Contemporary Practice in International Humanitarian Law,* Geneva, ICRC, (Vol. lll) (3rd edition), 2011.

Schmidt D., *Elements of Justice,* New York. Cambridge, Cambridge, University Press, 2006.

Schabas W. A., *Genocide in International Law,* Cambridge, 2000.

Shapo H. S. et al., *Writing and Analysis in the Law (3ʳᵈ edition)*, New York, The Foundation Press Inc., 1995.

Shaw M. N., *International Law (5ᵗʰ edition)*, Cambridge, Cambridge University Press, 2003.

Shute, S., and Hurley, S. (eds.), *on Human Rights*: The Oxford Amnesty Lecturer, 1993.

Sjoberg L. and Gentry C. E., *Mothers, Monsters, Whores: Women's Violence in Global politics*, London/ New York, Zed Books, 2007.

Sjocrona J. M., and Orie, A. A. M., *International Criminal Law*, Devenver, Strafrecht, 2002.

Sliedregt E. V., *The Criminal Responsibility of Individuals For Violations of International Humanitarian Law*, The Hague, T.M.C. Asser Press, 2003.

Solf W. A. and Roach J. A., *Index of International Humanitarian Law*, Geneva, ICRC, 1987.

Stiglmayer, A. (ed.), *Mass Rape: The War Against Women in Bosnia-Herzegovina*, 1994.

Than D. and Shorts, E., *International Criminal Law and Human Rights*, London, Sweet and Maxwell, 2003.

Tomasevski, K., Women and Human Rights (Women and Development Series), London, Zebi Books Ltd.,1993.

Tosh, C. and Chazan, Y., (eds.), Special Report: Sexual Violence in the Democratic Republic of Congo, The Hague, Institute for War and Peace Reporting, 2008, 12.

Udounwa S. E., *Boko Haram: Developing New Strategies to combat Terrorism in Nigeria*, 2013, (An unpublished Research Project submitted in partial fulfillment of the requirement of the Master of Strategic Studies Degree at the United States Army War College).

Uglon S., *Evidence*, London, Sweet & Maxwell Publishers, 1997.

Ugwu-Oju D., *What Will My Mother Say: A Tribal Girl Comes of Age in America*, Chicago, Bonus Inc., 1995.

Umozurike U. O., *The African Charter on Human and Peoples' Rights*, The Hague/Beston/London, Martinus Nijhoff Publishers, 1997.

Unegbu M. O., *From Nuremberg Charter To Rome Statute: Judicial Enforcement of International Humanitarian Law*, Enugu, SNAAP Press Ltd., 2015.

Unegbu M. O., and Okoronye (ed.), *Legal Developments in the New World Order: Essays on International Comparative and Public Law in Honour of Prof. Umozuruike.*

Uwechue R., *Reflections on the Nigerian Civil War: Facing the Future*, Paris, Jeune Afrique, 1971.

Valencia-Ospina E. (ed.), *International Court of Justice Year Book (1998-1999)*, The Hague, ICJ, 1999.

Valencia-Ospina E. (ed.), *International Court of Justice Year Book (2000-2001)*. The Hague, ICJ, 2001.

Valencia-Ospina E. (ed.), *International Court of Justice Year Book (2005-2006)*. The Hague, ICJ, 2006.

Vetlesen A. J., *Evil and Human Agency: Understanding Collective Evildoing*, Cambridge, Cambridge University Press, 2005.

Wardlaw G., *Political Terrorism*, Cambridge, Cambridge University Press.

Wallace R. M. M., *International Human Rights: Text and materials (2nd ed.)*, London, Sweet and Maxwell, 2011.

Weber, L., *The Holocaust Chronicle: A History in Words and Pictures*, Lincolnwood, Publications International Ltd., 2000.

Wilmshurst E. and Breau S., (ed.), *Perspectives on the ICRC Study on Customary International Humanitarian Law*, Cambridge, Cambridge University Press, 2007.

Women, Law and Development International, Gender Violence: the Hidden War Crimes, Washington D.C, Women Law and Development International, 1998.

Wyatt and Dashwood's *European Union Law*, London, Sweet and Maxwell Publishers, 2006.

Yarnell P. (ed.), *Sexual Orientation, Gender Identity and International Human Rights Law-Practitioners Guide No.4*, Geneva, International Commission of Jurists, 2009.

BOOK CHAPTERS

Askin K. D, "The International Criminal Tribunal for Rwanda and its Treatment of Crimes against Women", Carey J. et al. (ed.), *International Humanitarian Law: Challenges*, New York, Transitional Publishers, Inc., 2004.

Butler J., "Contingency Foundation", Benhabid S. et al., *Feminist Contentions: A Philosophical Exchange*, New York, Routledge, 1995.

Chukwumaeze U. U., "Protecting the Right of Women in Armed Conflict: A Legal Perspective", Njoku S. A. (ed.), *Essays on Contemporary Issues of Law*, Owerri, Peacewise Systems, 2010.

Connie de la Vega, "Customary International Law", Forsythe, D. P. (ed.), *Encyclopedia of Human Rights*, Oxford, Oxford University Press, (Vol. 1), 2009.

Enloe, C., "Afterword: Have the Bosnian Rapes Opened a New Era of Feminist Consciousness?", Stiglmayer, A. (ed.), *Mass Rape: The War Against Women in Bosnia-Herzegovina, 1994.*

Eruagu, O.O., "Inequality in Society and the Impact on Women", Azinge, E. and Uche, L. (ed.), *Law of Domestic Violence in Nigeria*, Lagos, N.I.A.L.S, 2012.

Erugo S., "Progressive Enforcement of International Human Rights Norms in Nigeria: The Question of Access to Justice", Ngwakwe, E. C. et al., (eds.), *Human Rights, Democracy and Development Revisited: Legal Essays in Honour of Professor Osita C. Eze*, Aba, KDVE – Publishers, 2012.

Falk, R.A, "Janus tormented: The International law of internal war", Rosenau, J.N., *International Aspects of Civil Strife,* Princeton University press, 1964.

Frug M. P., "Postmodern Feminist Legal Manifesto (An Unfinished Draft)", Bridgeman J. O., and Millns S., *Feminist Perspectives on Law: Law's Engagement with the Female Body,* London, Sweet and Maxwell, 1998.

Ibezim E. C., "Gender-Based Domestic Violence in Nigeria: A Socio-Legal Perspective", Azinge E., Uche L., *Law of Domestic Violence in Nigeria,* Lagos, NIALS, 2012.

Lavoyer J., "Implementation of International Humanitarian Law and the Role of the Red Cross", Carey J. et al, *International Humanitarian Law: Challenges,* New York, Transnational publishers, Inc., 2004.

Lindsey C., "The Impact of Armed Conflict on Women", Durham H. and Gurd T. (ed.), *Listening to the silences: Women and War,* Leiden, Martinus Nijhoff Publishers, 2005.

Messer-Davidow E., "The Philosophical Base of Feminist Literary Criticism", Kauffman L. and Blackwell, B. (ed.), *Gender & the Dialogues on Feminist Criticism,* New York, Bantam Books, 1989.

Ogwu J., "Women in Development: Options and Dilemmas in the Human Rights Equation", Kalu and Osinbajo Y. (ed.), *Perspectives on Human Rights,* Lagos, Federal Ministry of Justice, 1992.

Pejic J., "Status of Armed Conflicts", Wilmshurst, E. and Breau, S. (ed.), *Perspectives on the ICRC Study on Customary International Humanitarian Law,* Cambridge, Cambridge University Press, 2007.

Schuler, M., "Conceptualizing and Exploring Issues and Strategies", Schuler, M. (ed.), *Empowerment and the Law, Strategies of the Third World Women,* New York, O.E.F International, 1991.

Turshen M., "Women's War Stories", Turshen, M. and Twagiramariya, C. (ed.), *What Women Do in Wartime: Gender and Conflict in Africa,* London/New York, Zed Books Ltd., (1998).

Uche, O.L., "Effects of Domestic Violence on Children: A Nigerian Syndrome", Azinge, E. and Uche, L., *Law of Domestic Violence in Nigeria,* Lagos, N.I.A.L.S, 2012.

JOURNAL ARTICLES

Abraham G., 'Universal Jurisdiction and the African Union- The Wrong Side of History?', [2011], Abraham G. (ed.), *African Year Book on International Humanitarian Law.*

Abraham G., and others 'Ratification Table', [2014], Abraham G. (ed.), *African Year Book on International Humanitarian Law,* Claremont Juta and Company Ltd., 223.

Abresh W., 'A Human Rights Law of Internal Armed Conflict: the European Court of Human Rights in Chechnya', [2005], *European Journal of International Law,* (Vol. 16).

Adeyemi A. A., 'Legal/ Judicial Enforcement Mechanism for the protection of Women and Children's Rights', [2003], Rivers State University, *Journal of Public Law* (R/S UJPL, Vol. 1).

Adjami, M. and Mushiata, G., 'Democratic Republic of Congo: Impact of the Rome Statute and the International Criminal Court,' [May 2010], 27.

Akande J., 'Realizing Women's Rights', [1993], *Nigerian Current Law Journal, NCJL* (Vol.1, No. 1).

Akiyode-Afolabi, 'Gender justice in post conflict societies: an assessment of Sierra Leone and Liberia'. Ph.D Thesis, London, SOAS, University of London. [2013]

Arndt S., 'Perspectives on African Feminism: Defining and Classifying African Feminist Literatures', [2002], *Agenda: Empowering Women for Gender Equity*, (Vol. 17, No. 54).

Askin, K., 'Comfort women shifting shame and stigma from victims to victimizers', [2001], *International Criminal Law Review*, (Vol. 1, Nos 1-2), 5-22.

Badeji D. L. 'African Feminism: Mythical and Social Power of Women of African Descent', [1998], *Research African Literature*, (Vol. 29, No. 2).

Bar-Tal D. et al., 'A Sense of Self-Perceived Collective Victimhood on Intractable Conflicts', [June, 2009], *International Review of the Red Cross*, (Vol. 91, No. 874).

Barber R., 'Facilitating Humanitarian Assistance in International Humanitarian and Human Rights Law', [June, 2009], *International Review of the Red Cross*, (Vol. 91, No. 874).

Bartels, R., 'Time lines, borderlines and conflicts: The historical evolution of the legal divide between International and Non-International Armed Conflicts', [2009], *International Review of the Red Cross (IRRC)*, (Vol.91, No. 873), 50.

Barrow A., 'UN Security Resolutions 3125 and 1820: Constructing Gender in Armed Conflict and International Humanitarian Law', [March, 2010], *International Review of the Red Cross*, (Vol. 92, No. 877).

Bella A. et al., 'International Law and Armed, Non-State Actors in Afghanistan', [March, 2011], Bernard V. (ed.) *International Review of the Red Cross*, (Vol. 93, No. 881).

Bernard V. (ed.) 'Interview with David Kilcullen', [September, 2011], *International Review of Red Cross*, (Vol. 93, No. 883).

Birkeland N. M., 'Internal Displacement: Global Trends in conflict-induced Displacement', [March, 2011], *International Review of the Red Cross*, (Vol. 93, No.881).

Bongard P and Somer J., 'Monitoring Armed non state actor compliance with Humanitarian Norms: A look at International Mechanisms and the Geneva Call Deed of Commitment', [Sept. 2011], *International Review of the Red Cross*, (Vol. 93, No. 883).

Briggs O. E., 'Genderizing the Constitution', [2003], *Rivers State University Journal of Public Law* (R/S UJPL Vol.1).

Casalin D., 'Taking Prisoners: Reviewing the International Law Grounds for deprivation of Liberty by Armed Opposition Group', [Sept. 2011], *International Review of the Red Cross*, (No. 883).

Chelimo, G.C., 'Defining Armed Conflict in International Humanitarian Law', available at http://www.standentpulse,com/a?id=508 (accessed April 8, 2011, at 1 of 7).

Claus K., 'War Crime Committee in Non-international Armed Conflict and the Emerging system of International Criminal Justice', [2000], *Israel Year Book on Human Rights*, (Vol. 30).

Colvin, C.J., 'Ambivalent Narrations: Pursuing the Political through Traumatic Story telling', [2004], POLAR, (Vol. 27, No.1)

Cote J. A., 'International Criminal Justice: Tightening up the Rules of the Game', [March, 2006], *International Review of the Red Cross*, (Vol.88, No. 861).

Darcy, S., 'Assistance, direction and control: Untangling International Judicial Opinion on individual and State responsibility for war Crimes by non-State actors,' [2014], *International Review of the Red Cross*, (Vol. 96, No.893), 250.

Davis-Kimball J., 'Warrior Women of Eurasia', [Jan/Feb, 1997], *Abstracts*, (Vol. 50, No.1).

Davis, M.M., 'Helping to combat Impunity for Sexual Crimes in Democratic Republic of Congo: An Evaluation of the Gender

Justice Mobile Courts,' [2012], *Open Society Initiative for Southern Africa*, (Vol. 04).

Danladi K. M., 'The Imperative of Reviewing the fundamental Rights (Enforcement Procedure) Rules', [2006], *Ahmadu Bello University Law Journal (A.B.U.L.J)*, (Vol. 24-25).

Dankofa Y., 'The African Court of Human and Peoples Right: Re-Working the Human Rights Regime Of Nigeria', [2006], *Ahmadu Bello University Law Journal (A.B.U.L.J)*, (Vol. 24-25).

Doherty, T.A., 'Developments in the Prosecution of Gender-based Crimes- The Special Court for Sierra Leone Experiences', [2008], American University Journal of Gender, Social Policy and Law, (Vol.17, No.1).

Durham H., 'Women, Armed Conflict and International Law', [September 2012], *International Review of the Red Cross (IRRC)*, (No. 847).

Durham H., and O'Byrne, K., 'The dialogue of difference: gender perspective on international humanitarian law'. [2010], *International Review of the Red Cross*, (Vol. 92, No. 877).

Egede, E., 'Bringing Human Rights Home: An Examination of the Domestication of Human Rights Treaties in Nigeria', [2007], *Journal of African Law*, (Vol.51, No.2).

Enloe, C., 'Afterward: Have the Bosnian Rapes Opened a New Era of Feminist consciousness?', [1994], Stiglmayer, a. (ed.), Mass Rape: The War against women in Bosnian- Herzegovina, 1994.

Eze O. C., 'Africa, New World Order, Human Rights and Democracy', [1992], *An Inaugural Lecture*, Abia State University, Uturu.

Gardam, J. G. and Jarvis, M. J., 'Women, Armed Conflict and International Law', Kluwer Law International, the Hague, 2001, 137-138.

Gasser H., 'Humanitarian Law', [2009], Forsythe, D.P. (ed.), *Encyclopedia of Human Rights*, (Vol.2), Oxford, Oxford University Press.

Gender Equity Reports (Vol.23, No.2), July 1995.

Geoffrey A., 'Fleeing War and Relocating to the Urban Fringe-Issues and Actors: the Cases of Khartoum and Bogota', [Sept. 2009], *International Review of the Red Cross*, (Vol. 91, No. 875).

Gibney M., 'Refugees', [2009], Fosythe, D. P. (ed.), *Encyclopedia of Human Rights* (Vol.4), Oxford, Oxford University Press.

Gillard E., 'Reparation for Violations of IHL', [September, 2003], *International Review of the Red Cross (IRRC)*, (Vol. 85, No. 851).

Ginburg R. B., 'A Decent Respect to the opinions of (Human) kind: The Value of a Comparative Perspective in Constitutional Adjudication', [2005], *Cambridge Law Journal*, (Vol. 64, Pt. 3).

Haeri M. and Puechguirbal N., 'From helplessness to agency: examining the plurality of women's experiences in armed conflict', [2010], *International Review of the Red Cross (IRRC)*, (Vol. 92, No. 877).

Harmann I. and Palmieri D., 'Between Amazons and Sabines: a Historical Approach to Women and War', [March, 2010], Pfanner, T., *International Review of the Red Cross (IRRC)*, (Vol. 92, No.887).

Hogg N., 'Women participation in Rwanda genocide: mothers or monsters?' [2010], *International Review of the Red Cross (IRRC)*, (Vol. 92, No. 877).

Horovitz, S. 'DR CONGO: Interaction between International and National Judicial Responses to the Mass Atrocities', (2072), DOMAC (Vol. 14), 16.

Hortensia D.T., 'The Relationship between International Humanitarian Law and the International Criminal Tribunals', [March, 2006], *International Review of the Red Cross (IRRC)*, (Vol. 88, No. 61).

Human Rights Watch, 'Sierra Leone; "We'll Kill You If You Cry" Sexual Violence in the Sierra Leone conflict, [2003], Human Rights Watch, (Vol. 15, (A)), 55.

Ibezim E. C., 'Contemporary Challenges to International Humanitarian Law: the Private Military Companies', [2010], Abraham G. et al. (ed.), *African Year Book on International Humanitarian Law*, Cape Town, Juta and Co. Ltd.

Ibezim, E.C., 'Strategies for the Achievement of Gender Equality under the Law', [2007/2008], *Millenium Journal*, Imo State University.

Ibezim E. C., 'The Beijing Conference and the Human Rights Protection of Women: A Critical Review', [2000], (An unpublished LL.M Dissertation).

Imasuen E., 'Insurgency and Humanitarian Crisis in Northern Nigeria: The Case of Boko Haram', [July, 2015], *African Journal of Political Science and International Relations*, (Vol. 9(7)).

Jaccard, J., 'Reports and Documents: What's new in law and case law around the world?' [2014], *International Review of the Red Cross (IRRC)*, (Vol.96, No.893).

Josiporic I., 'Responsibility for War Crimes before National Courts in Croatia', [March 2006], *International Review of the Red Cross (IRRC)*, (Vol. 88, No.861).

Kellenberge J. 'Strengthening Legal Protection for Victims of Armed Conflicts: The ICRC Study on the Current State of International Humanitarian Law', [Sept. 2010], *International Review of the Red Cross (IRRC)*, (Vol. 92, No. 887).

Kisangani E. F., 'Democratic Republic of Congo', [2009], Forsythe, D. P. (ed.), *Encyclopedia of Human Rights*, (Vol. 2), Oxford, Oxford University Press.

Kuwali D., 'Human Rights: Enforcement of International Humanitarian Law by the African Court of Human Rights', [2011], *African Year book on International Humanitarian Law*.

Ladan M. T., 'Issues in Domestic Implementation of the International Criminal Court in Nigeria', [2003], *Rivers State University Journal of Public Law (R/S UJPL)*, (Vol.1).

Lindsey-Curtet C., 'Women and War', [September, 2000], *International Review of the Red Cross (IRRC)*, (N0. 839).

Ludwikowski R., 'Aspects of Terrorism', [2003], *Nigerian Journal of International Affairs*, (Vol. 29, No. 12).

Mackinnon, L., 'Crimes of War, Crimes of Peace' in Shuts, S. and Hurley S. (ed.) on Human Rights, Pg .83.

Malekian F., 'International Criminal Responsibility', [1999], Bassibuni, 157, footnote 32.

Manaugh S. 'The Vengeful Logic of Modern Criminal Restitution', [2005], *Law, Culture and the Humanities*, (Vol.1, No.3).

Matazu A. S. 'The Domestic implementation of International Humanitarian Law in Nigeria: Issues and Challenges', [2011], *African Year Book of International Humanitarian Law.*

Mcferson, F.M, 'Women and Post- Conflict in Sierra Leone'. [2012], *Journal of international Women studies* (Vol. 13, No. 1), 60.

Megwe P., 'Theorizing African Feminism(s): The Colonial question', [2008], *Journal for African Culture and Society*, (Vol. 3).

Meredith V. M., 'Victim Identity and Respect for Human Dignity: A terminological Analysis', [June, 2009], *International Review of the Red Cross (IRRC)*, (Vol. 91, No. 874).

Mordirezadeh N. K. et al, 'Humanitarian Engagement Under Counter-terrorism: A Conflict of Norms and the Emerging

Policy Landscape', [Sept. 2011], *International Review of the Red Cross (IRRC)*, (Vol. 93, No. 883).

Mujuzi, J.D., 'The Special Court for Sierra Leone and its Justification of Punishments in cases of serious violations of International Humanitarian Law and Human Rights Law: Reflecting on the Prosecution of the Special Court v Alex Tamba Brima, Brima Bazzy Kamara and Santigie Borbor Kanu in the Light of the Philosophical Arguments on Punishments [2007], *African Yearbook on International Humanitarian Law*, 105.

Munir M., 'The Layha for the Mujahideen: an Analysis of the Code of Conduct for the Taliban Fighters Under Islamic Law', [March, 2011], *International Review of the Red Cross (IRRC)*, (Vol. 93, No.881).

Niarchos, C.N., 'Woman, War and Rape: Challenges facing the International criminal Tribunal for the Former Yugoslavia,' [1995], *Human Rights Quarterly*, (Vol. 17), 672.

O'Cornell, 'Defining armed Conflict', [2009], *Journal of Conflict and Security Law*, (Vol. 13).

Ogbonna-Nwaogu I. M., 'Civil Wars in Africa: A Gender Perspective of the Cost on Women', [2008], *Journal of Social Sciences*, (Vol. 16, No. 3), 253.

Ogbu O. N., 'The incompatibility of Torture and Extrajudicial Killing with Democracy: The Nigerian Experience', [2003], *Rivers State University, Journal of Public Law* (R/S UJPL Vol.1).

Ooasterveld, V., 'Lessons from the special Court for Sierra Leone on the Prosecution of gender-Based Crimes,' [2009], Journal of Gender, Social Policy & Law, (Vol. 17, Issue 2), 7.

Olarinde E. S, 'Realizing Women's Right', [1993], *Nigerian Current Law Journal, (NCLJ)*, (Vol. 1, No.1).

Onyekwere, E., 'Culture based- Abuse of Women's Right', [1995], *Partnership for Development,* (Vol.1, No.2)

Oosterveld, V., 'Lessons from the Special Court for Sierra Leone on the Prosecution of Gender-based Crimes', [2009], *Journal of Gender,* Social Policy and Law, (Vol.2, Issue 2), 7.

Oosterveld, V., 'Gender and the Charles Taylor case at the Special Court for Sierra Leone', [2012], *Williams & Mary, Journal for Women and the Law,* (Vol.19, Issue 1), 31.

Open Society Initiative for Southern African, 'the Democratic Republic of Congo: military justice human rights – an urgent need to complete reforms (A discussion paper)', [2009], *An Open Society Institute Publications,* 3.

Oviasogie F. O., and Duruji M. M., 'State Failure, Terrorism and Global Security: An Appraisal of the Boko Haram Insurgency in Northern Nigeria', [2013], *Journal of Sustainable Society,* (Vol. 2, No. 1), 20.

Paulus A. and Vashakmadze M., 'Asymmetrical War and the Nature of Armed Conflict: A Tentative Conceptualization', [March, 2009], *International Review of Red Cross,* (Vol.91, No.873).

Pejic J., 'Status of armed conflicts', [2007], Wilmshurst E. and Breau S., (eds.), *Perspectives on the ICRC study on Customary International Humanitarian Law*, Cambridge University Press, 85.

Peterside Z. R., 'The Military and Internal Security in Nigeria: Challenges Prospects', [2014], *Mediterranean Journal of social sciences*, (Vol. 5, No. 27).

Pfanner T. 'Various Mechanisms and Approaches for Implementing International Humanitarian Law and Protecting and Assisting War Victims,' [June, 2009], *International Review of the Red Cross*, (Vol. 91, No. 874).

Plessis M. and Gevers C., ' Into the Deep End-The International Criminal Court and Sudan', [2006], *African Year Book of International Humanitarian Law*.

Poll L., 'The Emerging Jurisprudence on Sexual Violence Perpetrated against Women during Armed Conflict', [2007], *African Year Book on International Humanitarian Law*.

Powell C. H. and Abraham G., 'Terrorism and International Criminal Court and Sudan', [2006], *African Year Book of International Humanitarian Law*.

Rondeau S., 'Participation of armed groups in the development of the law applicable to armed conflicts', [September, 2014], *International Review of the Red Cross (IRRC), (Engaging Armed Groups)*, (Vol. 93, No. 883), 650.

Rosa A. and Wuerzner, 'Armed Groups, Sanctions and the Implementation of International Humanitarian Law', [June,

2008], *International Review of the Red Cross (IRRC)*, (Vol. 90, No. 870).

Rosenfeld F., 'Collective Reparation for Victims of Armed Conflict', [September, 2010], *International Review of the Red Cross (IRRC)*, (Vol. 92, No. 879).

Ruteere M., 'Sierra Leone', [2009], *Forsythe, D. P. Encyclopedia of Human Rights (Vol. 4)*, New York, Oxford University Press, 446.

Sassoli M., 'Transnational Armed Groups and International Humanitarian Law,' [2006], *Program on Humanitarian Policy and Conflict Research*, Harvard University, Occasional Paper Series, (No.6), Winter.

Scolnicov A., 'A Dedicated Follower of (Religious) Fashion?', [2005], *Cambridge Law Journal*, (Vol. 64, Pt. 3).

Shahram, D., 'The sentencing legacy of the special Court for Sierra Leone'. [2014], *Georgia Journal of international and comparative law*, (Vol. 42, no.3), 640.

Shepherd L. J., 'Women, armed conflict and Language – Gender, violence and discourse', [March, 2010], *International Review of Red Cross (IRRC)*, (Vol. 92, No. 877).

Sidorsky D., 'Contemporary Reinterpretation of the concept of Human Rights', [1979], Sidorsky, D. (ed.), *Essays on Human Rights* 88.

Singh S., 'Command Responsibility of Military and Civilian Superiors: An Examination of International Judicial Decisions', [2006], *African Year Book of International Humanitarian Law.*

Sjoberg L., 'Women Fighters and the "Beautiful Soul" Narrative', [March, 2010], *International Review of Red Cross (IRRC),* (Vol. 92, No. 877).

Stone A., 'Essentialism and Anti-Essentialism in Feminist Philosophy', [2004], *Journal of Philosophy,* (Vol. 1, No. 2).

Strydom H., 'The Lesson of Darfur'. [2006], *African Year Book of International Humanitarian Law.*

Tachou-Sipowo A., 'The Security Council on women in war: between peace building and humanitarian protection', [March, 2010], *International Review of Red Cross (IRRC),* (Vol. 92, No. 877).

Taiwo L.O., 'International Criminal Court, the United States and the Fight against Impurity', [2007-2009], Ahmadu Bello University, Zaria, *Journal of Private and Comparative Law, JPCL,* (Vol. 2 & 3).

Tamale S., 'Gender Trauma in Africa: Enhancing Women's Links to Resources', [March, 2005], *Journal of African Law.*

Twinning W., 'Have Concepts, Will Travel: Analytical Jurisprudence in a Global Contexts', [March, 2005], *International Journal of Law in Context,* (Vol.1, No.1).

Umozuruike, U.O., 'Application of IHL to Civil Conflicts,' [1992], *African Journal of International and Comparative Law,* (Vol.4,Pt.2).

Viljoen F. and Louw L., 'The Status of the Findings of the African Commission: from Moral Persuasion to Legal Obligation', [2004], *Journal of African Law*.

Vite S., 'Typology of Armed Conflicts in International Law: Legal Concept and Actual Situations', [March 2009], *International Review of the Red Cross (IRRC)*, (Vo.91, No. 873).

Zegveld L., 'The Inter-American Commission on Human Rights and International Humanitarian Law: A Comment on the Tablada Cases', [September, 1998], *International Review of the Red Cross (IRRC)*, (No. 324,).

Zegveld L. 'Remedies for War Victims of Violations of International Humanitarian Law', [September, 2007], *International Review of Red Cross (IRRC)*, (Vol. 89, No. 867).

INTERNET SOURCES/WEBSITES

'Boko Haram Actually Kills More People in Terror Attacks Than ISIS', available at http://www.huffingtonpost.com/entry/boko-haram-isis-us-564cd890e4b0ob7997f8c15d.

'Boko Haram Turn Nigerian Girls to Female Suicide Bombers', available at http:// www.naij.com/275853-boko-haram-nigerian-girls-suicide-bombers.html.

'Dahomey Amazons', available at en.m.wikipedia.org/wiki/dahomeyamazons.

'Effect of Boko Haram on Nigeria's Children', available at http://www.globalfundforchildren.org/effects-of-boko-haram-on-nigerias-children/.

'History of Women Warriors', available at www.womenhistory.about.com/od/boudicea/p/ boudicea.html.

'How Boko Haram has left Northeast Nigeria in Ruins: More than 1 million people have fled', available at http://www.huffingtonpost.com /2015/01/23/boko-haram-humanitarian-crisis_n_6510846.html.

'Initial report on the meaning of armed conflict in International Law', [2008], available at www.ilahq.org/en/committee/index.cfm/cid/1022.

'International Committee of the Red Cross (ICRC) Opinion Paper on how is the term "armed conflict" defined in International Humanitarian Law?' Opinion Paper, March 2008, available at www.icrc.org/web/eng/ citeengOnsf/htm/aa/armed-conflict.pd.

'Nigeria IDP Figures Analysis', available at http://www.internal-displacement.org/sub-saharan-africa/nigeriafigures-analysis.

'Nigeria suffers highest number of civilian deaths in Africa's war zones', available at http://www.theguardian.com/global-development/2015/jan/23/ boko-haram-nigeria-civilian-death-toll-highest-acled-african-war-zones.

'Prehistoric Warfare', available at en.wikipedia.org/wiki/prehistoric-warfare#Endemicwarfare.

'Rape in warfare', available at http://en.wikipedia.org/wiki/History-of-rape#Inwarfare.

'Statistics on Women in the Military, Women in Military Service for America Memorial Foundation Inc.', available at: http://www.Women'smomorial.org/PDFs/station/WIM.pdf.

'US Supreme Court, Hamdan v Rumsfeld, Secretary of Defence, et al., 29 June, 2006, 6, esp. (d) (ii), available at: http://www.supremecourt.gov/opinions/05pdf/05-184.pdf.

'War, Women and Druids: Eyewitness Reports and Early Accounts of the Ancient Celts', (2010), available at www.womenhistory.about.com/od/boudicea/p/boudicea.html.

'Why there are so few women warriors', [1983], available at www.Culture-of-peace.info/books/history/male-domination.html.

Appignanesi R. and Garratt C., *Postmodernism For Beginners*, 1995, 100-101, available at en.m.wikiadia.org.

Blogger Q. and Campbell J., 'Women and the Boko Haram Insurgency', available at http://blogs.cfr.org/campbell/2015/08/111/women-and-the-boko-haram-insurgency/.

Bridge, B., Gender and Armed Conflict (2003), Institute of Development Studies, www.bridge.ids.ac.uk (accessed 7-5-2019)

Bryne, B., Gender Conflict and Development, available at
www.bridge.ids.ac.uk> reports (accessed 7-5-2019)

Butler J., *Gender Trouble,* (1990), available at en.m.wikipedia.org.

Campbell J., 'Women and Boko Haram Insurgency', available at
http://blogs.cfr.org/campbell/2015/08/11/women-and-the-boko-
haram-insurgency/.

David-Kimball L., 'Warrior Women of Eurasia', [1997], *Abstracts,*
(Vol. 50, No. 1), available at www.Culture-of-
peace.info/books/history/pre-neolithic.html.

Fontanella-Khan, 'Women Fighters in Nepal', [September, 2009],
Financial Times, available at
http://www.ft.com/cms/s/2/57c05a/a-a719/11de-bd14-
00144feabdc0,dwp-uuid=a712eb94-dc2b-11da-890d-
0000779e2340.html.

Geneva Academy of International Humanitarian Law, The War
Report: Armed Conflicts in 2018 (15 April, 2019) available at
https://www.geneva-academy.ch>research (accessed on 10-5-
2019)

International Crisis Group, Beyond Victimhood: Women's Peace
building in Sudan, Congo and Uganda (2006) available at
https://www.crisisgroup.org>horn-africa (accessed 7-5-2019)

Klot, J.E., Gender Mainstreaming in Crisis Response and Recovery:
A Forward Looking Review, Social Sciences Research Council,
2006, available at academia.edu (accessed on 7-5-2019)

Krause, J., Women's participation in peace Negotiations and the Durability of

Michelle M., 'International Respect for International Humanitarian Law in Non-international Armed Conflicts', [February, 2008], Geneva ICRC, 11, available at http://www.icrc.org./eng/resources/documents/publications/po923.htm.

Okorie, H., The Protection of Women in Armed Conflict: An Examination, available at www.unmail.edu.ng>oer>law>Vol.2 (accessed on 10-11-2018

Oslo Norwegian Institute, The Impact of Armed Conflict on Women, Peace Research Institute Oslo, available at https://www.prio.org> (accessed on 10-5-2019)

Oslo Norwegian Institute, Women in Armed Conflicts – UNDP, available at www.undp.org?human-development (accessed 10-5-2019)

Prescott, J. M., Armed Conflict, Women , and Climate Change, available at www.internationallawobserver.eu>new(2019) (accessed 8-5-19)

Swaine, A., Conflict Related Violence against Women, (2018), available at https://www.cambridge.org>core>books (accessed 10-5-2019) (Cambridge University Press 2019)

UNHCR Handbook for the Protection of Women and Girls, available at https://cms.emergecy.unhcr.org

Writz, A., Gender-basaed violence in Conflict and displacement: Quantative Findings, available at https:www.ncbiinim.nih.gov 2014 (accessed 10-11-2018)

NEWSPAPERS / MAGAZINE

'Boko Haram: IDP's can't return to North East Now -UNHCR', [Tuesday, June 7, 2016], Dailysun Newspaper, 12.

'Boko Haram: Over 334 North East Households in Danger – OXFAM', [Tuesday, May 31, 2016], Dailysun Newspaper, 12.

Eze M., 'Boko Haram: 44 female insurgents surrender to Nigerian troops [Thursday, June 2, 2016], Dailysun Newspaper, (Vol. 12, No. 3419), 7.

Fontanella-Khan, 'Women Fighters in Nepal', [September, 2009], Financial Times.

Molomo D., 'Boko Haram: 40 girls abducted in fresh attack in Adamawa', [Thursday, October 23, 2014], Dailysun Newspaper, (Vol. 10, No. 2997), 7.

Olanrenwaju T., 'Borno: Boko Haram abducts 100 women, kids, teenagers', [Friday, December 19, 2014], Daily Newspaper, (Vol. 10, No. 3038), 14

Omonobi K. and Orakpo E., 'I was forced to fight for Boko Haram – 19 YR OLD WOMAN', [Tuesday, October 28, 2014], Vanguard Newspaper, (Vol. 25, No. 62262), 14.

The Punch of Monday, July 7, 2014, 9 & 10.

Yusuf U., 'Boko Haram stones captives to death', [Monday, May 4, 2015], Vanguard Newspaper, (Vol. 25, No. 62397), 5.